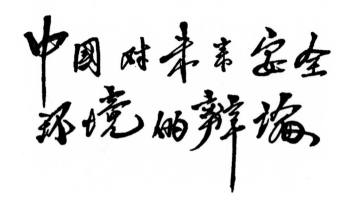

MICHAEL PILLSBURY

CHINA
Debates the Future
Security Environment

Advance praise for
China Debates the Future Security Environment

'*In this carefully researched and well crafted work, Dr. Michael Pillsbury has made another important contribution to our understanding of China's strategic thinking. Those who blithely assume that optimistic American views of global trends are normal and widely shared will be startled and educated. Contemporary Chinese predictions about Japan's ascendance and American decline will appear familiar but strangely anachronistic to those who recall the largely discredited American declinist school of the late Cold War. Other views will seem less familiar and even more disturbing, e.g., ideas about the high likelihood of fairly large-scale "local wars" in the next few decades, and the belief that the weaker local powers can prevail over stronger, more distant ones if the former adopt innovative and active military strategies.*"

—Thomas J. Christensen, Massachusetts Institute of Tehnology

'*The international politics of the twenty-first century will be shaped to a very considerable degree by the evolving relationship between the United States and the People's Republic of China. Yet we know surprisingly little about how China's top strategists think about us, about themselves, and about their place in the world. In this fascinating and disturbing book, Michael Pillsbury uses hundreds of recent Chinese books and articles to shed light on these critically important questions. Essential reading for anyone interested in the future of U.S.-China relations.*"

—Aaron L. Friedberg, Princeton University

"*This volume provides a useful reference for policymakers and scholars alike. It offers an extensive cross-section of Chinese viewpoints and provides a useful map of institutions, individuals, and publications which together form a core part of contemporary Chinese thinking on international security affairs.*"

—Bates Gill, The Brookings Institution

'Mike Pillsbury has done a terrific job presenting a range of Chinese voices and focusing our attention on how a combination of ancient historical analogies and traditional realpolitik analysis informs many public arguments about security today. Pillsbury's rich database sets an analytical agenda critical to a more nuanced understanding of China: How similar or different are U.S. and Chinese assessments? How does each construct images of the other? How do language and metaphor constrain Chinese debates? How authoritative and influential are individual Chinese institute analysts?"*

—Alastair Iain Johnston, Harvard University

This book illustrates very well that open sources can be used to understand crucial intelligence issues like Chinese strategic thinking. For our long-term policy of engaging China, we need to understand Chinese strategic perceptions. Mike Pillsbury's book is a major effort in that direction."

—The Honorable J. Robert Kerrey, Senate Intelligence Committee

"Dr. Pillsbury has performed a public service by highlighting what China's experts are saying about the Middle Kingdom's security policies and expectations and— equally interesting—who they see as a threat to those expectations (namely, the United States). It is time we stopped pretending China is our strategic partner and focused instead on what the Chinese are saying themselves. This book should be "must reading" for the next President of the United States and his security advisers."*

—The Honorable Trent Lott, Senate Majority Leader

Based on the reading of thousands of Chinese documents and on hundreds of hours of Chinese-language interviews, Pillsbury's ingenious account is the best book on Chinese military and strategic thinking of recent years."

—Arthur Waldron, University of Pennsylvania

CHINA
Debates the Future
Security Environment

一爭論就復雜了

Don't debate . . . Once debate begins, things become complicated
—Deng Xiaoping

實事求是

Seek truth from facts
—Deng Xiaoping quoting Mao Zedong

以劣勝优

The inferior can defeat the superior
—Fu Quanyou, Chief of Staff
of the People's Liberation Army

CHINA
Debates the Future Security Environment

MICHAEL PILLSBURY

University Press of the Pacific
Honolulu, Hawaii

China Debates the Future Security Environment

by
Michael Pillsbury

ISBN: 1-4102-1856-2

Reprinted from the 2000 edition

University Press of the Pacific
Honolulu, Hawaii
http://www.universitypressofthepacific.com

CONTENTS

PREFACE

The Office of Net Assessment, Department of Defense, is attempting to understand the long-term consequences of the rise of China as a major world power. As part of that effort, it seeks to understand the views of the most important Chinese authors who have analyzed the future security environment. Some Americans wrongly believe Chinese views reflect a mirror image of their own. This study suggests instead that the Chinese have their own unique perceptions, which may be difficult to appreciate.

The risk of mirror imaging our own views was an issue also present in the study of the Soviet Union. Andrew Marshall, Director of the Office of Net Assessment, cautioned against assuming that a foreign nation's strategic assessment is merely a reflection of America's: "Soviet calculations are likely to make different assumptions about scenarios and objectives . . . perform different calculations, use different measures of effectiveness, and perhaps use different assessment processes and methods. The result is that Soviet assessments may substantially differ from American assessments."[1] Marshall's cautionary note also applies to understanding Chinese assessments of the future.

This study offers over 600 selected quotations from the writings of over 200 Chinese authors published from 1994 to 1999. Analysis and interpretation are kept to a minimum so that the Chinese may speak for themselves. Many Chinese scholars assisted with this study by providing hard-to-get books and articles unfamiliar to most Westerners. Half the authors were interviewed in China. They explained some of the viewpoints in recent debates about the future security environment. Debates in China are generally concealed, and frequently authors pretend they do not exist. Conflicting views about the future nevertheless exist and merit attention if we are to understand the premises of China's national strategy and set a baseline from which to measure any future change in those premises.

Chinese policy debates are not easy to understand fully. Western studies in the past two decades have suggested various approaches. The selection of Chinese quotations in this study is based on the analytical foundation laid by the pioneering scholarship of A. Doak Barnett, Thomas J. Christensen,

---

[1] Andrew W. Marshall, "A Program to Improve Analytic Methods Related to Strategic Forces," *Policy Sciences* (November 1982): 48.

Banning Garrett, Bonnie Glaser, Carol Hamrin, Michael Hunt, Iain Johnston, Samuel Kim, Kenneth Lieberthal, Lyman Miller, Michel Oksenberg, Jonathan Pollack, Gilbert Rozman, Thomas Robinson, David Shambaugh, Michael Swaine, Allen Whiting, and Donald Zagoria.[2] One reason that the subject of Chinese policy debates is so complex and sensitive is because of the affiliations of the Chinese authors. They are not freewheeling scholars giving their personal views. The authors, who developed their writings in government-funded research institutes,[3] are either military officers who hold positions at China's Academy of Military Science (AMS), the National Defense University (NDU), and other research organizations affiliated with the People's Liberation Army (PLA), or civilian analysts from leading government institutes, such as the China Institute of Contemporary International Relations (CICIR).[4]

---

[2] A. Doak Barnett, *The Making of Foreign Policy in China* (Boulder, CO: Holt, Praeger, 1985); Thomas J. Christensen, *Useful Adversaries: Grand Strategy, Domestic Mobilization, and Sino-American Conflict, 1947-1958* (Princeton: Princeton University Press, 1996). Carol Lee Hamrin, *China and the Challenge of the Future, Changing Political Patterns* (Boulder, CO: Westview Press, 1990); Michael H. Hunt, *The Genesis of Chinese Communist Foreign Policy* (New York: Columbia University Press, 1996); Alastair Iain Johnston, *Cultural Realism, Strategic Culture and Grand Strategy in Chinese History* (Princeton: Princeton University Press, 1995); Samuel S. Kim, *China in and Out of the Changing World Order* (Princeton: Center of International Studies, 1991); Kenneth Lieberthal, *Central Documents and Politburo Politics in China* (Ann Arbor, MI: Papers in Chinese Studies No. 33, 1978); H. Lyman Miller, "Politics inside the Ring Road: On Sources and Comparisons," in *Decision-Making in Deng's China, Perspectives from Insiders*, eds. Carol Lee Hamrin and Suisheng Zhao (Armonk, NY: M.E. Sharpe, 1995); Michel Oksenberg, "Methods of Communication Within the Chinese Bureaucracy," *The China Quarterly*, no. 57 (January-March 1974): 1-39; Jonathan D. Pollack, The Sino-Soviet Rivalry and Chinese Security Debate (Santa Monica: Rand, 1982, R-2907-AF); Gilbert Rozman, *The Chinese Debate About Soviet Socialism, 1978-1985* (Princeton: Princeton University Press, 1987); Thomas W. Robinson and David Shambaugh, eds., *Chinese Foreign Policy, Theory and Practice* (Oxford University Press, 1994); David Shambaugh, *Beautiful Imperialist: China Perceives America, 1972-1990* (Princeton: Princeton University Press, 1991); Michael D. Swaine, *The Role of the Chinese Military in National Security Policymaking* (Santa Monica: Rand Corporation, 1996); Allen S. Whiting, *China Eyes Japan* (Berkeley: University of California Press, 1989); and Donald S. Zagoria, *The Sino-Soviet Conflict 1956-1961* (Princeton: Princeton University Press, 1962), especially "A Note on Methodology."

[3] Background on these institutes is provided in appendix 2.

[4] This book's bibliography lists over 300 Chinese books about future warfare and the future security environment. In addition, more than 100 Chinese military and civilian authors were interviewed during eight visits to Beijing and Shanghai from March 1995 to October 1998. Forty relevant articles appear in Michael Pillsbury, ed., *Chinese Views of Future Warfare* (Washington: National Defense University Press, 1997).

This study's main finding is that for these Chinese authors, the future security environment is remarkably clear, even if some aspects are still subject to debate. Surprisingly, this clear picture is consistent with what Chairman Mao and Premier Zhou Enlai told President Richard Nixon and Henry Kissinger 25 years ago: namely, a multipolar world was emerging and that four nations threatened China—Russia, India, Japan, and America.[5] Although there is some debate among them, Chinese authors consistently express suspicions about other foreign powers, especially the United States, Japan, and India. As Stanford Professor of Political Science Michel Oksenberg states, "China's leaders are naturally suspicious of foreign powers. They believe that foreign leaders tend to be reluctant to welcome China's rise in world affairs and would prefer to delay or obstruct its progress. They fear that many in the outside world would prefer to divide China if given the opportunity. . . . China's leaders retain in their minds a strategic map of the points on their periphery that make them vulnerable to foreign influence."[6]

Two important influences on Chinese assessments are Marxist-Leninist doctrine (though it is seldom mentioned explicitly) and China's own history, particularly its ancient historical statecraft. As will be discussed in the Prologue, Chinese authors are heirs to a 5,000-year-old written tradition of statecraft that has been distilled into a few classic texts.[7] Embedded in Chinese writing about the future are extensive references to this ancient statecraft. These allusions are often mistranslated. If the translator selects similar English language phrases, the translation will lose the reference to a specific historical meaning that was intended and that would be familiar to a Chinese. Obviously, this study cannot impart the subtle details of the entire corpus of Chinese ancient statecraft and its uses in China today, but important references to it will be pointed out. Indeed, in order to permit the reader to encounter Chinese views without delay, a number of issues have been treated in the Prologue and appendixes: appendix 1 defines what the strategic

---

[5]William Burr, ed., *The Kissinger Transcripts* (New York: The New Press, 1998), 216, footnote 57.

[6]Michel Oksenberg, *Taiwan, Tibet, and Hong Kong in Sino-American Relations* (Stanford, CA: Institute for International Studies, Stanford University, 1997), 56.

[7]See Alastair Iain Johnston, *Cultural Realism, Strategic Culture and Grand Strategy in Chinese History* (Princeton, NJ: Princeton University Press, 1995).

xvii

assessment process entails, and appendix 2 provides background about the major Chinese assessment institutions.

OBSTACLES

Some words of caution are advisable to any reader not fluent in Chinese or familiar with Chinese Government-sponsored documents. It is easy to set out the English language words with which Chinese analysts in government research institutes have described the future security environment. It is more difficult to attain a true understanding of the context and what these specific words actually signify to the Chinese. There are at least four obstacles to understanding Chinese views to keep in mind.

Precise Translation

Readers unfamiliar with the Chinese language may not appreciate how wide a range of choice an interpreter has in translating Chinese terms from ideographic symbols, the semantic content of which has developed in a 5,000-year-old cultural framework. For example, the Chinese word *sixiang* may be translated as "ideology," "thinking," "thoughts," and "doctrine," among other choices. Chinese verbs have no tense, so tense must be indicated by context, and Chinese nouns do not indicate singular or plural, again relying on context.

Some translation issues create only minor misunderstandings; others can be more significant. An example may help. Chinese writings on the future of warfare and the revolution in military affairs (RMA) frequently use three Chinese ideograms to signify something that can be used in a war that will surprise and overwhelm the enemy, vital parts of exploiting the RMA. The three ideograms (*sha shou jian*) literally mean "kill," "hand," and an ancient word for club, or "mace." U.S. Government translations have rendered this term as "trump card," "magic weapon," or "killer mace." None of these translations is wrong, but none captures the full meaning. The importance of the term can be seen in its continued usage over time, both originally in traditional Chinese novels and ancient statecraft texts, as well as today in the daily military newspaper. Behind these three ideograms may lie a concept of victory in warfare through possession of secret weapons that strike the enemy's most vulnerable point (called an acupuncture point), at precisely the decisive moment. This entire concept of how RMA technology can win a war cannot be fully conveyed by its simple English translation of "trump card."

The Changing Rules of the Chinese Communist Party about Debate

All authors quoted in this study are Party members with access to a system of confidential Party documents, many of which deal with assessment of the future security environment. Debate must remain within the limits of Party guidance. Books by Party members clearly will contrast with the freewheeling debates in American books about the future. In the United States, there is certainly no "party line" from the White House about the nature of world politics in 2020. Yet, as "scientific socialists," the leaders of the Communist Party of China are expected to have an official view of the future security environment and to disseminate this in confidential Party documents to members. The line may be unclear between narrow doctrines that Party scholars are expected to accept uncritically and broad areas that may be debated. Foreign readers, even if they know the Chinese language, can become lost in the woods if unfamiliar with Party context—which points are ideologically mandated and which are open to debate. One clue appears when there is extensive repetition by Chinese authors of "boiler plate" (*tifa*) phrases describing the future. Such repetition probably signals quotations from Central Party documents, but to foreign readers such terms may appear to be an uncanny coincidence of the same phrases used by dozens of Chinese authors.

The Party seems ambivalent about open debates. For 20 years, Party leaders have even debated whether or not to have open debates. The 20th anniversary on May 11, 1998, of the publication of the article, "Practice is the Sole Criterion of Testing Truth," led to numerous pieces in the Chinese press commemorating the debate over economic reform and opening up, that was ignited by the article.[8] Not only do they now praise the past debate, but they

---

[8]Some policy debates are not disclosed. For example, an article in the *New York Times* about China's bid to enter the World Trade Organization (WTO), reported, "China's top trade official, acknowledging for the first time that many lower level Chinese officials oppose the nation's proposed entry to the WTO, said in newspaper reports published on Monday that the government would begin a broad campaign to try to temper the internal discord. . . . Until now, Beijing's stance has been to pretend no opposition existed, even though many Chinese officials are known to be unhappy at the prospect of more open competition with international companies, one of the consequences of joining the trade organization." Seth Faison, "China Seeks to Win Over Dissenters on Joining Trade Group," *New York Times*, International Business Section, June 8, 1999.

Not only do Chinese analysts generally not admit publicly to the existence of debates, but usually they do not even refer to, let alone criticize, other author's views in their writings. For example, at the end of 1997, the Center for Peace and Development in Beijing hosted a conference on the situation in the Asia Pacific in which more than 15 Chinese scholars from

also advocate that in order to further carry out China's reforms, the country needs to "inherit the pioneering spirit of the debate . . . adhere to the ideological line of emancipating the mind and seeking truth from facts, and initiate a new stage for China's development."[9] One book written as part of the commemoration of the "criterion of truth" debate and the reforms that it brought about may itself even be ushering in a new open form of academic debate in China.[10] *Jiaofeng* (Crossing swords), by Ma Licheng and Ling Zhizhun, describes three periods of the "emancipation of the mind" since the end of the Cultural Revolution, in 1978, 1992, and 1997. According to a review in *Ching Pao*, the book broke all of the norms of Chinese veiled debates. "It criticizes people by name in total disregard of their 'face' or feelings. All parties involved in the sword crossing in the book are referred to directly by name and by the title of their works rather than by quoting and commenting on people's opinions as was usually the case in the past. It has been calculated that over 100 articles were cited. Even *Renmin ribao* and *Qiushi* [Party Central Committee publications] were cited. It is really clear where its spearhead is directed against."[11]

---

a variety of institutions presented different opinions without direct debate among themselves. See "1997 nian Yatai xingshi nianzhong yantaohui' (The 1997 year-end symposium on the situation in the Asia-Pacific), *Heping yu fazhan* (Peace and Development), 63, no. 1 (February 1998): 8-13. A similar conference on the international political situation, attended by 23 analysts, also lacked direct debate. "1997 nian guoji zhengzhi xingshi yantaohui fayan xuan deng" (Viewpoints as presented at the seminar on the international political situation in 1997), *Shijie jingji yu zhengzhi* (World Economics and Politics) 209, no. 1 (January 1998): 5-22.

[9]Beijing Xinhua Domestic Service, "Party Schools Commemorate Debate on the Criterion for Truth," May 14, 1998, in Foreign Broadcast Information Service (FBIS)-CHI-98-134, May 15, 1998. See also, "PRC Marks 20th Anniversary of Ideological Debate," Beijing Xinhua Domestic Service, May 3, 1998, in FBIS-CHI-98-123, May 6, 1998, and "Free Minds Essential to Reform," *China Daily*, May 5, 1998, 4.

[10]Ma Licheng and Ling Zhizhun, *Jiaofeng* (Crossing swords)(Beijing.: China Today Publishing House, March 1998).

[11]According to the *Ching Pao*, the editor-in-chief of the Chinese periodical *Zhongliu*, who was criticized by the book, retaliated by "accusing the authors of 'bullying,' 'baring their fangs,' 'breathing strong as a bull,' and 'becoming arrogant and overbearing.' " See Tsou Wang, "'Jiaofeng (Crossing swords) Gives Rise to Confrontation, Puts the Authorities in a 'Dilemma'," *Ching Pao* (The Mirror), August 12, 1998, in FBIS-CHI-98-224, August 13, 1998.

Premises about Statecraft Held by Chinese Analysts

The Prologue addresses several important examples of how ancient Chinese statecraft is used as a lesson or metaphor to assess the future. Chinese references to the "Warring States era" of 2,500 years ago remind Chinese readers never to forget the eternal verities of geopolitics and worst case scenarios. The Warring States era as a guide to the future is a rich subject, but it is never spelled out for foreign readers.[12] Though significant, the true meaning of "the words" is never made explicit in a way Westerners need to know in order to understand what is really meant.

The Taboo on Open Discussion of Future Chinese Security

This obstacle can truly confuse foreign readers. China's future role in international politics (which Western scholars often assume will be significant) is seldom mentioned. One explanation is that this sensitive subject can be dealt with only in secret Party documents, not in the open source books and journals upon which this study completely relies. Glimpses of these internal documents sometimes come as "leaks" to the press. In 1994, a Hong Kong magazine, *Cheng Ming,* disclosed that a confidential report about the period 2000 to 2010, "War to be Won," had been circulated to Party members by the Policy Research Office of the Chinese State Council, the Policy Research Office of the Central Military Commission, and the Policy Research Office of the Communist Party Central Committee. The main points are that China's Comprehensive National Power (CNP) will be among the top three in the world and that the two sides of the Taiwan Strait will be unified.[13] China's gross national product (GNP), excluding Taiwan, is estimated to become about U.S. \$2.5 trillion by 2010. China will have two to four aircraft carriers and a PLA of 1.5 million, reduced from today's 3 million. By 2010, manned

---

[12]The Warring States era (475-221 B.C.), which produced some of the classics of Chinese statecraft, was a period when a multistate competition to become "hegemon" featured stratagems, small wars, interstate conferences, treaties, and what Western scholars of international relations would label "anarchy."

[13]According to Professor Allen S. Whiting, "Although *Cheng Ming* is a Hong Kong journal, it has a good track record of acquiring authentic PRC classified documents." Allen S. Whiting, "East Asian Military Securities Dynamics," Asia-Pacific Research Center, Stanford University, February 1995, 49, footnote 9.

Chinese spacecraft will be launched and will have established a space station.[14] In May 1997, *Cheng Ming* leaked another report on Sino-U.S. relations, done by the Central Policy Research Center, the State Council's Policy Research Center, the Foreign Ministry and Defense Ministry. This second report predicted that war between China and the United States was possible in the future. According to *Cheng Ming*, the report asserted:

> With the return of Hong Kong and Macao to Chinese rule, the Taiwan issue will inevitably become China's major event around 2010. If the United States uses force to meddle in China's sovereignty and internal affairs, China will certainly fight a war against aggression, thus leading to a limited Sino-U.S. war. China must be prepared for this. With the change in the international situation, the United States will make use of islands, maritime space, and resources and will encourage and support Japanese militarists in provoking a war against China. . . . China is the U.S. number one political adversary at the turn of this century. China must make systematic preparations against the invasive war and military attacks unleashed by the United States under any pretext.[15]

If authentic, these documents represent rare samples of the kind of confidential forecasts Party members may be reading about China's future role that cannot be discussed in open books and journals.

These obstacles need not prevent all understanding, but together they limit the probability of fully comprehending China's assessment. Modesty is an appropriate attitude to adopt in any attempt to understand Chinese assessments. The need for further research and more extensive translations should be kept in mind.

PREVIEW OF FINDINGS

The central finding of this study is that China has developed a remarkably detailed picture of the future security environment. The concluding chapter provides details about the range of Chinese debates on the features of the future. The extent of the debate is very restricted when compared to the

---

[14]*Cheng Ming* (May 1994): 1.

[15]Li Tzu-ching, "CPC Thinks China and United States Will Eventually Go to War," *Cheng Ming*, no. 235 (May 1997): 15-16; in FBIS-CHI-97-126.

freewheeling give and take that exists in the West. The mutually exclusive "scenarios" employed by Americans to explore alternative possibilities for the future do not exist in Chinese writings.[16] China's clear picture of the future is an amalgam of Marxism and ancient Chinese statecraft from the Warring States era. All institute authors and PLA officers are members of the Chinese Communist Party, obligated to accept Party doctrine about the shape of the future. According to Deng Xiaoping, in order to preserve this clear picture of the future, Chinese should not "debate" because it can make things "complicated." Nevertheless, reformers continue to challenge orthodox ideological authors on sensitive issues. These debates are an important key to improving U.S. understanding of China.[17] Western understanding of Chinese debates has improved since 1949 because of the remarkable efforts of only a few scholars, mostly Chinese who have emigrated to the United States or Americans. This study highlights veiled debates between reformers and orthodox authors on:

- The future world structure in 2010-2030
- The rate of America's decline
- The future hierarchy of the major world powers in 2010
- Locations and causes of future wars
- Consequences of the RMA
- Prospects for Russia, India, and Japan.

---

[16]For examples of U.S. debates about the future, see Wendell Bell, *Foundations of Futures Studies* (New Brunswick, NJ: Transaction Publishers, 1987); Joseph F. Coates, John B. Mahaffie, and Andy Hines, *2025: Scenarios of U.S. and Global Society Reshaped by Science and Technology* (Greensboro, NC: Oakhill Press, 1997); and the annual publication, Earl H. Tilford, Jr., ed., *World View: The 1998 Strategic Assessment from the Strategic Studies Institute* (Carlisle Barracks, PA: U.S. Army War College, February 26, 1998). See also articles in *Futures Research Quarterly*, published by the World Future Society.

[17]An example of how differences between reform and orthodox views on China's future development resulted in "complications" was the debate over political and economic reform in the late 1980s, leading up to Tiananmen protests in 1989. For a discussion of this issue, see Benedict Stavis, "Contradictions in Communist Reform: China before June 1989," *Political Science Quarterly* 105, no. 1 (1990): 31-52. The Western press reported in 1998 that debate concerning political reform was once again emerging in China. See Steven Mufson, "Debate Blossoms in Beijing Spring, Open Discussion of Reform Spread to Universities, Media," *The Washington Post*, April 19, 1998, A1, A26; and Eric Eckholm, "Chinese Book on Political Reform Stirs Hopes for More Debate," *The New York Times*, August 25, 1998, A5.

The following section outlines additional findings of this study: measuring geopolitical hierarchy, dangers and opportunities for China, probable scenarios for future warfare, Leninist taboos, including absence of self-criticism, and the premise that capitalist nations trigger wars.

Measuring Geopolitical Hierarchy

Consistent with the texts of ancient statecraft, China's analysts believe in geopolitics. They try to calculate mathematically the hierarchy of the world's future major powers. At least two teams have done so at the orthodox Academy of Military Science and the reform-minded Chinese Academy of Social Science. According to the *military* forecast, China's CNP by 2020 will grow equal to that of the United States in a multipolar structure. Russia, Europe, and Japan will be "poles" three, four, and five, each with half the power level attained by the United States or China. According to the "reform" *civilian* forecast, the United States will lose its hegemony not to China but to Japan. Tokyo's national power will grow equal to that of the United States by 2010, followed closely by Germany. The *civilians* rate China only as number eight by 2010, not even one of the top five "poles." China and Russia score only half as high as the United States and Japan. Given these calculated power scores, Chinese analysts of the future focus intensively on assessing the intentions of Japan and the United States toward China, especially the strength of the "slanderous" and dangerous "China Threat Theory" in Tokyo and Washington.

China foresees a turbulent multipolar world. In contrast to wide-ranging Western debates about scenarios from the "long boom" to a more "dangerous world," since 1986, China's Communist Party has had an almost unchanging assessment of an "inevitable" multipolar future.[18] This Chinese assessment draws heavily on both Maoist, pre-Gorbachev Marxist-Leninism, and ancient Chinese statecraft. It sees a relative decline in U.S. power so that the world will be "multipolar," much like the Warring States era. American security alliances will weaken, the United States will decline to become a regional

---

[18]For Peter Schwartz' vision to 2020 of "unabashed technological optimism," see Steve Lohr, "Long Boom or Bust for Leading Futurist," *New York Times*, June 1, 1998. A pessimistic vision is Richard Kugler, *Toward a Dangerous World: U.S. National Security Strategy for the Coming Turbulence* (Santa Monica, CA: The RAND Corporation, 1995), 101-160. Additional reading includes Melville C. Branch, "Why We Simulate Long-Range Futures," *The Futurist* 32, no. 3 (April 1998): 52.

power, and the post-World War II rules and norms set mainly by the United States and the Allies will give way to China's proposed rules, known as the Five Principles of Peaceful Coexistence.[19] China's authors warn of future wars. There will be intense competition among major powers to build CNP and to develop the RMA. There will be a danger of frequent "local wars," from future small wars in Africa to wars on the scale of the Korean conflict and the Gulf War. The main cause of wars involving major powers will be competitive struggles over natural resources (oil and gas). The "Yalta System" of stable "spheres of influence" must be replaced by the Five Principles, which have already been adopted by "most countries," including Russia, but not the United States or Japan.[20] Without a new "system," turmoil like that during the Warring States era will continue indefinitely. "Systems" tend to last at least 40 years, according to some Chinese authors.

China calculates power ratios and predicts American decline. Ancient Chinese statecraft from the Warring States era emphasizes the need to calculate future power ratios mathematically. Chinese national security research analysts have quantitatively analyzed the relative power of the nations of this inevitable new "world structure" in which the United States will decline economically, socially, militarily, and internationally to become one of five "poles" in a "multipolar world." Nothing can save the United States from this fate, which will include serious conflict with its former NATO and Japanese allies, a failure to exploit the coming RMA, and a fading away of all U.S. security alliances. Orthodox Chinese analysts predict that 15 to 20 years will be sufficient; reformers argue that it may take longer. U.S. influence is already said to be declining because the multipolar power of other nations constrains U.S. ambition. A domestic Chinese radio broadcast explained, "Even though the United States is currently the most developed country in the world, this does not mean that it can dominate everything as it pleases; and this is

---

[19]Said to date from a 1954 agreement between China and India, they are Mutual Respect for Territorial Integrity, Nonaggression, Noninterference, Equality and Mutual Benefit, and Peaceful Coexistence. India violated them 8 years later and had to be taught a lesson by China, as did Russia (1969) and Vietnam (1979).

[20]Li Zhongcheng, "Emerging China's Role in World Politics," *Contemporary International Relations* 8, no. 2 (February 1998): 16. Li is a Research Professor in the Division for China and World Studies at CICIR.

specifically the inevitable outcome of the world's accelerated pace toward creating a multipolarized pattern after the Cold War."[21]

Dangers and Opportunities

This new multipolar world will present China with both dangers and major opportunities that parallel those of a rising power during the Warring States era.[22] Some rising states were brutally "extinguished" by the hegemon of the Warring States, a role the United States could play. Ancient strategists deceived or diverted the hegemon and even formed a coalition to balance it. As today's hegemon, the United States may already be maneuvering to prevent ("contain") China from entering this new multipolar world in which China's CNP continues to rise and grow closer to that of the United States. Orthodox authors argue that it is "too late" for the United States to "contain" China. They say U.S. military forces can be defeated through ancient strategic techniques known collectively as "the inferior defeats the superior" (*yiruo shengqiang*). Conversely, other authors assert that the inevitable process of America's decline has not gone far yet. One senior analyst created a probability chart of alternative policies China could pursue in order to delay for 10 years any U.S. military actions that would use force against a rising China to preserve American hegemony. Another author warns that this dangerous threat to China from the United States will not arrive until the decade 2020 to 2030, when the United States finally realizes the implications of becoming inferior to Chinese national power. Both orthodox and reform authors recommend tactical accommodation (including partnership) with the United States. However, both fear that if the China Threat Theory gains more influence in America, the United States will become so alarmed by China's rise that Washington will decide to contain, use strategic deception, or even attack China in order to preserve U.S. hegemony.

China's ancient statecraft urges the development and use of surprise "magic weapons" to win wars, a theory that today appears to influence China's view of the RMA. Five

---

[21]Yuan Bingzhong, "The Challenges the United States Confronts While Adjusting its Foreign Policy," Beijing Xinhua Domestic Service, December 17, 1997, in FBIS-CHI-97-352, December 20, 1997.

[22]Wu Rusong, "Zhanguo shidai duoji douzheng de zhanlue sixiang" (Multipolar strategic thought in the Warring States era), *Zhongguo junshi kexue* (China Military Science) 29, no. 4 (Winter 1994): 126. Colonel Wu stated in an interview with the author in August 1996 that he directs the ancient strategy section of the Strategy Department at AMS in Beijing. The article suggests parallels to the present.

books about the RMA published in 1996-97 are striking evidence of the importance of this subject to the Chinese military. Analysts assert that the *different rates* at which major nations exploit the radical changes in warfare will change the world balance of power, as occurred during the ancient Warring States era. These authors' books boldly predict the United States will lose its initial lead within a decade and then fall behind other nations in this RMA competition. Such a forecast about U.S. failure to take advantage of the opportunities of a potential RMA is consistent with the calculations of other Chinese authors about the future relative decline of the United States. Russia and Japan will surpass the United States in exploiting the RMA, they say. Thus, the effect of the RMA will reinforce the current "inevitable" trend toward multipolarity and the end of America's superpower status.

Future Warfare

There is some evidence that there are three distinct schools of debate about which type of future warfare China will most probably face. There is not a direct debate, so this study labels the different schools of thought the "RMA" advocates, the "Local War" advocates, and the more traditional "People's War," or "Active Defense," advocates. The RMA advocates complain that China's current military modernization is too slow and ought to be aimed instead at leapfrogging the other major powers. Since the mid-1980s, Local War advocates have been seeking to reduce ground forces and develop a better navy and air force. The advocates of continuing Chairman Mao's approach of Active Defense and People's War focus on ideological training, large, lightly armed infantry, and a national defense mobilization base.

There may be a tacit link among these three schools of thought and the debate about the future security environment. RMA advocates would prevail in a budget debate if forecasts of the future emphasized that China would face no local wars or major land invasions but would need to defend itself after two decades against a United States bent on dismembering China to prevent it from challenging U.S. hegemony. Local War advocates benefit from forecasts that China will indeed be challenged in the near term—such as by aggression on China's border with India or Vietnam, or in the South China Sea, or by a declaration of independence by Taiwan. People's War advocates benefit from forecasts that focus on the suspicious intentions of major powers (Japan or the United States) to invade or to dismember, justifying a 3-million-strong army and militia mobilization base.

Marxist Taboos

Some of the current strategic assessment was formulated secretly in the years between 1982 and 1985 through debate among the senior leadership in Beijing.[23] The procedure, which can be seen as China's "assessment cycle," brought about publication of a set of premises that began to shift during the decline of Deng Xiaoping in the early 1990s. There is now a new component—the United States as a potential threat to China's rise. It is remarkable that 20 years ago China saw the United States as a potential military ally and source of advanced weapons, yet today portrays the United States as a future long-term rival and even potential military opponent. Many Chinese note, however, that such changes were routine in the Warring States era.

There remain untested ideological taboos. One cannot publicly forecast certain scenarios. No Chinese author can today openly argue that the United States will grow relatively stronger than other major powers; U.S. relations will improve with capitalist Europe or Japan; Japan will weaken or remain a quasi-pacifist nation under its Peace Constitution; "multipolarity" as defined in China is unlikely; or it is wrong to suspect the United States of being a greedy hegemon seeking to dismember China's Tibet or Taiwan, because it continues to receive 70 percent of China's exports, remains among the top three foreign investors in China, and pledges to reduce arms sales to Taiwan.

One taboo prohibits forecasts or debates about China's own future security role. In sharp contrast to widespread Western interest and writing about the consequences of the rise of China, this subject cannot be addressed by Chinese analysts beyond certain boilerplate phrases used by senior leaders in international fora. There is no discussion of alternative scenarios about the rise of China as a great power. Analysts only repeat platitudes that China will never be a superpower, never seek hegemony, and always be a force for peace and stability.[24] Foreign commentary suggesting that China might behave as

---

[23]By 1986, an open source article described many of the key tenets of the current assessment of a multipolar world structure. See Gao Heng, "Shijie zhanlue geju zhengxiang duojihua fazhan" (Development of global strategic multipolarity), *Guofang daxue xuebao* (National Defense University Journal), no. 2 (1986): 32-34.

[24]For example, see Hu Ping, "Heping fazhan shi Zhongguo de changqi zhanlue quxiang" (Peaceful development is China's long-term strategic orientation), *Guoji zhanlue yanjiu* (International Strategic Studies) 46, no. 4 (October 1997): 4-6. Hu Ping is a Research Fellow at the China Institute of International Strategic Studies (CIISS).

other great powers have done has been harshly criticized and punished.[25] A top Chinese analyst agreed in 1987 with the prediction by the U.S. Commission on Integrated Long-Term Strategy that China will emerge by 2010 as the world's second economic power (after the United States and ahead of Japan and Russia). However, he warned that anyone who even considers unpleasant scenarios about China's future role, such as a "potential enemy," shows "a lack of sound strategic thinking."[26]

Candid Chinese views of China's own possible future role as a great power either do not exist or are not available in open sources. This topic is avoided. Instead, daunting challenges are emphasized.[27] China's leaders repeatedly warn that no one should be worried about China as a rising military power. Li Peng stated, "It will take more than 30 years for China to achieve modernization. Therefore, the China Threat Theory is not an objective view. It was spread by anti-China

---

[25]Foreign critics of China may be rebutted by name and accused of "slandering" China. Journals regularly assess the views of U.S. experts on China. The published writing of former U.S. Ambassador to China James Lilley has been criticized frequently in press articles. *The Coming Conflict With China*, by Richard Bernstein and Ross H. Munro, was harshly reviewed in China. For example, see Mi Zhenyu, "Stupid Lies—Commentary on 'The Coming Conflict With China' " (in Chinese), Beijing Xinhua Domestic Service, April 17, 1997. See also an article in *China Youth*, a collection of the views of leading analysts at CICIR, NDU, the Chinese Academy of Social Sciences (CASS), Beijing University, and other institutions, "Zhong-Mei chongtu ji jiang daolai ma?" (Is a Sino-U.S. conflict coming?), *Zhongguo qingnian* (China Youth), no. 8 (1997): 8-11. Even Russians must be criticized if they perceive a threat from China: "Some extreme nationalists in Russia also made trouble . . . [promoting] the theory Russia is getting weaker and China getting stronger." Shi Ze, "Lun xin shiqi de Zhong-E guanxi" (Perceptions of Sino-Russian relations in the new era), *Guoji wenti yanjiu* (International Studies) 60, no. 2 (April 1996): 7. There are also examples of Americans and Britons who publicly discussed a potential "China threat" and were then denied visas in the 1990s. Shi Ze is Vice President of the China Institute of International Studies (CIIS).

[26]Chen Zhongjing, *Guoji zhanlue wenti* (Problems of international strategy)(Beijing: Shishi chubanshe, 1988), 310-311. Chen, born in 1915, is one of the most distinguished Chinese strategic experts. Chen has been President of the Institute of International Relations and the Director of CICIR, a research institute affiliated with the Ministry of State Security. Some say he served as a vice minister of the Chinese foreign intelligence service.

[27]For example, see Ma Hong and Sun Shangqing, eds., *Jingji baipishu: Zhongguo jingji xingshi yu zhanwang: 1995-1996* (Economic white paper: China's economic situation and prospects: 1995-1996)(Beijing: Zhongguo fazhan chubanshe, 1996); Shi Bike, *Zhongguo da qushi* (China megatrends)(Beijing: Hualing chubanshe, 1996). For warnings on the need to conceal increasing national power, see Ma Jinsheng, *Junshi qipian* (Military deception)(Jinan: Junshi kexue chubanshe, 1992).

forces in Western countries with ulterior motives to contain China."[28] Apparently, some authors fear that a growing trend in America and Japan will be to prevent China's rise as a future power. "Within the U.S. Congress and the Clinton administration (such as the Defense Department and the intelligence departments), there are a number of experts, strategists, and government officials who do not consider issues from the angle of political strife but instead focus on preserving the U.S. world hegemonist status and proceed from long-term geopolitical strategic awareness in holding that the rise of China will be an enduring challenge and even a threat to the United States. They call for maintaining strategic alertness and instituting strategic precautions against China. They fabricate and publish all kinds of 'reports,' and stir up all kinds of 'cases' for which there is no factual evidence, in order to create strategic opinion for the 'China threat,' 'alertness against China,' and 'precautions against China,' in a bid to attain their strategic and political goals in the world, Asia, and China (including Taiwan)."[29] Chinese concern about the reaction of countries in the Asia-Pacific region to the development of its military force and a potential China Threat is one reason that a plan to build an aircraft carrier was postponed to the 2000-2005 Five-Year Plan. According to one officer, "We do not want our neighbors to misread the signals . . . but we need an aircraft carrier if we are to complete plans to modernize the navy. We have no plans to threaten anyone with an aircraft carrier."[30]

---

[28]"Li Peng on Domestic, International Affairs," Beijing Xinhua Domestic Service, January 2, 1996, in FBIS-CHI-96-002, January 3, 1996. Former Premier Li Peng added, "China will never practice hegemonism nor seek any spheres of influence. Even when it gets stronger in the future, it will, as always, maintain friendly relations with other countries."

[29]Chu Shulong, "Sino-US Relations Pushed into Perilous Waters," *Shijie zhishi*, no. 11 (June 1, 1999): 9-10; in FBIS-CHI-1999-0622, June 23, 1999. See also Song Qiang, Zhang Zangzang, and Qiao Bian, *Zhongguo keyi shuo bu—Lengzhan hou shidai de zhengzhi yu qinggan jueze* (China can say no—post-Cold War political emotional options)(Beijing: Zhonghua gongshang lianhe chubanshe, 1996), 6. The introduction states that "stemming both from its deep-rooted different ideological views, as well as from its ultra-hegemonic efforts to unilaterally dominate the world, the United States has increasingly shown agony and uneasiness regarding the rise of China . . . a big conspiracy on the part of the free world directed at China has begun to ferment and brew. . . . It is said to be a conspiracy because what the United States says is one thing and what it does is another."

[30]Quoted in Paul Beaver, "China Will Delay Aircraft Carrier," *Jane's Defense Weekly*, June 3, 1998.

No Self-Criticism

Chinese analysts have not engaged in public criticism about any aspects of China's foreign policy, in sharp contrast to the level of self-criticism in the USSR that Gorbachev permitted as early as 1987. No Chinese author has yet gone as far as Gorbachev's speech to the 19th Party Congress, which asserted, "It even happened that decisions of major importance were made by a narrow circle of persons. . . . This led to an inadequate reaction to international events and to the policies of other states and even to erroneous decisions."[31] No Chinese author has yet agreed with Gorbachev's call for "de-ideologization of interstate relations," or with Deputy Foreign Minister Anatoli Adamshin's rhetorical question, "Why is injecting ideology into foreign policy so dangerous? . . . It is no less incorrect to suppose oneself the bearer of historical truth, the possessor of a patent on the future."[32] Nor has any Chinese yet followed Gorbachev's speech on November 2, 1987, which challenged the Leninist view of international politics by suggesting that capitalist nations can do without militarism and neocolonialism.[33] Allen Lynch concluded after this speech, "One may even speak of the emergence . . . of a new Soviet theory of international relations," while Sylvia Woodby referred to it as a "new world view."[34] Not so in China.

China's commitment to its version of Marxism rules out the public use of purely Western international relations concepts to assess the future security environment. This ideology prohibits using certain concepts to assess the future. Deng's national security advisor on the State Council, Huan Xiang, wrote in 1987 that "bourgeois theories of international relations" were to serve the interests of imperialist foreign policies.[35] One well-known Chinese analyst observed,

---

[31]Quoted in Sylvia Woodby, *Gorbachev and the Decline of Ideology in Soviet Foreign Policy* (Boulder, CO: Westview Press, 1989), 36.

[32]Ibid., 16, 17.

[33]See Gorbachev's anniversary speech of November 2, 1987, on Moscow television, in FBIS, November 3, 1987. Cited in Woodby, *Gorbachev and the Decline of Ideology in Soviet Foreign Policy.*

[34]Allen Lynch, *Gorbachev's International Outlook: Intellectual Origins and Political Consequences* (New York: Institute of East-West Security Studies, 1989), 37; and Woodby, *Gorbachev and the Decline of Ideology,* 23. See also Galia Golan's work on the subject, *Gorbachev's "New Thinking" on Terrorism* (New York: Praeger, 1990; published with the Center for Strategic and International Studies, Washington).

[35]Huan Xiang, "Preface to the Chinese Translation of Dougherty and Pfaltzgraff, Contending Theories of International Relations," *Shijie zhishi* (World Knowledge), no. 8 (1988): 12.

"Differing from Western international relations theorists such as Hans Morgenthau, China's theory of international relations is based on dialectical and historical materialism."[36] Textbooks of international relations in use in China, such as a recent book by Liang Shoude and Hong Yinxian, emphasize the interpretations of Marx, Lenin, Mao, and Deng Xiaoping.[37] Liang asserts that the foreign policies of nations depend on whether the bourgeoisie or the proletariat is in power.

Capitalist Nations Trigger Wars

Chinese textbooks state that bourgeois states are greedy and constantly plot war and intervention; they are blocked from this course only by the socialist states, who desire peace and development. Students in China from high school on are examined on these principles. Liang Shoude headed the commission that drafted the national syllabus in international politics for all universities. Chinese have publicly rejected Western international relations theory, including the school of thought known as Realism or Neo-Realism, which began to be discussed in 1982 in China.[38]

In contrast to Western research that suggests miscalculation and misunderstandings may be the leading cause of war, Chinese analysts assert that "scrambling for resources" causes war. "Economic factors are . . . the most fundamental cause triggering

---

[36]Wang Shuzhong, "The Post-War International System," in *As China Sees the World: Perceptions of Chinese Scholars*, ed. Harish Kapur (London: Francis Pinter Publishers, 1987), 22.

[37]Liang Shoude and Hong Yinxian, *Guoji zhengzhixue gailun* (General theory of international politics)(Beijing: Zhongyang bianshi chubanshe, 1994).

[38]See Chu Shulong, "Guanyu guoji guanxixue xueke jianshe de ji ge wenti" (Several issues concerning the establishment of the subject of international relations), *Xiandai guoji guanxi* (Contemporary International Relations) 66, no. 4 (April 1995): 59-63; Yang Zheng, "Shixi guoji guanxixue de yanjiu duixiang wenti" (A tentative analysis of the object of the study of international relations), *Xiandai guoji guanxi* (Contemporary International Relations), 66, no. 4 (April 1995): 64-67; and David Shambaugh and Wang Jisi, "Research on International Studies in the Peoples Republic of China," *PS* (Fall 1984): 758-64. According to an interview in Beijing with Wang Jisi in June 1995, the first article on Western theory was by Chen Lemin entitled "Western International Relations Theory" in *Research on International Problems*, the journal of CIIS. Chu has a Ph.D. from George Washington University; Wang, from Oxford University.

war."[39] This view may make it difficult for Chinese analysts to appreciate the role of miscalculations and misperceptions in causing war.

Chinese analysts often assert that signs of future trends are hidden in current events. For example, the Bosnia conflict is said to reveal a struggle between the United States and the European Union (EU) to dominate Europe and to re-divide the former Soviet sphere of influence.[40] The hidden intent behind U.S. policies of NATO enlargement and revision of the U.S.-Japan defense guidelines is to challenge the spheres of Russia and China from both the east and west flanks.

Will another 25 years of Sino-American "strategic dialogue" and military-to-military exchanges eliminate the Chinese misperceptions identified in this study? American exchange programs have been effective and need to be increased in the future. However, China may not be willing to modify its most dearly held beliefs about traditional statecraft and the future.

---

[39]Liu Mingde, "Changes in the Forms of War and Their Implications After the Disintegration of the Bipolar Pattern," *International Strategic Studies* 24, no. 2 (June 1992): 9. Liu is a Research Fellow at CIISS.

[40]Chen Feng, "1997 nian di guoji zhanlue xingshi" (The Strategic situation in 1997), *Guoji zhanlue yanjiu* (International Strategic Studies) 47, no. 1(January 1998): 3-7. According to interviews, Colonel Chen served in the Situation Room of the Chinese military intelligence headquarters in Beijing. He is now at the Chinese mission to the United Nations in New York.

PROLOGUE:
Ancient Lessons

To reduce the potential for misunderstanding or mirror imaging discussed in the preface, this prologue draws together examples from nine authors in five key research institutes who draw upon concepts from ancient statecraft. Their comments about the future security environment would be difficult to understand without extensive knowledge of the metaphors of Chinese ancient statecraft. The Chinese language is rich in idioms from ancient statecraft. Moreover, Chinese writing about the future security environment describes the future in terms of the Warring States era in Chinese history.[1] The age in which the classics of Chinese statecraft were produced was a time when a multistate competition to become "hegemon" featured stratagems, small wars, interstate conferences, treaties, and what Western scholars of international relations would label "anarchy." One set of "lessons" (among many) was how to become a hegemon; another was how to survive destruction at the hands of a predatory hegemon.

One specific Chinese premise from the ancient statecraft of the Warring States era seems to influence Chinese authors who write about the United States today—the concept of how to diagnose and deal with a powerful "hegemon" (*ba*) that seeks to dominate several other less powerful states. The way hegemons conducted themselves during the Warring States period of ancient China forms one of the sources of the classic lessons of Chinese statecraft. Unfortunately, lessons from Chinese statecraft about dealing with a predatory hegemon are little known in the West, and there is no guide for Westerners to the famous stories in Chinese traditional statecraft so well known to all our authors.[2] According to interviews with Chinese military

---

[1] The Warring States era (475-221 B.C.) was "the flowering age for the Chinese fable and exerted a definite influence on works of later centuries," according to K. L. Kiu, *100 Ancient Chinese Fables* (Taipei: Taiwan Commercial Press, 1993), 8.

[2] A forthcoming study for OSD Net Assessment discusses Chinese military writings published since 1993 on the contemporary relevance of ancient Chinese statecraft, including the following books: *Sanshiliu ji gujin tan* (Ancient and modern discussions on the 36 stratagems), *Zhisheng taolue—Sun Zi zhanzheng zhixing guanlun* (Strategies of superiority—Sun Zi's views on knowledge and action in war), *Bu zhan er qu ren zhi bing—Zhongguo gudai xinlizhan sixiang ji qi yunyong* (Conquest without combat—ancient Chinese psychological warfare thought and usage), *Zhongguo lidai zhanzheng gailan* (An outline of warfare in past Chinese dynasties), *Quanmou*

officers, these stories are embedded in Chinese culture just as the West has its own history, its own literature, and its own Bible stories. This prologue selects only one subject among many from the lessons of the Warring States—how China in the future should assess and deal with a powerful hegemon.

China's military authors have called the future multipolar world "amazingly" similar to the Warring States era and declare that China's future security environment resembles the Warring States era in several ways. A representative article by Colonel Liu Chungzi of the National Defense University Strategy Department states that Sun Zi's *The Art of War* was "the product of the multipolar world structure in China 2500 years ago," that "there are a surprising number of similarities between Sun Zi's time and the contemporary multipolar trend,"and that "in the 1990s, the world entered a multipolar era very similar to the time of Sun Zi."[3] General Gao Rui, former Vice President of the Academy of Military Science (AMS), writes that the era is "extremely distant from modern times, but still shines with the glory of truth" and "the splendid military legacy created through the bloody struggles of our ancient ancestors . . . [today] has a radiance even more resplendent."[4] Others claim that China should study "treasuries" of strategies from the Warring States. Many books have been published in the last 5 years as a revival of interest in ancient statecraft has been officially blessed by a large commission of China's generals. The director of research at the General Staff Department of the People's Liberation Army published six volumes of studies on ancient statecraft in 1996 that contained specific advice on how to comprehend the current and future security environment.[5]

---

shu—*Shujia yu yingjia de jiaoliang* (Power stratagems—a contest of losers and winners), *Sun Zi bingfa yu sanshiliu ji* (Sun Zi's the art of war and the thirty-six stratagems), *Zhongguo gudai bingfa jingcui* (The essence of the ancient Chinese Art of war), *Sun Zi bingfa de diannao yanjiu* (Computer studies on Sun Zi's the art of war), and *Ershiwu li junshi moulue gushi jingxuan* (A selection of 25 stories on ancient military strategy).

[3]Liu Chungzi, "*Sun Zi* yu dangdai junshi douzheng" (*Sun Zi* and contemporary military struggles), *Zhongguo junshi kexue* (China Military Science) 33, no. 4 (Winter 1995): 136.

[4]Gao Rui, *Zhongguo shanggu junshi shi* (Chinese ancient military history)(Beijing: Junshi kexue chubanshe, 1995), 2.

[5]See the three two-volume sets by Chai Yuqiu, *Moulue jia* (Strategists), *Moulue lun* (Strategic theories), and *Moulue ku* (Treasury of strategies)(Beijing: Guangxi renmin chubanshe, 1995).

GEOPOLITICAL CALCULATIONS

An essential aspect of assessing the security environment is said to be determining the rank order of the power held by the various warring states. Although today's Chinese concept of Comprehensive National Power (CNP) was invented in the early 1980s, it originally stemmed from Chinese traditional military philosophy. Authors who currently assess the CNP of different nations can find precedents in the ancient classics. For example, Sun Zi identified "five things" and "seven stratagems" that govern the outcome of war, and Wu Zi wrote about six conditions in which, if the other side's strength was greater, war should be avoided. Colonel Wu Chunqiu of AMS writes that these six points "are relatively complete, they simply are the epitome of [today's concept of] Comprehensive National Power."[6]

However, much like current times, Chinese ancient strategists also attempted to help their country achieve dominance through nonwarfare methods. According to Wu Chunqiu, calculating CNP can aid a nation not just for war but also to "coordinate a political and diplomatic offensive, to psychologically disintegrate the enemy forces and subdue them." Assessing one's own CNP can also aid a country in promoting development and growth.

Two studies by the late Herbert Goldhamer of the RAND Corporation sought to outline some of the content of Chinese statecraft and China's unique perceptions.[7] One of Goldhamer's insights relevant to this study is his emphasis on how China's ancient statecraft demanded efforts to calculate the future. He points out that ancient China's first Minister was called "The Universal Calculator"; that the philosopher Han Feizi demanded that strategy be based on cost-benefit calculations; and that the philosopher Mozi persuaded an enemy general to surrender by showing he could calculate through a "seminar game" what the outcome of the battle would be.[8]

---

[6]Wu Chunqiu, *Guangyi da zhanlue* (Grand strategy)(Beijing: Shishi chubanshe, 1995), 98.

[7]Herbert Goldhamer, *The Adviser* (New York: Elsevier, 1978); Herbert Goldhamer, *Reality and Belief in Military Affairs: A First Draft* (Santa Monica, CA: The RAND Corporation, 1979).

[8]Goldhamer, *The Adviser*, 130-132.

The Warring States era had the equivalent of general staffs, which calculated the strengths and intentions of players in this multipolar world.[9] Sun Zi warned that victory depended on calculations and estimates of enemy strength and weaknesses made in advance by advisers in the temple council; Mozi taught his students the future could be known.[10] Two of ancient China's greatest advisers on statecraft, Lord Shang and Li Si, warned of the need for calculating the future in a multipolar strategic environment. Li Si wrote a famous memorandum to the ruler of Qin, the man who would unify China and become its first emperor, warning, "This is the one moment in ten thousand ages. If your Highness allows it to slip away . . . there will form an anti-Qin alliance."[11]

With regard to calculating the future, Goldhamer suggests that political writings from ancient China contained "principled predictions," not just intuition or guess work. For example, Lord Shang, a famous adviser in Qin, warned that the price for neglecting quantitative calculations would be that even a state with a large population and a favorable geographical position "will become weaker and weaker, until it is dismembered. . . .The early kings did not rely on their beliefs but on their figures."[12] The subject of Chinese statecraft in a multipolar world explored by Goldhamer remains important to China's process of strategic assessment, especially judging by the sharp increase of Chinese military publications about the relevance of ancient statecraft in the last few years.

GEOPOLITICAL STRATEGY

Warring states that rose too fast suffered attack, dismemberment, and even complete extinction. In the final phase of the Warring States era, as every literate Chinese knows, a brilliant strategist formed a coalition that stood for

---

[9]Goldhamer, *Reality and Belief in Military Affairs*, 32-33.

[10]Huang Yingxu, "*Manyi Zhongguo gudai junshi sixiang zhong de minben jingshen*" (A discussion on the spirit of relying on the people in Chinese ancient military thought), *Zhongguo junshi kexue* (China Military Science) 34, no. 1 (Spring 1996): 121-125. Colonel Huang describes the change from divination to calculation in the Spring and Autumn era. He is a Research Fellow in the department of Mao Zedong Military Thought at AMS.

[11]Goldhamer, *The Adviser*, 121.

[12]Ibid., 135-136.

several decades against the predatory hegemon Qin. Chinese authors today apparently believe the United States is this kind of hegemon, which, if provoked, will attack or "contain" China to preserve its hegemony.

The existence of a dangerous and predatory hegemon is the context of Deng Xiaoping's advice, which employs expressions from the Warring States and other ancient texts to guide future Chinese leaders on strategy. China must *"tao guang yang hui,"* which, literally translated, means "Hide brightness, nourish obscurity," or, as the official Beijing interpretation translates the four-character idiom, "Bide our time and build up our capabilities." China at present is too poor and weak and must avoid being dragged into local wars, conflicts about spheres of influence, or struggles over natural resources. Deng's much-quoted advice also is to "yield on small issues with the long term in mind."

How is Deng's advice about dealing in the future with a dangerous hegemon actually applied? Dr. Yan Xuetong, Director of the Center for Foreign Policy at the China Institute of Contemporary International Relations (CICIR), China's largest international research institute, warned in an article in 1997 that the probability of China's avoiding war for at least 10 more years will increase the more China avoids any confrontation not only with the current global hegemon but with at least two of the other major powers. Like his colleague at CASS, Liu Jinghua, who warns about the dangerous decade from 2020 to 2030, when the U.S. leadership will finally realize that China's power is about to surpass America's, the CICIR center director warns that from ancient times, the hegemon will form a coalition to strangle to death (*e mo*) a rising power when he fears he is to be replaced. Deng Xiaoping's additional word of advice was *bu chu tou*—never be the leader or, literally translated, "Don't stick your head out."

President Jiang Zemin has issued traditional-style, poetic statements in sets of 16 Chinese characters that continue Deng's cautious advice about avoiding confrontation with the hegemon.[13] Under Jiang Zemin, an additional set of writings (five books in 1996) has advocated that China's military programs be focused on the potential revolution in military affairs (RMA)

---

[13]The 16-character policy put forward by Jiang is, "To enhance confidence, decrease troubles, promote cooperation and avoid confrontation" (*zengjia xinren, jianshao mafan, fazhan hezuo, bugao duikang*). Quoted in Lu Zhongwei, "On China-U.S.-Japan Trilateral Relations—Comments on Their Recent Exchanges of Top-level Visits," *Contemporary International Relations* 7, no. 12 (December 1997): 9.

rather than improving current weapons. According to these books, the potential RMA will not "mature" until at least 2030, by which time Chinese military authors calculate that China (or possibly Japan) will score highest in the world in CNP and be well positioned, as General Mi Zhenyu has written, to "get ahead of all the others."[14]

Deng Xiaoping's call for caution is not the only lesson based on ancient statecraft. Other Chinese authors (called hotheads by their critics) want to take the initiative to form a coalition against the United States, Warring States style. This is the opposite of not sticking your head out, or biding your time. China's ultranationalist and well-connected author He Xin advocates that China, "under the banner of opposing the hegemon" should align with every anti-American nation in the world, explicitly citing the powerful precedent of the Warring States coalition. Critics of He Xin, especially authors from his former employer, CASS, point out that the Warring States era ended when a more brilliant statesman adroitly broke up the coalition and became the founding emperor of China, which may be just what He Xin fears. He predicts that the future ambition of the United States is to impose world domination.

He Xin's critics, however, project a sharp decline in the global role of the United States, asserting that in two decades or so:

- The United States will inevitably decline to one of five powers.
- Japan, the European Union, Russia, and China will each equal the United States.
- The United States, Russia, and China will have nuclear equivalence.

From this viewpoint, dealing with the dangerous hegemon is only a temporary problem. Within two or three decades, or so, the problem will solve itself, as happened many times in the Warring States era.

Patience and caution are thus seen to be wiser than aggressive coalition building against the United States. Dr. Yan Xuetong, of CICIR, has argued that the ruling American hegemon can be kept from using force to contain China's rise as long as certain policy goals are maximized: annually increasing exports up to 9 percent and avoiding simultaneous confrontation with the

[14]Mi Zhenyu, *Zhongguo guofang fazhan gouxiang* (China's national defense development concepts) (Beijing: Jiefangjun chubanshe, 1988). Excerpts translated in Michael Pillsbury, ed., *Chinese Views of Future Warfare* (Washington: National Defense University Press, 1997), 361-381. Mi Zhenyu is a former Vice President of the Academy of Military Science (AMS).

United States and two other powerful nations. Using the following imaginative table of probabilities, Dr. Yan predicts that China can avoid war for at least 10 years by adopting these two policies. However, his table shows that as China's annual share of export markets declines and the number of powerful nations China confronts increases, the probability that China will become involved in war with the United States increases rather sharply.

Table 1. *The Rank and Index Numbers of Individual Indexes*

The international environment for a rising power	Outcome			
	Very favorable	Relatively favorable	Relatively unfavorable	Very unfavorable

Index Numbers of Individual Indexes

Index	4	3	2	1	Unit
Anticipated time of being drawn into a war	>10	>5 ≤10	>0 ≤5	0	Year
Unity with the strategic interests of other powers	Be in unity with the United States and one power	Be opposed to the United States and in unity with three powers	Be opposed to the United States and one power	Be opposed to the United States and two powers	Country
The increasing share of export markets	>0.3	>0.1 ≤0.3	>0 ≤0.1	≤0	%

Source: Yan Xuetong, "Zhongguo jueqi de guoji huanjing pinggu" (An Assessment of the international environment of China's rise), *Zhanlue yu guanli* (Strategy and Management) 20, no. 1 (1997):18, 20, 23.

Not all authors are as optimistic as Dr. Yan. Indeed, his fellow author at CICIR, Zhang Wenmu, presents a more pessimistic diagnosis also based on Warring States premises. The hegemon needs resources, and such a hegemon presents a set of dangers China will face because of America's desperate need for access to new oil and gas resources, especially in Central Asia. According to Zhang's assessment of U.S. future strategy, the United States has begun to interfere in the Tibet issue as part of a larger scheme involving the enlargement of NATO and the redefinition of the U.S.-Japan Defense Guidelines. Zhang believes U.S. strategy is always to "follow the oil." In World War II, the United States did not intervene until Japan changed its strategy and moved toward oil supplies. Similarly, before the Gulf War, the United States ignored Iraqi expansion toward the North and West and even "pretended" not to notice, but when Saudi and Kuwait oil was threatened, the United States went to war. Zhang writes that in 1998 the United States had a "two arms" strategy to contain both Russia (with NATO enlargement) and China (with the new Japan Defense Guidelines and promoting the China Threat Theory).

In addition, Zhang predicts that the United States wants to screen off both Chinese and Russian access to Central Asian oil and gas. To accomplish this strategic goal, the United States will promote the future independence of Tibet from China. If there is internal turmoil in Tibet or farther north in Muslim Xinjiang, Zhang predicts that the United States will try to set up an international no-fly zone as it did after the Gulf War. In a disguised manner, this would amount to "dismembering" Tibet and Xinjiang, the hub or pivot of China's geopolitical position. This is particularly dangerous because the Soviet collapse started with the independence of the Baltic states. A chain reaction from Tibet and Xinjiang would affect China's industrial southwest and cause the loss of the high plateau, which provides natural protection to the west. Zhang therefore recommends that China take the lead in settling the Afghan civil war (which he says the United States is prolonging through covert aid to the Taliban fundamentalists). At the same time, Zhang advocates more caution. China must get the Central Asia oil market oriented to China. It is better to place high priority on land transport of oil and gas, which China's superiority in ground forces can protect, rather than depend in the future on sealanes for oil supplies that the United States and Japan will threaten with their powerful navies.[15] These recommendations had their counterparts in the Warring States era.

---

[15]Zhang Wenmu, "Meiguo de shiyou diyuan zhanyue yu Zhongguo Xizang Xinjiang diqu anquan" (America's geopolitical oil strategy and the security of China's Tibet and Xinjiang regions), *Zhanlue yu guanli* (Strategy and Management) 27, no. 2 (1998): 100-104.

Zhang Wenmu and Dr. Yan Xuetong contrast sharply with the strategic diagnosis and recommendation based on the Warring States period offered by one of China's most colorful and controversial strategic authors, He Xin, who frequently uses analogies to the era.[16] Reformers despise him and orthodox analysts tend to distance themselves from his outspoken nationalistic writings, which run against Deng Xiaoping's advice to "bide our time" and "never take the lead." Nevertheless, there is no better example of how statecraft from the Warring States era can affect China's assessments of the future. Among many other articles, He Xin has written a call for a Chinese-led coalition against today's hegemon before it is too late. He Xin cites the precedent of the Warring States era, because "the past can help us understand the present" and outlines key points:[17]

- "The world situation, after the severe changes in the Soviet Union and Eastern Europe, in form actually appears amazingly similar to the situation in the latter period of the Warring States, where there were six powerful countries facing each other and one country dominating."[18]
- The United States "will sacrifice different countries' national interests and independent sovereignty, take the entire world and change it into an American World Empire. . .[and] become the director, arbitrator, the final

---

[16]He Xin himself has been compared by a Western analyst to the strategists of the Warring States era that he so admires: "The Party leadership throughout its history has relied on intellectuals and ideologues to rationalize the quirks of its decisionmaking. The more talented and astute intellectuals of this kind serve a function not dissimilar to that of the advisers to the imperial court; or perhaps their role can be likened to that of the itinerant 'lobbyists' (*youshui zhi shi*) or the 'strategists' (*zonghengjia*) of the Warring States period. Sometimes these hired hands have proved to be highly capable men, as the case of Chen Boda, Chou Yang, and Hu Qiaomu in the 1940s and 1950s, or Yao Wenyuan in the 1960s. Though he has yet to achieve the prominence of the above-listed figures, over recent years another intellectual has appeared on the scene to vie with clever young things employed by Zhao Ziyang and his supporters. His name is He Xin." See He Xin, "A Word of Advice to the Politburo," translated, annotated, and introduced by Geremie Barme, *The Australian Journal of Chinese Affairs*, no. 23 (January 1990): 50.

[17]He Xin, *Zhongguo fuxing yu shijie weilai* (China's rejuvenation and the world's future)(Chengdu: Sichuan renmin chubanshe, 1996), 41.

[18]In addition to the one superpower (the United States) and four powers (Japan, China, Germany, and Russia) usually cited by Chinese authors, He Xin also includes France and England. Ibid., 30.

decider of all problems—the highest dictator of world economics and politics."[19]

• "In the early period [of the Warring States era], the six countries 'joined horizontally,' and for a number of decades effectively resisted the powerful Qin threat. However, in the later period, one after another they accepted Qin protection and were willing to become its satellite countries. The result was their collapse in 10 years. They were each destroyed by the Qin threat. . . . It is now necessary to form a modern strategy of 'joining horizontally.' "[20]

• "China must pay close attention to those countries that are opposed to American interests, or are potential strategic enemies. It must be borne in mind that the enemies of enemies are one's own allies."

• "China should do all that it can to warn and help these countries, and prevent them from being destroyed by the United States as the Soviet Eastern European bloc was. It must bring together the world antihegemonism force under the flag of fighting hegemonism."

• "Know this: the more the United States encounters trouble in other places in the world, the more difficult it is for it to concentrate its power on dealing with China and the greater the opportunities for China's existence and development."

• "China must seek allies among all countries that could become America's potential opponents today or in the future. The following three regions are especially worth serious attention: Japan (America's future potential strategic opponent in the Asia-Pacific); Germany (America's future potential strategic opponent in Europe); and the South Asia peninsula (a border region that is of important strategic significance to China). I solemnly put forward a three-point plan, 'Join Japan, work with Germany, stabilize the South.' "[21]

Somewhere between the cautionary advice of Deng Xiaoping, Dr. Yan, and Zhang Wenmu, and the bold demand of He Xin for anti-U.S. coalition building, lies the strategic advice offered by Liu Jinghua, of CASS. While less

---

[19]Ibid., 31.

[20]Ibid., 41.

[21]Ibid., 41-42.

dramatic than He Xin's proposal for a global anti-U.S. coalition, his suggestion deals with the same problem of preventing the predatory, hegemonic United States from containing China's rise, or worse, and is also firmly in the tradition of Warring States statecraft. Liu warns that by 2020 to 2030, serious confrontations will begin among the major powers. At present, it is wise to *tao guang yang hui* (conceal abilities and bide time), in order to eliminate the China Threat Theory, but by 2020 that policy will not be sufficient. The United States (and Europe, too) will by then begin seriously to attempt to contain China. Then, "once the flood begins, we must have a 'Great Wall' that cannot collapse." One part of this "Great Wall" must be a partnership with Russia to defeat Western containment of China, which will be attempted by restricting access to capital markets and technology, promoting Western values and using military power "as the core" against China.[22] Implicit here, too, is that China has plenty of time and needs mainly not to provoke the hegemon in the intervening two decades until the Great Wall can be made ready.

Another diagnosis and recommendation projects onto the United States the kind of knowledge from ancient statecraft that a true predatory hegemon ought to have. This is a kind of mirror image from the Warring States. According to General Li Jijun, one of China's most distinguished military authors and a former Vice President of AMS, the greater danger to a nation's survival is not warfare but *zhanlue wudao*—"strategic misdirection"—in the current multipolar world structure. General Li describes the United States as being particularly adept at this strategy, as powerful hegemons used to be.

According to Genera Li, the United States brought about the collapse of the Soviet Union with strategic misdirection. Washington deceptively stimulated the Soviets to increase their defense budget to great heights through various means, including the Strategic Defense Initiative ("Star Wars"), which the United States had no intention of deploying, Li writes. The United States also supported the opposition in Poland and Afghanistan, drove down the price of oil to cut off the main source of Soviet foreign exchange, and exacerbated the domestic Soviet political crisis. In 1990, Washington again used strategic misdirection against Saddam Hussein, in order to contain his rising power in the Gulf. As supposedly revealed by an American author,

---

[22]Liu Jinghua, "Ershi yi shiji ershi sanshi niandai Zhongguo jueqi ji waijiao zhanlue xueze" (Diplomatic strategic alternatives for a rising China in 2020 to 2030), *Zhanlue yu guanli* (Strategy and Management) 4, no. 3 (1994), 119.

Washington deliberately lured Saddam into invading Kuwait, in part through deliberately deceptive comments to Saddam by the U.S. Ambassador in Baghdad, to the effect that the United States did not care if he invaded Kuwait. General Li, comparing the strategic cultures of all the major powers, concludes that the preferred "strategic cultural" approach of the United States is strategic misdirection. Citing the lessons of history, General Li warns that "unconsciously accepting an opponent's strategic misdirection causes a nation to be defeated or collapse, and not know why."[23]

General Li is not the only PLA officer to hold this view. Following the NATO bombing of the Chinese Embassy in Belgrade in spring 1999, a Chinese journal interviewed several PLA generals about the attack; they stated that one reason for the United States to bomb the embassy was strategic misdirection. An article in the June issue of *Zhongguo Pinglun* concludes, "The Western forces are attempting to drag China into the mire of the arms race. The United States is planning to pursue a TMD [theater missile defense] system . . . so that the Chinese will step into the shoes of the former Soviet Union. In an arms race with the United States, China will consume its national power, and collapse without a battle."[24] A key strategy of the Warring States was to attempt to do just this to an opponent.

Having made the point that these nine authors from five key research institutes use lessons and metaphors from the Warring States era and ancient statecraft, the first chapter presents several debates underway among many authors about the exact nature of the future "multipolar" security environment China will face in the decades ahead.

---

[23]Li Jijun, "Zhanlue wenhua" (Strategic culture), *Zhongguo junshi kexue* (China Military Science) 38, no. 1 (Spring 1997): 8-15.

[24]"China Must be Ready to Fight a World War—PLA Believes That the West is Hatching Six Major Conspiracies Against China," *Sing Tao Jih Pao* (Hong Kong), May 28, 1999, b14, in FBIS-CHI-1999-0528, June 1, 1999.

CHINA
Debates the Future
Security Environment

1 : THE MULTIPOLARITY DEBATE

THE VISIONS OF MORE THAN 30 AUTHORS are presented in this chapter about the geopolitical features of the future. They reveal debates between orthodox and reformist authors about which nations will be the most powerful by 2020, what kinds of international alignments will form, and the nature of the post-Cold War transitional pattern.

THE CURRENT ASSESSMENT, 1986-99

China's current assessment of the future security environment is based on the kind of calculations Sun Zi and the Warring States strategists would recognize. It was issued before the collapse of the Soviet Union and the end of the Cold War and can be dated to early 1986. The assessment characterizes the present world as being in a "new era" of transition that will last several decades. During this period, great rivalries will emerge among the powers, and many local wars will be fought (as large as Korea in 1950 or the Gulf War in 1991), as a "re-division of spheres of influence" and a struggle for world leadership takes place. Bosnia is one example of the strife that typifies the era, because the Bosnia conflict is frequently called a "struggle between the United States and the European Union for domination of Europe." NATO enlargement, which China opposes, is another example of this "struggle to re-divide spheres of influence." The outcome of this transitional period of "turbulence" will have the following eight features:

- After the transition period is complete, there will no longer be any "superpowers" but instead a "multipolar world" in which five major nations—China, the United States, Japan, Europe and Russia—will each have roughly equal Comprehensive National Power (CNP).[1]

• The nations that will do "best" in competitive terms during the transitional period will pursue "peace and development" and enhance their economic competitiveness. By avoiding local wars, they can decrease defense expenditures and avoid the damage of warfare. Chinese authors frequently assert that the collapse of the Soviet Union and the decline of the United States are due in large part to extremely high defense spending and diminishing competitiveness in CNP.

• Today's "sole superpower" is in severe decline. The United States risks declining so extensively in contrast to the rise of other nations that it will fall to the level of a mere "common major nation."[2] This continual weakening of U.S. strength in the decades ahead is an important feature of the Chinese assessment, so this study provides more details on this subject than on China's views of other major powers.

• After the transition to the multipolar world, a new "world system" will emerge to govern international affairs, one that will probably resemble the current Chinese proposal of the "Five Principles of Peaceful Coexistence." Chinese authorities assert that world politics since the 1800s always has had a "system" or a "strategic pattern." Under those rules, there is a competition among powers that includes a global division of spheres of influence. Chinese historical textbooks discuss the "Vienna System" of 1815-70; an intermediate system when Germany and Italy each unified and Japan launched the Meiji Reform; the "Versailles

---

[1] An American view of the prospects for world multipolarity is found in Charles Krauthammer, "The Unipolar Moment," *Foreign Affairs* 70, no. 1 (America and the World, 1990/1991): 23-33. Krauthammer argues that there is but one first-rate world power and he forecasts that "no doubt, multipolarity will come in time. In perhaps another generation or so there will be great powers coequal with the United States . . . But we are not there yet, nor will be for decades." Similarly, Joseph Nye, Jr., in *Bound to Lead: The Changing Nature of American Power* (New York: Basic Books, 1990), 235, argues, "At one extreme multipolarity merely refers to the diffusion of power. At the other it refers to a number of roughly equal powers, able and willing to shift alliances frequently to maintain their equilibrium."

[2] He Fang, "Guodu shiqi de guoji xingshi" (The international situation during the transition period), in *2000: Shijie xiang hechu qu?* (2000: where is the world going?), ed. Yang Zheng (Beijing: Zhongguo guangbo dianshi chubanshe, 1996), 319.

System" of 1920-45; the "Yalta System" of 1945-89; and the present "transition era."

● The new Chinese-style world system of the Five Principles will be much better than systems of the past and present, because there will be harmony, no "power politics," and no more "hegemony."[3] This harmonious world requires a transition away from capitalism in the major powers toward some type of "socialist market economy." Just as China has modified the doctrines of Marx, Engels, Lenin, and Stalin to produce what Deng Xiaoping called "Socialism with Chinese Characteristics," so will the United States, Germany, Japan, and Russia ultimately develop their own socialist characteristics.

● Some Chinese military authors believe that there is now underway a revolution in military affairs (RMA) that will radically change future warfare. Several recent Chinese books assert that the United States may not exploit the RMA as well as other nations in the decades ahead.[4] China's generals "plan to be better, to be ahead of everyone . . . and become latecomers who surpass the old-timers" in the new revolution.[5]

● A major global nuclear war is highly unlikely for two decades. This official forecast is a sharp change from the forecasts of Chairman Mao that a global nuclear war was inevitable.[6] Therefore, China claims to have cut its defense spending from more than 6 percent of gross national

[3]Chen Xiaogong, a senior military intelligence officer and former U.S. Atlantic Council visiting fellow, has written that the question of the transition period will be "Should the world be built into a peaceful and stable place based on the Five Principles of Peaceful Coexistence, one which is beneficial to economic development in an absolute majority of countries?" In Chen Feng and Chen Xiaogong, "The World Is in the Transition Period of a New Strategic Pattern Replacing the Old," *Jiefang jun bao* (Liberation Army Daily), January 4, 1991, 3, in FBIS-CHI-91-021, January 31, 1991, 11-15.

[4]Chinese views of the RMA will be treated in detail in chapter 6.

[5]Mi Zhenyu, *Zhongguo guofang fazhan gouxiang* (China's national defense development concepts) (Beijing: Jiefangjun chubanshe, 1988). Excerpts translated in Michael Pillsbury, ed., *Chinese Views of Future Warfare* (Washington: National Defense University Press, 1997), 361-381. Mi Zhenyu is a former Vice President of the Academy of Military Science (AMS).

[5]Mao's assessment predicted an inevitable Soviet-American war in Europe, in which Soviet forces would drive NATO forces toward the Channel and result in a "Dunkirk" or evacuation under fire of the United States from continental Europe.

product (GNP) in the 1960s and 1970s, to between 2 and 3 percent when the current assessment came into force by the mid-1980s, and down to about 1.5 percent of the GNP in the 1990s. This claim by China that it has drastically reduced defense spending, which included cutting the People's Liberation Army (PLA) from 7 to 3 million, is based on China's expectation that it can remain above the fray of local wars during the turbulent transition era ahead.

● There are many global forces at work for *luan* (turbulence, a word that also may be translated as chaos), including the potential for nationalist, militarist takeovers of Japan and India. The "main trend" in the world is toward "peace and development," but "potential hot spots exist which could lead to the involvement of major powers and regional powers in direct military confrontation."[7] As suggested by one writer, this is true even in Asia: "Although the Asia-Pacific region has been relatively stable since the end of the Cold War, there are also many uncertainties there. If certain hot-spot problems are not handled properly, they may cause conflicts, confrontations, and even war in this region, thus wrecking the peace, stability, and prosperity of the region."[8]

Within the framework of this strategic assessment, China's analysts discuss a number of subjects in their journals and books.[9] For example, the

---

[7] Major General Pan Zhengqiang, "Current World Military Situation," *Renmin ribao* (People's Daily), December 23,1993, 7, in FBIS-CHI-94-005, January 7, 1994, 27-29. Pan is Director of the Institute for National Security Studies of the National Defense University (NDU) in Beijing.

[8] Zhu Chenghu, "Focus Attention on the Converging Points of Interest of China and the United States" (in Chinese), *Jiefangjun bao* (Liberation Army Daily), June 19, 1998, 4. Zhu is Deputy Director of the Strategic Research Institute of the National Defense University, Beijing.

[9] For examples of comprehensive studies on the current and future security environment sponsored by three different institutions, the Chinese Academy of Social Sciences, the Shanghai Institute for International Studies, and the China Institute of Contemporary International Relations, see Xi Runchang and Gao Heng, eds., *Shijie zhengzhi xin geju yu guoji anquan* (The new world political structure and international security)(Beijing: Junshi kexue chubanshe, 1996); Chen Qimao, ed., *Kua shiji de shijie geju da zhuanhuan* (Major changes in the world structure at the turn of the century)(Shanghai: Shanghai jiaoyu chubanshe, 1996); and Li Zhongcheng, *Kua shiji de shijie zhengzhi* (Trans century world politics)(Beijing: Shishi

question frequently arises about how current events fit into the framework. Some Chinese authors see the following examples of the "turbulent period of transition" as suggesting that former spheres of influence are being "re-divided." While not all Chinese authors included in this volume would agree with all these findings, the examples demonstrate how the framework of the assessment of the future is applied in practice:

- The United States is exploiting Russian weakness by enlarging NATO in order to increase its domination of its European NATO allies.
- The United States ("its hegemonistic ambitions further inflated") is forcing Japan to increase its financial support for U.S. bases and forces in Japan under the guise of the Defense Guidelines.[10]
- The United States arranged the Bosnian settlement at Dayton to dominate further its European NATO allies.
- Japan is seeking to embroil the Unites States and China in a struggle that will weaken both Washington and Beijing.[11]
- Some in the United States are fearful of China and seek to contain or block China's gradually increasing influence by promoting the China Threat Theory. This is wrong because "China has neither the strength nor the will to compete with the United States and other big powers in global affairs."[12]
- Central Asia may be the location of political struggles and wars among the big powers as the former Soviet sphere of influence is re-divided. For example, a recent article stated, "Following the Soviet Union's disintegration, the United States has cast its covetous eyes on Central Asia, the 'second Middle East of the next century,' with the goal

---

chubanshe, 1997).

[10]Zhang Taishan, "Ri-Mei junshi guanxi de xin fazhan" (New developments in the Japan-U.S. military relationship), *Guoji zhanlue yanjiu* (International Strategic Studies) 46, no. 4 (October 1997): 16-18. Zhang is a Research Fellow at the Chinese Institute of International Strategic Studies CIISS.

[11]Feng Shaokui's article on this issue is discussed below.

[12]Chen Peiyao, "Big Power Relations in the Asia-Pacific Region," *SIIS Journal* 1, no. 3 (November 1995): 1.

of eventually controlling most of the energy resources in Central Asia." The article asserts that in 1998 "Russia and the United States continued their contention in Central Asia by covert and overt means. The basic situation is still that 'the United States is on the offensive while Russia is on the defensive.' What has changed is that Russia has switched its 'passive defense' to 'active defense.' " The author concludes that this change means the United States will "find it difficult to have a free rein in Central Asia."[13]

• NATO airstrikes against Yugoslavia in spring 1999 were a part of a U.S. plan to gain control over Eurasia. "On the surface, the 'salvation' of the ethnic Albanians in Kosovo by NATO troops seems to be out of 'humanitarian considerations' but some important geostrategic interests are undoubtedly hidden behind this operation."[14] An article entitled, "What are NATO's Motives in Bombing the Federal Republic of Yugoslavia," explained, "Kosovo is located in the middle of the Balkan Peninsula and the peninsula is at the meeting point of Europe, Asia, and Africa. It is an important corridor joining the north, south, east, and west and leading to Asia and Africa. . . . The United States knows full well the importance of the Balkan region and has regarded it as a 'new priority for consideration'. . . . In this region, it can strengthen its security system in the Mediterranean and the North Atlantic to the west; can consolidate the 'southern wing of NATO' to the south through converging it with its Middle East strategy; can infiltrate and expand in the Black Sea and the Caspian Sea regions to the west, that is, the outer Caucasus and Central Asia regions, weakening and squeezing out Russian forces and influence, and taking a step further, can press on to China's northwestern boundary to coordinate from afar with its Asia-Pacific strategy; and finally, can exercise restraints on its European allies to the north, especially the NATO move southward. In this way, the United States will be able to

---

[13]Zhou Xiaohua, "Roundup: Overt and Covert Russia-U.S. Rivalry in China," Beijing Xinhua Domestic Service, December 28, 1998, in FBIS-CHI-99-004, January 4, 1999.

[14]Wang Yizhou, "A Warning Issued at the End of the Century," *Shijie Zhishi*, no. 10 (May 16, 1999): 7-10, in FBIS-CHI-1999-0623, June 24, 1999.

properly fulfill its ambition of making Europe more important and practicing hegemony in the world."[15]

MULTIPOLARITY PROCLAIMED IN 1986

Chinese analysts do not observe international scholarly standards by footnoting each other or providing bibliographical information. Most authors write as if they were the sole Chinese to ever deal with an issue, in sharp contrast to Western scholarly books and articles, where the author is expected to make clear his debt to earlier work and narrowly and modestly to describe his new contribution. Thus, no Chinese author writing in the 1990s refers to the origins of the current view of the future security environment. Interviews have established that it was Huan Xiang, Deng Xiaoping's national security adviser, who had both access to scholarly experts from Shanghai as well as experience as China's ambassador to Britain, who announced its features in early 1986, just after the U.S.-Soviet summit. Huan's speeches and articles in 1984 and 1985 described a world structure that was changing, but it was still unclear what actions the major players would take and its characteristics were not yet determined:

● "The two largest military powers are weakening and declining . . . militarily they are developing in the direction of multipolarization . . . if the Star Wars plan develops, multipolarization could develop toward bipolarization, and could again return to bipolarization. If secondary

---

[15]Yan Zheng, "What Are NATO Motives in Bombing the Federal Republic of Yugoslavia?," *Renmin Luntan*, no. 4 (April 15, 1999): 37-39, in FBIS-CHI-1999-0516, May 16, 1999. See also Zhang Dezhen, "On U.S. Eurasian Strategy," *Renmin Ribao*, June 4, 1999, 6, in FBIS-CHI-1999-0605, June 4, 1999. "The recent aggressive war flagrantly waged by the U.S.-led NATO forces against the Federal Republic of Yugoslavia has laid bare the fact that the United States would not hesitate to make a reckless move to pull out the last 'nail' in Europe and to place the Balkan region and the entire Europe under its control. . . . By expanding its sphere of influence at both the east end and the west end of Eurasia, the United States has succeeded in encircling Eurasia in two directions and in bringing pressure to bear on the Eurasian countries. In view of the U.S. infiltration into and the U.S. control over the Gulf-Caucasus-Caspian Sea-Central Asian region, it could be said, the United States has attained step by step its strategic goal of first placing Eurasia and then the whole world under its control."

ranked countries want to carry out a Star Wars plan, it will be very difficult. The position of those countries will immediately decline."[16]
- "The old world order has already disintegrated and the new world order is now taking shape, but up to now it still has not yet completely formed."
- "U.S. domination of the Asia-Pacific will end."
- "Japan knows what role it should take, but it still hesitates. . . . China must go through a long period of hard work . . . 30 to 50 years time will make it truly powerful."[17]

Beginning in January 1986, the uncertainty about the future world structure had disappeared, and its transformation and transition had definite traits and stages.[18] Huan explained, "Future international politics and economics are facing a new period."[19]

- "In the confrontation between the two superpowers, changes that are deeper and more significant than those of the past have occurred."[20]

---

[16]Huan Xiang, "Xin jishu geming dui junshi de yingxiang" (The influence of the new technological revolution on military affairs), in *Huan Xiang wenji* (The collected works of Huan Xiang)(Beijing: Shijie zhishi chubanshe, 1994), 2: 1263. This article was originally published in *Liberation Army Daily*, June 7 and June 14, 1985.

[17]Huan Xiang, "Yatai diqu xingshi he Mei-Su de zhengduo zhanlue" (The situation in the Asia-Pacific region and U.S.-Soviet rivalry strategy), in *Huan Xiang wenji*, 1115. This article originally appeared in *Guoji zhanwang* (International Outlook), no. 14 (1984).

[18]Soon after Huan Xiang began to discuss the new multipolar era, another analyst described many of the key tenets of the current assessment of the multipolar world structure in an open source article. See Gao Heng, "Shijie zhanlue geju zhengxiang duojihua fazhan" (Development of global strategic multipolarity), *Guofang daxue xuebao* (National Defense University Journal), no. 2 (1986): 32-33.

[19]Huan Xiang, "Wo guo 'qiwu' qijian mianlin guoji zhengzhi jingji huanjing de fenxi" (An analysis of the international political and economic environment that China is facing during its seventh five-year plan), in *Huan Xiang wenji*, 1300. Originally an interview with a reporter from the *Shanghai shijie jingji dabao*.

[20]Huan Xiang, "Zhanwang 1986 nian guoji xingshi" (Prospects for the 1986 international situation), in *Huan Xiang wenji*, 1291. Originally published in *Liaowang*, no. 1 (1986).

● "Even though the two superpowers still are the two countries with the most solid actual strength, . . . the new stage of U.S.-Soviet relations will further weaken their ability to control and influence their respective allies. More and more of their allies will seek an even greater level of independence . . . within the two blocs, there are also increasingly developing trends of economic and political friction and being at odds with the leadership. . . . The world's political multipolarity trend will further develop."[21]

● "The focal point of the competition has been raised from the past emphasis, which was solely on the struggle for military superiority . . . to a contest of entire economic, scientific and technological, military and political comprehensive strength. Thus for the next several years . . . strengthening Comprehensive National Power will be the main task."[22]

● "The development toward multipolarity is divided into two steps. The first step is the big triangle . . . China, the United States and the Soviet Union. . . . After China's national might and military prowess greatly developed during the Korean War and the Indo-China war, the world had to recognize that China is a very powerful nation. Currently, after revision of its domestic and international policy, its position in the three poles is definite. Western Europe and Japan also are regarded as poles, but they have not completely formed the power of a pole. To form a single pole force, it must be seen if they can be independent with the initiative in their own hands. . . . As the world moves toward a multipolar world, both in the first large triangle stage, and in the future as it moves toward a five pole world, when the United States and the Soviet Union are considering problems, they must think about the China factor, and also the other poles."[23]

---

[21]Ibid., 1292-1293.

[22]Ibid., 1291-1292.

[23]Huan Xiang, "Dui shijie xingshi fazhan qushi de fenxi ji junwei tichu zhuanru 'heping shiqi' zhanlue juece de lillun yiju" (An analysis of the development trends in the world situation and the theoretical basis of the central military commission's strategic decision concerning the shift to the "period of peace"), in *Huan Xiang wenji*, 1327-1328. Originally published March 1, 1986.

- "Militarily there still are two poles, the United States and the Soviet Union. . . . Economically, there currently are four centers: the United States, the Soviet Union, Japan, and Western Europe. . . . Politically, the Sino-U.S.-Soviet large triangular relationship is currently the major factor most able to influence the development of the international situation. In regional issues there are two squares. In the Far Eastern Asia-Pacific region, there is China, the United States, the Soviet Union and Japan. . . . In Europe the square is the United States, the Soviet Union, Eastern Europe, and Western Europe."[24]

- "Japan considers the United States to be its main economic opponent, for deployment of its offensive and for making challenges. It not only wants to strive to be on equal footing with the United States economically and politically, but further, it is deliberately planning, when the time is ripe, to surpass the United States and replace America's world economic hegemony. Once it has economic hegemony, political, and military hegemony would not be too difficult."[25]

China's national security analysts became very concerned about Bush administration proposals for a "new international order" and held a conference in 1991 to discuss their own views.[26] The phrase "New World Order" was first used by then Soviet President Mikhail Gorbachev at the November 1990 Conference on Security and Cooperation in Europe (CSCE) Summit in Paris and at the U.N. General Assembly speech on December 7, 1988, when he announced severe reductions in Soviet military forces, including Soviet forces stationed in the Warsaw Pact countries, which, according to a congressional research study, may have stimulated the unraveling of support for the Communist parties in Eastern Europe and "the

---

[24]Huan Xiang, "Kexue juece yu guoji huanjing" (Scientific decisionmaking and the international environment), in *Huan Xiang wenji*, 1395-1396.

[25]Ibid., 1400.

[26]Two articles on the subject are Ye Ru'an, "Conceptions of the World's Future: On Different Propositions Concerning the new International Order," *Shijie zhishi* (World Knowledge), no. 13 (July 1, 1991), in FBIS-CHI-91-140, July 22, 1991; and speeches at a symposium on this issue by 18 Chinese analysts published in *Shijie zhishi* (World Knowledge), no. 12 (June 16, 1991), in FBIS-CHI-91-141, July 23, 1991.

demise of the Warsaw Pact."[27] Multipolarity in the 21st century was forecast by a senior scholar in 1991.[28]

REVISIONIST MULTIPOLARITY

Challenging the Orthodox View

As mentioned, Chinese authors rarely refer to each other and almost never criticize other authors by name, but in 1997, two unusual articles broke this apparent taboo in two national journals. The episode began when Yang Dazhou, a well-known senior analyst at the Institute of American Studies of the Chinese Academy of Social Science (CASS), published a direct and detailed criticism of the orthodox assessment of the coming world of multipolarity.[29] It is difficult for any foreign observer to know whether the article remained within the bounds of scientifically "seeking truth from facts" that Deng Xiaoping demanded in 1978, or whether it was a "poisonous weed" that threatened Communist Party doctrine, because Central Party documents, which authoritatively set the range of debate, are never made public. Some of those interviewed said the article tested the outer limits of Party orthodoxy about the future world.

The article met with a vigorous response from a senior general in military intelligence. In a departure from the tradition of merely stating a view without debating anyone else, the PLA general actually quoted long passages from the reformer's article. The general then wrote that these views were ridiculous, without foundation, and unsupportable and, worst of all, played into the hands of the United States.[30]

---

[27]Stanley R. Sloan, "The U.S. Role in a New World Order: Prospects for George Bush's Global Vision" (Washington: Congressional Research Service, March 28, 1991).

[28]Luo Renshi, "Strategic Structure, Contradictions and the New World Order," *International Strategic Studies* 19, no.1 (March 1991): 1-6.

[29]Yang Dazhou, "Dui lengzhan hou shijie geju zhi wo jian" (My opinion on the post-Cold War world structure), *Heping yu Fazhan* (Peace and Development) 60, no. 2 (June 1997): 41-45.

[30]Huang Zhengji, "Shijie duojihua qushi buke kangju" (The inevitable trend toward multipolarity), *Guoji zhanlue yanjiu* (International Strategic Studies) 46, no. 4 (October 1997): 1-3. This article parallels the same author's views in an article entitled "Volatile World Situation," *International Strategic Studies* 24, no. 2 (June 1992): 1-5. The journal is published by

Several Chinese authors commented in interviews on both the style and the issues of this unusual "debate." They acknowledged that the two articles reflect a difference among the senior leadership of China about *the pace* of the decline of the United States and *the rate* of the rise of "multipolarity." At least a few influential civilian analysts are said to have written sensitive internal studies for the senior leadership of China, concluding that the United States may remain a superpower for as long as 50 more years. However, analysts stated that no one is willing yet to openly publish the view because of resistance by the military and some civilians who cling to the conventional assessment. This "debate" may have been addressed at the 1997 traditional annual month-long meeting of China's most senior leaders. If so, it highlights the importance of these contradictory two articles on the future security environment.

In his article, Yang Dazhou heretically argues against each of the key features of the orthodox view of the future security environment, putting forward a reformist scenario:

- The United States will maintain its superpower status for at least three decades.
- The United States will maintain its alliances with Japan and Germany.
- There will not be a period of "uncertainty" in the next two or three decades.
- There will not be an extended transition period featuring a trend toward multipolarity.
- A "pluralistic" world structure of "one superpower and four powers" already exists.
- Only the United States is really a "pole" able to decide key issues in any region, as it did with the Dayton Accords. "The United States plays a leading role that no other nation can replace . . . the only country that is a 'pole.' "
- China "does not have sufficient qualifications to be a 'pole.' "
- For more than 20 years, no other nations, including those in the Third World, will emerge as major powers to challenge the five strongest,

---

CIISS and is sponsored by Chinese military intelligence, in which General Huang served.

therefore the phrase used by many analysts "'one super many strong' is actually not appropriate."[31]

- It is not likely large local wars will break out among nations.[32]

The Orthodox Counterattack

According to an interview the author of this volume conducted in Beijing in May 1998, the editor of the PLA journal *International Strategic Studies* decided that an unsolicited article by General Huang Zhengji merited publication even though it was very "sharp" (hostile in tone) and "out of the ordinary" in style. General Huang quoted passages from Yang's article without directly citing it and reasserted the orthodox view on each of these points:

- U.S. decline is inevitable and continuing; U.S. global influence is already severely limited.
- Five-pole multipolarity is inevitable, especially as friction grows between the United States and Japan and Germany (as proved by the new summits between the European Union (EU) and Asia, which excluded the declining United States).
- The rise of the Third World has transformed world politics and will continue to restrain the United States.
- Local wars are certain, even though "'peace and development' is the main trend" during the transitional period of uncertainty in the decades ahead.

---

[31]Yang Dazhou, "Dui lengzhan hou shijie geju zhi wo jian," 43-44.

[32]Yang may have an ally in the author of a book published by the China Institute of Contemporary International Relations (CICIR). On its last page, the author concludes, "The future multipolar structure's principal parts will be the five powers, the United States, Russia, China, Japan, and Germany. The United States will no doubt become 'one pole in the multipolar world,' but its comprehensive strength will be comparatively more powerful than that of other poles, its relations with the other poles also probably will be friendlier than the mutual relations between the four other poles, and its ability to conform to changes probably will be a little bit stronger. Therefore, can it be said: the U.S. in the future is 'one pole in the multipolar world,' but we also can say it is 'the first pole.' " See Lin Huisheng, *Gei shanmu dashu suan yi gua* (Telling Uncle Sam's fortune)(Beijing: Shishi chubanshe, 1995), 229.

According to interviews, the orthodox forecast of the future security environment continues to dominate in all Chinese international studies journals. It is as if the reformist views of Yang Dazhou's article had never appeared. Two methods reinforce the orthodox view. First, new developments are assembled to "prove" the orthodox view. For example, a typical review of 1997 supposedly provided clear evidence not only of the "acceleration" of the inevitable trend toward multipolarity, but also of America's declining international influence: the Association of South East Asian Nations (ASEAN) refusal of U.S. demands that Burma not be admitted as a member of ASEAN; Russian and European defiance of U.S. pressure not to trade with Iran; and Brazil's blocking of U.S. efforts for a free-trade zone in South America.[33]

The second method to reinforce the orthodox and ignore the reform view is repetitive articles by senior officials. One novel example is the publication of a speech given at Harvard University in December 1997 by the Deputy Chief of the General Staff of the PLA, General Xiong Guangkai, that contained all the features of the orthodox view. According to interviews in Beijing, the use of Harvard as the location and a senior PLA policy maker as the "awesome" vehicle was an emphatic message to reformers. It is useful to

---

[33]Chen Feng, "1997 nian di guoji zhanlue xingshi" (The strategic situation in 1997), *Guoji zhanlue yanjiu* (International Strategic Studies) 47, no. 1 (January 1998): 3-7. According to interviews, Colonel Chen served in the Situation Room of the Chinese military intelligence headquarters in Beijing. He now is at the Chinese mission to the United Nations in New York. Shen Qurong, Director of CICIR, provides similar examples of how U.S. foreign affairs activities have been rebuffed around the world: "During the Iraqi crisis of nuclear weapons inspection, the United States did not hesitate to spend several billion U.S. dollars and amassed a large number of naval and air units trying to launch military attacks against Iraq, and stopped short only because of opposition from the majority of the countries around the world including Russia, France, and China. At the Geneva meeting on human rights, the United States was forced to drop its anti-China human rights proposal for lack of support, and its motion against Cuba was also voted down by the conference. The United States has tried to dominate the peace process of the Middle East, but Europe and Russia wanted to share the leading role with it, and Israel did not energetically cooperate with it. In handling the crisis resulting from India's nuclear tests, the United States did not give a strong enough response and the eight-nation group had a divergence of opinion, so Pakistan was forced to follow suit, seriously undermining the international nuclear nonproliferation system advocated by the United States over a long period." See Shen Qurong, "The World is Experiencing the Tests of Crises," *Liaowang*, no. 27 (July 6, 1998): 6, in FBIS-CHI-98-216, August 6, 1998.

quote at some length the words Xiong used to reinforce the orthodox view of the future:

- "Peace and development have become the main theme of the current epoch. However, we cannot but note that the world is still not tranquil."
- "Since the beginning of the 1990s, as many as 68 local wars or armed conflicts have broken out in all parts of the world."
- "Any efforts for seeking hegemony and world domination can only result in accumulating contradictions and fermenting war."
- "Only by facing up to and promoting such a trend as the co-existence of multipolarity can we bring about peace and prosperity."
- "The practice of resolving contradictions among countries by relying on augmenting military blocs, strengthening military alliances or engaging in military confrontation is not conducive to preserving peace and safeguarding security."
- "It is necessary to develop a new concept. I think the Five Principles of Peaceful Coexistence, which has been consistently initiated by the Chinese Government for years, shall constitute an important foundation for establishing a global security system in the 21st century."
- As to the extent of future local wars, Xiong states the death toll was 14 million in the First World War, 60 million in the Second World War, and as high as 24 million in the "40 years of the Cold War."[34]

TECHNIQUES FOR SHOWING DISSENT

As stated, the orthodox and reform views rarely confront each other. Therefore, the open "debate" between Yang Dazhou and Huang Zhengji was without precedent in dealing with such core issues as to whether:

- The United States is really declining
- Local wars will arise

---

[34]Xiong Guangkai, "Mianxiang 21 shiji de guoji anquan xingshi yu Zhongguo jundui jianshe" (Gearing toward the international security situation and the building of Chinese armed forces in the 21st century), *Guoji zhanlue yanjiu* (International Strategic Studies) 48, no. 2 (April 1998): 1-4.

- China is even a "pole"
- Nations other than the 5 strongest can become poles
- There continues to be any "transitional era" of uncertainty about the future.

This is not to say that there are no differences or variances in opinion about the above issues; merely, other authors do not mention anyone else's views, let alone criticize them. Sometimes a "neutral" author alludes to the existence of different points of view on an issue, or a journal will publish the comments of several scholars from a conference in a way that shows disagreements exist. For example, in *2000: Where is the World Going?*, Yang Zheng sets forth six different scenarios for the future world structure, but he only provides a scholar's name in one scenario, does not distinguish between the views of Chinese and foreign analysts, and does not examine or give his own opinion on the feasibility of these possible scenarios.[35]

In 1997, a very senior analyst at CICIR, Li Zhongcheng, outlined three different views of the future world structure by analysts at CICIR and CASS. Although they are not described as being part of a debate, their conflicting

---

[35]The six scenarios are: One, the world is currently in a transition era toward a future multipolar world. Two, there will be a "multilayered multipolar world" (*duo cengci de duoji shijie*), because "the multipolar structure is not a unilevel equal rank system." Rather, in different fields different countries will have greater power. For example, the United States and the Commonwealth of Independent States (CIS) will be the military poles; the United States, Japan and Europe will be the economic poles; and the United States, the CIS, China, Europe, Japan, and the Third World will be the political poles. Third, there will be no poles in the future world structure. "In the foreseeable future, the world will be a world of sudden changes, a turbulent and unstable world. . . . In this world without poles, there are no centers, and there is a great lack of stability." However, there will be "a completely new, large unified international structure." Fourth, there will be a "three pole era" formed by the United States, Europe and Japan. Fifth, there will be "the age of the Comprehensive National Power competition," where strength "will not again be determined by superiority in one single area, such as economics, politics or military affairs." Sixth would be "Han Suyin's unique view" of serious economic and financial confrontation, military interventionism, and the pervasive influence of Western culture and models. Yang Zheng's only ambiguous remarks are, "In brief, having 'left Yalta,' the world is seeking a direction and center of resistance, each tentative idea exists in two of the above possibilities and feasibilities, and all have put forward their various anticipated theoretical and factual foundations. However, the development of history often does not change according to people's subjective wishes; its laws of motion frequently are difficult to dictate." See Yang Zheng, ed., *2000: Shijie xiang hechu qu?*, 22-24.

arguments fall into the opposing sides of the Yang Dazhou-Huang Zhengji dispute. The first scenario is depicted in the writings of Xi Runchang of CASS, who, like Yang Dazhou, refers to the world pattern following the collapse of the Soviet Union as "one super, four strong," and believes that this pattern constitutes a world structure: "Currently there has already basically formed a new embryonic structure supported by the five powers . . . in the 21st century, this new structure will further form and be perfected."[36]

The views of Yan Xuetong of CICIR are representative of the second scenario, "the theory on finalizing the basic design of multipolarity." He asserts, "The basic establishment of the great nations' strategic relations in 1996 caused the post-Cold War transition from a bipolar structure to a one super many strong structure to be completed."[37] Finally, the writings of Song Baoxian and Yu Xiaoqiu of CICIR offer a third scenario, which is more similar to that of Huang Zhengji and the orthodox camp, that "multipolarity is forming" and that countries other than the five most powerful are growing in strength. They argue, "The development of the multipolarity trend is accelerating" and "a new group of powers will rise" that will have a "restricting role with regard to the five major powers, [and] will cause the multipolarity trend of the world structure to be even more attractive and varied."[38] Li does not directly criticize any of the authors whose concepts he presents, although his own views appear to be much closer to those represented in the third scenario.

Authors sometimes resort to citing respected foreign experts in order to dissent. For example, in 1997 in a book published by CICIR, the three authors, who are presumably aware of the orthodox position that there can

---

[36]Xi Runchang, "Shijie zhengzhi xin geju de chuxing ji qi qianjing" (The embryonic form of the world's new political structure and its prospects), *Heping yu fazhan* (Peace and Development), no. 1 (1997), cited in Li Zhongcheng, *Kua shiji de shijie zhengzhi* (Trans century world politics)(Beijing: Shishi chubanshe, 1997), 29.

[37]Yan Xuetong, "1996-1997 nian guoji xingshi yu Zhongguo duiwai guanxi baogao" (A report on the 1996-1997 international situation and China's foreign relations), *Zhanlue yu guanli* (Strategy and Management), supplementary issue (1996-1997), cited in Li Zhongcheng, *Kua shiji de shijie zhengzhi*, 31.

[38]Song Baoxian and Yu Xiaoqiu, "Shijie duojihua qushi jishu fazhan" (The world's multipolarity trend continues to develop), *Renmin ribao* (People's Daily), December 28, 1994, cited in Li Zhongcheng, *Kua shiji de shijie zhengzhi* , 32.

only be five poles, hinted that Henry Kissinger holds a reform view: "Kissinger predicted that the future world will have six poles—America, Japan, China, Russia, Europe, and India. . . .[Today] India's military power is only fourth behind the United States, Russia and China, and India's Comprehensive National Power is continually increasing."[39]

Another innovative technique to avoid debate of the orthodox view is to rise above it by inventing new definitions of orthodox terms. Yan Xuetong of CICIR writes, "The new international structure has some special characteristics, the most important of which is the replacement of 'poles'(*ji*) by 'units' (*yuan*). The nature of 'poles' is long-term stable confrontation, but the nature of 'units' is that the dominant position of key countries is determined by the nature of specific affairs."[40] These definitions elude the orthodox line. Much of Yang Dazhou's article challenged the orthodox view by employing this very tactic of establishing and clarifying definitions for key words and phrases, such as "pole," "transition era," "pluralization" (*duoyuanhua*) versus "multipolarization" (*duojihua*), and "major nation" (*daguo*) versus "a power" (*qiangguo*).

For example, Yang defined what constitutes a "pole" based on the standards of the Cold War era, when the United States and the Soviet Union were the only two poles. The "four strong," consequently, are not poles because "when compared to the Soviet Union, there still is a great distance."[41] Similarly, in his argument against those who claim that the world is in a transition era that will go on for an undetermined long period of time, Yang argues that by definition a transition is not indefinite. "Some people believe that the post-Cold War transition period could continue for 20, even 30 years. This type of argument is not appropriate; a 'transition period' always has an ending time. Suppose the 'transition period' goes on for 20 or 30 years, then

---

[39] Wu Hua, Shen Weili, and Zhen Hongtao, *Nan Ya zhi shi—Indu* (The lion of South Asia—India)(Beijing: Shishi chubanshe, 1997), 2.

[40] Yan Xuetong, *Zhongguo guojia liyi fenxi* (Analysis of China's national interests)(Tianjin: Tianjin renmin chubanshe, 1996), 55.

[41] Yang Dazhou, "Dui lengzhan hou shijie geju zhi wo jian," 43.

this itself already constitutes a new structure different from that of the Cold War period."[42]

DIFFERENCES WITHIN THE ORTHODOX CAMP

Differences of opinion clearly exist between the reform and orthodox camps over whether or not a world structure has already been established, but even among scholars who adhere to the orthodox line and believe that the world is in a transition period, various views can be found on how long it will last. No real consensus appears to exist on the subject. Many authors simply make vague predictions without giving a time frame of when multipolarity might emerge, other than "in the early 21st century." For example, He Feng of the State Council International Studies Center writes, "Because the replacement of the old world structure by a new one is taking place under peaceful conditions, this transition era certainly will be comparatively long," and he believes that it will "continue into the early part of the next century."[43]

Chen Qimao, former president of the Shanghai Institute for International Studies (SIIS) breaks down the transition period into three stages, which the world will go through before a multipolar structure is established. The first stage was from 1989 to 1991, when the fall of communism in Eastern Europe and the Soviet Union brought about the end of the Cold War. Currently, according to Chen, the world is in the second phase, from the Soviet collapse to "the basic formation of the new multipolar structure." He writes that during this stage, where "the old structure has already ended, but the new structure has not yet formed, . . . a situation of 'one super (the United States) many strong (the European Union, Japan, Russia, China),' or the so called 1-2-3-5 layered structure has emerged—1 (one superpower, the United States), 2 (two military powers, the United States and Russia), 3 (three economic powers, the United States, Japan, and Europe), 5 (five political powers, the United States, Europe, Japan, Russia, and China)." He foresees the world will be "complex and changeable, turbulent and unstable" until "the beginning of the next century," when "the period of major changes will come to an end, and

---

[42]Ibid., 42.

[43]He Fang, "Guodu shiqi de guoji xingshi," in *2000: Shijie xiang hechu qu?*, 318.

a new balance will be established." The world will then begin the last phase of the transition, "the formation and finalization of the foundation of the multipolar structure, a stage where a new international political and economic order suited to the requirements of the new structure will be established and adjusted."[44] However, Chen does not predict when the final transition stage will end.

Some analysts have even revised their own estimates. In the early 1990s, Lieutenant General Li Jijun, Vice President of the Academy of Military Science (AMS), wrote, "Because of the fast development and globalization of science, technology and economics, the dispersion of world power will speed up." Therefore, the creation of a " world structure of multipolar coexistence . . . might take 10 or 20 years to take shape."[45] However, a few years later, he extended the timetable for the transition period. "By the mid-21st century, I believe, the world will have gradually built a real multipolar structure and a mature security structure as well so that absolute hegemonism will have declined and this is likely to dictate a global trend in the second half of the 21st century."[46]

Other differences of opinion exist about who will be a pole once the world has gone through its transition period and finally formed a multipolar structure. For example there is the issue of a European pole. Some authors, such as Gao Heng of CASS, believe that Germany as an independent nation will be one of the world's five poles, not the EU. The First Secretary at the Chinese Embassy in Germany, Shang Jin, regards unified Germany as "the biggest winner of the Cold War" and the future overlord of Europe's economy.[47] Several authors assert that Germany is striving for domination of

---

[44]Chen Qimao, "Qianyan" (Introduction), in *Kua shiji de shijie geju da zhuanhuan* (Major changes in the world structure at the turn of the century), ed. Chen Qimao (Shanghai: Shanghai jiaoyu chubanshe, 1996), 1-2.

[45]Li Jijun, *Junshi lilun yu zhanzheng shijian* (Notes on military theory and military strategy) (Beijing: Junshi kexue chubanshe, 1994), in Pillsbury, *Chinese Views of Future Warfare*, 222.

[46]Li Jijun, "This Century's Strategic Heritage and Next Century's Strategic Trend," *Jiefangjun bao* (Liberation Army Daily), July 28, 1998, 6, in FBIS-CHI-98-229, August 18, 1998.

[47]Shang Jin, "Tongyi sannian hou de Deguo" (Germany, three years after reunification), *Heping yu Fazhan* (Peace and Development) 47, no. 1 (February 1994): 42-44.

Europe in order to establish itself as a pole. However, it is running into opposition from Britain and France. According to Qi Deguang of CICIR, the struggles among the European powers are manifested through leadership conflicts, such as over how to proceed in the Bosnia crisis. He claims Germany supported the Bosnian Croats in order "seize the leadership of Europe," but France and Britain "would not bow out in favor of Germany." London and Paris therefore "invoked the provision in the German Constitution that forbids Germany from sending its troops abroad" and supported NATO instead. The French and British decision to send peace-keeping troops to Bosnia was also "meant to belittle Germany."[48]

Other analysts argue that while Germany may be the strongest of the Western European nations, it still is no match for the United States; only Europe has that potential. In a study conducted by SIIS, Wang Houkang asserts that none of the Western European nations individually has the power to constitute a pole, but the joint strength of the European Union not only provides it with "pole" qualifications, but once its integration process has progressed and solidified, it will then be able to contend with the United States for global influence:

> Each independent country in the European Union, including Germany, which is the most powerful, when viewed globally, is at most a regional power, but the European Union taken as a whole, is a force that can be completely equal to the United States . . . if Europe wants to surpass the United States and play the role of a future world leader, . . . the most important basic condition is European unity. This is to say, Europe must not only realize economic integration, but also political integration, and during this process establish a powerful military force. As of today, the European Community and the European Union still are alliances of sovereign nations.[49]

---

[48]Qi Deguang, "The Bosnian Civil War: Retrospect and Prospect," *Contemporary International Relations* 4, no. 8 (August 1994): 10-11. Qi is an Associate Research Professor at CICIR.

[49]Wang Houkang, "Lengzhan hou Ouzhou geju de bianhua" (Post-Cold War changes in Europe's structure), in *Kua shiji de shijie geju da zhuanhuan*, 153-154.

While noting the difficulties in the integration process and predicting that it will be long in duration, Wang also believes that its eventual completion is inevitable: "The trend of European integration will not stop or reverse, this point is certain." Finally, Wang questions the potential for Europe to be the dominant world power in the future: "In the 18th and 19th centuries, Europe . . . was the acknowledged leader of the world for several hundred years. In the 20th century it declined and the U.S. moved ahead of it. In the 21st century can it rise again? People can not eliminate this possibility."[50] His view is shared by a Senior Research Fellow at CIISS, Shen Guoliang, who writes, "Today not a single country in Europe, including such European powers as Germany, France and Britain, can possibly be independent of European integration and cope with the complex and fierce challenges independently. Europe can only become one of the poles in the world by way of integration and playing a role in the multipolar order."[51]

Whether or not Third World countries will play a significant role in the future multipolar world also is an issue where Chinese authors have differed. Like Yang Dazhou, Chen Qimao believes that the CNP of Third World countries will continue to grow in the early part of the next century but does not see their strength increasing fast enough to allow them to come close to the power of the five poles. Chen, however, predicts that they will rise somewhat more quickly than Yang, "The power of India, Brazil and ASEAN will greatly increase, but until the early 21st century (before 2010) there is no prospect for any of them to become one of the world's poles."[52] In contrast, He Fang estimates that great changes involving Third World countries will have occurred in the world by the end of the next decade. He writes, "The rise of the developing countries shows even more so the irreversible trend of relative U.S. decline. . . . By 2010, seven of the world's ten economic powers

[50]Ibid.

[51]Shen Guoliang, "Prospects for the Development of the European Union," International Strategic Studies 45, no .3 (July 1997): 30.

[52]Chen Qimao, "Qianyan" (Introduction), in Kua shiji de shijie geju da zhuanhuan, 9.

will be developing countries. . . . Regional powers will be elevated to world powers and world powers will decline to regional ones."[53]

POST-KOSOVO DEBATE

The NATO strikes on Yugoslavia and the NATO bombing of the Chinese Embassy in Belgrade in the spring of 1999 have given prominence to the debate concerning the future world structure. One of the biggest outgrowths of the Kosovo crisis and the bombing is that they led to reevaluation of previous assessments of the pace of U.S. decline and the rate at which the world is moving toward multipolarization. It appears that the reformist view, represented by Yang Dazhou, gained support as a result of U.S. and NATO actions in Yugoslavia. A clear post-Kosovo trend has been the number of Chinese authors admitting that the transition to multipolarity has been delayed: "An analysis of the situation at the present stage shows that . . . the deeds of the United States have slowed down the multipolarization process and made it more difficult for the international community to build a new political and economic order in the next century."[54] A key element in the new assessment is the corresponding issue of why the time frame for the transition to the new world structure has been greatly extended—the United States remains powerful. Not only are some authors no longer focusing on current U.S. decline, but rather, they are predicting that its strength may even continue to increase:

> The United States, as the sole superpower, occupies a relatively prominent, single, superpower position of domination, and it will for some time maintain the momentum of expansion. . . .Right now multipolarization has lost its momentum for "accelerated development." Multipolarization in the course of history may be more complicated and tortuous than once thought. It would be more appropriate for us to describe today's world as "single-superpower pluralism" than "multiple powers with one

---

[53]He Fang, "With Multipolarity Now Evolving, the Superpowers are Going to Become History," *Shanghai Jiefang Ribao* (Shanghai Liberation Daily), April 22, 1996.

[54]Li Donghang, "Dangerous Attempt to Resist Multipolarization Process," *Jiefangjun bao* (Liberation Army Daily), May 26, 1999, 5, in FBIS-CHI-1999-0604, May 26, 1999.

superpower." The early part of the 21st century may see a situation characterized by "single superpower domination, and pluralistic disputes."[55]

Chinese authors explain U.S. dominance as stemming from a number of factors. Current U.S. economic and technological superiority is at the top of their list. "The United States is at the peak of a financial monopoly of capital. Moreover, being propelled by a contemporary technological revolution, it is in the leading position in most high and new technological fields, in addition to enjoying relative superiority in the technological industry and economic strength."[56] According to Xiao Lian of the North American Institute at CASS, future U.S. economic domination may last many decades because of the success of U.S. strategy. He gives several reasons. First, "no matter how the European economy is reorganized or integrated, Europe will be unable to control the Japanese and the Asia-Pacific economies unless the United States participates in this process. By the same token, no matter how the Asia-Pacific economic cooperation zone is built, Europe will be unable to play a significant role in the Asia-Pacific economy unless the United States takes part in this process." The second reason Xiao lists is that "United States has all along controlled the WTO [World Trade Organization], the World Bank, and has had a bigger say in the IMF [International Monetary Fund] to date. . . . United States has time and again succeeded in consolidating and enhancing its control over the world economy." This success includes "controlling and manipulating the foreign exchange markets the world over" in order to get "huge profits by virtue of its economic and financial strength and the special position of the U.S. dollar."[57]

Another argument put forward by Chinese authors to explain the delay in multipolarization is that the other poles do not yet have the strength to independently stand up to the United States. For example, Shen Jiru, Director of the International Strategic Studies Office of the Institute of World

---

[55]Wang Zhuxun, "Effects of Kosovo on Global Security," *Liaowang*, no. 20 (May 17, 1999): 8-10, in FBIS-CHI-1999-0622, June 23, 1999.

[56]Ibid.

[57]Xiao Lian, "On U.S. Economic Expansion and Hegemonism," *Renmin Ribao*, June 8, 1999, 7, in FBIS-CHI-1999-0610, June 8, 1999.

Economics and Politics at CASS, describes the EU position in international activities rather negatively. He writes, "In world affairs, it has always remained a political shorty and a military dwarf. . . .So far, the EU has yet to develop any independent defense strength which can be of some real use; and the EU still has to largely depend on NATO for its defense."[58] Consequently, Chinese authors assert, the United States has taken advantage of the relative weakness of European countries and Japan to create some powerful alliances. These partnerships are an additional factor boosting current American dominance. One author stated, "Internationally, the United States has formed a collective hegemonist alliance, turning some international political, economic, and military organizations into U.S. tools for hegemony."[59] Shen Jiru agrees, claiming that it is an "ill omen that the unipolar world dominance of the United States takes the form of a U.S.-Europe and a U.S.-Japanese joint hegemony." According to Shen, because the U.S. share of the world economy will drop in the future, "this means that its economy will be unable to provide adequate backing for its hegemonist practices," so it must rely on its allies to maintain its superiority. "In order to establish a unipolar global dominance, the United States needs a group of helpers no matter whether it is viewed from the political, economic, or military angle." However, Shen cautions, while "this group of helpers"— NATO and Japan—may "look like joint hegemony outwardly," it "is actually dominated by the United States in reality; in other words, a unipolar hegemony still dominated by the United States. Such a practice can considerably prolong the life of the U.S.-dominated unipolar hegemony and greatly put off the formation of a multipolar world setup."[60]

Other Chinese analysts, while recognizing that the pace of the multipolarization process has decreased, and predicting further increases in U.S. power, also emphasize that the current trend does not mean that the U.S.

---

[58]Hsu Taochen, "World Facing Seven Ill Omens at Turn of Century—Interviewing CASS Research Fellow Shen Jiru (part 2 of 3)," *Ta Kung Pao* (Hong Kong), May 20, 1999, A6, in FBIS-CHI-1999-0608, June 10, 1999.

[59]Wang Zhuxun, "Effects of Kosovo on Global Security."

[60]Hsu Taochen, "World Facing Seven Ill Omens at Turn of Century—Interviewing CASS Research Fellow Shen Jiru."

will be able to establish a unipolar world. It is only a setback in the transition to a new world structure: "For the world to advance toward multipolarization is the inevitable trend of history. Although twists and turns and ups and downs may occur in the process of the development of this trend, no force can block the tide of development of multipolarization."[61] Another author writes:

> A few years ago, people were over-optimistic about the "multipolar" trend. They thought that the "multipolar" trend would "move faster and faster." Some even thought that the multipolar world had already taken shape. After NATO use of force against Yugoslavia and its attack on the Chinese Embassy, some people went to the other extreme and believed that the 'unipolar' trend now reigned supreme and the world remained a unipolar world. Both views are rather biased. Judging from the present situation, the multipolar pattern has not yet taken shape, but the trend cannot be changed. Recent developments only serve to show that the trend of multipolarism is obviously slowing down and that the U.S. pole will be further strengthened, but the plots of the United States to build a "unipolar world" where it can dominate everything can never succeed.[62]

The reason cited by most authors for the ultimate success of multipolarization is that the other poles will become more powerful and come into greater conflict with the United States: "The true essence and the vital point of the U.S. pursuit of hegemonism is to establish an international order under U.S. dominance, but the developing countries will not allow this, and even its allies will not allow it."[63] Another author writes, "Although cooperation and coordination between Europe and the United States are obviously growing, conflicts and differences remain," and asserts that the same situation also applies to the U.S. relationship with Japan.[64] Zhang

---

[61]"On the New Development of U.S. Hegemonism," *Renmin Ribao*, May 27,1999, 1, in FBIS-CHI-1999-0527, May 27, 1999.

[62]Xiao Feng, "World Trends Under U.S. Global Strategy, Part One of Two," *Renmin Ribao*, May 31, 1999, p.6; in FBIS-CHI-1999-0601, May 31, 1999.

[63]"On the New Development of U.S. Hegemonism.

[64]Xiao Feng, "World Trends Under U.S. Global Strategy, Part One of Two."

Zhaozhong, Director of the Science and Technology Teaching and Research Section of NDU, concurs: "NATO is by no means totally united, and it is certain that splits will occur in the future, and multipolarization remains a trend. France will not follow the United States for ever, Germany has become stronger since reunification and it too is not willing to always follow the United States; since the Europeans have organized the euro, this will naturally match the dollar."[65]

SHANGHAI'S ELABORATE STUDIES

The "orthodox" features of the future security environment can be found in many books and articles of the 1990s, but those from Shanghai frequently are very thorough and elaborate. According to interviews conducted by the author in Beijing, open-source assessments are based on internal Chinese Government documents approved by Deng Xiaoping in the mid-1980s. Several officials pointed out that President Jiang Zemin has endorsed all the features of Deng's assessment. SIIS has a close relationship with Jiang, developed while he was mayor of Shanghai. Perhaps because of this personal relationship (and because Shanghai is far from the rigid, official climate of Beijing), SIIS publications often provide extensive details about the future security environment.[66] SIIS publications, particularly those by its former President Chen Qimao, who has also written articles for *Qiu Shi*, the journal of the Central Committee of the Communist Party, are authoritative and add greater detail and background about the future security environment.[67] It is

---

[65]Ma Ling, "The Attempt Behind the 'Bombing in Error'— Interview with Renowned Military Commentator Zhang Zhaozhong," *Ta Kung Pao* (Hong Kong), May 17, 1999, A4, in FBIS-CHI-1999-1518, May 17, 1999.

[66]For example, see Chen Qimao, *Kua shiji de shijie geju da zhuanhuan* (Major changes in world structure at the turn of the century)(Shanghai: Shanghai jiaoyu chubanshe, 1996).

[67]For example, see Chen Qimao, "Lengzhan hou daguo zhengzhi juezhu de xin dongxiang" (The New direction of the post-Cold War political rivalry of the major powers], *Qiushi*, no. 6 (1995): 39-44. Chen has also presented his views on the future security environment in American publications. See Chen Qimao, "New Approaches in China's Foreign Policy—the Post-Cold War Era," *Asian Survey* 32, no. 3 (March 1993): 237-251. During his time as President of SIIS, Chen was a foreign relations advisor to former Shanghai mayors Wang Daohan and Jiang Zemin. More recently, he has been a visiting Research Fellow at California State University and Princeton University and currently is president of the Shanghai

possible that the view from Shanghai tends to be both orthodox and elaborate, because scholars there can draw more from Central Committee documents, or maybe because they helped draft these documents and therefore have been permitted leeway to present them.

An example of the extensive details of the future world structure provided by SIIS can be found in "The Roots of the Transitional Era," which focuses on turbulence and wars. Former SIIS President Chen Qimao states,

> Historically speaking, the disintegration of an empire is a long and painful process. The Eastern Roman Empire began to decline at the end of the 12th century and was destroyed by the Ottoman Empire in 1461. The whole process took more than 200 years, during which class conflicts were intensifying, [and] . . . invasions from the outside constantly took place.[63]

Chen then compares the decline of the Ottoman Empire to the collapse of the Soviet Union. Chen points out that the full process of the decline of the former Soviet Union is not complete. He notes that there are still 25 million Russians living in republics outside Russia and 20 million other nationalities in Russia. He forecasts, "Due to the rise of nationalism, this situation may lead to a great deal of explosive potential." The process of reform and the completion of the process of disintegration of the former Soviet Union, Chen argues, will "become one of the important causes of turbulence in the transitional era." He reminds us that the former Soviet Union was a superpower and in World War II it "utterly routed the imperial fascist Germany."

Chen draws on several episodes of Chinese history to illustrate how the process of the emergence of a new era can take many decades. He begins with the decline of the Eastern Han Dynasty (25 B.C.-220 A.D.) to the establishment of the Western Jin Dynasty (265-316 A.D.), a period of about 80 years during which the "war lords fought each other, the Three Kingdoms dominated their own territories, while the masses lived in dire poverty." China

---

International Relations Society.

[68]Chen Qimao, "The Transitional Era: Roots of Turbulence and Features of International Affairs," *SIIS Journal* 1, no. 2 (1994): 15-32. All other quotes in this section are from this article, unless otherwise noted.

saw another long period of turbulence when the Tang Dynasty (618-907 A.D.) collapsed.

Looking to the several decades that lie ahead for the emergence of a post-Cold War world strategic pattern, Chen points to Central Eurasia as a conflict zone where "religious frictions and national disputes are interlocking, leading to a lot of historic grievances." This is also where two world wars were fought. This whole zone in the past century or more has been dominated by tsarist Russia, the Ottoman Empire, and the Austro-Hungarian Empires. According to Chen, contradictions among these three empires produced several wars. He states, "Territorial issues were always so sensitive that a little disturbance could have resulted in enormous turbulence, thus leading to the danger of another world war." Chen adheres to the concept put forth by many Chinese analysts that the Vienna System built upon the Anti-Napoleon War, the Versailles System established after World War I, and the Yalta System built upon World War II created new political maps and divided spheres of influence among the great powers relatively rapidly, because of the international conference agreements that these great powers were able to work out after the wars.

Without such a war or international conference to mark the end of the Cold War, Chen states that a new world system cannot be created by way of victorious powers' conferences, "nor can spheres of influence be divided quickly." Thus, Chen believes violence is ahead, and the "re-division of spheres of influence will be a long-term and tortuous process . . . the struggle among big powers for spheres of influence is under way." Russia wants to maintain as its sphere all its former Soviet boundaries, while "there is little doubt that Western nations want to have East European countries joining NATO and to put them under the protection of the West." Besides the struggle for redividing spheres of influence in Europe, Chen states that "struggles between the United States and Japan for the dominating role in the Asia-Pacific as well as struggles among Germany, France, and Britain for the dominating role in Europe have not yet surfaced, but they do demonstrate themselves through a series of signs." Such struggles involve re-division of influence spheres and "will become significant roots for the emergence of turbulence in the transitional world."

In Europe, Chen agrees with many Chinese analysts that Germany was the major winner of the Cold War and has the best prospects to become a great power in the new era. He traces the origins of the Bosnia Conflict to "Germany's support for the independence of Slovenia and Croatia, without taking into account American objections and other European allies' reservations. Germany also went together with Austria to supply a great deal of weapons to Slovenia and Croatia, quickening the pace of disintegration of the former Yugoslavia and aggravating the turbulence in the Balkan Peninsula." However, Chen goes on to use the Bosnia case study as an "indirect demonstration of the struggle between the United States and the European Union" over who will dominate the future of Europe.

Chen, like many Chinese analysts, directly attacks the concept that the United States is the sole superpower and that there is a unipolar strategic pattern. Will there be American hegemony? According to Chen, "Enormous facts emerging after the end of the Cold War have proved that kind of view wrong." He believes that many issues "demonstrate that America's ability to control its allies has decreased." However, "The Yalta System in the Asia-Pacific region was not so complete and solid as that in Europe." Chen argues that a looser, multipolar system has long existed in Asia because of the American failure in the Vietnam War and the Soviet failure in the Afghan War, which reduced the two superpowers' influence. He states, "Their capacity to control the region was already much less than that in Europe. Because of these developments, many contradictions and disputes in the Asia-Pacific region were not covered by the bipolar system." Of course, he acknowledges that the Asia-Pacific region has a number of uncertainties, such as territorial disputes, the Korean problem, the Taiwan issue, and the leadership succession in several countries. However, the region has actually become a place where "the centers not only are relatively independent but also in mutual check and balance" among the United States, Russia, Japan, China, and ASEAN.

Using the indicators of CNP (described in chapter 5), Chen believes that "the heyday when the United States dominated the Asia-Pacific region has gone forever." Thus, the multipolar structure has begun to take shape earlier in the Asia-Pacific than in other regions of the world, so that it's possible already to say that "no single power can have the final say in the Asia-Pacific region." This has been achieved without a Yalta, a Versailles, or a Vienna conference. The role of China has become a source of regional stability because of its rapid economic growth and its adherence to the Five Principles of Peaceful Coexistence. Chen believes China's role has been important in encouraging this transition to take shape in Asia first.

Chen's argument that the rise of China will bring peace and stability is strengthened by an article from another former SIIS President, Liang Yufan. Liang states that because China was the "prey of imperialist aggression for more than a century, the rivalry of great powers inside China was once a major cause of persistent instability and turmoil and wars in East Asia." The implication is that a strong, unified China eliminates the influence of foreign great powers (who caused wars), so Chinese stability will help to end the era of transition and bring the new era to East Asia first.[69]

FIFTY-YEAR STRUCTURES

One of the important premises on which Chinese assessments about the future security environment are based is the concept of "world structures" (*zhanlue shijie geju*).[70] This term is used to refer to the design of the world pattern, which, according to Chinese, generally exists for several decades before undergoing a major transformation. Each "world structure" is based on the organization and state of relations among the great nations in the world. The process by which one world strategic pattern gives away to another usually is a major war. One author writes, "A world pattern is the relatively stable international structure formed by the interrelations and interaction between the main forces in the world during a certain historical period. . . . The changes in the world pattern are based on the changes in the relations of the world's main contradictions, and they accompany international and social phenomena such as turbulence, division, alignment and crises, that result in conflicts and war."[71] The basic Chinese catechism identifies four major "world strategic patterns" during the past 200 years. One scholar at CICIR has put together a grid (table 2) illustrating characteristics of the world order in the 20th century.

---

[69]Liang Yufan, "The Rise of Asia and Asian Regional Security," *SIIS Journal* 1, no. 1 (1994): 13.

[70]This Chinese phrase has been translated by Chinese authors as "structure" or "pattern" or "regime." The terms are used interchangeably in this volume.

[71]Yang Zheng, ed., *2000: Shijie xiang hechu qu?*, 25.

Table 2. *International Security Systems in the 20th Century*

Systems and Models	Period			
	Between World War I & II	*Post World War II*	*1970s-80s*	*1990s*
International relations systems	Multipolar system	Bipolar system	Bipolar, pluralist system	Pluralist coexistence system
Types of war or disputes	World War	Cold War and local war	Cold War, local war, and economic war	Economic disputes, national and religious wars
International security models	Military alliance and balance of power	Military blocs and nuclear deterrence	Alliance, nuclear deterrence, and balance of power	U.N. and multilateral security dialogue
Goals	Domain and colony	Orbit and global hegemony	Comprehensive strength of state	Comprehensive strength and social stability
Decisive factors of forces	Military and diverse empires	Military and two superpowers	Military, economic and pluralist powers	Economic, pluralist harmony and military force
World economic systems	Plantation system and discriminatory economic blocs	Two large closed markets of socialism and capitalism	Transitional global market economy	Harmony of globalism and regionalism in world economy
Nature of international relations	Struggle for hegemony	Power politics	Power politics and inter-dependence	Interdependence and power politics

Source: Liu Jiangyong, "On the Establishment of Asia-Pacific Multilateral Security Dialogue Mechanism," *Contemporary International Relations* 4, no. 2 (February 1994): 32. Liu is a Senior Fellow and Director of the East Asia Division at CICIR.

The first world structure, called the "Vienna System" by the Chinese, lasted 40 to 50 years and was set up by the victorious nations who defeated Napoleon. These four powers (Russia, Austria, Prussia, and Britain) established a world structure that was centered entirely on Europe and characterized by mutual bargaining and the use of "spheres of influence" to preserve stability. The second structure, which also lasted 40 to 50 years, was created by internal events in Japan, Italy, Germany, and the United States that destroyed "the original proportions and distributions of strength" and in so doing broke out of the strategic configuration confined to Europe.[72] Although still centered on Europe, this new pattern also expanded to North America and Asia. Briefly, the major developments were the rapid advancement of capitalism in the United States after the Civil War, the Meiji Restoration in Japan, and the political unification of Italy, as well as the unification of Germany in 1870 and its defeat of France in the Franco-Prussian War in 1871.

The third world structure derived from the conduct of the powers that won World War I. In a manner similar to the creation of the Vienna System Pattern, the new Versailles System was established by the strong victorious powers (the United States, Britain, France, Italy, and Japan). As had occurred with the Vienna Conference after the Napoleonic Wars, the Paris Peace Conference of 1919 "redivided the world" and laid down the rules for the next "era." However, the October Revolution established the Soviet Union in this period and Moscow participated in the Versailles System, which "broke the pattern whereby imperialism ruled the whole world."[73] When discussing this era, several Chinese authors refer to it as the Versailles-Washington System, arguing that the three major treaties signed at the Washington Conference of 1921 played a major role in shaping the world structure of the time.[74]

The fourth world structure is known in China as the Yalta System, a name derived from the Yalta Summit involving the United States, Britain, and the Soviet Union in February 1945. Most Chinese claim this conference "carved out the spheres of influence in Europe and Asia for the United States and the Soviet Union." With respect to China, the Yalta Summit included Soviet recognition of "U.S. control over Japan," while the United States in turn "satisfied the Soviet Union's wishes to regain Sakhalin Island, enabled Outer Mongolia to become independent, and enlisted northeast China into the

---

[72]Chen Feng and Chen Xiaogong, "The World is in the Transition Period of a New Strategic Pattern Replacing the Old," 11-15.

[73]Ibid., 3.

[74]For example, a discussion of the Versailles-Washington System, as well as the Vienna and Yalta Systems, can be found in Yang Zheng, *2000: Shijie xiang hechu qu?*, 24-36.

sphere of influence."[75] The Chinese state that the decline of British strength reduced its sphere of influence, so that the Yalta System actually established a world structure of two poles, Washington and Moscow, whose relationship largely determined world politics. The Yalta System endured until 1991, nearly 50 years. Because the core of the Yalta Agreement was the division of Europe and Germany into two parts, Chinese date the end of the Yalta System to the reunification of Germany in 1991. Although the Chinese say the Yalta System has "basically disintegrated," they recognize it continues in Northeast Asia in the division between North Korea and South Korea and in the unresolved territorial dispute between Moscow and Tokyo over the northern territories. There have been some Chinese references to the unresolved problem of Taiwan's sovereignty also being a part of the Yalta System because Taiwan's legal status was not resolved either at Yalta or the 1951 San Francisco Peace Conference.

Within a world structure there is also what is known as a world order (*shijie zhixu*), or the ways and means by which nations interact and deal with each other:

> A world structure refers to a relatively stable international framework and strategic situation formed on the foundation of a certain power balance. A world order then refers to, on the basis of the world structure, the mechanisms and rules of the motion of international relations (such as handling international affairs and international contact). The two have both generalities (both take the power balance as their base) and differences (they

---

[75]Chen Feng and Chen Xiaogong, "The World is in a Transition Period of the New Strategic Pattern Replacing the Old," 3. Yang Dazhou of CASS offers a different version of the events that led to the formation of the post-World War II Cold War structure, which he says was established in 1949. "In 1949 three major events occurred, making that year the symbolic year of the new structure: First, the Western nations, with the United States as the head, established NATO, which was directed against the Soviet Union, revealing the prelude to the Cold War. Second, the Soviet Union successfully exploded a nuclear bomb, giving the Soviets the military means to contend with the United States. Third, new China was established, causing changes to occur in the world's power balance, which greatly benefitted the 'socialist camp.' " Yang Dazhou, "Dui lengzhan hou shijie geju zhi wo jian," 42.

do not adapt to one another; if the old structure collapses, the old order probably continues to exist).[76]

FUTURE WARS

Rivalries, Struggles, and Local Wars

The future world structure will depend on the outcomes of competitions in both military strength and CNP. The struggle for "peace and development" will shift the competitive rank orders of various nations according to their CNP, which is based on the economic and technology policies they pursue. At the same time, in the military domain there are different rules to the international competition, including the use of force and the competition for military superiority. This field has been addressed primarily by military authors in China, although a few civilian analysts have also written about the consequences of local war and the development of military technology.[77]

The rivalries and struggles to achieve CNP and military superiority will greatly contribute to the turbulence that characterizes the transition period, say Chinese analysts. As a consequence, the "new era" will feature destabilizing factors and inevitable local wars that will last for several decades. In fact, many Chinese articles mention the current trend of "relaxation," and then warn that there are prospects for more wars in the future. Three NDU analysts write, "The overall situation is one in which frequent regional conflicts are the outcome of the changing strategic pattern and international political disorder."[78]

The certainty of future local wars does not seem to be debated. On the contrary, all Chinese analysts expect frequent local wars in the decades ahead.

---

[76]He Fang, "Guodu shiqi de guoji xingshi," in *2000: Shijie xiang hechu qu?*, 322. He Fang is at the State Council International Studies Center.

[77]This topic is discussed further in chapter 6; forecasts of how the United States will fare in the military competition are found in chapter 2.

[78]Xia Liping, Wang Zhongchun, Wen Zhonghua, and Xu Weidi, "Shijie zhanlue xingshi de zhuyao tedian yu qushi" (The world strategic situation—characteristics and trends), *Heping yu fazhan* (Peace and Development) 47, no. 1 (February 1994): 14-18. The authors are from the National Defense University Strategy Institute.

Liao Yonghe of CASS writes, "With the further reduction of the danger of a global world war, regional armed conflicts and limited wars will become the main field of military conflict."[79] In the available literature, the definition of local war includes the conflicts in Korea (1950-53), Vietnam (1964-69), and the Gulf War (1991). This is an important premise of Chinese views of the future security environment: international wars on at least the scale of Korea, Vietnam, and the Gulf War are virtually certain in the decades ahead. Furthermore, there are many explicit references to the level of destruction caused by each of these past local wars. Different measures of destructiveness have been used, including logistics. In 3 years of war in Korea, 600,000 bombs were used; Vietnam required twice that number; and the Gulf War consumed nearly 8 million tons of supplies. Chinese articles on the "revolution in science and technology" expect future wars to have still higher levels of destruction.

Not only have Chinese authors noted that the intensity and scope of local wars are escalating, but they cite another major trend in the accelerating frequency with which they have been occurring since the Cold War period. According to Li Zhongcheng of CICIR, "In the 40 years of the Cold War, there were 190 regional conflicts, an average of four per year. In the first 7 years after the end of the Cold War there were 193, an average of 28 per year, seven times that of the former year average."[80] Other authors, in order to predict future trends, have tracked the specific number of conflicts per year, distinguishing between wars that are new and those that are continuations from the previous year. Li Qinggong, a Research Fellow at CIISS, writes,

> Throughout the world in 1997 there were altogether 38 armed conflicts and local wars of various scales, an increase of 8 in comparison with the 30 that occurred in 1996, but a decrease of 8 from the 46 that took place in the peak year of 1995. Of all these local conflicts and wars, 8 new ones occurred in 1997, an increase of 2 in comparison with the number of 6 in 1996, but a decrease of 8 in comparison with the number of 16 at the peak

---

[79]Liao Yonghe, "Pingmian duojihua yu liti duojihua qianxi" (On the new pattern of world politics), *Shijie jingji yu zhengzhi* (World Economics and Politics) 184, no. 12 (December 1995): 67-69. Liao is on the staff of the European Institute at CASS.

[80]Li Zhongcheng, *Kua Shiji de shijie zhengzhi*, 185.

time of 1993. . . . This shows that after the Cold War, conflicts and wars have passed the "frequently occurring period" and entered the "period of ups and downs," with the new feature of "sometimes many, sometimes few, sometimes rising, sometimes falling."[81]

In contrast to Western nations, there appear to be few Chinese articles or books on the international security situation that express optimism about the future role of arms control or the United Nations in building international trust or reducing the probability of the use of force. Since 1980, China has entered global economic institutions like the World Bank and International Monetary Fund but has never accepted the jurisdiction of international security arrangements such as U.N. peacekeeping forces.[82]

Chinese authors appear to assume other nations share their views about the future role of military force. Chinese assessments about future military competition suggest they see other countries preparing themselves for the era of regional wars. For example, an article by two PLA analysts claims that the United States thinks "a new threat surpassing the confrontation between the East and the West in the past 45 years" is emerging. With regard to Russia, they argue, "The Russian military thinks that the process of easing up does not have an irreversible nature and that the danger of war still exists in the world." Japan, they assert, "faces military threats and serious competitors. Therefore, Japan will continue to beef up military strength and improve weapons and equipment." Concerning India, the PLA analysts claim that India thinks "India's security situation in the 1990s is still very grim, therefore it will continue to improve overall military strength and strategic deterrence

---

[81] Li Qinggong, "Dangqian de guoji junshi anquan xingshi" (The current international military security situation), *Guoji zhanlue yanjiu* (International Strategic Studies) 47, no. 1 (January 1998): 9.

[82] Chinese analysts are not entirely negative about the role of the United Nations in the future world structure. For example, Sa Benwang, a Senior Researcher at CIIS, when predicting what the world pattern will be like in 2015 or 2020, writes, "International organizations such as the United Nations will continue to exist and be strengthened." Sa Benwang, "Perspectives of International Strategic Patterns in the 21st Century," *Liaowang*, no. 37 (September 14, 1998): 41-42, in FBIS-CHI-98-268, September 29, 1998. See also the section, "Can the U.N. Become the World's Government?" in Guo Longlong, "Xin shiqi Lianheguo de diwei he zuoyong (The position and role of the United Nations in the new period)," in *Kua shiji de shijie geju da zhuanhuan*, 357-359.

strength." During the transition era some PLA analysts thus conclude that various countries "view the use of military strength as an important means to support their international status and safeguard their national interests."[83]

After the U.S. accidental bombing of the Chinese embassy in Belgrade, some authors seemed to question whether the main trend of the times still is peace and development. For example, Yang Chengxu, President of CIIS, writes, "Simply put, NATO will have the right to interfere anywhere in the world. As an ideological organization, it is laying down some hidden troubles for the outbreak of World War III. The world has become more turbulent."[84]

An article in *Zhongguo Pinglun*, which interviewed generals from several military research institutes, brought up a similar issue, warning that "China must be ready to fight a world war." It said, "after NATO attacked the Federal Republic of Yugoslavia, Chinese strategists believe that before peacetime truly comes, world war could erupt at any moment. China must be fully prepared for it."[85] However, although the potential for a third world war was mentioned following U.S. and NATO actions in Yugoslavia, the majority of Chinese authors still claim that ultimately peace and development will prevail. Shen Jiru of CASS argues, "The military actions taken by NATO will hardly change the general trend of peace and development" for three reasons:

- "First, economic globalization is a powerful material force to restrict large-scale wars."
- "Second, the outcome of a war is determined by the balance between economic and military strength, public attitudes, and moral support of the two sides. We do not deny the great destructiveness of modern weapons, as well as the unprecedented cruelty of modern warfare. Nevertheless, it has been proven in history that wars are not necessarily won by military strength. France did not win the Algerian War with its advanced weapons

---

[83]Chen Feng and Chen Xiaogong, "The World is in a Transition Period of the New Strategic Pattern Replacing the Old," 3.

[84]"Experts on NATO's New Strategy and Related Issues," *Beijing Review*, no. 23 (June 7, 1999).

[85]"China Must Be Ready to Fight a World War—PLA Believes That the West Is Hatching Six Major Conspiracies Against China," *Sing Tao Jih Pao* (Hong Kong), May 28, 1999, b14, in FBIS-CHI-1999-0528, June 1, 1999.

nor did the United States win the Vietnam War with its advanced weapons. The more destructive a war, the more restrictive it is to the aggressors."

● "Third, peace and development are the common wishes of all people in the whole world. . . .The will of the people is the fundamental safeguard for maintaining world peace and development. We firmly believe that world peace and development can be won by the joint struggle of all people in the world."[86]

As before the Kosovo crisis, Chinese analysts maintain the seeming contradiction that regional wars will continue to exist even though peace and development are the main trend. "For the 21st century, peace and development will still be the theme of the times. We should not doubt or waver in this judgment. . . . However, limited war will be unavoidable since the roots of war will still be there."[87]

Sources of Wars

What will be the causes of the regional wars that will occur throughout the transition period as the new world structure is in the process of replacing the old one? Where will they take place? Who will be involved? Chinese analysts explain the outbreak of local wars in the 1990s as having two major reasons: first, the ethnic, religious, historical, and territorial disputes previously covered up and restricted by the U.S.-Soviet confrontation were free to emerge following the end of the Cold War; and second, as the new world structure is forming, there is competition and contention for power, influence, and economic resources. As the transition period progresses, the hot spots where local wars are focused will not be static but are expected to shift as some conflicts come to an end and new ones emerge, and as relations between the powers develop. Former SIIS president Chen Qimao explains:

---

[36]Hsu Tao-chen, "United States Still Makes Old Mistakes, Exclusive interview with Shen Jiru," *Hong Kong Ta Kung Pao*, May 21, 1999, p. A6; in FBIS-CHI-1999-0604, May 21, 1999. Shen is a Research Fellow and director of the International Strategic Research Section of the Institute of World Economics and Politics, CASS.

[87]Wang Zhuxun, "Effects of Kosovo on Global Security."

These hot spots must go through a process, from breaking out, to intensifying, to relaxing, to resolution. Currently, their development still is not very even; some have already relaxed, some are intensifying, some have just broken out, some have not yet shown their heads; they still are in a stage where "as one falls another rises.". . . Internationally, following the end of the Cold War, the various forces have been re-dividing and uniting, and relations between the powers are very unstable, which also is a very significant source of the turbulence in the transformation period. Therefore, the current world still is not stable.[88]

Consequently, the local wars will occur for a variety of reasons, with the participants ranging from small groups to major powers, and at locations worldwide.

Several Chinese authors have suggested that the fault lines of future war in the multipolar security environment will not be the same as during the bipolar Soviet-American confrontation. Following the end of the Cold War, the main area where local wars were focused was in Central and Eastern Europe and the former Soviet Union. However, most Chinese analysts, while not predicting protracted peace and stability, consider the region's turmoil and armed conflicts to have subsided to some extent and see the main local war hot spot as shifting to Africa. A *People's Daily* article reported that for 1997, "According to statistics, nearly half of all the local wars that took place worldwide this year happened in Africa. . . . Though these conflicts were of the nature of civil wars and were local, they have nevertheless posed a certain threat to peace and stability and have caused the concern of the international community."[89] Chinese analysts do not foresee the problems in Africa disappearing any time in the near future and expect that there will continue to be frequent wars. For example, Li Zhongcheng of CICIR writes, "At the turn of the century, and the early part of next century, it is extremely possible that there will appear in the African Great Lake region a situation where as one

---

[88]Chen Qimao, "Qianyan," 2.

[89]Zhang Dezhen and Zhu Manting, "Relations Among Big Nations Profoundly Adjusted and Multipolar Trends Quickened," *Renmin Ribao* (People's Daily), December 15, 1997, 7, in FBIS-CHI-98-001, January 1, 1998.

racial or sectional conflict ends another begins."[90] The Middle East is another area mentioned by Li and other authors as a current hot spot:

> The Palestinian-Israeli peace process can only through repeated reversals slowly progress. At the same time, aside from the Palestinian-Israeli and Arab-Israeli contradictions, other Middle Eastern regional conflicts will gradually develop and intensify, becoming the sources of the Middle Eastern region's continued turbulence and intranquility, and its continued and frequent regional conflicts.[91]

Many Chinese analysts point out that the proliferation of local ethnic, religious, and territorial wars has not meant that the major powers have not been involved in the conflicts. In fact, a number of analysts cite hegemonism and military interventionism as contributing to and exacerbating local wars. Wang Xuhe of the Strategy Department at AMS stated, "The factors threatening international security are pluralizing, becoming more complicated, and have more layers, but hegemonism and power politics will for a considerably long period still be the major threats to international security."[92] With regard to the two current hot spots, Africa and the Middle East, Chen Feng, a Senior Research Fellow at CIISS, writes,

> The conflicts in Africa and the Middle East have their respective causes, e.g., the complicated ethnic or cultural contradictions, frontier resource disputes and internal struggles, etc. However, if analyzed from a deeper perspective, these conflicts reflect the struggle to control these regions between the great powers. Conflicts in these regions all have the intervention from those powers involved. The United States, making full use of the chance that France had adjusted its African policy, tried various means to create its own agents in Africa and to drive the French forces out of its sphere of influence. In the Middle East, because the U.S. policy is

---

[90]Li Zhongcheng, *Kua Shiji de shijie zhengzhi*, 192.

[91]Ibid., 191.

[92]Wang Xuhe, "Dangqian guoji anquan xingshi de zhuyao tedian" (The main characteristics of the current international security situation), *Shijie jingji yu zhengzhi* (World Economics and Politics) 209, no. 1 (January 1998): 7.

biased toward Israel, it has put the peace process in a stalemate, and its influence in the Arab world has declined.[93]

Other examples of hegemonism and intervention on the part of the major powers are cited by another CIISS Research Fellow, Li Qinggong: the United States sending aircraft carriers to the Gulf when Iran crossed the "restricted airspace" to attack Iraq's Kurdish region; in Bosnia, "the U.S. peacekeeping forces clashing with local people and shooting a number of Serbian residents"; the United States "sending an 'expeditionary air force' to Bosnia to terrorize psychologically the Serbian people;" and France "continuously engaging in military intervention against the Republic of Central Africa."[94]

Following NATO military strikes against Yugoslavia in spring 1999, there was a tremendous increase in criticism and alarm about U.S. hegemonism being a source of war. One author writes, "Hegemonism and power politics are still developing, and there will be no peace under heaven in the 21st century."[95] Wang Jincun, a senior researcher at CASS portrays the United States as "striving to build a single-polar world and to strengthen its hegemony." After the U.S. accidental bombing of the Chinese embassy in Belgrade, Wang wrote that the United States is employing military methods as one means for achieving its goal: "What deserves more attention is that the United States, not yet satisfied with its Cold War achievements, seeks to gain more advances through military means. Therefore, there has appeared an even closer growing link between the new Cold War and 'hot war.' The military interference by the United States in Iraq, Somalia, Haiti, and Bosnia-Herzegovina, the bombing against Sudan and Afghanistan, and especially the ongoing air strikes against Yugoslavia, serve as prominent examples."[96]

Chu Shulong of CICIR pointed out, "The number of times and the frequency with which the United States has used force in various parts of the

---

[93]Chen Feng, "1997 nian de guoji zhanlue xingshi," 5.

[94]Li Qinggong, "Dangqian de guoji junshi anquan xingshi," 10.

[95]Wang Zhuxun, "Effects of Kosovo on Global Security."

[96]Wang Jincun, "Global Democratization—Camouflage of U.S. Hegemony," *Xinhua*, May 27, 1999, in FBIS-CHI-1999-0527, May 27, 1999.

world in just a few years have rarely been seen before in the history of U.S. foreign policy and in the history of international relations."[97] An explanation offered by one author for the sudden increase in U.S. intervention is that it has a "Gulf War syndrome:" "The United States, the world's sole superpower, developed a 'Vietnam syndrome' on account of its defeat with heavy casualties in the Vietnam war, and became careful and cautious for a time about getting involved in overseas conflicts. Success in the 1991 Gulf War produced a 'Gulf War syndrome' in the United States and it became enthusiastic about military intervention activities."[98] One article noted that, "Since 1990, the United States has dispatched troops more than 40 times, and 10 of them were strong military interventions." It concludes, "Given the large amount of indisputable evidence, the United States has become the world's major source of war by its arms expansion and implementation of hegemonism and power politics, and it has become a major threat to the world's peace. It is predictable that more countries will become test spots for the high- and new-technology weapons of the United States and the victims of its war machine."[99]

---

[97]Chu Shulong, "Sino-US Relations Pushed into Perilous Waters," *Shijie zhishi*, no. 11 (June 1, 1999): 9-10, in FBIS-CHI-1999-0622, June 23, 1999.

[98]Luo Renshi, "What about the 'New Gunboat Policy'," *Jiefangjun bao*, May 20, 1999, 5, in FBIS-CHI-1999-0526, May 20, 1999. A more extensive description of the history of the rise and decline of U.S. interventionism comes from Wang Zhuxun, who states, "The United States . . . is riding on the third expansionist upsurge in its history. During the first upsurge, which lasted from the end of the 18th century to early 19th century, the United States capitalized on endless internal strife brought on by the revolutionary movement and the War of Napoleon in the old European continent, and put forward the Monroe Doctrine. It went full force to expand in the Western Hemisphere, and tried its best to turn America into the Americans' America. During the second upsurge, which lasted from the end of the 19th century to the early 20th century, the United States developed from free capitalism to monopoly capitalism, and increased its national strength tremendously. Under the guidance of Mahan's theory on sea power, it vigorously expanded overseas. . . . Now, the United States is in a new period of expansion. Factors such as the weakening of its Cold War opponent and its sustained economic growth have placed the United States in a new window of strategic opportunity.' The Kosovo War was launched in this strategic backdrop. This will be an important factor that impacts on the direction headed by the international strategic situation in the 21st century." Wang Zhuxun, "Effects of Kosovo on Global Security."

[99]"Just See How the United States Expands its Arms and Prepares for War," *Xinhua*, June 1, 1999, in FBIS-CHI-1999-0603, June 1, 1999.

For Chinese analysts, the question is not whether the U.S. will once again interfere overseas, but where. In its pursuit of global hegemony and a unipolar world order, U.S. military intervention is expected to continue to occur throughout the transition period. According to Colonel Zhang Zhaozhong of NDU, "Gangster logic is now emerging ever more prominently. We should realize from this that at the turn of the century we are in an extremely unstable strategic pattern, and the United States is also testing the water. At present it is in midstream, not knowing if it can get to the opposite bank and whether there will be any dangerous rocks or reefs. I believe that this testing of the water will go on for several years, and we need to observe whether Chechnya or the Korean peninsula will be next."[100] An article in the *Liberation Army Daily*, after asserting that U.S. "gunboat policy will inevitably lead to endless wars and disorder all over the world," predicted that U.S. military interference may not be limited to smaller nations in the future. "The target today may be a small nation, but it could be a big country tomorrow! The target may be Kosovo today, but it could be any country that does not meet U.S. desires tomorrow. . . . War increasingly will become the major means adopted by the United States to establish a polarized pattern. Wars are not far away from us."[101]

In addition to hegemonism and power politics and ethnic, religious, and territorial reasons, Chinese analysts see the struggle for economic resources as another major source contributing to local wars in the transition era. As Colonel Liu Mingde states, "The Marxists hold that the conflict of economic interests is the root of war." He explains that the Arab-Israeli dispute "has to do with Israel's heavy reliance on the Jordan River" and that the Iran-Iraq war and the Gulf War were about petroleum. Similarly, the civil war in Yugoslavia is a war between the "poor" Serbs and the "rich" Slovaks and Croats. Liu concludes, "Competition in Comprehensive National Power has aggravated

---

[100]Ma Ling, "The Attempt Behind the 'Bombing in Error'—Interview with Renowned Military Commentator Zhang Zhaozhong."

[101]Bi Changhong, "Polarization Attempt and Danger of War," *Jiefangjun bao*, May 21, 1999, 4, in FBIS-CHI-1999-0528, May 21, 1999.

the scrambling for resources among nations."[102] An even bleaker forecast about the rivalry over economic resources is predicted by He Xin, who draws an analogy to the Warring States era of Chinese history:

> The energy and natural resources crises of the early 21st century will unavoidably lead to the economic decline of industrial countries, and cause the intensification of economic and political wars as countries contend for natural resources and markets. In this situation, the world probably will enter a new "Cold War" (economic, political war), even a "Warring States era" with numerous local and regional hot wars emerging.[103]

It is this struggle for economic resources that could lead to direct conflicts between the major powers. While many Chinese authors imply that there will not be a war among the five major powers, that they very likely will participate in the regional wars but probably not against each other, there is another viewpoint that believes the potential for conflict exists.[104] Three analysts at the Strategy Institute at NDU write, "The majority of regional conflicts in the world are civil wars, social turmoil, and civil coups. Although there are influence and interference from some other countries, these interventions do not develop into military confrontations between large countries." However, they warn that, "Potential conflict areas do exist that may possibly involve direct military confrontations between large countries or regional powers. If large-scale armed conflicts and local wars happen in these regions, it can result in drastic changes in the world situation and harm the global strategic situation."[105]

A likely area for future conflict among the powers will be Central Asia where "abundant natural resources will become the target of a struggle"

---

[102]Liu Mingde, "The Implications of the Changes in Warfare After Disintegration of the Bipolar Structure," *International Strategic Studies* 24, no. 2 (June 1992): 7-8.

[102]He Xin, *Zhongguo fuxing yu shijie weilai*, 8.

[104]For an example of the former view, see General Pan Zhengqiang, "The Current World Military Situation," *Renmin ribao* (People's Daily), December 23, 1993, 7, in FBIS-CHI-94-005, January 7, 1994.

[105]Xia Liping, Wang Zhongchun, Wen Zhonghua, and Xu Weidi, "Shijie zhanlue xingshi de zhuyao tedian yu qushi," 14-18.

between the major powers. Yang Shuheng from the U.S. Institute at CASS writes that the United States wants the region's energy resources, but Russia is unwilling to "drop to the status of a second-rank country" and will resist the United States. However, pursuing economic interests is not the only U.S. goal in the region—another is "squeezing Russia out."[106] She explains, "The rivalry over the Caspian Sea region's oil and natural gas . . . is part of the U.S.-Russian rivalry over strategic interests and spheres of influence in the Eurasian hinterland." Yang predicts, "The number of countries involved will increase. The European Union also regards the Central Asian region as an energy resources base that can replace the Gulf in the future . . . . International forces covet the treasure chest that is Central Asia."[107]

The NATO bombing of Yugoslavia was seen by a number of Chinese authors as part of the organization's efforts to gain influence and control in the region. Li Yonggang, a scholar at the Chinese Society for Strategy and Management, says geopolitical, economic, and energy interests were the motivations for NATO actions, for once NATO controlled the Balkans it had a direct path to Central Asia. He writes,

- "From the angle of geopolitics, Kosovo is located in the middle of the Balkan Peninsula, which is situated among the three continents of Europe, Asia, and Africa; as such, Kosovo has a decisive strategic position. To NATO, with control over the Balkans, it can advance westward to the Mediterranean and North Atlantic, and southward, it can consolidate the 'southern wing of NATO,' offering a link to its strategy in the Middle East. Eastward in the region of Black Sea and Caspian Sea, that is, the region of outer Caucasus and Central Asia, NATO can infiltrate, expand, and weaken and push out the power and influence of Russia."

- "Viewed from the angle of economic interests, NATO European powers have been quietly, secretly enthusiastic about getting through the

---

[106]Yang Shuheng, "Lengzhan hou daguo he diqu liliang dui Zhongya de zhengduo" (The struggles over central Asia by major nations and regional forces in the post-Cold War period), *Heping yu fazhan* (Peace and Development) 60, no. 2 (June 1997): 26-29.

[107]Ibid., 45.

Balkan corridor in the south to extend their sphere of economic influence to Central Asia and even further. . . . Although the European powers are still in line with the United States on several important issues, the building of a united, powerful, and eventually independent Europe to contend with the United States is still the long-term strategy of these countries. . . . Once the Euro has reached the bank of the Caspian Sea, it can enter the hinterland of Russia and can also come into contact with the five countries in Central Asia. This will have extremely far-reaching political, economic, and cultural significance. This is the general political, economic, and financial strategy of Europe."

● "What should also be noticed is that by putting the Balkans under control and moving westward, there is the possibility of manipulating a vast geographic area rich with oil and natural gas."[108]

An additional source of instability in Central Asia has been pointed out by Gao Heng of CASS, who believes that "the development of Islamic resurgence activities" could lead to conflict.[109] Moreover, Chen Feng of CIISS argues that the contention in Central Asia could be exacerbated by the military activities and exercises of foreign troops. For example, when the United States, "for the first time since the end of World War II, sent regular troops (more than 500 personnel of one battalion under the 82nd Airborne Division) to the region to take part in military maneuvers, it indicated that the struggle to control the region between the big powers has spread from economic and political fields to military and security fields."[110]

---

[108]Li Yonggang, "Looking at the U.S. World Strategy Against the Backdrop of the Kosovo Crisis," excerpt published in *Zhongguo Tongxun She* (Hong Kong), May 27, 1999, in FBIS-CHI-1999-0528, May 27, 1999.

[109]Gao Heng, "Shijie daguo guanxi de xin tedian" (New characteristics of the relations between the world's major nations), *Shijie jingji yu zhengzhi* (World Economics and Politics) 209, no. 1 (January 1998): 8.

[110]Chen Feng, "1997 nian de guoji zhanlue xingshi," 5.

Central Asia is one of two regions Chinese analysts predict will emerge as a new hot spot in the future; the other is the Asia-Pacific.[111] There are, however, differing views concerning the potential for future wars in Asia. While some authors are concerned about the possibility that major conflicts could erupt, others emphasize the recent greater stability in the region as compared to other parts of the globe. Zhang Changtai, a Research Fellow at CIISS believes, "In a relatively stable security environment, the Asia-Pacific remains one of the regions in the world with fewer cases of armed conflicts and such a situation can still be maintained in the years to come." His views are backed up by the few number of local wars in the region. He writes:

> For a long time, especially in the post-Cold War era, the Asia-Pacific has been a comparatively stable region. Statistics show that in 1991 prior to the end of the Cold War, 29 armed conflicts and local wars occurred in the world, out of which 6 were in the Asia-Pacific. In 1997 the total number of armed conflicts in the world increased to 38, while it was kept to 6 in the Asia-Pacific, namely the internal armed conflicts in Afghanistan, Sri Lanka, Cambodia, the Philippines and Myanmar, as well as that between India and Pakistan in Kashmir. The armed conflicts in the Asia-Pacific not only remain the least in the world, but also have decreased to some extent in intensity.[112]

However, many authors argue that despite the low number of local wars and greater stability in the 1990s, there still is serious potential for the Asia-Pacific to become a hot spot.

Chen Peiyao, president of SIIS has pointed out, "During the Cold War, East Asia was the region where military conflicts and local wars were constantly seen. The end of the Cold War did not bring an end to all the

---

[111]For example, Colonel Xu Weidi of the NDU predicts that the two great zones of war will be the East Asian littoral (because of territorial disputes) and the Eurasian zone, including Central Asia and the Persian Gulf. See Colonel Xu Weidi, "Post Cold War Naval Security Environment," *World Military Trends* (Beijing: Academy of Military Science, no date).

[112]Zhang Changtai, "1997 nian yatai diqu xingshi zongshu" (Roundup of the Asia Pacific situation in 1997), *Guoji zhanlue yanjiu* (International Strategic Studies) 47, no. 1 (January 1998): 20.

regional problems."[113] His argument is furthered by Shen Qurong of CICIR, who states, "The Cold War in the postwar Asia-Pacific was never 'cold' and peace in post-Cold War Asia-Pacific has been only lukewarm. The issue of regional peace awaits a fundamental solution. Beneath the surface of relative stability lie destabilizing factors. . . . In the 50 postwar years, the two largest local wars in the world both broke out in the Asia-Pacific region . . . the Asia-Pacific has now entered a stage of 'Cold Peace.' "[114] According to Li Zhongcheng, of CICIR, major issues such as the Korean peninsula, Taiwan, the Nansha Islands, and the Diaoyu islands "make it clear that in the East Asia-Pacific region there exists the kindling for regional conflicts."[115]

The Japanese parliament's adoption of the U.S.-Japan Security Guidelines, in spring 1999, also is considered to be a source of future conflicts. Not only does it signify the rise of militarism in Japan, considered by some to be a serious potential factor for instability in the region, but it also "increased the capacity of the U.S. military to intervene in the Asia-Pacific . . . [for] without Japan as a forward base, U.S. military forces would have to retreat east to Hawaii and south to Australia." Lu Guangye, a fellow at the Chinese National Defense Strategic Institute, claims that together with NATO, the U.S.-Japanese military alliance has become one of "the two black hands helping the tyrant to do evil." He sees NATO military strikes in Yugoslavia and the bombing of the Chinese embassy as omens of future U.S. and Japanese actions. "Everything that NATO does can be regarded as the most direct and most realistic mirror of what we understand as the substance of the Japanese-US military alliance and of how Japan and the United States will act in the Asia-Pacific region. The 'experiment' carried out in the Federal Republic of Yugoslavia by US-led NATO also provides a vivid example for the Asia-Pacific countries."[116]

---

[113]Chen Peiyao, "East Asian Security: Situation, Concept and Mechanism," *The SIIS Journal* 3, no. 2 (July 1997): 2.

[114]Shen Qurong, "Post-War Asia Pacific: Historical Lessons and Common Efforts for a Bright Future," *Contemporary International Relations* 5, no. 11 (November 1995): 7.

[115]Li Zhongcheng, *Kua shiji de shijie zhengzhi,* 192.

[116]Lu Guangye, "Going Against the Tide of History, Threatening World Peace," *Jiefangjun bao,* June 6, 1999, 4, in FBIS-CHI-1999-0617, June 18, 1999.

Another potential cause of war in the Asia-Pacific has to do with China's rise as a global power. Several authors have written about U.S. efforts in the next decade or two to contain China's development and prevent its rise in international affairs. Colonel Zhang Zhaozhong of NDU was asked in an interview why he considered "the next 10 to 15 years will be the most difficult and most important period in China's development." His reply was, "The United States has already realized that this is the best period for containing China, and so it produces stuff like the theory of the Chinese threat to suppress China. If the United States is unable to curb the momentum of China's development in the next 10 to 20 years, it will have wasted a lot of effort. During this period, therefore, the United States may devise all kinds of ways to cause trouble." However, Colonel Zhang does not foresee China and the United States going to war in the near term. "Unless there are major changes over Taiwan or other issues, the United States at present does not have the gall to take the initiative in attacking China's territory. But we must be vigilant."[117] Chu Shulong of CICIR also predicts that efforts to contain China could lead to problems, "Negative and extremist trends in U.S. domestic politics, external strategy, and diplomacy toward China are extremely dangerous for world peace and development and for the present and future of Sino-US relations."[118] These views are echoed in the yearly *Study Reports on the International Situation—1997-1998*, published by the Chinese Society for Strategy and Management, where Yan Xuetong of CICIR warns of potential conflicts between China and the United States, as China's power increases and the "desperate" United States struggles to maintain its leading position:

> In history, the rise of a new world power often leads to large-scale international wars, but these wars are not necessarily caused by the expansion of a rising power. Some of them resulted from the military policies of a hegemonic power in maintaining its hegemony. The U.S.-British War (1812-1814) is a typical example. In order to constrain the rise of the United States, Britain blocked American shipments to Europe . . .

---

[117]Ma Ling, "The Attempt Behind the 'Bombing in Error'—Interview with Renowned Military Commentator Zhang Zhaozhong."

[118]Chu Shulong, "Sino-U.S. Relations Pushed into Perilous Waters."

(just like) the case of the U.S. blocking Chinese ships, such as the Yinhe event of 1993.[119]

The predictions of Yan and others tend to modify Deng Xiaoping's earlier assertion, discussed below, that China will never be a "source" of war. Yan and many authors are worried that the United States could somehow force a war upon China in order to contain its rise or dismember its territory.

Deng Xiaoping Thought

In the mid-1980s, Deng Xiaoping apparently described, in still-unreleased documents, four alternative scenarios, each of which was based on a different "basic contradiction" that would characterize the new era. He summarized a series of major conflicts in the world that might lead to war in four Chinese characters: "East, West, South, and North." The first set of conflicts, East-West, is posited as the conflict between the United States and the Soviet Union—that is, between socialism and capitalism; the second scenario suggests West-West conflicts between developed capitalist countries; in the third scenario South-North conflicts are between the developing Third World countries and the developed capitalist countries; and the fourth alternative view sees South-South conflicts as differences between Third World countries that can lead to warfare. In 1989 Deng predicted that two of these sets of conflicts could result in new Cold Wars. "I hope the Cold War will end, but I am disappointed. Perhaps when one cold war ends, two more cold wars have already started. One is directed against the south and the third world, the other against socialism."[120]

A crucial part of Deng's formulation of the sources of future warfare is that China will never be a source of war, nor does China aspire to become a superpower, even though Chinese officials since 1988 have explicitly accepted

---

[119]Yan Xuetong, "The International Security Environment of China's Rise," in *Guoji xingshi genxi baogao—1997-1998* (Study reports on the international situation—1997-1998)(Beijing: Zhanlue yu guanli chubanshe, 1998), 82-83. This book has 10 authors, four from CASS, three from CICIR, one from CSSM, and one unidentified.

[120]*Selected Works of Deng Xiaoping*, vol. 3, 344, quoted in "Hegemonism Should Never be Allowed to Act Willfully," *Qiushi*, no. 11 (June 1, 1999): 6-7, 10, in FBIS-CHI-1999-0617, June 18, 1999.

the Iklé-Wohlstetter Commission estimate that China will have the world's largest economy around 2020. The one exception to these comments on the sources of war appears to be Taiwan; many authors echo the long-standing question of Taiwan's status as a national threat. According to Gao Heng of the usually moderate CASS,

> If Taiwan (no matter what name or form it uses) publicly or officially flies a "Taiwan independence" flag, it will lead to a major crisis in relations between the two shores. On that occasion, if the United States, Japan, or other countries publicly intervene, it will lead to a serious armed conflict, or escalate to a local war. Its influence will go beyond the Asia-Pacific region, and have global and historical impact.[121]

CHINA'S ROLE IN MULTIPOLARITY

Chinese analysts assert that China need not be purely passive but can assist the trend toward multipolarity and increase its pace. For example, it can help Europe move toward becoming a pole. One author argues that the EU wants to play a bigger international role as a "powerful independent pole" in an unfolding multipolar world, so it is "seeking at the same time to tighten its bond with the world's major powers," and issued an important policy document entitled, *Building a Comprehensive Partnership with China*, in March 1997. Feng Zhongping of CICIR calls this "a strategic partnership." According to Feng, this new relationship with China will "help the EU in its long cherished endeavor to assert itself on the world stage and become an independent 'pole' in world affairs." The reason the EU can become a "pole" is because of "China's status in the unfolding world power balance."[122] A similar argument is put forward by Shen Yihui, who states that "the EU needs to count on China for support," because "West Europe's building closer ties with China will enable itself to play a bigger part in international affairs. It is also conducive to quickening the process of world multipolarization as far as

---

[121]Gao Heng, "Dongbei Ya de anquan geju ji weilai qushi" (Northeast Asia's security structure and future trends), *21 shi ji* (21st Century), no. 6 (1995): 36.

[122]Feng Zhongping, "An Analysis of the China Policy of the European Union," *Contemporary International Relations* 8, no. 4 (April 1988): 1-6. Feng is Deputy Director of the Division for Western European Studies at CICIR.

international politics is concerned." Shen adds that not only can China help the EU gain power in world affairs, but improved Sino-EU relations can also benefit the EU in other areas as well. He states that, economically, "The Chinese market is needed to catalyze Europe's economic growth." Even in the area of security, he claims, "China can be used to build a 'crescent' security zone around the EU."[123]

FINDINGS

The current assessment of the future security environment publicly emerged in 1986, following the U.S.-Soviet summit, and can be attributed to Deng Xiaoping's national security advisor, Huan Xiang. Its orthodox tenets about a future multipolar world are subject to muted revision and debate. Among the disagreements which this chapter has examined in some detail: who will form the poles of a coming multipolar world; how "pole" should be defined and on what basis classifications should be made; the transition to a multipolar world and how to characterize the turmoil and world structure of such a transition period; and finally, how Chinese analysts interpret and construe recent events as evidence for the prevailing orthodox view, or conversely for the reformist view.

The Basic Framework

The Chinese assessment of the current and future security environment depicts the present world as being in an era of transition to a new world structure. During this period, great rivalries will emerge among the powers, and many local wars will be fought, as a struggle for world leadership takes place. Chinese authorities assert that world politics since the 1800s always has had a "system" or a "strategic pattern" (the "Vienna System" of 1815-70; an intermediate system when Germany and Italy each unified and Japan launched the Meiji Reform; the "Versailles System" of 1920-45; the "Yalta System" of 1945-89; and the present "transition era.") Under those rules, there is a

---

[123]Shen Yihui, "Cross-Century European-Chinese Relations," *Liaowang*, no. 14 (April 6, 1998): 40-41, in FBIS-CHI-98-114, April 24, 1998. For an additional article discussing improving Sino-EU relations see Wang Xingqiao, "A Positive Step Taken by the European Union to Promote Relations with China," Beijing Xinhua Domestic Service, July 1, 1998, in FBIS-CHI-98-191, July 10, 1998.

competition among powers that includes a global division of spheres of influence. Some examples of the current rivalries to carve out spheres include:

- The United States arranged the Bosnian settlement at Dayton to dominate further its European NATO allies.
- The United States is forcing Japan to increase its financial support for U.S. bases and forces in Japan under the guise of the Defense Guidelines, so that it can challenge the Russian and Chinese spheres of influence from the east, while NATO challenges them from the west.
- Japan is seeking to embroil the Unites States and China in a struggle that will weaken both Washington and Beijing.
- NATO air strikes against Yugoslavia in spring 1999 were a part of a U.S. plan to gain control over Eurasia.

The decline of U.S. power and influence is a key feature of the current era, so that after the transition period is complete, there will no longer be any superpowers but instead a "multipolar world" in which five major nations—China, the United States, Japan, Europe and Russia—will each have roughly equal comprehensive national power. International affairs in the new multipolar "world system" will be governed by the "Five Principles of Peaceful Coexistence," and hegemons and power politics will no longer prevail.

Debates

Chinese authors rarely refer to each other, seldom provide footnote or bibliographical information, and hardly ever mention or admit to the existence of debates or differences of opinions, let alone criticize other authors by name. The precedent was broken however in 1997 when two national journals carried two articles, one reformist in nature, and the other orthodox, which openly challenged and criticized the other point of view about the current transition period and the coming world of multipolarity. Yang Dazhou, a senior analyst at the Institute of American Studies of CASS, initiated the debate, when he published a direct and detailed criticism of the orthodox assessment of the future security environment. The article met with a forceful response from a senior general in military intelligence, Huang Zhengji.

Although he did not directly cite Yang's article, Huang refuted it by quoting long passages of it. The two articles reflect a debate among Chinese analysts about:

- The *pace* of the decline of the United States
- The *rate* of the rise of "multipolarity"
- Whether there currently is a transition period of uncertainty
- Whether the United States will lose its allies
- What the future role of Third World nations will be.

In his article, Yang Dazhou put forward a reformist scenario of the current and future security environment, which conflicted with the majority of the key features of the orthodox view. He argued:

- The United States will maintain its superpower status for at least three decades.
- The United States will maintain its alliances with Japan and Germany.
- There will not be a period of "uncertainty" in the next two or three decades.
- There will not be an extended transition period featuring a trend toward multipolarity.
- A "pluralistic" world structure of "one superpower and four powers" already exists.
- Only the United States is really a "pole" and able to decide key issues in any region.
- China "does not have sufficient qualifications to be a 'pole.' "
- For more than 20 years, no other nations, including those in the Third World, will emerge as major powers to challenge the five strongest.
- It is not likely large local wars will break out among nations.

In turn, General Huang reasserted the orthodox view by contesting each of Yang's points:

- U.S. decline is inevitable and continuing; U.S. global influence is already severely limited.

- Five-pole multipolarity is inevitable, especially as friction grows between the United States and Japan and Germany (as proved by the new summits between the EU and Asia, which excluded the declining United States).
- The rise of the Third World has transformed world politics and will continue to restrain the United States.
- Local wars are certain, even though "'peace and development' is the main trend," during the transitional period of uncertainty in the decades ahead.

Other differences or variances in opinion also exist about the above issues, however, rather than engaging in a direct debate, some Chinese authors employ more subtle techniques for showing dissent, such as by citing foreign experts in order to show an opposing view, or rising above the debate by inventing new definitions of orthodox terms. Sometimes a "neutral" author might set forth conflicting scenarios or different points of view held by other authors, or a journal will publish the comments of several scholars from a conference in a way that shows disagreements exist.

The NATO strikes on Yugoslavia and the NATO bombing of the Chinese Embassy in Belgrade in spring 1999 highlighted the debate concerning the future world structure, because they resulted in the reevaluation of previous assessments about the current transition period. The reformist view clearly gained support on the issues of the pace of U.S. decline and the rate of multipolarization. This new trend was manifested through a number of articles admitting that the transition to multipolarity has been postponed. The cause for the delay was largely attributed to the fact that the United States remains powerful. Not only were some authors no longer focusing on current U.S. decline, but rather they predicted that its strength may even continue to increase. However, other Chinese analysts, while recognizing that the pace of the multipolarization process has slowed, also emphasize that the current trend does not mean that the U.S. will be able to establish a unipolar world. It is only a temporary setback, the basic premise about the world moving toward a relatively equal multipolar structure has not been altered.

Regional Wars

Chinese analysts are largely in agreement that before multipolarity and peaceful coexistence prevail, the current transition period will be characterized by turbulence and instability. Despite the mantra that "peace and development are the main trend" of the times, regional wars are expected to be frequent. In general, a major world war is not predicted, although after the Kosovo crisis and Chinese embassy bombing in spring 1999, warnings were expressed by a few authors about the possibility of a third global war.

The regional wars that will prevail throughout the current period are noted to be increasing in intensity, scope and frequency. According to Chinese authors, they stem from three major sources:

- Ethnic, religious, historical and territorial disputes.
- Hegemonism and military interventionism, particularly on the part of the United States.
- The competition for power, influence and economic resources as the new world structure is formed.

While a number of authors stress that the major powers will not be involved in wars against one another, other authors cite struggles over resources as conflicts that could lead to such types of confrontations.

New regional war "hot spots" are expected to emerge as the transition period progresses, and aside from the current problem areas such as the Balkans, Africa, and the Middle East, Central Asia and the Asia Pacific are considered to be potential candidates. Whether or not the Asia-Pacific will remain stable is a subject for debate among Chinese analysts. The Korean peninsula, Taiwan, the Nansha Islands, and the Diaoyu islands, are cited as conceivable seeds for major conflicts, all of which could somehow involve China. Although Deng Xiaoping asserted that China would never be a source of war, China's rise as a global power is considered to be another possible cause of instability. Several authors have written about U.S. efforts, in the next decade or two, to contain China's development and prevent its rise in international affairs. They warn of potential conflicts between China and the United States, as China's power increases and the "desperate" United States struggles to maintain its leading position.

A number of analysts cite hegemonism and military interventionism as contributing to and exacerbating local wars. Following the NATO military strikes against Yugoslavia in spring 1999, for example, there was a tremendous increase in criticism and alarm about U.S. hegemonism being a source of war. Chinese analysts assert that in its pursuit of global hegemony and a unipolar world order, the United States will continue to intervene militarily throughout the transition period.

While many authors imply that there will not be a war among the five major powers, there is another viewpoint that believes the potential for conflict exists among the major powers. A likely area for future conflict among the powers will be Central Asia, due to its strategic position and vast natural resources.

The current debates among Chinese security analysts all might be said to elaborate on the four alternative scenarios Deng Xiaoping described in the mid-1980s. Each was based on a different "basic contradiction" that would characterize the new era. Deng summarized a series of major conflicts in the world that might lead to war in four Chinese characters: "East, West, South, and North." The first set of conflicts, East-West, is posited as the conflict between the United States and the Soviet Union—that is, between socialism and capitalism; West-West conflicts are characterized as being between developed capitalist countries; South-North conflicts are expected to be between the developing Third World countries and the developed capitalist countries; and South-South conflicts are defined as the differences between Third World countries that can lead to warfare. A crucial part of Deng's formulation of the sources of future warfare is that China will never be a source of war, nor does China aspire to become a superpower.

As noted, the formulation used by Chinese authors during the 1990s to forecast the future security environment is similar to the authoritative statements first made 15 years ago by Deng. Huan Xiang, his national security adviser, first announced the features of the current view of the future security environment in early 1986, just after the U.S.-Soviet summit:

- "The new stage of U.S.-Soviet relations will further weaken their ability to control and influence their respective allies. . . . The world's political multipolarity trend will further develop."

- "As the world moves toward a multipolar . . . five pole world, when the United States and the Soviet Union are considering problems, they must think about the China factor, and also the other poles."
- Japan "not only wants to strive to be on equal footing with the United States economically and politically, but further, it is deliberately planning, when the time is ripe, to surpass the United States, replace America's world economic hegemony. Once it has economic hegemony, political and military hegemony would not be too difficult."

2: AMERICA'S DECLINING ROLE

CHINA'S SECURITY ANALYSTS HAVE BEEN PREDICTING U.S. DECLINE for a long time. In fact, the idea that U.S. strength is weakening and that its policies will no longer be effective throughout the world is not new in the 1990s. Using internal Chinese documents, Professor Robert S. Ross has shown it was alleged in the early 1980s. For example, U.S. concessions in what formed the August 17, 1982, communique between the United States and China were explained as due to U.S. "power decline." Ross cites one analyst who argued at that time that the U.S. "position of strength is declining" and U.S. policy will "lead to failure everywhere."[1]

According to official Chinese Marxism, a "capitalist" United States cannot avoid decline forever. Even in military strength and technology, including the development of the revolution in military affairs (RMA), areas where the United States currently is considered to hold the leading position, Chinese military experts claim that there are several reasons the United States is destined to fall behind other nations. This "inevitable" decline of the U.S. hegemon is a decisive feature of China's assessment of the future. Without U.S. decline, there will be no multipolar structure in which a rising power can seek protection. Without the fading away of U.S. military alliances with Europe and Japan, a rising power will have no new partners with which to align. Additionally, without U.S. decline, Chinese Marxism would be proven false.

Since 1991, some Chinese military authors have described specific U.S. military weaknesses and forecasted that after two decades the superpower

---

[1] Robert S. Ross, "China Learns to Compromise: Change in U.S.—China Relations, 1982-1984," *China Quarterly* 28 (December 1991): 742-773.

status of the United States will end. This chapter, which cites the views of 70 authors, divides its survey of U.S. decline into three subjects:

- How and why the United States will fail to exploit the promise of a potential RMA
- People's Liberation Army (PLA) assessments of how U.S. logistics and operational weaknesses in the Gulf War are indicators of American decline and the problems it will face in future wars
- How U.S. military weakness is one factor affecting overall U.S. decline.

This is the first of several chapters to deal with Chinese writings about the future implications of the RMA, which is also an important factor in the chapters about Comprehensive National Power (CNP), Japan, Russia, and future wars. PLA authors assert that the United States will do well in the RMA only in its initial period of a decade or so, then other nations like Russia and Japan will surpass America in developing future RMA-type forces.[2] Failure with the RMA will affect victory in future war, because "Non-RMA troops will not possess the qualifications for future high-technology warfare."[3]

The assessment of U.S. military decline is reinforced by Chinese civilian authors. As mentioned in chapter one, authoritative civilian analysts forecast a decline in America's diplomatic role in the 21st century, as multipolarity opens up the potential for new alignments and "partnerships," and Japan and Europe seek to improve their relations with China. According to the ancient statecraft of the Warring States era, a too-powerful hegemon could easily destroy a rising rival. However, a coalition or a series of "strategic partnerships" could save a rising power from such destruction if the hegemon were declining. Chinese authors claim, "Today the trend toward multipolarization in the world is quickening, which prevents the United States

---

[2]For a discussion of the implementation of the RMA in Russia, Germany, France, England and Japan, see Li Qinggong, "1997 nian di guoji junshi anquan xingshi" (The international military security situation in 1997), *Guoji zhanlue yanjiu* (International Strategic Studies) 47, no. 1 (January 1998): 10-11.

[3]Su Zhisong, *Kua shiji de junshi xin guandian* (New military points of view at the turn of the century)(Beijing: Junshi kexue chubanshe, 1997), 14.

from achieving world dominance. In fact the United States is declining relatively in the world. The gap between insufficient power and overly lofty goals fundamentally frustrates its scheme to create a single-pole world."[4]

FAILURE TO IMPLEMENT THE RMA

Chinese authors define an RMA as they believe the United States does, emphasizing the potential invention of radical new forms of warfare, enhanced information warfare, networks of systems, and "digitized" combat forces.[5] However, while Chinese analysts acknowledge America's current leading position in the field, many also point to existing and future weaknesses, how they can be exploited, and why other countries will surpass the United States. For example, the scope of negative predictions about how the United States will implement an RMA varies little among five books published by PLA authors at the Academy of Military Science (AMS) in the last 4 years.[6] Their critiques of the United States range from technology issues to the ways in which U.S. military and government attitudes and philosophies will restrict and limit creativity, development, and implementation of the RMA. Several of the authors emphasize the greater potential of other countries, including China, in the area of innovation. Gao Chunxiang writes that U.S. weaknesses

> provide us with the train of thought in future information warfare on how to stay clear of the enemy's main force and strike at his weak points, avoid his strengths and attack his weaknesses, adopt his good points and avoid his shortcomings, use the indigenous to create the foreign, seek the cause to

---

[4]Zhang Linhong, "U.S. Global Strategy Seeks World Domination," *Zhenli de zhuiqiu*, no. 9 (September 11,1997): 2-4, in FBIS-CHI-97-350, December 18, 1997.

[5]See chapter 6 for a detailed discussion of Chinese views on the RMA.

[6]Wang Pufeng, *Xinxi zhanzheng yu junshi geming* (Information warfare and the revolution in military affairs)(Beijing: Junshi kexue chubanshe, 1995); Li Qingshan, *Xin junshi geming yu gao jishu zhanzheng* (The new revolution in military affairs and high-technology warfare)(Beijing: Junshi kexue chubanshe, 1995); Gao Chunxiang, ed., *Xin junshi geming lun* (On the new revolution in military affairs)(Beijing: Junshi kexue chubanshe, 1996); Zhu Xiaoli and Zhao Xiaozhuo, *Mei-E xin junshi geming* (America, Russia, and the new revolution in military affairs) (Beijing: Junshi kexue chubanshe, 1996); Han Shengmin, ed., *Zouxiang 21 shiji de waiguo jundui jianshe* (Foreign military development toward the 21st century)(Beijing: Junshi kexue chubanshe, 1996).

respond with a plan. . . . In future information warfare, if we only dare to blaze new trails there will be no need to be afraid of anyone.[7]

Other authors point out how long it will take the United States to realize fully the RMA. General Wang Pufeng estimates it will take until 2050 for all U.S. forces to be "digitized" and part of a "system of systems," because of the slow pace to date and U.S. interservice rivalry.[8]

According to Han Shengmin, the United States faces the following four major obstacles in "establishing a digitized battlefield:"[9]

- Interservice rivalry. The U.S. Air Force and Navy do not want to join the U.S. Army's digital forces experiments and have a "negative-passive attitude." Both houses of the U.S. Congress are also said to be obstacles, as indicated by the statement, "Senate Armed Services Committee, Air-Land Forces Subcommittee Chairman, John Warner, believes that 'troops still lack the technical skills to use digitized equipment in combat.' " Another Senator is quoted as saying, "Army troops are too reliant on digitized battlefields, and as soon as a digitized network is destroyed, they would be unable to fulfill their combat missions."[10]
- Insufficient funds. The U.S. defense budget has been decreasing for many years, and recently even for digital forces.
- The technology is too complex. "If you want to build a digitized battlefield, you must resolve the following six technical issues: converting sensors information into digitized coded form; processing digitized information; making digitized connections; joining digitized systems of

---

[7]Gao Chunxiang, ed., *Xin junshi geming lun*, 202.

[8]Wang Pufeng, "Yingjie xinxi zhanzheng de tiaozhan" (The challenge of information warfare), *Zhongguo junshi kexue* (China Military Science) 30, no. 1 (Spring 1995): 8-18, in Michael Pillsbury, *Chinese Views of Future Warfare* (Washington: National Defense University Press), 317-326.

[9]Han Shengmin, ed., *Zouxiang 21 shiji de waiguo jundui jianshe*, 47.

[10]Ibid., 47.

different combat platforms; developing digital display equipment; and establishing digital links between troops and platforms."[11]

● Information networks are easily damaged. "The control nodes of information networks after being attacked are easily damaged, causing the entire system to break down. . . . Local network systems' security is poor, and they are easily subject to electronic attacks."[12]

Another important example of Chinese beliefs is *America, Russia, and the Revolution in Military Affairs,* by two officers at the AMS, who argue that the United States will at first be successfully innovative during the initial decade of the RMA but later will be surpassed by one (or more) vigorous nations. They explain that the United States will ultimately lose its status as a military superpower because it will fail to exploit the RMA for several reasons, including:

● American military arrogance following the Gulf War will inhibit fundamental innovation, especially in the area of new operational concepts which are crucial for an RMA.
● Information technology and other new military technologies will be universally available through commercial enterprises and cannot be restricted by the U.S. Government, so the United States will lose its current advantage.
● Smaller defense budgets have historically produced more innovation than the giant U.S. budgets.
● New, innovative "measures of effectiveness" tend to drive innovation, and nations other than the United States are experimenting more in this area, even when they have to buy weapons from more advanced nations.[13]

Wang Zhenxi, a Senior Adviser at the China Institute of International Strategic Studies (CIISS), provides additional insight into why, despite its

---

[11]Ibid., 47-48.

[12]Ibid., 48.

[13]Zhu Xiaoli and Zhao Xiaozhuo, *Mei-E xin junshi geming,* 41-45.

advanced technology, other countries may surpass the U.S. in exploiting the RMA. He argues that not only could other nations put forward new technologies or doctrines before the United States, but that military factors are not the only ones affecting the outcome of the RMA. Instead, a variety of components, such as the factors that make up a country's CNP, also contributes to a country's ability to develop the RMA:

> Counting on its technical superiority, the United States claims itself to be the forerunner in the military revolution and that it even has such a great lead of 30 to 50 years over other nations that no country can catch up and advance shoulder to shoulder with it before 2020. We say that military technology is an agent behind the military revolution, but not the only one.

Wang next employs the same definition of RMA used by Andrew W. Marshall and other American proponents:

> It depends on the combined action of social, political, economic and scientific and technological factors for a military revolution to take place and proceed smoothly. . . . And in the military field it hinges on the joint innovation of the military technology, doctrines and organizational structure.

To the surprise of Westerners, Wang differs from Americans and does not expect the United States to be the world's leader in the RMA:

> It is not necessarily the existing most technologically advanced country that will eventually achieve the best results in the military revolution. And it can not be ruled out that in the current military revolution certain countries may advance new military thoughts or doctrines, thus pinning down the technological supremacy the U.S. primarily expects to possess in the era of information. . . . If the social, political, economic, scientific and technological, and military thought factors are taken into account, then it is not absolutely limited to the United States as the only country that can wage a military revolution.[14]

---

[14]Wang Zhenxi, "The New Wave of the World Revolution in Military Affairs, *International Strategic Studies* 44, no. 2 (April 1997): 8-9.

Chinese analysts also use the most recent public review of United States defense strategy, the *Quadrennial Defense Review* (*QDR*), as the basis to suggest increasing military challenges the United States may not be prepared to face. First, there is the issue of homeland defense. Lu Dehong from the CIISS writes, "It is the first time since the end of the Cold War that the United States emphasizes that the U.S. homeland is not free from external threats." Second, Lu points out that the United States is making only a modest effort to exploit the RMA: "How to balance investment in the present versus the future was the fundamental contradiction facing the U.S. Department of Defense." The QDR examined three different strategic paths to solve this tough problem: the QDR chose a third path—to strike a balance between the present and the future "that embraces the RMA in an evolutionary way. . . . Continuing to exploit the RMA has been adopted as the general principle of U.S. military development of the QDR."[15]

The Chinese criticize the U.S. Army for already "being trapped in the blind alley of technology." A *Liberation Army Daily* article states, "The Army which the U.S. is developing is no more than the use of a nation's technology to transform the *existing* units as well as the *existing* weaponry and equipment of the Army, and the U.S. Army is already trapped in the blind alley of technology." The article warns, "If the United States goes on with the present practice, the military revolution it is engaged in will not be a thorough going one," and predicts "The United States will not exploit the RMA very well."[16]

According to some Chinese military authors, the United States already knows China can defeat it in 2020. General Pan Junfeng states that the United States will not have formed a full information warfare force until the middle of the 21st century. He explains three ways that in future wars American computers can be very vulnerable. "We can make the enemy's command centers not work by changing their data system. We can cause the enemy's headquarters to make incorrect judgments by sending disinformation. We can dominate the enemy's banking system and even its entire social order."

---

[15]Lu Dehong, "Meiguo xin 'si nian fangwu pinggu baogao' pouxi" (An analysis of the U.S. new report of the quadrennial defense review), *Guoji zhanlue yanjiu* (International Strategic Studies) 46, no. 4 (October 1997): 7-10.

[16]Zhang Feng, "Historical Mission of Soldiers Straddling Twenty-First Century," *Liberation Army Daily*, January 2, 1996, 6.

General Pan states that the United States already realizes these three points and that on January 30, 1994, *Defense News* reported that in war games between the Chinese military and the U.S. Navy in the Pacific, at the U.S. Naval War College, the Chinese forces defeated U.S. forces. General Pan puts forward five suggestions for ways in which China can strengthen its development and implementation of the RMA:

- Increase research on military doctrine
- Establish operational theory
- Train high-quality people in advanced degrees
- Establish combat laboratories and learn from the six laboratories the United States has created
- Create *sha shou jian*, or "magic weapon trump cards"[17]

FUTURE MILITARY WEAKNESSES

Some Chinese authors have treated the question of America's future extensively as they analyze the future security environment, so it is important to know the baseline of how China assesses the United States today. In general, Chinese authors assert the following points about current U.S. military weakness:

- The United States barely won the Gulf War.
- Saddam could have won with a better strategy.
- The United States today cannot "contain" Chinese power.
- The United States is unable to execute its military strategy of two major regional contingencies.
- U.S. munitions cannot damage deep underground bunkers (like those in China).

---

[17]General Pan Junfeng, "Dui xin junshi de jidian kanfa" (Several views on new military affairs), *Zhongguo junshi kexue* (China Military Science) 35, no. 2 (Summer 1996): 111. General Pan is Director of the Foreign Military Studies Department of AMS in Beijing. Similar proposals for how China can exploit U.S. weaknesses and improve its position in the RMA are offered in Gao Chunxiang, *Xin junshi geming lun*, 199-202, and Wang Pufeng, *Xinxi zhanzheng yu junshi geming*, 201-203.

Chinese books on the U.S. military are plentiful and largely descriptive.[18] Some Chinese military textbooks about the U.S. Armed Forces begin with a sentence that declares U.S. military technology is the best in the world,[19] but this apparent praise is misleading. The main point of all writings about U.S. forces is to emphasize their weak points and their vulnerability to defeat by China. Not one of the more than 200 books reviewed for this study admitted that the United States could defeat China by force in any scenario—but many techniques can supposedly defeat U.S. forces.[20] There are frequent references to China's "defeat" of U.S. forces in both Korea and Vietnam. The United States is said likely to fall behind others in the RMA. It is said that even Japan

---

[18]Relevant books include: Chen Haihong, *Meiguo junshi liliang de jueqi* (The rise of American military strength)(Huhehaote: Nei Menggu daxue chubanshe, 1995); Cui Shizeng and Wang Yongnan, *Meijun lianhe zuozhan* (U.S. military joint operations)(Beijing: Guofang daxue chubanshe, 1995); Hu Siyuan and Chen Hu, *Meijun hangtian zhan* (U.S. military space warfare) (Beijing: Guofang daxue chubanshe, 1995); Pan Xiangting and Sun Zhanping, eds., *Gao jishu tiaojian xia Meijun jubu zhanzheng* (American military local warfare under high-technology conditions)(Beijing: Jiefangjun chubanshe, 1994); Wang Fang and others, *Shiji chao ba—Meilijun* (The century's ultra-tyrant—America)(Beijing: Shishi chubanshe, 1997); Wang Guoqiang, *Meiguo youxian zhanzheng lilun yu shijian* (U.S. limited warfare theory and practice)(Beijing: Guofang daxue chubanshe, 1995); Wang Zhuo, *Xiandai Meijun houqin* (Modern U.S. logistics)(Beijing: Guofang daxue chubanshe, 1995); Yin Chengkui, Gao Guixiu, Li Ligang and Su Yusheng, *Meijun gao jishu wuqi zhuangbei yingyong yu fazhan* (Use and development of U.S. high-technology weaponry)(Beijing: Guofang daxue chubanshe, 1995).

[19]See the 10-book Modern U.S. Military Studies Series (*Xiandai Meijun yanjiu congshu*) published by authors from China's National Defense University in 1995. Hu Siyuan and Dai Jinyu, *Xiandai Meiguo kongjun* (The modern U.S. Air Force)(Beijing: Guofang daxue chubanshe, 1995), 1, state, "The U.S. Air Force is the most modern Air Force in the world today." Similarly, Wang Zhongchun, Zhao Ziyu, and Zhou Bailin, *Xiandai Meiguo lujun* (The modern U.S. Army) (Beijing: Guofang daxue chubanshe, 1995), write, "The U.S. Army is the army with the highest level of modernized equipment in the world today." Yin Gu, Li Jie, and Lei Xiangping, *Xiandai Meiguo haijun* (The modern U.S. Navy)(Beijing: Guofang daxue chubanshe, 1995), 1, state, "The United States is currently the world's only maritime superpower." Finally, Wang Baofu, *Meiguo tezhong zuozhan budui yu tezhong zuozhan* (U.S. Special forces and special warfare)(Beijing: Guofang daxue chubanshe, 1995), 1, states, "The U.S. Special Combat Units have the best equipment and the largest scope of any special combat force in the world."

[20]In January 1998, a weekly column entitled "Future Warfare" began to appear in the *Liberation Army Daily* that included advice on how an "inferior" national force can defeat a "superior" force.

is developing better military technology than the United States in several areas and that the United States is "dependent" on Japan for military technology.[21]

The devaluing of U.S. military power is accompanied by frequent references in military books and the prestigious journal, *China Military Science*, to the importance of ancient Chinese statecraft, especially to the early centuries of Chinese history, when several warring states adroitly manipulated a balance of power until one state achieved primacy and assumed the name "China." Both the challenge of new military technology and the need to use traditional Chinese statecraft figure in this story of the founding of China; both are also often mentioned when Chinese authors address the 21st century.

In general, most Chinese analysts since 1991 have acknowledged that the United States is the "sole military superpower" and has the most technologically advanced army, navy and air force in the world. Somewhat humorously, one analyst writes, "In the last 20 years, people have turned pale at the mere mention of U.S. military strength."[22] However, they suggest that this characterization of narrow technological superiority would mean very little in a U.S. conflict with China. Chinese authors repeatedly emphasize that major, fatal weaknesses characterize the American Armed Forces. Almost all universally cite Chairman Mao's requirement that the dialectical aspect of Chinese military science requires assessment of weakness as well as strength.

The Chinese view is that the United States suffers from fundamental logistics weaknesses and several operational weaknesses. Chinese authors believe Saddam Hussein, using Chinese-style strategy, could have exploited these weaknesses in order to defeat the United States.

---

[21]"Riben: Junshi jishu lingxian Meiguo" (Japan: leading the U.S. in military technology), *Junshi wenchai* (Military Digest) 4, no. 2 (1996): 18. This article asserts that Japan has modified its fighter aircraft to exceed the turn rate of U.S. fighters; that F-117 exteriors and 95 per cent of U.S. military electronics depend on Japan and that Japan could shift the Russian-American balance of power in missile accuracy if it sold the same electronics to Russia that it does to the United States.

[22]Wu Chi, "Gulf War Reveals U.S. Weak Points," *Hong Kong Ta Kung Pao*, March 20, 1991, 3, in FBIS-CHI-91-058, March 26, 1991, 2.

WEAKNESSES IN LOGISTICS

In order to denigrate the image of the United States as a superpower colossus, a number of Chinese articles focus on American logistics limitations.[23] Many Chinese analysts cite statistics and examples from the Gulf War in order to point out the problems the United States would face in a potential war in Asia. Other authors examine the evolution of U.S. military strategy, arguing that it illustrates the gradual weakening of U.S. power since World War II.

The United States is described as a country that "must cross the Atlantic or Pacific Oceans and go to Europe or Asia" before any serious war starts. From 1961 to 1968, Presidents Kennedy and Johnson incorporated a flexible response strategy for fighting two-and-a-half wars simultaneously. Chinese military authors refer to these as a war with the Soviet Union and Europe, a war with China and Asia, and half a war with a regional power in an area such as the Middle East. As America's overall national strength declined, however, from 1969 to 1980, Presidents Nixon, Ford, and Carter realized that "strength fell short of ambition" to fight two-and-a-half wars, so U.S. military strategy shifted to fighting one-and-a-half wars. Chinese called this "fighting the big war either in Europe or Asia, and at the same time a small war in some other region."[24]

The Chinese posit that American weakness can be seen from the U.S. definition that the Gulf War should have been a "half war," but in fact it required almost all America's conventional weapons, its reserves had to be called up, 6 months were needed for the United States to complete the deployment of troops in the Gulf, and it had to hire foreign ships to carry troops, equipment, and supplies. Chinese analysts point out that nearly 50 percent of the weapons and equipment for the Gulf War had to be carried by foreign ships and foreign aircraft because the United States lacked strategic airlift and sealift. After detailing the extent of U.S. dependency on foreign transportation, one author wrote, "Huge inputs were [needed] merely in order to guarantee one battlefield's requirements; if it had to simultaneously ensure the requirements of two battlefields, the current U.S. transportation

---

[23]For example, see Su Enze, "Haiwan zhanzheng Meijun 'Shipa' " ("Ten fears" of U.S. forces during the Gulf War), *Junshi wenzhai* (Miliary Digest), no. 13 (1995): 24.

[24]Wu Chi, "Gulf War Reveals U.S. Weak Points," 2.

capabilities clearly are insufficient."[25] More importantly, Chinese articles point out that in the Gulf War, oil, which accounts for 50 percent of the materials consumed by the U.S. Armed Forces, could basically be arranged in the region rather than having to rely on vulnerable lines of supply. One author asks, "If it were a long, drawnout war, with many casualties and losses, could the United States promptly replenish troops, equipment, and materials and maintain the troops' fighting ability?"[26]

They cite other U.S. advantages in the Gulf War, not to be repeated again, such as the cooperation of the 28 countries in the coalition and the role of 120 countries in imposing a blockade against Iraq. Chinese analysts also note that America's "strong dependency on allies" is a potential vulnerability in future multination joint combat operations because of problems inherent in alliances. One author writes that during the Gulf War, "Due to differences among the various allied countries' troops, in the areas of war interests, combat ideology, weaponry, culture, and language, numerous difficulties inevitably existed in command coordination. This could provide the opponent with a few opportunities it could exploit, including dividing and disintegrating the alliance politically, and destroying the countries militarily one by one."[27] In addition, Chinese military specialists also point out that in spite of all the advantages provided by the alliance, it took Iraq only several hours to capture Kuwait, but the allied forces took more than 30 days to recover Kuwait.

One important assessment concludes that if it was so difficult for the United States to win a "half war" against Iraq with so many advantages from its coalition forces, the United States would not do well fighting alone against China and Asia. A PLA author asserts that it would be "hard to predict the result" of a United States war with China and Asia:

> If we have to predict, then the chance of its winning is only 30 percent, because the U.S. Forces have never fought a "whole" war overseas, while

---

[25]Zhen Xi, *Kelindun junshi zhanlue yu di er ci Chaoxian zhanzheng shexiang* (Clinton's military strategy and the scenario of a second Korean war)(Beijing: Junshi kexue chubanshe, 1996), 69.

[26]Wu Chi, "Gulf War Reveals U.S. Weak Points," 2.

[27]Li Qingshan, *Xin junshi geming yu gao jishu zhanzheng* (The new revolution in military affairs and high-technology warfare)(Beijing: Junshi kexue chubanshe, 1995), 188-189.

the "half wars" they have fought ended sometimes in victory and sometimes in defeat. The two sides fought to a draw in the Korean War; the Vietnam War was lost; and the Gulf War was a victory, but fought by 28 countries.[28]

Even looking back on World War II, the Chinese assessment is that, although the United States was in a "whole" war, it fought only "half of it" because of its limited participation, which began with Pearl Harbor. According to the Chinese assessment, "The relentless pressure of the Russians was driving the Germans farther and farther back, and the defeat of Germany was almost a certainty" before the United States opened the second front in Normandy. Even in the European theater, the United States was joined by both the Soviet Union and Britain, while in the Asian theater the United States enjoyed the combat cooperation of "China, Britain, and the Soviet Union."[29]

NORTH KOREA CAN DEFEAT AMERICA

Chinese military authors also appear to devalue the effectiveness of U.S. forces in a future Korean scenario. According to a colonel at AMS, several factors ensure U.S. defeat "if in the next few years a Korean War erupted." His main points are:

● The United States will not have 6 months to deploy and train forces. Instead, "the Korean People's Army will surprise attack South Korean air bases, ports and communication lines."
● "U.S. casualties will not be as low as in the Gulf War. . . . On the Korean peninsula, the population is dense, with river networks and mountains, roads are few, unsuitable to armor . . . casualties will be extremely high."
● "North Korea's mountains are wrapped in clouds and mist; it will be difficult for the U.S. Air Force and high-technology weaponry to give full play to their vast superiority."

---

[28]Wu Chi, "Gulf War Reveals U.S. Weak Points," 2.

[29]Ibid., 2.

75

- Temperatures of negative 40 degrees centigrade "provide excellent conditions" for guerrilla warfare.
- North Korea will not allow the United States to land in the rear.
- U.S. forces lack numerical strength. During the Korean War, U.S. troops reached over 400,000, but the result was not victory. In the 1960s and 1970s, in the Vietnam War American forces were 663,000 and had great technical superiority, but the result also was defeat. U.S. forces in year 2000 will be 70 percent of today.[30]

WEAKNESSES IN THE GULF WAR

The Chinese perception of American strategic weakness based on logistics is further compounded by the assertions of many Chinese military authors that American operational weaknesses could one day make U.S. forces extremely vulnerable to a Chinese style strategy. An overall assessment of the war comes from the Vice President of AMS, Li Jijun, who writes that during the Gulf War,

> U.S. Armed Forces revealed many weak points. For example, the combat consumption was too great, and it could not last long. There was great reliance on the allied countries. The high-tech equipment was intensive and its key links were rather weak; once they were damaged, combat effectiveness was greatly reduced. Also if the adversary of the United States was not Iraq, if the battle was not fought on the flat desert, if the Iraq Armed Forces struck first during the phase when U.S. Armed Forces were still assembling, or if Iraq Armed Forces withdrew suddenly before the U.S. Armed Forces struck, then the outcome of the war might have been quite different.[31]

Several books published in the mid-1990s purport to analyze U.S. military weaknesses in detail. One published in May 1996 by Major General Li Zhiyun, Foreign Military Studies Director at the National Defense University, contains

---

[30]Zhen Xi, *Kelindun junshi zhanlue yu di er ci Chaoxian zhanzheng shexiang*, 66-68.

[31]Li Jijun, *Junshi lilun yu zhanzheng shijian* (Notes on military theory and military strategy)(Beijing: Junshi kexue chubanshe, 1994), in Pillsbury, 227.

articles by 75 PLA authors who describe in detail an extended list of joint warfare weaknesses of the U.S. Army, Navy, and Air Force:[32]

- Interservice rivalries limit coordination.
- Intelligence does not reach operators rapidly.
- Space satellites are vulnerable to direct attack.
- Command control nodes are exposed to attack.
- Ports and airfields are vulnerable in initial deployment.
- Each high-tech weapon has its own weakness.
- Aircraft carriers depend on E6 Prowlers.
- U.S. forces are optimized for deserts, not mountains.

These represent a common theme in PLA views of future warfare—America is proclaimed to be a declining power with but two or three decades of primacy left. U.S. military forces, while dangerous at present, are vulnerable and can be defeated by China with the right strategy. That strategy is "defeating the superior with the inferior" (*yiruo shengqiang*). Part of the recommended approach in some of this PLA writing is the requirement for "the inferior" to pre-emptively strike the "superior" in order to paralyze his nerve centers and block his logistics. Chinese military books and articles on U.S. weaknesses date back at least to the Gulf War in 1991 and continue to appear, drawing on analysis of that conflict. Ten strategies that could have been employed to exploit U.S. operational weaknesses during the Gulf War were cited by Chinese military analysts.

- *Fortify positions*. One representative analyst states, "Nothing can better reflect an Army's fighting ability than combat involving attacks on fortified positions." The Chinese explain American success in attacking Iraqi fortifications as due to the terrain in Kuwait and Southern Iraq, which is "a flat desert" where it is "difficult to build long-term solid fortifications" because the sand layer is so thin. Even with this advantage of Iraqi weakness, "The United States took a long time to tackle them . . . in 38 days they flew 10,000 sorties, and eliminated only 40 percent of the

---

[32]Li Zhiyun, *Meiguo lianhe zuozhan yanjiu* (Studies on U.S. Joint operations theory)(Beijing: Guanfang daxue chubanshe, 1995).

77

Iraqi forces." To the Chinese, the important point about American weakness is that U.S. forces could not overcome the following defenses: cities and mountains deep in the hinterland, the underground command post, garrisoned tunnels, underground warehouses, and aircraft and strategic missile bunkers that, according to the Chinese analysis, were "relatively safe." Only a few civilian bunkers and "some hangars which were not solid enough" were destroyed. U.S. conventional munitions cannot destroy fortifications with walls greater than 10 meters thick or deep underground facilities, especially in mountainous areas. The Chinese analyst concludes, "If the Iraqi forces could have relied on mountainous areas and built tunnels with layers more than 10 meters or even dozens of meters thick, then even if the U.S. forces could have cut several meters away from the peak, they could not have hurt the Iraqi forces one little bit."

Using this measure of effectiveness, Chinese analysts belittle American capabilities to "penetrate or blow up a protective layer several meters thick" or the battleship *Wisconsin*'s 1-ton shells that can destroy "a reinforced concrete protective layer as thick as 4 meters."[33] Chinese underground bunkers are portrayed as invulnerable to American attacks. If press reports are accurate, China has a series of underground tunnels in the mountainous area west of Beijing that protect a national underground command center. Chinese use of tunneling and mountainous areas for command centers and protection of army, navy, and air force equipment dates back to the Korean War and is often described with pride in Chinese historical accounts. It is therefore likely that Chinese military leaders take comfort in this American operational weakness.

● *Exploit weaknesses.* Several Chinese articles criticized the Iraqi military commanders for not exploiting well-known American weaknesses.[34] The Vietcong and North Vietnamese knew how to play on American weaknesses, but the Iraqis did not learn from those lessons. For example,

---

[33]Wu Chi, "Gulf War Reveals U.S. Weak Points," 2-3.

[34]Ho Poshih, "The Chinese Military is Worried About Lagging Behind in Armament," *Hong Kong Tang Tai*, March 9, 1991, 17-18, in FBIS-CHI-91-050, March 14, 1991, 30-32.

the Iraqis did not conduct harassment attacks behind American lines at bases in Saudi Arabia, unlike the Vietcong's extensive operations. The Iraqi officer corps was not sufficiently trained in technology to master the advanced equipment that it had purchased.[35]

One way to defeat U.S. Air Force and Naval air power is to strike at American-controlled airbases, according to former Chief of Staff of the PLA, General Su Yu: "However strong a combat capability, an Army unit does not have any combat capability before entering its position." According to past examples of local wars, the Israeli Air Force succeeded in launching surprise attacks in several wars because of its "strict training and meticulous planning and preparations" and because "the other party slackened their efforts, lowered their guard, had insufficient training, and issued inappropriate combat commands."[36] Another crucial area where Chinese analysts criticized Iraq for not making surprise attacks was pointed out by Gao Chunxiang. When discussing the complexities of logistics safeguards, he stated, "If the Iraqi military had made a surprise attack on the rear of the U.S. military and multination troops, then the end of the war could have been rewritten."[37]

● *Prevent specialized training.* According to the Chinese, the Iraqis allowed the U.S. Armed Forces to conduct special training for several months before the war and to remain on a high state of alert. "This undoubtedly helped to win superiority and take the initiative." According to Chinese analysts, "Air power's relative strength is complicated. It includes the quality and quantity of weapons, the training level and fighting will of personnel, the logistics support capabilities, and combat operational concepts." These are referred to as "a balance of static forces" which Chinese analysts do not believe is as useful a measure of effectiveness as

---

[35]Song Xinzhi and Su Qingyi, "Reassessing Constraints on Air Power," *Jiefangjun bao* (Liberation Army Daily), January 25, 1991, 3, in FBIS-CHI-91-029, February 12, 1991, 39-40.

[36]Ibid., 40.

[37]Gao Chunxiang, *Xin junshi geming lun*, 201.

the "balance of dynamic forces." The dynamic balance "has a great deal to do with how both parties actually employ their power."[38]

● *Use special measures.* A particular example of how one side in combat can greatly strengthen its superiority in a "balance of dynamic strength" is to adopt "special measures." Although the U.S.-led coalition had static balance superiority in terms of air power, if the Iraqis had followed a North Vietnamese example, during the Gulf War they could have released "smoke screens supplemented by the spray of water." The Vietnamese used these "screens" to "make it impossible for the laser-guided bombs dropped by the U.S. Air Force to hit the Hanoi electric power station." Some Iraqi special measures were effective, however. Quoting a U.S. Government source, Chinese analysts state, "Only a dozen or so of the 700 Iraqi aircraft were destroyed in the first 2 days of air raids," because of the effectiveness of air defense self-protective measures, camouflage, and "air defense exercises in cities." In the long run, Chinese analysts trust the use of protracted and guerrilla warfare to wear down the invader. Harassing attacks can create confusion, cause losses, and damage the morale of the political system.[39]

● *Study high-tech weapon vulnerability.* A series of Chinese articles describes how individual U.S. high-tech weapons systems each have their own particular weaknesses and flaws that must be studied and exploited. Even the U.S. Tomahawk cruise missile can be shot down by Chinese surface-to-air guided missiles. Chinese missiles have "on several occasions downed U.S.-made U-2 high-altitude reconnaissance planes, causing a great shock to the United States." The HQ-2 surface-to-air guided missile made by China is acclaimed to have a "killing probability" of "no less than 90 percent" when three missiles are launched simultaneously within the effective range of about 30 kilometers.[40]

● *Camouflage tanks.* Another measure of effectiveness showing American military weakness involves Iraqi tanks and American efforts to destroy

---

[38]Song Xinzhi and Su Qingyi, "Reassessing Constraints on Air Power," 40.

[39]Ibid., 40.

[40]Ho Tawei, "Exclusive Report: China-Made Weapons Display Their Might in the Middle East," *Hong Kong Tang Tai,* January 26, 1991, 10, in FBIS-CHI-91-024, February 5, 1991, 25-26.

them. According to Zhai Zhigang, a military Research Fellow, in order to attack Iraqi troops successfully, U.S. troops would have had to achieve a three-to-one superiority in order to "insure a quick battle to force a quick decision." Zhai then listed the obstacles to American success. First, Iraqis had built antitank ditches filled with gasoline and with mines laid densely around them; thus, "even if the 2,200 U.S. tanks break through the many Iraqi tank positions and gallop to northern Kuwait, they will fight an engagement with nearly 1,000 T-72 tanks from five of the best Presidential Republican Guard divisions." According to Zhai, "A tank in a defilade can usually cope with two to three offensive tanks with similar capabilities." There were 4,000 Iraqi tanks in Kuwait that had been concealed in "solid defilades." Therefore, Zhai estimated, only 40 percent of a tank in a defilade was exposed, and camouflaging made it hard to discover or hit directly.[41]

What is the significance of these military calculations? Zhai's comments confirm the use of operations research by Chinese analysts. Trading off one tank vs. two to three tanks when the defending tank is in defilade is a good example. The suggestion that the 2,200 U.S. tanks that penetrated Northern Kuwait would not be able to successfully destroy 1,000 T-72 tanks contains a number of miscalculations, including the determination that a U.S.-crewed M-1 tank is roughly equivalent to an Iraqi-crewed, 20-year-old, Soviet-made T-72 tank and that even a 2.2-to-1 superiority is inadequate.

• *Destroy the nonlinear.* U.S. combat theory for high-tech local wars was criticized by one Chinese analyst, who believes that the nonlinear form of combat, where "fairly large gaps can emerge between the flank and rear of one's own troops," means there is the potential for "annihilation." Li Qingshan writes, "During the Gulf War, the U.S. military frontal attack from the coast of the Persian Gulf . . . was approximately 300 kilometers. In this 150,000-square-kilometer combat area, the U.S. military deployed 17 divisions, and the average interval between each division was 94 kilometers. It is thus clear that the gaps exposed by the nonlinear form of

---

[41]Zhang Chunting, "Chinese Military Research Fellows on the Gulf War," *Liaoyang* (overseas edition) 28 (January 1991): 7, 8, in FBIS-CHI-91-022, February 1, 1991, 6-7.

combat can provide opportunities for the one side to be carved up, surrounded, and even destroyed by the other."[42]

• *Establish sound economic structure.* A Chinese military Research Fellow, Han Ren, pointed out that Iraq had an important economic-based weakness. "Iraq's economic structure is irrational, and 80 percent of its food, 60 percent of its medicines, and the majority of its modern weapons are imported." Han described Iraq's overall military disadvantage by comparing the static totals. His comparisons are particularly interesting because Iraq's quantitative military indicators approach those of China. Han said that Iraq had 1.1 million troops, 5,500 tanks, 780 combat planes, and 40 to 50 naval vessels. U.S. and coalition forces counted 700,000 troops, 3,100 tanks, 2,200 planes, and some 200 naval vessels superior in quality and capability to Iraq.[43]

• *Establish a nuclear deterrent.* The Chinese media (and interviews by the author) stress that Iraq did not have a nuclear deterrent and that the United States needed to make nuclear threats in order to achieve victory over Iraq. According to the Chinese, Saddam treated seriously a comment to the British Broadcasting Corporation by Vice President Dan Quayle, on February 1, 1991, that he "would not rule out using nuclear weapons in the war against Iraq." This assertion seems to suggest that the conventional forces alone of the U.S.-led coalition could not have defeated Iraq without a nuclear threat, which presumably would not be so successful in deterring China.

• *Assess air power.* Chinese assessments of American air power also include specific measures of effectiveness and imply the use of operations research. U.S. airborne warning and control systems (AWACS) have "raised by more than 30 percent the probability of attacking aircraft hitting their targets." This would be effective even for old aircraft models. Chinese assessments of the Falklands War emphasized that "even though Argentina did not enjoy advanced air power, it achieved the glorious distinction of downing 18 British ships and won widespread notice in the

---

[42]Li Qingshan, *Xin junshi geming yu gao jishu zhanzheng*, 189.

[43]Zhang Chunting, "Chinese Military Research Fellows on the Gulf War," 6.

international community."[44] Sun Hongwei points out that "even in the Gulf War, in which the largest amount of new weaponry was used, aircraft dating from the 1960s made up the biggest proportion of the total used by coalition forces." The point seems to be that by combining new and a majority of old fighter aircraft with the force multiplier of AWACS and others listed in the article (electronic jamming aircraft sometimes made up as much as 25 percent of each formation), superiority can be achieved.

This misperception allows an obsolete 30-year-old fighter aircraft (the majority of China's Air Force) to become effective by adding a few AWACS aircraft and electronic jamming aircraft, which China is in the process of acquiring. This is not a proper approach to assessing the balance of air power and could lead to a major miscalculation. If Chinese military leaders actually use such concepts, they would greatly underestimate the damage that advanced fighter aircraft can do to a nation defended by obsolete fighters.

U.S. AIRCRAFT CARRIER VULNERABILITIES

The aircraft carrier battle group still is the "epitome" of combat forces and is second to none on the ocean, writes Ying Nan. But according to his analysis of how the weak can defeat the strong, aircraft carrier battle groups have numerous "weaknesses." A weaker opponent can still achieve the result of "the mouse will rule the elephant" (*laoshu zhi daxiang*). His main points are:[45]

● The entire aircraft carrier battle group has numerous radar reflections and infrared and electromagnetic signatures, so it is very difficult to effectively conceal them.

---

[44] Sun Hongwei, "New Developments in the Use of Air Power," *Jiefangjun bao* (Liberation Army Daily), March 22, 1991, 3, in FBIS-CHI-91-072, April 15, 1991, 55-57.

[45] Ying Nan, "Hangmu de biduan ji fan hangmu zuozhan" (Aircraft carrier defects and anti-aircraft carrier operations), *Xiandai junshi* (Contemporary Military Affairs) (January 1998): 13-15. See also Liu Xinghai, "Hangkong mujian bingfei zhan wu bu sheng" (Aircraft carriers are not invincible), *Junshi shilin* (Military History), no. 7 (1998): 28-30.

- Aircraft carrier battle group capabilities drop following the deterioration of natural conditions (such as weather), and the nighttime flying capability of pilots of carrier-based planes is only about 50 percent of their daytime ability.

- Aircraft carrier battle group flexibility is limited by numerous islands and reefs, or when water is shallow and when close to the coast.

- While getting supplies at sea, their defense capability clearly drops. For example, U.S. aircraft carriers generally use MKC-13-1 steam launchers, and each launch requires 1.5 to 2 tons of fresh water; after every 500 launches, specialized technical personnel ground the aircraft and overhaul it at sea for 1-2 days; after every 2,500 launches, the aircraft is returned to home port for 3 to 6 weeks of repairs.

- Aircraft carriers need 1 to 4 special supply ships that frequently are the target of an enemy's attack.

- The antisubmarine and antimine capability of an aircraft carrier battle group is relatively poor. During World War II, nine aircraft carriers—36 percent of the total number of aircraft carriers that sank—were bombarded and sunk by submarines.

- Since the 1980s, new high technology in submarines has caused the threat of submarines to aircraft carriers to increase.

- Although it is difficult for mines to directly sink and destroy an entire aircraft carrier, the damage and deterrent role created by mines still make the navies of all countries uneasy.

- Elevators, catapult launchers, and arresting devices all are extremely vulnerable. The elevators move planes to the deck, so if they are damaged, the aircraft carrier is unable to do anything.

- The U.S. Navy has reduced the number of S-3 aircraft and escort ships accompanying aircraft carriers.

- AWACS aircraft operating from a carrier will be the priority targets of other navies wishing to attack aircraft carriers.

- Unmanned planes can repeatedly launch attacks against the aircraft carrier battle group, forcing the ship's catapult launcher to continuously launch fighters for take off, causing it to lose large amounts of power and fresh water.

- Aircraft carriers are vulnerable to electronic equipment aboard medium and small ships, on offshore islands and reefs, and on air balloons, which can continuously create confusion in the electromagnetic environment.

OVERALL U.S. DECLINE

The effect of U.S. military decline will reinforce the trend toward multipolarity and the end of America's superpower status, because, according to Chinese assessments, U.S. military weaknesses are just one part of the overall fall in U.S. CNP. In fact, Chinese analysts see U.S. decline in virtually any arena. For example, in a discussion about how the newest and highest skyscrapers in the world are all being built in Asia, and many in China, one author writes, "As the 20th century fades, the United States seems to be ceding skyscraper supremacy to the East. Does that imply that the coming century and the coming millennium will belong to the Orient?"[46] However, as was true of the debates on the period of transition to a multipolar world, Chinese authors do differ in their views on the extent and rate of U.S. decline. Some analysts focus on the concrete, specific aspects of American weaknesses, while others examine overall U.S. power and compare it with that of other nations.[47]

One of the authors of a major study on the changing world structure by the Shanghai Institute for International Studies (SIIS) asserts that U.S. decline is relative. He explains, "Position of strength is a relative concept; whether a country's position of strength is high or low, strong or weak, can be shown only through a comparison with other countries. In general, the relative decline of America's position of strength is the contrast between the power of the United States and that of other major nations." The author goes on to state that at present, no country will increase its strength quickly enough to surpass the United States before the early 21st century. The rise of Japan, Germany, and other major European and Asian countries "subjected America's position of strength to new challenges, but they still do not constitute a major threat to America's superpower status. This situation will

---

[46]Li Haibo, "Heading for the 21st Century," *Beijing Review* 37, no. 39 (September 26-October 2, 1994): 9.

[47]For a discussion on how the Kosovo crisis and the NATO bombing of the Chinese Embassy in Belgrade in spring 1999 led to a re-evaluation of previous assessments of the pace of the U.S. decline, see chapter one, the section titled "Post-Kosovo Debate."

be maintained at least until the beginning of the next century."[48] The former president of SIIS, Chen Qimao, points out that U.S. power can be declining compared to other countries even though its economy and science and technology are strong. "Overall, the U.S. position of strength will continue its relative decline, but in recent years, the U.S. economy has picked up, its economic structure has been adjusted, and, in areas such as the science and technology revolution that takes information as its core, it is at the forefront of the Western nations; therefore, the process of its relative decline will be convoluted, not direct."

He goes on to claim that "Certain far-sighted intelligent U.S. personages have already clearly pointed out that in the new century the U.S. will be transformed from a superpower to a common power (*putong daguo*)."[49] He Fang, at the State Council International Studies Center, also believes that the United States will be a common power in the future; however, he provides a possible exemption for U.S. military strength. He writes, "The transition period will be America's evolution process from a superpower to a common power; its military force perhaps will not be included, but its military role is declining."[50]

Social issues are frequently cited by Chinese analysts as an area where the United States has serious troubles. Particularly when compared to other countries, the United States is depicted as leading the world in social problems.[51] For example, one author referred to America as the "Drug

---

[48]Ding Xinghao, "Shijie geju zhuanxing qi zhong de Meiguo" (The United States during the transformation of the world structure), in *Kua shiji de shijie geju da zhuanhuan* (Major changes in the world structure at the turn of the century), ed. Chen Qimao (Shanghai: Shanghai jiaoyu chubanshe, 1996), 118.

[49]Chen Qimao, "Qianyan" (Introduction), in *Kua shiji de shijie geju da zhuanhuan*, 8.

[50]He Fang, "Guodu shiqi de guoji xingshi" (The international situation during the transition period), in *2000: Shijie xiang hechu qu?* (2000: where is the world going?), ed. Yang Zheng (Beijing: Zhongguo guangbo dianshi chubanshe, 1996), 319.

[51]A comparison of how the United States stands up to the European Union (EU) in social issues, economics, science and technology, and military affairs comes from an SIIS study: "In the future world structure, Europe and Japan are the only forces that have the qualifications to struggle with the United States for the leading world position, as will be compared below. Europe has more advantageous conditions than Japan; Japan's weak points are Europe's strong points. . . . The population of the EU is more than half that of the United States, its GNP

Superpower."[52] A book entitled *American Social Diseases* conveys the impression that pure economic decline would be the least of the problems Americans will face in the future. The author forecasts American weakness based on:

- "The great disparity between rich and poor"
- "The homeless"
- "Wide racial gaps"
- "Right-wing extremist groups (militias and white supremacist groups)"
- "Destruction of the family and the problems of children and women"
- "Crime and drug use"
- "Generation gaps"
- "Spiritual and moral crisis ('spiritual deficit' and 'moral extinction,' 'excessive sexual indulgence')"

[gross national product] surpasses Japan's and is comparable to America's. The EU share of world trade has already exceeded America's. The European savings rate is equal to that of Japan and long ago greatly outstripped that of the United States. Europe's science and technology have very strong competitive power, based on Japanese statistics; in the world's 110 important technology areas, Europe is in the leading position in 34. Europe's reliance on the world is not as great as Japan's, it has comparatively vast territory, the trade among the countries of Europe is very vigorous, and natural resources can be obtained through many channels. . . . In Europe, on the basis of sovereign nations, each country already has suitable military force; if in the future after they establish a common military structure, if they further engage in arms expansion, it will not, like Japan, give rise to contrary political consequences. When comparing internal conditions, Europe surpasses the United States in numerous areas. The standard of living of the people in Western and Northern Europe is not poorer than in the United States and there are far fewer city evils than in the United States. There are not as many racial and national problems as in the United States. The slums often seen in the United States almost cannot be found in Western and Northern Europe. According to statistics, of American children, 22 percent live in poverty, but in Germany it is only 5 percent. The quality of Europe's middle and elementary school education is higher than America's, and the crime rate and number of drug users are less than in the United States. Western and Northern Europe, in the social welfare areas of medical insurance, old-age pensions and unemployment subsidies also are better than the United States." See, Wang Houkang, "Lengzhan hou Ouzhou geju de bianhua" (Post-Cold War changes in Europe's structure), in *Kua shiji de shijie geju da zhuanhuan*, 153-154.

[52]Yang Zheng, ed., *2000: Shijie xiang hechu qu?*, 110.

- "Crisis of political confidence (lack of trust in the government and congress, disappointment and dissatisfaction with both parties, 'lost faith' in the current political mechanism)."[53]

The author concludes that U.S. decline is both relative and actual:

America's international position and influence continue to relatively weaken . . . due to the quickening development of the world's multipolar trend, so that internationally, the U.S. is subject to greater challenges and restrictions; on the other hand. . . . America's own deep social problems and crises are becoming more and more revealed to the world, so that U.S. international influence is naturally declining.[54]

LOSS OF ALLIES

What are the long-term consequences of the United States declining while others rise? Chinese authors assert that as Japan and Western European nations gain more and more power, they will seek influence in international affairs commensurate with their strength and demand equality in their relationships with the United States. In keeping with the world's transition toward multipolarity, the decreasing gap between U.S. CNP and that of Japan and Europe means America's allies will be asserting themselves as poles, unwilling to remain the subordinate partners of the United States and submit to its "Unipolar World Strategy."[55]

An article by four analysts at the China Institute of Contemporary International Relations (CICIR) states, "As a result of their economic growth, more and more countries now dare to say 'no' to the United States. Gone are

---

[53]Wan Guang, *Meiguo de shehui bing* (American social diseases)(Chengdu: Sichuan renmin chubanshe, 1997), 1-5.

[54]Ibid., 311.

[55]Wang Naicheng, "Beiyue dongkuo dui Mei-E-Ou guanxi de yingxiang" (The impact of NATO's eastward expansion on relations between the United States, Russia and Europe), *Guoji zhanlue yanjiu* (International Strategic Studies) 46, no. 4 (October 1997): 18.

the days when one or two powers could sit upon high and dominate."[56] Yuan Peng, also of CICIR, agrees, "It is proved in practice that, although the absolute strength of the United States has almost peaked, its international influences and its capability of dominating global affairs have not synchronously increased. On the contrary, they are noticeably not as good as in the past. The multipolar system proposed by China, Russia, France, and other countries has posed a direct challenge to the unipolar strategy of the United States. . . . Of more concern to the United States is the fact that its traditional European allies, Japan, etc., are also gradually drifting away and are hardly of one heart and one mind with the United States on major issues."[57]

For its part, the United States, with its "global domination mentality," is expected to fight to hold on to its position of world leadership and supremacy, leading to direct conflicts and struggles with Japan and Europe.[58] Although America will be able to maintain its alliances in the short term, Chinese analysts foresee that in the long run:

- The United States will lose its global prominence.
- The United States will gradually lose its powerful alliances with Europe and Japan as the three powers descend into fierce economic and political rivalries.
- As their conflicts with the United States increase, Japan and Europe will work to improve their relations with China.

Jin Dexiang, a senior analyst at CICIR, believes, "Changes in the relative economic status of the United States, Japan, and Germany have exerted a far-reaching impact not only on their external and internal policies but also on

---

[56]Yan Xiangjun, Yang Bojiang, Chu Shulong and Dao Shulin, "A Survey of Current Asian Pacific Security," *Contemporary International Relations* 8, no. 7 (July 1994): 1, 2.

[57]Yuan Peng, "An Arrogant and Lonely Superpower—The Tradition and History of Hegemony," *Zhongguo Qingnian Bao*, May 26, 1999, 3, in FBIS-CHI-1999-0609, June 10, 1999. Yuan is at CICIR.

[58]Yan Tao, "U.S. Determination on Use of Force and Its 'Global Domination' Mentality," Beijing Xinhua Domestic Service, February 15, 1998, in FBIS-CHI-98-046, February 20, 1998.

world economics, world politics, and international relations."[59] Jin argues that while the U.S. economic growth rate and share of world trade declined greatly from its post-World War II levels, due in large part to its arms race with the Soviet Union, the economies of Japan and Germany grew. Subsequently, Japan and Germany were no longer satisfied with economic power but desired influence in other realms as well. "Bulging money bags have whetted the appetite of both Tokyo and Bonn for a larger global role in the political arena." According to Jin, Japan therefore is "beefing up its military muscle" and "filling up the vacuum left behind by U.S.-Soviet military retrenchment" in the Asia-Pacific region. Germany, too, is seeking a major political role through several tactics. It is striving for a Bonn-centered European Economic Zone while "trying its best to overtake Japan and catch up with the United States in the 21st century." Jin believes, "The scramble for the political leading role already exists among America, Europe, and Japan," concluding that "rivalry and contention among the three economic power centers of America, Europe, and Japan promise to replace U.S.-Soviet contention and the arms race as an all-important world issue."[60]

While Jin argues that simply the economic power of Germany has provided it with the foundation to assert itself on the world stage, other authors point to the fact that the joint economic strength of the EU is even greater than that of the United States according to some indicators. When discussing the economic contention and friction that exist between the EU and United States, for example, Yang Dazhou of the Chinese Academy of Social Sciences (CASS) writes, "Europe already possesses the economic strength to contend with the United States; the GNP of the European Union nations already exceeds America's."[61]

In addition to economic considerations, another major factor cited by many authors that has contributed to the increasing rivalry between the United

---

[59]Jin Dexiang, "America vs. Japan and Germany: Why are There Growth Imbalances? What is Next?," *Contemporary International Relations* 2, no. 5 (May 1992): 8; other quotes in this paragraph are from 10-12. When he wrote this article Jin was Vice President of CICIR.

[60]Ibid.

[61]Yang Dazhou, "1997 nian guoji zhengzhi xingshi de tedian" (The characteristics of the 1997 international political situation), *Shijie jingji yu zhengzhi* (World Politics and Economics) 209, no. 1 (January 1998): 6.

States and Japan and Europe is the disintegration of the former Soviet Union. To quote Jin Dexiang, the end of the Cold War resulted in the "removal of the glue cementing Western unity."[62] Sa Benwang, a Senior Researcher at the China Institute of International Studies (CIIS), agrees. He believes "the demise of the 'common threat' and 'common enemy,' and the subsequent demise of the 'common target' of the U.S.-European-Japanese 'Cold War alliance'," reduced the possibility of coordination and compromise, so that "'west-west' contradictions between the United States and Europe and Japan will be on the rise."[63] Three CICIR analysts claim that the combination of "eroded alliance cohesion" and the growth of the EU means

> a transformation process has been underway to turn the transatlantic partners into strategic rivals. . . . This results in transatlantic bickering and quarrels in political, security, economic and trade fields. Bilateral tensions grew over Bosnia, NATO, trade and other issues with never-ending disputes. Thus the demise of a common strategic goal had put the alliance built up in the Cold War in jeopardy and pushed it close to the verge of collapse.[64]

Several analysts at CICIR argue that the United States realizes its "leadership capacity and cohesive force" are weakening and therefore it has to "cotton up" to its allies by supporting Germany and Japan to become permanent members of the U.N. Security Council, allowing Europe to build a certain amount of self-defense strength and encouraging Japan to play a greater role in Asia. They explain that the United States does this "to achieve 'soft control' over these countries."[65] Most authors, however, believe that the

---

[62]Jin Dexiang, "America vs. Japan and Germany, 12.

[63]Sa Benwang, "Perspectives of International Strategic Patterns in the 21st Century," *Liaowang,* no. 37 (September 14, 1998): 41-42, in FBIS-CHI-98-268, September 29, 1998.

[64]Yang Mingjie, Gan Ailan, and Cao Xia, "Groping for a New Trans-Atlantic Partnership," *Contemporary International Relations* 6, no. 4 (April 1996): 4. The authors are Assistant Research Professors at CICIR.

[65]Xu Zhixian, Zhang Minqian, and Hong Jianjun, "On the Foreign Strategy and Trends of China Policy of the U.S., Western Europe and Japan at the Turn of the Century," *Contemporary International Relations* 8, no. 3 (March 1998): 12-14.

United States will be more active in its efforts to maintain power. For example, Yang Shuheng at the Center for Peace and Development, argues that the United States intends to establish its dominant position.[66] According to Qi Deguang of CICIR, the United States "purposefully took an attitude of aloofness" toward the Bosnia crisis to "wait to see the fun when they failed."[67] After the European effort to reduce the crisis failed, the United States started to proclaim that it must play the leading role and bombed the Bosnian-Serb position to show that the United States was seizing overall control.

Another analyst suggests that a key factor causing the United States to enlarge NATO is that "the United States finds its national power weakened, . . . [and] it seeks to rely on NATO to continue its leading role in the world."[68] According to Chinese analysts, America's goal through the NATO eastward expansion is both to weaken and encircle Russia, and to provide itself with a means of consolidating and furthering its leadership position in Europe. Zhang Liangneng, an analyst at CICIR, states "NATO eastward expansion is a vital strategic step for the United States to control Europe and contain Russia." However, Zhang asserts that the United States may not be able to realize its aspirations where Europe is concerned, because

> The Western European countries, particularly France and Germany, have already realized that the era when they had to rely purely on the United States to maintain regional security in Europe is gone. Only by promoting economic and political integration, enhancing military and defense cooperation, establishing united defense institutions and military forces and

---

[66]Yang Shuheng, "Ou, Mei, E zai Bohei de juezhu" (The rivalry among Europe, the United States, and Russia in Bosnia), *Heping yu fazhan* (Peace and Development) 49, no. 3 (August 1994): 29-32.

[67]Qi Deguang, "The Bosnian Civil War: Retrospect and Prospect," *Contemporary International Relations* 4, no. 8 (August 1994): 10-11. Qi is an Associate Research Professor at CICIR.

[68]Wan Shirong, "Shi ren zhumu de beiyue zuzhi dongkuo wenti" (NATO's eastward expansion, an issue attracting world attention), *Guoji wenti yanjiu* (International Studies) 59, no. 1 (January 1996): 12-17.

forging a solid "European pillar," can Europe's security and stability, as well as other interests, be truly protected.[69]

Zhang's argument is supported by another CICIR analyst, who believes that European nations not only intend to create a more unified military force independent of the United States, but also plan to utilize NATO to do so: "Although both the United States and Western Europe advocate NATO eastward expansion, they are not entirely the same in regard to the concrete objective, style and pace of the extension. While the United States attempts to make use of the NATO move to maintain its own leading position in European affairs, Western Europe wants to build up its own 'defense pillar' through NATO expansion so as to get rid of American control."[70] A Senior Research Fellow at CIISS, Wang Naicheng, expects that this "U.S.-European contradiction of control and counter-control" will become more and more acute, because each side will intensify its efforts to establish its position. "Europe is striving to change its role during the Cold War period as the little partner utterly controlled by and dependent upon America. It is demanding that power be shared in order to establish an equal, true partnership with the United States, but the United States refuses to concede and instead is becoming even more domineering, trying vigorously to consolidate its position as the overlord in NATO."[71]

Europe is not the only place where Chinese authors predict a U.S.-EU struggle for leadership; they also foresee conflicts between the two Cold War allies around the globe as Europe moves to expand its influence. Asia in particular is pointed to by Chinese as an area where European nations are striving to establish closer ties. An article by three CICIR analysts states,

Euro-American contention will be even more fierce in areas beyond the transatlantic region, especially in the Asia-Pacific. The European Union has

---

[69]Zhang Liangneng, "Western Europe and NATO Enlargement," *Contemporary International Relations* 7, no. 5 (May 1997): 19. Zhang is an Associate Research Professor at CICIR.

[70]Feng Yujun, "Moscow vs. NATO: Compromise Will Not Dispel Apprehensions," *Contemporary International Relations* 7, no. 5 (May 1997): 13. Feng is an Assistant Research Professor at CICIR.

[71]Wang Naicheng, "Beiyue dongkuo dui Mei-E-Ou guanxi de yingxiang," 18, 20.

initiated an omnidirectional strategy for expanding its foreign relations through thrusting southward to the Mediterranean Sea and North Africa, advancing eastward to Eastern and Central Europe and Russia, and designating Asia as the key area for contention with the United States.[72]

The first Asia-Europe Summit Conference in Thailand (March 1996) was considered by the authors to be a symbol of greater closeness between the two regions, presaging further decline in U.S. global influence. They write that in addition to seeking "stability and equilibrium in world political and economic order," one of the main goals of the summit was to "further weaken U.S. dominance in the global economy and international relations and frustrate U.S. attempts to seek post-Cold War global hegemony."[73] Chen Feng, a Senior Research Fellow at CIISS, pointed out that the Asia-Europe summit meant that "for the first time the United States, as the only superpower in the world, was unable to take part in this significant international conference."[74]

As the desire to be independent poles grows among European nations and in Japan, Chinese analysts predict that they will work to improve their relations with China. Three CICIR analysts conclude that the result of the power struggles among the Cold War allies will be that America, Western Europe, and Japan will "attach more importance to the China factor in their foreign strategies" because of the "enhancement of China's Comprehensive National Power and the extension of China's international influence."[75] Li Zhongcheng, also at CICIR, agrees that China will become a new focus in international relations because of its increased strength, but argues that China's growing importance may actually be one of the factors that comes between the allies. "With the improvement of its political big power status, Japan will gain more independence in dealing with regional and international affairs. Therefore, even though more stress has been laid on keeping vigilance over China within the U.S.-Japanese alliance, it will be very difficult for Japan and the United

---

[72]Yang Mingjie, Gan Ailan, and Cao Xia, "Groping for a New Transatlantic Partnership," 8.

[73]Ibid., 8.

[74]Cheng Feng, "Retrospects and Prospects of the International Strategic Situation," 12.

[75]Xu Zhixian, Zhang Minqian, and Hong Jianjun, "On the Foreign Strategy and Trends of China Policy," 12-14.

States to act synchronously and speak in one voice on their China policy. Worse still, they could even become major rivals to each other in vying for economic dominance in the Asia-Pacific."[76] Gao Heng of CASS asserts that Japan is not only working on its relations with China, but is also focusing on Russia. "Under pressure from the United States, Japan accepted the new policy of the U.S.-Japan Security Treaty. However, for its own interests (to serve as a world level power), Japan could not but try its best to improve its relations with Russia and China."[77]

According to Gao, Germany is also focusing on improving its relations with Russia in order to expand its influence, even though it is "America's 'leading partner' in Europe."[78] Gao, like other authors, mentions the developing closeness in German-French-Russian relations and the recent creation of a large triangular relationship among the three. Wu Guoqing of CASS explains that "political triangles" such as the German-French-Russian one "constitute new geopolitical centers" that alter Europe's geopolitical structure.[79] Hu Ning of the Center for Peace and Development argues that Germany, France, and other Western European nations are seeking to improve relations with Russia at the same time that NATO is pursuing its eastward expansion, because Russia can serve as a counter to the United States. Europe "needs to draw support from Russia's power to oppose the U.S. domination of European security affairs, with the aim of building a U.S.-Russian-Western European 'multipolar restrict and balance' situation."[80]

[76]Li Zhongcheng, "The Role of an Emerging China in World Politics," *Contemporary International Relations* 8, no. 2 (February 1998): 13. Li is a Research Professor in the Division for China and World Studies.

[77]Gao Heng, "Shijie daguo guanxi de xin tedian" (New characteristics of the relations between the world's major nations), *Shijie jingji yu zhengzhi* (World Economics and Politics) 209, no. 1 (January 1998): 8.

[78]Ibid., 8.

[79]Wu Guoqing, "Xi Ou lianhe you you xin jinzhang, duli zizhu jinyibu zengqiang" (There is new progress in the unification of Western Europe, and its independence and initiative is further strengthened), *Shijie jingji yu zhengzhi* (World Economics and Politics) 209, no.1 (January 1998): 17.

[80]Hu Ning, "Beiyue dongkuang xianxi" (A brief analysis of NATO eastward expansion), *Heping yu fazhan* (Peace and Development) 64, no. 2 (May 1998): 31.

Chinese authors quote Yeltsin as stating that if he had to choose, he would side with Europe over the United States: "President Yeltsin . . . said during the Denver Summit, 'If conflicts occur somewhere between Europe and the United States, Russia will favor the position of Europe, sharing weal and woe together.' "[81]

Despite the extensive writing by Chinese analysts about the trends of growing rivalries and conflicts between America and Japan and Europe, most expect the alliances to endure in the short term. Regarding the United States and Europe, for example, Wang Naicheng of CIISS writes that, although "their contradiction has intensified," he believes that "in the foreseeable future . . . coordination and cooperation will remain the central point in their relations." Because of Russia's existence as a common potential threat and Europe's continued, though decreasing, dependence on the United States in security affairs, and because of economic interdependence, "it is difficult to change in a short time the feature of the relationship where the United States is the principal and Europe is the subordinate. . . . Nevertheless, the cohesive force linking America and Europe in NATO from the beginning of the post-Cold War era has weakened with each passing day, and the contradiction, quite intense at times, has been developing continuously." He believes that as EU integration continues, the pattern of the U.S.-EU relationship will change. "With the progress in EU political, economic and defense cooperation, certainly Western European countries will pose even graver challenges to U.S. hegemony."[82]

Wang's views are shared by Sa Benwang of CIIS, who sees the weakening of the alliances between America and Japan and Europe as inevitable but believes that they will not abruptly end: "The centrifugal trend of Europe and Japan away from the United States as head of the alliance will further increase, and the tendency of the alliance to weaken will be hard to stop. Of course, this will also be a tortuous and complex process; it is expected that alliance relations will be maintained up to 2015."[83] Views similar to those held by the above two analysts are presented more strongly by three CICIR analysts who

---

[81]Quoted in Wang Naicheng, "Beiyue dongkuo dui Mei-E-Ou guanxi de yingxiang," 20.

[82]Ibid., 20.

[83]Sa Benwang, "Perspectives of International Strategic Patterns in the 21st Century," 41-42.

predict that major U.S.-EU confrontations only await the growth of EU unified CNP:

> There simply does not exist any room for fundamentally harmonizing such mutually contradictory strategic goals. This divergence can be covered up at a time when Europe still falls short of U.S. strength. However, once Western Europe succeeds in catching up in strength with the United States, serious conflicts will flare up between the two sides over their strategic goals.[84]

SELF-PROPHECY OF DECLINE

Chinese analysts quote American authors out of context to suggest that distinguished Americans agree with China's assessment. It is true that American authors frequently predict drastic decline for their country, but these warnings are always linked to a set of recommendations that, if followed, will save the day and avert the fall. Chinese authors omit these linked recommendations, thereby giving their readers the impression that many sage Americans predict their nations's own inevitable weakening.[85]

Henry Kissinger has been quoted as stating that America will now be only a "beggar policeman," because the United States sought coalition funding for the Gulf War. A glowing review of a book by Zbigniew Brzezinski, *Out of Control*, in China's most prestigious military journal subtly distorted a key point of the book. Brzezinski suggests that the United States will risk losing its global leadership role if it does not improve its materialistic values and present a more attractive model civilization than it does at present. According to Colonel Pan Jiabin of the Academy of Military Science, the book "is certainly representative of Western thought, especially that of high-level U.S. Government views." Pan then misquotes Brzezinski: "The U.S. position as a

---

[84]Yang Mingjie, Gan Ailan, and Cao Xia, "Groping for a New Transatlantic Partnership," 6.

[85]Chinese analysts do this for other countries, as well as for Taiwan. See Tai Baolin, *Taiwan shehui qiwen daguan* (The unheard of magnificent spectacle of Taiwan society)(Beijing: Hongqi chubanshe, 1992).

global power is in imminent danger."[86] Pan omits Brzezinski's recommendations, which, if followed, would assure America's superpower status. Colonel Zhang Zhaohong, of NDU, cites Samuel Huntington on American weaknesses. He writes, "This U.S. leadership group lacks the ability to sit in a tent and devise successful strategies. Huntington's latest book, *The Lonely Superpower*, includes some views with which I rather agree. The book points out that when the power of the sole superpower reaches a considerable degree, it has too much trust in its own strength, does not take a broad view of anything, and is prone to make many mistaken policy decisions."[87]

Paul Kennedy's book, *The Rise and Fall of the Great Powers*, is another example of American writing frequently cited by Chinese analysts. Kennedy argues that high military spending leads to the weakening of the U.S. and the Soviet Union, while low military spending allowed Germany and Japan to rise. CICIR analyst Jin Dexiang, quotes Kennedy on the link between large defense budgets and the decline of a country's economy and overall national power. "If . . . too large a proportion of the state's resources is diverted from wealth creation and allocated instead to military purposes, then that is likely to lead to a weakening of national power over the longer term. In the same way if a state overextends itself strategically . . . it runs the risk that the potential benefits from external expansion may be outweighed by the great expense of it all—a dilemma which becomes acute if the nation concerned has entered a period of relative economic decline." Jin then puts forward his own belief that the United States is already entrapped in the danger zone predicted by Kennedy. "As a matter of fact," he writes, "Washington today does not merely 'run the risk' of weakening national power, it is actually bogged down in the quagmire of relative decline. Relentless expansion of war industry has entailed

---

[86]Pan Jiabin, " 'Shiqu kongzhi: 21 shiji qianye de quanqiu hunluan'—Burejisiji dui guoji geju yanbian de fenxi yu renshi" (Out of control: global turmoil on the eve of the 21st century—Brzezinski's analysis and understanding of the evolution of the international structure), *Zhongguo junshi kexue* (China Military Science) 30, no. 1 (Spring 1995): 158, 160. Pan is at the Foreign Military Studies Department of AMS.

[87]Ma Ling, "The Attempt Behind the 'Bombing in Error'—Interview with Renowned Military Commentator Zhang Zhaozhong," *Ta Kung Pao* (Hong Kong), May 17, 1999, A4, in FBIS-CHI-1999-1518, May 19, 1999. Zhang is Director of the Science and Technology Teaching and Research Section of NDU.

. . . disastrous consequences on the long-term development of the U.S. economy."[88]

LORD OF THE EARTH

Chinese authors have repeatedly pointed out that one important cause of America's future decline is its conscious choice of a mistaken foreign policy. After the bombing of the Chinese Embassy in Belgrade, the depiction of America's foreign policy in the official Communist Party newspaper became particularly vivid. For example, the United States was likened to Nazi Germany in eight specific ways in a long article that concluded that the pursuit of such Nazi-like policies would end in "complete failure."[89]

In lieu of excerpting many other articles that also describe U.S. foreign policy as a search for world domination, this one will be quoted in sufficient detail to reveal the Chinese assessment of American goals clearly. It begins by responding to the rhetorical question of how the United States today and Nazi Germany are alike:

- "First, their self-centeredness and ambition to seek hegemony are exactly the same. In his notorious book, *Mein Kampf*, Hitler advocated 'ethnic superiority' and 'living space,' maintaining that human society was one that observed the law of the jungle, and that ethnic Germans should expand and become the 'lord of the earth.' If we ask which country in the world wants to be the 'lord of the earth' like Nazi Germany did in the past, there is only one answer, namely the United States, which upholds hegemonism."

- "Second, the United States has outdone Nazi Germany with respect to increasing military budgets and expanding its armament. Although the United States has yet to launch a new world war, the size of its armament expansion and the frequency of its use of military strength overseas have far exceeded those of Nazi Germany in the past."

---

[88]Jin Dexiang, "America vs. Japan and Germany," 3.

[89]Observer, "We Urge Hegemonism Today To Take a Look at the Mirror of History," *People's Daily*, June 22, 1999, in FBIS-CHI-1999-0622.

- "Third. . . . When Hitler came to power, he made anti-Communism both his strategic goal and tactical means for realizing his ambitions of engaging in arms expansion and war preparations and of contending for world hegemony. . . . It was also precisely under the guise of possessing 'common values' that the United States and Japan have reinforced their military alliance, so that the latter will play the role of the 'NATO of the Far East.' What substantive differences are there between this kind of expansionist tactic and the Nazism of the past?"

- "Fourth, the trend toward replacing global international organizations with military alliances is not without precedent. After World War I, on the proposal of then-U.S. President Wilson, 44 countries formed the League of Nations in 1920. . . . Germany was a permanent member of the league's executive council. It withdrew from the league in October 1933 due to restrictions on its program of arms expansion and war preparations. . . . Of course, the United States and its allies will not withdraw from the United Nations. But is not the way they have repeatedly bypassed the United Nations and wantonly intervened in other countries through their military alliance or bloc very similar to the Fascist way of Germany?"

- "Fifth, the strategic priorities and directions of global expansion are basically similar. Hitler made Europe a strategic priority. . . . Today, Europe is also the U.S. global strategic priority . . . the United States has reinforced its military alliance with Japan in Asia, making Japan an important accomplice in its armed intervention against other Asian countries. This is also an attempt to gain control of the European and Asian continents from the Western and Eastern fronts, with the ultimate goal of fulfilling its strategy of dominating the world."

- "Sixth, the methods they employed in dismembering other countries' territories and encroaching upon their sovereignty through exploiting their ethnic contradictions were very similar. Hitler, to secure the passageway for taking over the Balkans, plotted in June 1937 the 'Green Project' of annexing Czechoslovakia by employing its ethnic issues. Czechoslovakia was a multiethnic country and its Sudetenland was inhabited by some Germans. Gorpel [name as transliterated] clamored that 3.5 million Germans in Sudetenland were 'tortured' and Germany could not afford to 'watch as an onlooker'. . . . In less than five months, Nazi Germany took over the entire Czechoslovakia. Today, the U.S.-led NATO is attempting to dismember and control the Federal Republic of Yugoslavia by taking advantage of its ethnic problems. . . . Is it not exceedingly clear from what the United States and NATO did during the Kosovo crisis who was acting like Nazi Germany?"

● "Seventh, utilization of advanced technology to slaughter peaceful citizens is by no means less barbaric. . . . Hitler not only used in war what were considered to be the most advanced weapons of the time, such as airplanes, tanks, and long-range artillery, to massacre peaceful citizens in anti-Fascist countries, but also built concentration camps in Auschwitz and in other areas to slaughter Jews and prisoners of war with 'advanced' technology. Executioners drove hundreds and thousands of people into gas chambers and poured cyanide through air holes in the roof, killing them all. Today, the U.S. hegemonists used high-tech weapons to attack FRY civilian facilities several hundred miles away from the battlefield, or, with laser and global position systems several thousand meters above the sky, treated innocent and peaceful citizens as live targets. The flagrant use of missiles by the U.S.-led NATO to attack the Chinese embassy in Yugoslavia was a barbaric atrocity that the then-Nazi Germany had not dared to commit."

● "Eighth, there is no difference between brazen undermining of international law and aggressive acts. What is the difference between the modern-day hegemonists who willfully undermine international law and the erstwhile Nazi Germany?"

● "When we read world history, we know that many empires that had dominated for some time finally ended in decline. Particularly in this century, the worldwide colonial system that the Western powers built for several hundreds of years has collapsed. They employ the wishful thinking that fortune is now on their side and that it seems to be the turn of the United States—the sole superpower in the world—to dominate the world and to become 'the master of the globe'. . . . Even though they may run rampant for a while, they will eventually end in complete failure."

Although this article is harsher in tone and more intemperate than others, it does not deviate much in substance from Chinese authors who also condemn the "hegemonic" goals of the United States. Some authors seem to hold out hope that Washington will someday change its foreign policy goals, but this debate is muted at present.

FINDINGS

Differing only in their views of exactly how fast and in what ways America's powers will decline, Chinese analysts agree in asserting that the U.S. is losing economic, political, and military influence around the world, and therein, its status as a superpower. As evidence, analysts cite American military vulnerabilities, including failure to invest fully in the RMA, weak strategies and logistics, intractable domestic problems, and frequent inability to prevail diplomatically.

Chinese authors emphasize several problem areas that the United States faces in implementing the RMA and maintaining its leading position: Their main criticisms of American weaknesses are outlined below.

- Interservice rivalry
- A decreasing defense budget
- Complex technology
- The universal availability of technology through commercial enterprises after its development
- Easily damaged information networks
- The greater potential of other countries in the area of innovation.

Several Chinese analysts suggest that China can exploit the above U.S. weaknesses and improve its own development of the RMA. Chinese military analysts also use examples from the Gulf War to illustrate U.S. weaknesses. Many state that the outcome of the Gulf War could have been different if Iraq had employed different tactics and exploited the following U.S. weaknesses:

- The United States had insufficient means of transportation.
- U.S. munitions cannot damage deep underground bunkers.
- Various U.S. weapons systems have their own specific weaknesses.
- The United States did not have superiority in its efforts to destroy Iraqi tanks.

- The U.S. nonlinear form of combat makes it vulnerable to being surrounded and divided by the other side.

In addition to Iraq's economic weakness and its lack of a nuclear deterrent, Chinese analysts criticize Iraq for:

- Not making surprise attacks on U.S. airbases and the U.S. rear
- Permitting the United States time to build up its logistics and conduct special training for several months before the war
- Not employing "special measures," such as harassing attacks.

It should be noted, however, that Chinese assessments do not treat the United States as "weak" in any absolute sense at the present time. They characterize the United States as a true hegemon in every way today. For example, a series of books on the U.S. Armed Forces asserts U.S. technological superiority in practically every field, despite U.S. reductions since 1991.[90] Nevertheless, they assert that the United States will fall behind in military innovation after 2010.

U.S. military vulnerabilities are only one contributing factor in the overall process of U.S. decline depicted by Chinese analysts. While some authors focus on specific areas where America is weakening, such as in military affairs or domestic social problems, other analysts argue that the country's decline is relative, that it is only declining compared to other nations whose power is increasing. One predicted outgrowth of this trend of falling national strength is that the U.S. is expected to lose its allies. As the power of Europe and Japan increases, and they no longer must depend upon America either militarily or economically, they are expected to come into greater conflict with the U.S. Consequently, rivalries and struggles are expected to gradually cause the alliances to weaken and fade. Moreover, at the same time that their relationships are deteriorating with the U.S., Chinese analysts predict that Japan and Europe will be striving to improve their ties to China.

---

[90]The United States has cut defense personnel by 40 percent, to the smallest level since 1950. Weapon purchases have declined nearly 70 percent. The 1999 defense budget will be about 40 percent below its 1985 level in real terms, with only 3.1 percent of gross domestic product for defense, the smallest share since 1940.

After the Kosovo conflict in spring 1999, a number of Chinese authors debated the length of time that the United States would be able to sustain its "unipolar" hegemonic domination and hold back the global trend toward multipolarity. However, agreement about the central trend was not reversed. The debate was only about the length of time it will take for these tendencies and trends to unfold.

Chinese national security specialists have been describing America's role in the future security environment in the same way for a decade: dangerous but declining. In the picturesque terms of ancient Chinese statecraft, America is a decaying hegemon whose leaders are as yet unaware that their fate is unavoidable, so the U.S. leadership is pursuing several dangerous but doomed strategies, such as:

- Attempting to limit Russia's recovery and access to resources
- Practicing limited containment of China's rising influence
- Fomenting conflict between China and Japan
- Investing (too slowly) in a potential RMA
- Using the Bosnia conflict to maintain domination of Europe
- Falsely spreading the China Threat Theory in ASEAN
- Seeking military bases and new NATO allies in Central Asia
- Aiding separatist movements in Tibet, Taiwan, and Xinjiang.

China's authors propose a number of countermeasures to these alleged American maneuvers. Deng Xiaoping's public proclamations were to "remain coolheaded" and to *"taoguang-yanghui"*—bide our time and build our capability—to avoid conflict with the United States during the decades it suffers inevitable decline. Other authors sound more stringent warnings. The Vice President of AMS urges vigilance, because the declining United States will attempt "strategic deception" of other major powers, including China, as it did the Soviet Union with the phony "Star Wars" threat, and as it did when it tricked Iraq into invading Kuwait so the United States could dismantle Iraq's growing power. The Director of the Foreign Policy Center at China's largest security research institute warns that the United States may form a coalition to "strangle" China if the proponents of the China Threat Theory become strong in the United States.

Other proposals are more defensive. For example, China's forecasted energy needs will be enormous in 2020, which could make China vulnerable to the United States. Therefore, one author urges that China's energy must be sought through pipelines to Russia and Central Asia, because China's relative military superiority in ground forces can better protect these energy assets, rather than through oil purchases from the Persian Gulf, which rely on sea lanes that America (and Japan) could threaten in the future. Perhaps the most aggressive advice about how China should deal with the declining American hegemon has been couched in specific analogies to ancient statecraft. A well-connected scholar proposes China help to form a global anti-U.S. coalition with any and all nations opposed to the United States. His colleagues criticize him for such alarmist proposals. Several analysts have written that it is already "too late" for the United States to contain China.

3: JAPAN AND INDIA
Dangerous Democracies

THE INEVITABLE RISE OF JAPAN AND INDIA

CHINA'S ASSESSMENT OF JAPAN AND INDIA differs sharply from America's, as will be seen in this chapter's survey of 82 Chinese authors on the future role of these two countries. Chinese authors have addressed Japan's predicted rise to become the strongest or second-strongest world power by 2020, its alleged ambitions to dominate China, its drive to attain equivalence with the United States in both nuclear and conventional weapons, its prospects to implement a revolution in military affairs (RMA), and its efforts to contain China's rise by instigating conflict between China and the United States. Differences do exist among Chinese analysts about Japan's future, but the range of debate is not extensive. There are those who see only "some elements" in Japan having the above-mentioned ambitions, rather than a dedicated Japanese elite.[1] Chinese assessments of India resemble (on a smaller scale) their views of Japan's future role, suggesting that similar premises are at work in the way China's authors examine its two democratic and capitalist neighbors. Following India's nuclear tests in May 1998, in particular, numerous Chinese authors have accused India of pursuing a policy of military expansion since attaining independence, in order to become a military power, contain China, and dominate and control South Asia and the Indian Ocean.

---

[1] For example, Shen Qurong, the President of the China Institute of Contemporary International Studies (CICIR), writes that only "some elements" in Japan are trying to promote conflict between the United States and China. Feng Shaokui of the Chinese Academy of Social Science (CASS), however, writes that it is Japan's official policy goal to do so.

In the short term, Chinese authors (and the Chinese Government) advocate good relations with both Japan and India, through "shelving" territorial disputes for later resolution. However, in the long term, Chinese analysts appear to hold exaggerated estimates of the prospects of future geopolitical threats to China from both Japan and India, including the threat of their supporting "dismemberment" of China. India could join the United States in aiding Tibetan independence, and Japan might support an independent Taiwan.[2] One reason for this wariness may be that Chinese Marxism counsels suspicion of the predatory motives of any capitalist power. Another may be that ancient Chinese statecraft recommends vigilance toward nearby rivals, especially those with whom one has disputed territory, as China does with Japan and India. Chinese authors themselves suggest that an additional cause for concern has to do with history and culture, particularly the still prevalent memories of past wars. For example, an extreme assessment comes from General Li Jijun, Vice President of the Academy of Military Science (AMS), who writes that Japan's strategic culture is fundamentally ruthless, bloodthirsty, and a "self-made freak."[3] While not as bad as the Japanese, the Indians as a culture are also described as ambitious. A report written by the late Premier Zhou Enlai described India's "blood relationship" (interbreeding) with the British and explained that the Indian middle classes "took over from British imperialism this concept of India as the center of Asia," and want to have "a great Indian empire" that dominates Asia.[4]

---

[2]Zhang Wenmu, "Meiguo de shiyou diyuan zhanlue yu Zhongguo Xizang Xinjiang diqu anquan" (U.S. petroleum—geostrategy and the regional security of China's Tibet and Xinjiang), *Zhanlue yu guanli* (Strategy and Management) 27, no. 2 (1998): 100-104. Zhang is on the staff of CICIR.

[3]Li Jijun, "Lun zhanlue wenhua" (Strategic culture), *Zhongguo junshi kexue* (China Military Science) 38, no. 1 (Spring 1997): 8. Lieutenant General Li is Vice President of AMS.

[4]*The Sino-Indian Border Dispute* (Beijing: Foreign Languages Press, 1962), 103. Views on how India inherited the British imperialist philosophy continue to be expressed today; for example, an article in the *Liberation Army Daily* claimed that, "India has always considered itself to be a 'natural successor to the great British empire.' It believes that since the Indian Ocean was formerly the 'lake of Britain,' it should now be included in the sphere of influence of India." See Liu Yang and Guo Feng, "What is the Intention of Wantonly Engaging in Military Ventures—India's Military Development Should be Watched Out For," *Jiefangjun bao* (Liberation Army Daily), May 19, 1998, 5, in FBIS-CHI-98-141, May 23, 1998.

The Chinese Academy of Social Sciences (CASS) calculates that by 2010 Japan will become equal to the United States in Comprehensive National Power (CNP), at a growth rate that will allow it to surpass the United States by 2020. Prior to May 1998, Chinese military authors had been predicting that India would become a nuclear power; now they estimate that Japan will follow suit and that both countries will each maintain at least two aircraft carriers. They assert these two democracies will probably become nationalistic, aggressive military powers. In other words, the fact that Japan and India are democracies counts for little in the eyes of Chinese analysts assessing the future security environment. Instead, several Chinese authors use ancient statecraft and strategic culture arguments to portray Japan and India in derogatory terms usually reserved for totalitarian regimes. Japan's national goal is purportedly to replace the United States as world hegemon, while India is merely in pursuit of regional hegemony. No author says so, but it appears that few welcome Japan or India as a potential strategic partner for China. Instead, these two are "nearby" powers to be opposed rather than "distant" states with whom to seek partnerships.

India's CNP will remain inferior to China's, according to civilian analysts, but military analysts write that India is already ahead of China in naval power and defense spending. Japan's prospects with respect to the RMA are rated as high. Japan is expected to become a major nuclear and conventional military power, co-equal or superior to China, Russia, and the United States. Japan's future military equivalence to the United States can come through its superior CNP or through its implementation of the RMA, and "Japan's Self Defense Forces will strive to be on an equal footing with the United States in the area of conventional military forces."[5] A more nationalistic Chinese author, He Xin, warned in 1989 about Japan's long-term goals in harsher terms: "Japan in the overall strategic arrangement will completely carve up and isolate China. Casting off the United States, nibbling at China, fostering cordial relations with the Soviet Union, and striving for world hegemony very likely will be

---

[5]Han Shengmin, ed., *Zouxiang 21 shiji de waiguo jundui jianshe* (Foreign military development toward the 21st century)(Beijing: Junshi kexue chubanshe, 1996), 75-76. Several Chinese books on the RMA stress Japan's potential.

Japan's basic strategic world policy."[6] Such Chinese predictions about Japan's intentions and capabilities contrast sharply with orthodox American views of Japan.

A provocative article by Feng Zhaokui, a Japan specialist at CASS, appeared in 1997 alleging that Japan is seeking to engineer a severe conflict between China and the United States. Following a classic Warring States tactic of "Murder With a Borrowed Knife" (the third of the 36 Stratagems),[7] Japan's long-term strategy for the future multipolar world is said to be devious efforts to turn the United States against China in the decades ahead so that Japan can "sneak" past the United States in CNP while the United States is distracted by the pseudo threat of China.[8] Japan's motive is said to be to continue its historical ambition to dominate Asia, in pursuit of which it must weaken China's CNP and also break free of its dependency on the United States. Both these goals can be achieved if Japan (or India) succeeds in persuading the Americans that China is a threat and a challenge to American world leadership. Even the usually moderate *Beijing Review* asserted in 1997 that the sinister China Threat Theory was manufactured first in Japan in 1990 for just this purpose.[9]

---

[6] He Xin, *Zhongguo fuxing yu shijie weilai* (China's rejuvenation and the world's future)(Chengdu: Sichuan renmin chubanshe, 1996), 3.

[7] The text of the "Murder with a Borrowed Knife" *(jie dao sha ren)* strategy is, "When the enemy's intention is obvious and the ally's attitude hesitant, induce the ally to fight the enemy while preserving one's own strength." According to a translation of the *36 Stratagems* by Sun Haichen, the purport of this strategy is, "To avoid getting incriminated for his act of murder, a person can sometimes conduct the act with a 'borrowed knife,' which generally refers to someone who holds a grudge against the victim. By inducing a third party to commit the murder, one will be able to achieve one's goals without being held responsible for it. In military contexts, the idiom advises the commander to exploit the conflicts among various powers. To fight a strong enemy, he should find out the power groups that are at odds with this enemy and thereby induce them to fight it in his stead. In this way, he will get twice the result with half the effort." Sun Haichen, ed. and trans., *The Wiles of War: 36 Military Strategies from Ancient China* (Beijing: Foreign Languages Press, 1991), 24-25.

[8] Feng Zhaokui, "Ri-Mei anbao tizhi yu Riben de daguo zhanlue" (The Japan-U.S. security system and Japan's strategy for world power status), *Shijie jingji yu zhengzhi* (World Economics and Politics) 204, no. 8 (August 1997): 47-49. Feng serves in the Japan Institute of CASS.

[9] Wang Zhongren, "China Threat Theory Groundless," *Beijing Review* (July 16, 1997): 14-20. The Japanese protagonist was Professor Murai of the National Defense Academy (NDU).

India, too, is seen to have menacing designs for the future multipolar world and also is said to employ the tactic of playing the China Threat card. An article by Zhang Wenmu of the China Institute of Contemporary International Relations (CICIR) asserts that India's intention is to separate Tibet from China, because, "Tibetan independence will create a buffer zone between China and India and enable India to take bolder action on the South Asian continent, and subsequently, in the Indian Ocean region, without the fear of being attacked front and rear." Consequently it used the China Threat as its excuse for conducting nuclear tests in May 1998. Zhang argues India realized that "in order to ease pressure from the United States (regarding its nuclear tests), India must challenge China," because India and the West have similar strategic aims concerning containing China. Zhang writes,

> In the next century, to split China's western part, or more specifically, to split China's Tibetan region . . . is probably the target of the Western world's geopolitical strategy. Having pushed Russia northward, creating a political barrier like Tibet or Xinjiang between China and the oil-producing countries in Central Asia conforms to the strategic interests of the West to control permanently the world's geographic and energy center. This dovetails with India's political plot to create a Tibetan buffer zone between China and India. Currently, India is pulling out all the stops to convince the West that it is willing to play the vanguard for the West's effort to achieve this goal, under the prerequisite that the West will adopt an appeasement policy towards its nuclear option.

According to Zhang, the mutual objective explains why the sanctions imposed on India by the West were not as harsh as those inflicted on Iraq for a similar problem.[10]

Chinese authors assess the future roles of Japan and India in the international security environment mainly as future rivals of China, based both on a belief in their sinister long-term hegemonic strategies and on the military power they will use to back up their plans. Although in overall CNP there are definite differences in the three countries' scores, in terms of military power,

---

[10]Zhang Wenmu, "The Issue of South Asia in Major Power Politics," *Hong Kong Ta Kung Pao*, September, 23, 1998, B1, in FBIS-CHI-98-293, October 21, 1998.

both Japan and India are today assessed as roughly equal to China; Japan is slightly superior while India slightly inferior. AMS estimates that:

- Japan's national defense strength is slightly stronger than China's.
- China's national defense expenditures are only 17.8 percent of Japan's.
- In average national defense expenditures per person and annual per capita defense expenditures, China's figures are 1.6 percent and 1.9 percent, respectively.
- In the comprehensive comparison of national defense power, Japan's value is 62.42 and China's, 48.32.[11]

AMS assessments of India show that China is:

- Inferior to India in naval power (India has two aircraft carriers)
- Stronger than India in long-range missiles
- Inferior to India in overall weapons technology
- Lower than India in defense spending per capita
- Higher than India in overall defense, scoring 48.32 vs. India's 41.37
- Superior, but "the superiority is not great."[12]

These current "scores" comparing China to India and Japan are not static in Chinese assessments. Instead, many authors focus on the probability of ultranationalist, militarist takeovers of the governments of either Tokyo or New Delhi, or both. In such scenarios, China could find itself facing military giants to the east and south, two nations that might even form a coalition against China. A stream of articles in the 1990s by Chinese specialists on Japan and India tends to ignore the democratic and even pacifist sentiment on which Western analysts focus. Rather, the Chinese seem to be debating among themselves as to how soon current indicators of political, economic, and

---

[11]Huang Shuofeng, *Guojia shengshuai lun* (On the rise and fall of nations)(Changsha: Hunan chubanshe, 1996), 496.

[12]Ibid., 497.

religious trends will result in nationalistic, militarist regimes in Japan and India.

JAPAN

Future Rivalries

Chinese authors do not lack knowledge of Japan; they cite Japanese language sources and interviews in Japan. They predict Japan's future based on its domestic development and other factors that will make Japan, like all capitalist nations, behave in a predatory imperialist fashion.[13]

The Chinese have not always been so negative in their views of Japan's military development and actually encouraged it in the 1970s. Indeed, it was not until the mid-1980s that China reassessed its support (offered since 1972) for Japanese military modernization. Chinese military figures had encouraged Japan to increase its defense spending to meet the Soviet threat. At one point the Chinese deputy chief of the general staff encouraged Japan to increase its share of defense expenditures from 1 percent of the gross national product (GNP) up to 3 percent, nearly triple Japanese defense expenditures. If this advice had been followed by Tokyo, Japan's budget today would not be U.S. $40 billion but U.S. $150 billion, more than 20 times China's claimed military budget.

Deng Xiaoping told a Japanese delegation to Beijing in September 1978, "I am in favor of Japan's Self Defense Force buildup."[14] At that time, China faced a threatening security environment, and its support for Japan's enlarged defense efforts may have been related in part to Beijing's interest in acquiring Japanese weapons and defense-related technology. China also was clearly

---

[13]For an overall study of Japan's politics, society and economics see Liu Jiangyong, ed., *Kua shiji de riben—Zhengzhi, jingji, waijiao xin qushi* (Japan across the century—new political, economic, and foreign relations trends)(Beijing: Shishi chubanshe, 1995). The editor of this major collection is the CICIR director for Japan studies. See also Chen Shao, "Zhanhou Riben zonghe guoli de fazhan ji pinggu" (An assessment of Japan's postwar comprehensive national power development), *Taipingyang xuebao* (Pacific Journal), no. 3 (December 1995): 96-101. Chen is on the staff of IWEP at CASS.

[14]Cited in Michael Pillsbury, "A Japanese Card?," *Foreign Policy*, no. 33 (Winter 1978-1979): 6.

interested in recruiting a new partner to their united anti-Soviet front.[15] However, 10 years later, China's security environment had changed, and by the time Japan announced in January 1987 that it would actually increase its defense spending slightly above 1 percent of GNP, the Chinese reacted strongly, attributing it to Japan's larger military ambitions. One of the first strong criticisms of Japanese military goals that authoritatively reversed earlier encouragement of Japan came from Huan Xiang, who served as Deng's national security advisor.[16]

Today, Chinese security experts seem united in the view that in the future security environment, Japan will be primarily locked in a long-term competitive struggle with the other great capitalist power centers, Europe and America; this is a consistent Chinese Marxist-Leninist view of Japan. In 1986, Deng Xiaoping's national security adviser, Huan Xiang, declared that America's allies would all begin to free themselves from U.S. domination. Japan's future strategy toward China and Russia is seen in this larger global geopolitical framework of a powerful Japan now escaping from an ever-declining America, but also colliding with America's escaping European capitalist allies. The 1990s have seen no change since Huan Xiang's assessment in 1986. For example, Japan's present and future geopolitical goals are treated as being the same in five subsequent annual reviews of the international security environment conducted by CICIR, which, as part of its duties for the Ministry of State Security, publishes an annual "World Outlook" article. The authors are not the same each year, but their views on Japan's future role appear to be consistent:

> 1993: "Japan and Germany, the twin rising economic giants, are cashing in on the golden opportunity of the demise of the former Soviet Union, the end of the Cold War, and the relative decline of the United States . . . in pursuit of the status of major powers in the year ahead."[17]

---

[15]Ibid., 16.

[16]See Huan Xiang, "Sino-U.S. Relations Over the Past Year," *Liaowang* (January 11, 1988), in FBIS-CHI, January 15, 1988.

[17]Li Zhongcheng and Guo Chuanlin, "World Trends 1993," *Contemporary International Relations* 3, no. 1 (January 1993): 2. Li and Guo are Research Fellows at CICIR.

1994: "Changes will occur in the tripartite relationship among America, Europe, and Japan . . . and contention for supremacy among the trio will flare up accordingly."[13]

1995: "The United States . . . is confronted with an enlarged and deepening European Union and a Japan seeking to become a major political power. . . . Washington intends to dominate global affairs and constrain any major power from challenging its 'leadership role,' but its intentions are greater than its power."[19]

1996: "The United States, Europe, and Japan will encounter new competition with each other in the context of economic regionalism. The European Union (EU) will speed up its involvement in the East Asian economy, which will inevitably lead to a triangular competition. . . . The intensified efforts made by Europe and Japan to infiltrate Latin America will also pose a threat to the dominant position enjoyed by the United States in its 'backyard.' In short, the unfolding competition among the United States, Europe, and Japan within the framework of their existing relationships will cause more troubles to America in its endeavor to maintain its leading position."[20]

1997: "The United States will strive for maintaining global unipolarity with its status as the sole superpower intact. Its strong desire for world leadership will meet with ever-mounting challenges and rejection. The EU, armed with increasing CNP, will try hard to reach out for the center of the world stage. Japan will come up with more measures for winning the status of a great power."[21]

---

[13]Yang Mingjie, Ouyang Liping, and Bing Jinfu, "World Outlook 1994," *Contemporary International Relations* 4, no. 1 (January 1994): 9. Yang, Ouyang, and Bing are researchers in the Division for Comprehensive International Studies at CICIR.

[19]Li Zhongcheng and Wang Zaibang, "World Outlook 1995," *Contemporary International Relations* 5, no. 1 (January 1995): 7-8. Li is Director of the Division for Comprehensive International Studies and Wang is a Doctor of Laws at CICIR.

[20]Wang Zaibang and Yang Mingjie, "World Political Outlook 1996," *Contemporary International Relations* 6, no. 1 (January 1996): 5-6. Wang and Yang are both on the staff at CICIR.

[21]Li Zhongcheng, "World Politics," *Contemporary International Relations* 7, no. 1 (January 1997): 1.

Chinese analysts often write about the increasing friction in the U.S.-Japan relationship and how Japan is no longer willing to be America's unequal partner. Gao Heng of CASS writes that the United States recognizes the growing threat from Japan and is attempting to use their alliance to diminish the danger. "Political power that dares to say 'no' to the United States is converging into a powerful historical trend. Under these conditions, the United States has begun to use the 'military political alliance' to contain Japan's development. Especially in military affairs, the United States wants to firmly control the scale and direction of its use." However, he explains, the effectiveness of U.S. strategy is limited, because "Facts make clear that the move toward further relaxation in the Japanese-U.S. military and political alliance is a difficult-to-reverse trend."[22] Some analysts, such as Feng Zhaokui, also from CASS, suggest Japan's nuclear ambitions will estrange it from the United States and "will very likely damage the 50-year-old U.S.-Japan security relationship."[23] An article in the *Liberation Army Daily* predicts, "taking the long-term view, this relationship may be a 'two-edged sword.' Japan's move in strengthening its military alliance relationship with the United States is a means and not an end for becoming one of the world's poles. . . . as Japan spreads its wings and gradually advances toward becoming one of the world's poles, its tendency to break away from the United States will grow."[24]

An article in the foreign ministry journal *World Knowledge* also points to Japan's increasing power and confidence in the relationship. It forecasts that American-Japanese relations "have entered the most turbulent period in the postwar era, and Japan no longer plays the obedient lamb of the United States." However, like other analysts, the author claims that there is no urgency to this problem: "Although there are contradictions of sorts in U.S.-Japanese relations, no radical change in the basic pattern of relations between

---

[22]Gao Heng, "Dongbei Ya de anquan geju ji weilai qushi" (Northeast Asia's security structure and future trends), *21 Shiji* (The 21st Century), no. 6 (1995): 34.

[23]Feng Zhaokui, "Lengzhan jiexu dui Ri-Mei keji guanxi de xiangying" (The impact of the end of the Cold War on U.S.-Japan relations in science and technology), *Heping yu fazhan* (Peace and Development) 48, no. 2 (May 1994): 5-13.

[24]Liang Ming, "A New Trend that Merits Vigilance," *Jiefangjun bao*, June 5, 1999, 4, in FBIS-CHI-1999-0616, June 17, 1999.

the two countries is on the horizon in the foreseeable future."[25] According to some Chinese analysts, the reason that the relationship will not be greatly altered in the near term, despite the increasing discord and Japan's growing power and ambitions, is Japan's continued economic, political, and security dependency on the United States. One author explains that while "there are obvious economic conflicts between Japan and the United States," and "the United States is worried that it may lose out to Japan. . . . Due to mutual political and military needs, with Rightist forces in Japan wishing to rely on the United States to achieve their target of building Japan into a political and military power and the United States wishing to rely on Japan to consolidate its 'line of defense' in East Asia, the two countries have come closer together in recent years."[26] A CICIR analyst elaborates further: "For a long time Japan will not part company with America, although it will change its policies toward the latter. This is because Japan's economy relies heavily on the United States. Its security and politics also need support from the United States. In the new times the Japanese-U.S. relationship is one of cooperation and competition, and of conflict and coordination."[27]

However, Japan's dependency on America will be greatly reduced and overcome, if the assessments of other Chinese analysts regarding Japan's current and future development are correct. For example, one of the major areas in which many Chinese believe Japan holds the world's most advanced position is high technology. Praising the progress it has made in research and innovation, one author writes, "This basic research will be in a leading position in the future science and technology competition, especially nuclear energy, space navigation, civil aviation, ocean development, bio-engineering, superconduction, the magnetic suspension train, fiber-optics communications,

---

[25]Zi Jian, "Two Problems in U.S.-Japanese Relations," *Shijie zhishi* (World Knowledge)(July 1, 1990), in FBIS-CHI, August 6, 1990: 1-2.

[26]Xiao Feng, "World Trends Under US Global Strategy, Part One of Two," *Renmin Ribao*, May 31, 1999, 6, in FBIS-CHI-1999-0601, May 31, 1999.

[27]Xu Zhixian, "*Xin shiqi Riben waijiao zhanlue de tiaozheng*" (Readjustment of Japan's foreign policy in the new era), *Xiandai guoji guanxi* (Contemporary International Relations) 74, no. 12 (December 1995): 12.

high-definition television, and fifth-generation computers, etc."[28] Even in the area of military technology, Chinese authors write that Japan is encroaching on U.S. dominance. A 1996 article, "Japan: Leading the U.S. in Military Technology," stated, "Japan has had great progress in the area of military computer application . . . Without Japan's technology, the U.S. military's F-117A stealth fighter, which was tremendously intimidating in the Gulf War, essentially would not have been created."[29]

Not only do Chinese authors emphasize specific areas in which they believe Japan already is superior to America, but some perceive Japan to be catching up and even pulling ahead of the United States in overall national power. According to an article in *World Knowledge*, the major U.S. competitive adversary is shifting to Asia, specifically to Japan, because a number of indicators show "Japan is swiftly shrinking its gap with the United States in the fields of economics and science and technology, and engaging in sharp competition with the United States":

- Japan has outstripped the United States in per capita GNP.
- Japan's domestic fixed-assets investment has topped that of the United States to rank first in the world.
- Japan's per-capita savings rate is higher than that of the United States, ranking first in the world.
- In certain high-tech fields, Japan has caught up to or surpassed the United States.
- The United States is in an adverse trade position with Japan.
- International loans by Japanese banks exceed those by U.S. banks.
- The United States has become the world's largest debtor nation, while Japan has become the world's largest creditor nation.
- Japan provides more foreign aid than the United States and is the country that provides the most foreign aid in the world.

---

[28]Chen Shao, "Zhanhou Riben zonghe guoli de fazhan ji pinggu," 99.

[29]"Riben: Junshi jishu lingxian Meiguo" (Japan: leading the U.S. in military technology), *Junshi wenzhai* (Military Digest) 4, no. 2 (1996): 18.

This article seems to "favorably" forecast Japan's catching up to the United States in the future. For example, it goes on to assert, "By 2010, Japanese direct overseas investment will account for about one-third of global transnational direct investment. Japan is going to exploit these advantages to catch up to the United States faster . . . by 2025 the Japanese economy will overtake the U.S. economy. Even in purchase price parity power, by 2045, the Japanese economy will overtake the U.S. economy."[30] As will be discussed in chapter five, Chinese analysts who quantitatively measure CNP also have predicted that Japan will surpass the United States in the future.

However, it must be pointed out that in the late nineties negative assessments of Japan's short-term development have been appearing in Chinese journals, particularly when comparing its economic situation with that of its leading rivals, the United States and Europe. As an example, Chen Feng, a senior Research Fellow at the China Institute of International Strategic Studies (CIISS), suggests, "Japan's performance is rather bad among the developed nations. Suffering from the aftermath of the collapse of the bubble economy, the Japanese economy has been weak in recovery with repeated fluctuations and is estimated to barely maintain growth by 1 percent."[31] Another author, Jian Yuechun of the China Institute of International Studies (CIIS), forecasts, "The Japanese economy will be weak for a long time. The period of real recovery for the Japanese economy will not come for some time."[32] The Deputy Director of the Division of East Asian Studies at CICIR has even written that the country's economic problems are having a negative impact on its rivalry with the United States and Europe for global dominance: "The unstable political situation and weak economy shook the pillars supporting Japanese diplomacy, and the 'Japan can say no' position that used

---

[30]Li Changjiu, "The Asian Century and the Shift to Asia in the Focus of U.S. Foreign Trade Relations," *Shijie zhishi* (World Knowledge)(July 1, 1994): 1-7.

[31]Chen Feng, "1997 nian de guoji zhanlue xingshi" (The international strategic situation of 1997), *Guoji zhanlue yanjiu* (International Strategic Studies) 47, no. 1 (January 1998): 3.

[32]Jiang Yuechun, "Features, Causes and Prospects of the Protracted Japanese Recession," *International Studies*, no. 2-3 (1995): 18. Jiang is the Deputy Head of Asia Pacific Studies at CIIS.

to be seen in its relations with big powers vanished."[33] However, the former president of the Shanghai Institute for International Studies (SIIS), Chen Qimao, predicts that the diminishing of Japan's diplomatic capabilities is not permanent, and that in the long term its strong overall CNP will allow it to overcome its current problems:

> In the past, Japan regarded its sound economic foundation as a diplomatic pillar. Now that the Japanese economy has reached a low ebb, I believe that Japan's diplomatic development will be slowed down. However, I believe that with its comprehensive national strength, Japan will tide over these temporary economic problems sooner or later. In this sense, we must not underestimate Japan's diplomatic development.[34]

Contrasting Views

Before going into a discussion of Chinese views on Japanese militarism, it is useful to contrast a carefully selected "mainstream" American view of Japanese strategic policies with the Chinese "mainstream" view.[35] There is no more respected American specialist on Japan than the late Edwin Reischauer, who served as President John F. Kennedy's Ambassador to Japan after more than two decades at Harvard University, where he trained a generation of American scholars in Japanese studies. He is the co-author with John K. Fairbank of a college textbook on East Asia used for three decades. In addition to his scholarly writings, Reischauer frequently wrote essays on Japan,

---

[33]Yang Bojiang, "The Trans-Century Tendencies of Japan," *Contemporary International Relations* 8, no. 8 (August 1998): 17.

[34]Chiang Feng, "Japan Is Not Cross-Strait Relations Mediator—Interviewing Chen Qimao, Shanghai International Relations Society President," *Hong Kong Ta Kung Pao*, February 16, 1998, in FBIS-CHI-98-055, February 26, 1998.

[35]There are dissenters from the U.S. mainstream whose views are closer to those of the Chinese. For example, in *Blindside: Why Japan is Still on Track to Overtake the U.S. by the Year 2000* (Tokyo: Kodansha International, 1997), 324, Eamonn Fingleton states, "The world seems headed for a truly dramatic change in the balance of power in the next two or three decades. . . . Japan could be outproducing the United States by a factor of two or three times by the year 2050." However, Fingleton avoids claiming this is inevitable and prescribes several policies the United States can employ to save itself. See also George Friedman and Meredith Lebard, *The Coming War with Japan* (New York: St. Martins Press, 1991).

including the centerpiece for a *Life* cover story.[36] Reischauer saw the American occupation of Japan (1945-50) as "restoring" democracy to a Japan that had already been operating well as a democracy in the 1920s. He wrote that the Japanese are a "populace devoted to the concepts of individual human rights, democracy, and world peace," concluding by stating, "Most important, we have come to share much the same ideals. With such shared ideals, we are inevitable partners."[37] Reischauer's emphasis on the 1920s is important. In that period, Japan's military spending was low compared to later years, it seemed to have active political parties and a lively parliament, and the role of the military in politics was extremely limited. Japan agreed at the Washington Conference (1921-22) to limit its naval development for a decade. In Reischauer's view, the American occupation purged Japan of the Fascist and military leaders of the 1930s and returned Japan to its roots in democracy and responsible diplomacy of the 1920s. However, this is not the Chinese assessment.

Future Militarism

There is a range of debate among China's leading Japan specialists about the direction of Japan's future development.[38] Almost all see it as inevitable that Japan will seek and assume a greater international political role commensurate with its global economic influence, and that an increase in its military power will accompany this new position. What is debated, however, is the extent to which the country's drive to be a world power and its growing military force will affect its democracy and foreign policy. Will the conservative rightists in Japanese society and politics gain the ascendency and Japan once again head down the "road to militarism?" Chinese analysts question whether Japanese

---

[36]*Life*, September 11, 1964, 27-28.

[37]Some American scholars dissent from Reischauer's positions, as shown by Henry Rosovsky, who argues that Japanese and Western models of capitalism and democracy are quite different. Henry Rosovsky, *Asia's New Giant: How the Japanese Economy Works* (Washington: Brookings Institution, 1976), 10-12.

[38]In interviews, He Fang of the State Council's International Study Center was cited as a moderate about Japan's future, while Major General Pan Junfeng is perceived to be more alarmed about the future threat of Japanese militarism. Pan heads the AMS Foreign Military Studies Department.

democracy is enduring and stable. One author writes, "Objectively speaking, Japan's becoming a major political nation is the general trend of the times, and no individual's will can change that. The question is, what kind of major political nation will it become? What kind of role will it play?"[39]

In 1995, Liu Jiangyong, chief of Japan studies at CICIR, published a lengthy criticism of Japanese democracy and called into question the extent to which the American occupation influenced the Japanese political system. Its implications for Japanese future policy is as pessimistic as Reischauer's is optimistic.[40] According to Liu Jiangyong, "Japan's militarism has never been thoroughly exposed and criticized." He acknowledges that the American occupation took "some measures for Japan's demilitarization and democratization, such as disbanding its armed forces, arresting the war criminals, as well as supervising the formulation and adoption of Japan's postwar constitution of peace." However, in Liu's view, the American occupation failed to terminate the century-old force of Japanese militarism. A class-A war criminal was released and became Japan's prime minister in 1957. Troop 731, which had engaged in biological warfare experiments, was exempted from trial. In March 1950, all remaining class-A Japanese war criminals in custody were released, thus "preserving the remnants of Japanese militarism."[41] More recently, in 1995 "Japan's right-wing forces have collected and published a series of materials in preparation for reversing the verdict." Liu was particularly concerned that Japan's prewar imperial perception of history still has considerable influence. This theory first appeared in a message of the Meiji emperor, when the government claimed, "The emperor is the supreme deity who has been Japan's ruler ever since the birth of the universe." Liu writes that the myth was "derived from Japan's earliest fairy tale, Kojiki." Today, Japanese "right wingers" are still "deeply immersed in the imperial perception of history and now want to amend Japan's constitution to restore

---

[39]Zheng Yin, "Duoyuanhua de Yatai diqu xin geju" (The Asia-Pacific region's new pluralized structure), in *Kua shiji de shijie geju da zhuanhuan* (Major changes in the world structure at the turn of the century), ed. Chen Qimao (Shanghai: Shanghai jiaoyu chubanshe, 1996), 199.

[40]Liu Jiangyong, "Distorting History will Misguide Japan," *Contemporary International Relations* 5, no. 9 (September 1995): 1-11.

[41]Ibid., 3.

the old imperial system." Liu criticizes members of the Japanese cabinet who have payed homage at the Yasukuni Shrine, which was established in 1979 and used for "spiritual mobilization for further aggressive expansion in China."[42]

Liu writes that because Japan has become "an economic power, it is now moving toward becoming a great military power." He sees "a contempt for Asia" in past and present Japanese policies. The scholar who originated many of these Japanese concepts, Yukichi Fukuzawa, even defined the Chinese-Japanese War of 1894-95 as a "war between civilization and barbarism," in which Japan found itself with a sense of superiority against a "barbarian" China. Liu argues that Japan's "sense of superiority" has again "gained ground" and is "daily expanding." Liu lays emphasis on the 1995 effort by the Japanese prime minister to pass a resolution in parliament in symbolic opposition to war and aggression. Nearly 40 percent of the membership of the parliament opposed passage of the resolution, and two associations collected more than five million signatures, 4 percent of Japan's population, to oppose it. Liu notes the significance of the Diet members who voted against the resolution, including a number of "second-generation heredity Diet members" who are "influenced by their fathers in their perception of war."

Liu is also concerned that Japanese right-wing organizations, 237 of which were disbanded in 1945, have made a comeback since the mid-1990s and now number 1,900. Some have "propaganda vans on the streets of Tokyo shouting slogans to sing praises of the holy war for greater East Asia." Some of these organizations have collectively published the book, *Listen! Japan's Innocent Cry,* which is aimed at blocking any further investigation into the Emperor's responsibility for the war. Liu contrasts Japan's attitude with the anti-Nazi legislation of Germany, a law passed in 1994 that sentences to 5 years in prison anyone who denies the truth of the Holocaust. He writes, "People cannot help thinking that Japan has legally retained the freedom for the right-wing forces to reverse the verdict on Japan's history of aggression."[43]

---

[42]Ibid.

[43]Ibid., 10. In another article concerning Japanese militarism, Liu argues that in the 1990s, "when Japanese politics are sharply turbulent, divisive, and in the midst of reorganization, a neonationalist ideological trend is lifting its head in Japan." His main example is of a Japanese leader who wishes to "have Japan become an ordinary country" that can send troops abroad

Liu is not alone in his analysis of Japan; other scholars point to similar issues in their assessments. For example, a Research Fellow at CIISS, also is alarmed by the Japanese cabinet members who visited the Yasukuni Shrine and "have been increasingly spreading fallacies denying Japan's history of militarist aggression." The author goes on to state,

> This demonstrates fully the fact that within Japan there is quite a batch of militarists refusing to conscientiously plead guilty, and attempting to revive the old dream of the so-called "Greater East Asian Co-prosperity Sphere."
> . . . The trend of politically right deviations in Japan has aroused grave worries and high vigilance among the peoples of Asia.[44]

The release in Japan in May 1998 of "Pride, The Fatal Moment," a movie eulogizing one of the great advocates of the Co-prosperity Sphere and a Japanese class-A war criminal, Hideko Tojo, drew numerous attacks in China for "boisterously glorifying" Tojo and the "Japanese evil war of aggression" and was cited as an example of the continued existence and pervasiveness of militarism. "The making of this reactionary movie is not something accidental. It reflects the continuing existence of militarist thinking in Japan. The ideas expressed in it are not anything new, but belong to the same category promoted by Japan's postwar ultrarightist force. What is worrying after all is

---

and take part in international conflicts just like the United States, Britain and France. According to Liu, this leader has suggested adding a Section 3 to the Japanese Constitution following Article 9, Section 2, the substance of which is that Japan could "possess self-defense forces aimed at peace making as well as an international joint mobile force that would operate at the invitation and under the command of the United Nations." Liu says that "this would open a channel for Japan to intervene militarily in international matters, creating the external terms for Japan to strengthen its military force, and giving itself defense forces that can really use force." He adds that "there is a 'great debate' among all Japanese circles over these suggestions. See Liu Jiangyong, "Japanese Politics and Hata's Diplomatic Alignment," *Xiandai Guoji Guanxi* (Contemporary International Relations), no. 6 (June 1994): 6-10.

[44]Zhang Changtai, "Some Views on the Current Situation in the Asia-Pacific Region," *Guoji zhanlue yanjiu* (Strategic International Studies) 43, no. 1 (January 1997): 31-32. Zhang is a Research Fellow at CIISS. In August, the Chinese press did report that Prime Minister Obuchi and other Japanese Ministers stated they would not visit the Yasukuni Shrine this year, "to avoid stirring criticism from neighboring countries." See the Beijing Xinhua Domestic Service report of August 7, 1998, "Xinhua Reports Obuchi Not To Visit Yasukuni Shrine," in FBIS-CHI-98-219, August 19, 1998.

that the ultra-rightist force does still have some following in Japan. Otherwise, this reactionary movie would not have been screened for the public."[45]

The adoption of the U.S.-Japan Security Guidelines by the Japanese parliament and the passage of relevant bills in spring 1999 also raised concerns about the growing strength of the right-wing and militarism. An article in the *Liberation Army Daily* warns:

> Rightist forces in Japanese politics are on the rise, and certain right-wing politicians have come out from behind the stage to the front and are trying to sway Japan's policy directions. . . . and in recent years more and more agitation for revising the constitution has been stirred up; following the passage of the bills related to the new guidelines, quite a number of people in Japanese political circles have again clamored for revising the constitution, babbling that the constitution enacted 50 years ago can no longer meet the demands of the development of the times. Under their agitation, many people in Japan agree that the constitution should be revised; and once this is done, the development of Japanese military strength is bound to become "uncontrollable."[46]

Some Chinese authors temper their discussions of Japanese militarism by pointing out that it is only one segment of Japanese society and politics that advocates extreme nationalism, not the general public. For example, Gao Heng of CASS believes that the American occupation did not eradicate militarism in Japan, and worse, because the United States wanted to use Japan to counter the Soviet Union, North Korea, and China during the occupation, "It preserved Japan's entire national machinery and war machinery (although the names were changed)." Today, he writes, "In the Northeast Asian region, the greatest undetermined factor is Japan. Facts make clear that the people who advocate that Japan should restore the militarist line are continuously getting more power." However, Gao believes the general Japanese public does not support the militarists, although he warns, "If Japan's domestic society

---

[45]Da Jun, "A Japanese Movie Confusing Right and Wrong," Beijing Xinhua Domestic Service, May 23, 1998, in FBIS-CHI-98-143, May 27, 1998. See also, "No Whitewashing for War Criminals—Comment on Japanese Reactionary Movie 'Pride, the Fateful Moment'," *Renmin ribao* (People's Daily), May 14, 1998, 6, in FBIS-CHI-98-135, May 15, 1998.

[46]Liang Ming, "A New Trend that Merits Vigilance," 4.

and the international society lose vigilance, and lack a restricting mechanism, then the possibility that Japan will follow the same disastrous road to militarism still exists."[47] The Deputy Director of the Division for East Asian Studies at CICIR, Yang Bojiang, believes that currently the political trend of militarism is on the decline in Japan. "Generally speaking, the influence on Japanese politics of the conservative hard liners, who are pursuing a domestic policy of cooperating with conservatives and a foreign policy of carrying out extreme nationalism, is decreasing." However, he also cautions, "Taking the Japanese diplomatic environment into account, in the next 5 to 7 years, if political and economic development is not smooth, nationalism is likely to continuously rise. For example, some Japanese will possibly spread extreme views regarding the country's historical acts of aggression, some will even raise the question of revising the Constitution."[48]

Lu Guangye, a fellow at the Chinese National Defense Strategic Institute, argues that a revival of militarism is not inevitable in Japan, because not only are the Japanese people opposed to it, but it runs counter to the main trend of peace and development in the world today: "The main current in the world today . . . is peace and development, and the cries of the people of the whole world in demanding justice and equality and the establishment of a new international political and economic order cannot be blocked. The Japanese

---

[47]Gao Heng, "Dongbei Ya de anquan geju ji weilai qushi," 35-36. A similar argument concerning the view that overall Japanese society and politicians are not advocates of military expansionism, can be found in Zheng Yin, "Duoyuanhua de Yatai diqu xin geju," 200. "It should be pointed out that although the ideological trend of militarism in Japan is deep-rooted and continuously crops up in Japan's political circles, this does not illustrate that this trend of thought already occupies a political position in Japan. All previous governments in post war Japan have upheld and effectively carried out the policy of light arms, strong economy . . . Japan cannot easily change this policy, the Japanese people will not again be easily pulled down the road to militarism. In the future, Japan will still mainly rely on its economy, science and technology strength, coordinated foreign affairs, culture and other various means, as well as appropriate military force to realize its strategic objectives."

[48]Yang Bojiang, "The Trans-Century Tendencies of Japan," 17. For an extensive study on the Japanese Constitution and efforts to revise it see, Song Zhangjun, *Riben guo xianfa yanjiu* (Studies on Japan's Constitution)(Beijing: Shishi chubanshe, 1997).

people dearly love peace and will absolutely not permit the country to again march into the abyss of war."[49]

Impact of Militarism

The prospects of future Japanese militarism are worrisome for the Chinese because of the role Japan may try to play in the Asia-Pacific. Japan is viewed as breaking free of its links to the West and shifting its focus to Asia. One author writes, "A historical issue that has confronted Japan ever since the Meiji Restoration is this: should Japan exist as part of Asia or part of the United States and Europe?" He suggests that for the "third time Japan has changed its national direction." The author continues to say that recently Japan has decided to become more involved with Asian economic affairs, and "this strategic shift naturally has attracted profound concern in nations around the world, particularly its neighbors in Asia."[50] Therefore, the issue for Chinese analysts becomes how will Japan act with regard to its new focus. An article by four CICIR analysts states, "Japan is now on the third historical turning point since the Meiji Restoration. A debate is well under way in the country on whether Japan should grow into a 'peaceful country which emphasizes making contributions to the world' or 'a mini superpower with a military role to play.' "[51]

Of even greater concern to the Chinese is how Japan may view China and Chinese national interests as it strives to become a major political and military

---

[49]Lu Guangye, "Going Against the Tide of History, Threatening World Peace," *Jiefangjun bao*, June 6, 1999, 4, in FBIS-CHI-1999-0617, June 18, 1999. Lu's argument is echoed by other authors. For example see, Wang Dajun, "An Important Step in Pursuit of Power Politics," *Xinhua*, May 24, 1999, in FBIS-CHI-1999-0526, May 24, 1999. "The path that Japan chooses today is very similar to one that led it to war many years ago. Whereas many years ago Japan promoted the so-called 'Greater East Asia Co-Prosperity Sphere,' now it has consorted with the United States to engage in their so-called 'new world order.' Such a practice apparently runs counter to the wishes of the majority of peace-loving people in Japan, to the wishes of Japan's neighboring countries that want mutual respect and peaceful existence, and to the tide of the times."

[50]Zhang Dalin, "Economic Regionalism, Protectionism Drive Japan's Move Back to Asia," *International Studies* (January 1994): 17-21.

[51]Yan Xiangjun, Yang Bojiang, Chu Shulong and Dao Shulin, "A Survey of Current Asian Pacific Security," *Contemporary International Relations* 4, no.7 (July 1994): 3.

power and, particularly, how will it react to the rise of China. The Vice President of CICIR, Lu Zhongwei, points out, "In Asia's diplomatic history, there has never been such a precedent as the coexistence of a strong China and a strong Japan."[52] Cooperation between the two powers is not considered to be a likely option, he argues, because of the "two T's (Taiwan and the security treaty between the U.S. and Japan)," and because China considers itself to be in an unfavorable position in the Sino-U.S.-Japan trilateral relationship. Several Chinese authors mention that in recent years Japanese politicians have stated that Sino-Japanese relations are equally as important to Japan as U.S.-Japanese relations. However, Lu writes that despite these assurances, "It would be very hard for Japan to manage deftly to put the two relationships on an equal footing when it has to make a strategic decision."[53] Other authors argue that Japan sees the relationships as being of equal importance, only because, in its efforts to become a power, it intends to take advantage of China's strength and international standing, while at the same time working to contain China and intervene in its development and affairs:

- "Japan needs to use China's power and influence to improve its own status while on the path to becoming a political power, but at the same time it wants to have a louder voice in the bilateral relationship."
- "It hopes that China can maintain political stability, while intending to interfere in China's democratization and human rights."
- "Japan supports China's economic reforms and open-door policy through providing assistance, while imposing restrictions."
- "In the international community, Japan welcomes China's participation while trying to reduce China's influence on neighboring countries."
- Japan is "attempting to have a breakthrough in ties with Taiwan, and to develop a 'quasi-official' relationship with Taiwan. Recent years have witnessed a growing pro-Taiwan force in Japan."

---

[52]Lu Zhongwei, "On China-U.S.-Japan Trilateral Relations—A Comment on Their Recent Exchanges of Top-Level Visits," *Contemporary International Relations* 7, no. 12 (December 1997): 7.

[53]Ibid., 3, 5.

● "In security issues, Japan has spread the opinion of a 'Chinese military threat.' "

● Japan is "constraining China's territorial policy and interfering in China's sovereignty over the Nansha Islands and the Diaoyutai Island."[54]

Additionally, there are the dual concerns that "some elements in Japan also intend to utilize the United States to restrain China" and that the United States wants to use Japan for the same end.[55] At AMS, the director of the foreign military studies department, a Japan specialist, has described the history of Japanese militarism and its consequences for Japan's future military role in Asia. He and others worry that "Attempts by the United States to restore its hegemony by playing China and Japan against each other will be dangerous. The United States may try to encourage differences among the Western Pacific countries."[56]

When asked by outsiders about the prospects for Chinese cooperation with Japan on security issues in the future, the typical Chinese answer

---

[54]Xu Zhixian, "Xin shiqi Riben waijiao zhanlue de tiaozheng,"13. Japan's need of China could also be viewed from a different angle, as a sign of weakness; for example, "There is every indication of Japan's four 'worries' at present when considering its China policy. First, in the general setting of the successive fixes of the Sino-Russian relationship, Sino-French relationship and Sino-American relationship, the sustained laggard in the Japan-China relationship is bound to lighten Japan's weight in the foreign policy of China, which will put Japan in a disadvantageous position. Second, the excessive reliance on the United States will not only cause damage to Japan's image, but will also be detrimental to the future development of Japan-China relations. Third, Japan may fall short of its desire to become the permanent member of the U.N. Security Council for lack of the necessary support from China. Fourth, if by any chance the development of Japan-China economic relations cannot be rationalized, Japan will lose its geoeconomic superiority. Therefore, Japan has no choice but to enhance China's status in its diplomatic agenda, making the Japan-China relationship the backbone second only to the Japan-U.S. relationship, for it needs help from China in geostrategies, economic interests, and the pursuit of a position as a political big power." Xu Zhixian, Zhang Minqian, and Hong Jianjun, "On the Foreign Strategy and Trends in the China Policy of the United States, Western Europe, and Japan at the Turn of the Century," *Contemporary International Relations* 8, no. 3 (March 1998): 16.

[55]Shen Qurong, "Postwar Asia Pacific—Historical Lessons and Common Efforts for a Bright Future," *Contemporary International Relations* 5, no. 11 (November 1995): 5, 7.

[56]Liu Jiangyong, "On the Establishment of Asia-Pacific Multilateral Security Dialogue Mechanisms," *Contemporary International Relations* 4, no. 2 (February 1994): 28.

generally includes a discussion of the problem of Japanese latent militarism and the growing strength of the "right wing" in Japan. In balance of power terms, it would be in China's interest to avoid a rivalry with Japan that could be exploited by other powers. As East Asia's two great powers, China and Japan could reap benefits from cooperation to prevent Asian instability; it is thus interesting that Chinese perceptions of several Japanese initiatives in the 1990s have been negative. The Chinese believe the initiative of Japanese Prime Minister Miyazawa in 1992-93 brought to an end the postwar doctrine of Prime Minister Yoshida, who advocated that Japan concentrate on economic development at home and investment in Asia, while relying on the U.S. security umbrella, with Japan's own defense concentrating solely on the home islands. The so-called Miyazawa doctrine to form a regional forum to discuss Asian security issues modeled on the Conference On Security and Cooperation in Europe (CSCE) was criticized by Chinese authors as a thinly veiled effort to contain China. When Japan then supported American efforts in Iraq and passed the Peace Keeping Operations Law, which authorized Japanese forces in U.N. missions for 1 year, Chinese analysts described this as yet another step in the return to militarism in Japan.

When Japan's Self-Defense Forces participated in the U.N. mission in Cambodia, Beijing objected even though Japan sent only unarmed engineers. Beijing seems divided between those who wish to discourage Japan's military buildup and believe it may be underway, and the more pessimistic view that Japan's militarization is inevitable and can only be postponed at best.[57]

China's national security research organizations seem united in the view that in the future Japan will play an independent role as a major military power.[58] This is in sharp contrast with most American views of Japan. Richard Nixon, for example, raised the prospect of a Chinese-Japanese quasi-alliance that could dominate East Asia economically and militarily.[59] According to some calculations, the arithmetic combination of the Japanese and Chinese

---

[57]Li Defu, *Daoguo kun bing—Riben* (The hard pressed soldiers of the island nation)(Beijing: Shishi chubanshe, 1997).

[58]Lu Lei, Wu Youchang, and Hu Ruoqing, *Riben fu guo zhi mi* (The riddle of Japan, the wealthy country)(Beijing: Jiefangjun wen yi chubanshe, 1994).

[59]See the interview with Richard Nixon in *Time*, April 2, 1990, 49.

gross national products in the year 2020 would surpass the GNP of the United States. In China, this concept of a China-Japan alliance seems absurd.

One Chinese journal claimed that the United States had itself begun to become wary about Japan's longer term military ambitions, including the possible event of "Japan taking the road of a military power."[60] The article stressed that the United States had tried but perhaps failed "to control Japan (and to make) Japan its important strategic partner forever." A kind of Marxist economic concept was used to explain that "the present Japan-United States economic frictions have not reached the stage of endangering the strategic cooperation between both sides." In other words, an increase in Japanese-American economic friction beyond a certain threshold may well lead to Japan becoming an independent military power. Nevertheless, *The New York Times* reported that a Chinese official revealed that the Chinese military has asked for additional defense spending in the 5-year plan to deal with Japanese military capabilities.[61] In November 1995, China called for the closing of American bases in Okinawa and called into question the need for a U.S.-Japan mutual security treaty in the post-Cold War environment.

Against this backdrop, the recent revisions of the U.S.-Japan Security Guidelines have proved especially worrisome for China, because the scope of the alliance was expanded in ways that China felt directly threatened its national interests. One author writes, "Last April, the United States and Japan signed a joint declaration on security guarantees to strengthen their military cooperation. This was aimed at preventing China from rising, getting stronger, and positing a challenge to the United States."[62] In the *Study Reports on the International Situation—1997-1998*, a yearly compilation of the views of authors from a variety of institutes published by the Chinese Society for Strategy and

---

[60]Zhao Jieqi, "The Present Status and Prospect of Japan—U.S. Military Relations," *International Strategic Studies* (English edition), no. 4 (1989): 12-15. See also Ge Gengfu, "Changes in the Development of Japan's Defense Policy and Defense Capabilities," *International Studies* (English edition), January 13, 1989, in JPRS-CAR-89-032, 6-12.

[61]See Nicholas D. Kristof, "China, Reassessing its Strategy, Views Japan Warily," *New York Times*, October 23, 1993.

[62]Zhu Chun and Xie Wenqing, "The U.S. China Policy and Sino-U.S. Relations Moving Toward the 21st Century," *International Strategic Studies* (English edition) 43, no. 1 (January 1997): 36. Zhu and Xie are Senior Research Fellows at CIISS.

Management, Liu Jiangyong of CICIR points out that the Defense Institute of the Japanese Defense Agency has issued a report, "Long-Term Forecast for Japan's Security at the End of 1996." This report asserts, "By 2015 it is almost certain that China will become a great power economically, militarily, and politically. At any time it will constitute a threat to Japanese navigation passage from the Malacca Strait to the Bashi Channel. The South China Sea will become a Chinese sea." According to Liu, "obviously in revising the defense guidelines with the United States the purpose of Japan and America is to strengthen the strategic deterrence against China . . . China becomes a so-called imaginary enemy under the Japanese-American Security Treaty."[63]

One of the chief causes for Chinese concern is that the new agreement indicates, both in terms of geographic coverage and time of action, that the United States and Japan plan to involve themselves in China's affairs. First, the wording referring to the geographic area encompassed by the guidelines changed from the "Far East" to "Japan's surrounding areas," which means that not only is Taiwan included, but the Nansha Islands as well. Second, the time of joint Japan-U.S. military operations is no longer limited to an attack on Japan, but now includes both peacetime and contingencies in the "surrounding areas." Many Chinese analysts were particularly angered by the comments of Japanese officials on the subject. Zhang Changtai of CIISS stated, "Japanese Chief Cabinet Secretary Siroku Kajiyama openly declared that 'Japan's surrounding areas should naturally include the Taiwan Strait' and that 'Japan will not sit idle if the U.S. troops set out for the Taiwan issue,' thus exposing clearly their intents of interfering in China's internal affairs by means of the new guidelines."[64]

At present, China is most concerned about a possible Japanese manipulative role in Taiwan politics, possibly encouraging Taiwan to move toward independence and a close relationship with Japan. Zbigniew Brzezinski has revealed in his memoirs that China insisted on a promise from the United

---

[63]Liu Jiangyong, "Sino-Japanese Relations and the New U.S.-Japan Defense Guidelines," in *Guoji xingshi genxi baogao—1997-1998* (Study reports on the international situation—1997-1998)(Beijing: Zhanlue yu guanli chubanshe, 1998), 121.

[64]Zhang Changtai, "1997 nian Yatai diqu xingshi zongshu" (Roundup of the Asian-Pacific situation in 1997), *Guoji zhanlue yanjiu* (International Strategic Studies) 47, no. 1 (January 1998): 23. Zhang is a Research Fellow at CIISS.

States that it would prevent Japan from forming a defense relationship with Taiwan.

Another extremely troublesome aspect of the new U.S.-Japan security guidelines for the Chinese is that Japan's military functions in the alliance have been broadened. Its activities are no longer solely confined to defending its own territories, but include providing the United States with logistic support. According to the Deputy Director of the Institute of Japanese Studies at CASS, "During the Cold War, . . . Japan played the role of a 'shield' and America that of a 'spear.' The new strategic assignment the Joint Declaration has allotted to Japan is through providing logistic support, to play a corresponding military role in preventing disputes in the Asia-Pacific region. In other words, the role of Japan has changed from a 'shield' in the past to one of an auxiliary 'spear.' "[65] The Chinese fear is that Japan's expanded role and functions will further fuel the development of militarism and the growth of the Right. A Research Fellow at CIISS writes that there is a direct connection between U.S.-Japan security cooperation and the efforts of some Japanese to put their country back on the road to militarism:

> Adjustment in Japan-U.S. military relations will enable Japan to have the opportunity to achieve a new breakthrough in military policies and further encourage the turn to the right in domestic politics in Japan. . . . For quite some time, there has been growth of the rightist tendency in seeking reversal of the verdict on the history of Japan's aggression and trying to rid itself of the status of the vanquished nation. Although this is a stubborn manifestation of the rightist forces in Japan, it should also be noted at the same time that it is closely related to Japan's strengthening of its military relations with the United States, which indicates that there are indeed some people in Japan attempting to seek a military upswing by strengthening its military relations with the United States.[66]

---

[65]Zhao Jieqi, "'Redefinition' of Japan-U.S. Security Arrangements and its Repercussions," *Waijiao jikan* (Foreign Affairs Journal), no. 41 (September 1996): 36-37.

[66]Zhang Taishan, "Ri-Mei junshi guanxi de xin fazhan—Cong Ri-Mei xiugai fangwei hezuo zhidao fangzhen kan" (New developments in the Japan-U.S. military relationship—a perspective on the revision of the Japan-U.S. defense cooperation guidelines), *Guoji zhanlue yanjiu* (International Strategic Studies) 46, no.4 (October 1997): 17.

Similarly, CICIR's Liu Jiangyong writes that if America and Japan actually implement the Security Treaty, "it will lead to political turmoil in Japan." [67]

Following NATO military strikes in Yugoslavia and the Japanese parliament's adoption of the U.S.-Japan Security Guidelines in the spring of 1999, Chinese authors expressed even graver concerns about the U.S.-Japanese military relationship. "This NATO of the Asian version has brazenly included 'emergencies in areas surrounding Japan,' including China, into the sphere of its military intervention and is attempting to include China's Taiwan into its 'theater missile defense system,' thus sowing the seed of trouble for the future peace and stability of the Asia-Pacific region." [68] Lu Guangye, a fellow at the Chinese National Defense Strategic Institute, went so far as to warn:

> The NATO bloc and the Japanese-US military alliance have become the two black hands helping the tyrant to do evil. . . . Everything that NATO does can be regarded as the most direct and most realistic mirror of what we understand as the substance of the Japanese-US military alliance and of how Japan and the United States will act in the Asia-Pacific region. The "experiment" carried out in the Federal Republic of Yugoslavia by U.S.-led NATO also provides a vivid example for the Asia-Pacific countries. [69]

He Xin: A Dissenting View

At the "high end" of alarm about Japan's future intentions and capabilities toward China, one must count He Xin, perhaps China's best known hypernationalist author and an advisor to then Premier Li Peng. In an article

---

[67]Liu Jiangyong, "Sino-Japanese Relations and the New U.S.-Japan Defense Guidelines," 118.

[68]"Commentary on U.S. Intention," *Xinhua*, June 6, 1999, in FBIS-CHI-1999-0606, June 6, 1999.

[69]Lu Guangye, "Going against the Tide of History, Threatening World Peace," No. 3 in series, "Experts Comment on the Strengthening of the Japanese-U.S. Military Alliance," *Jiefangjun bao* (Liberation Army Daily), June 6, 1999, 4, in FBIS-CHI-1999-0617, June 18, 1999. See also Zhang Jinfang, "Serious Threats to China's Security," No. 1 in series, "Experts Comment on the Strengthening of the Japanese-U.S. Military Alliance," *Jiefangjun bao* (Liberation Army Daily), June 4, 1999, 4, in FBIS-CHI-1999-0616, June 17, 1999; and Liang Ming, "A New Trend that Merits Vigilance," No. 2 in series, "Experts Comment on the Strengthening of the Japanese-U.S. Military Alliance," *Jiefangjun bao* (Liberation Army Daily), June 5, 1999, 4, in FBIS-CHI-1999-0616, June 17, 1999.

written at the end of 1988, He Xin predicted that Japan's predatory need for resources would cause it try to "colonize" China. The only hope for China's survival would be comprehensive cooperation with the Soviet Union.[70] He Xin forecast the following:

- "In the early 21st century, only Japan will have global power."
- "Since the 19th century, Japan has never abandoned its long-established global strategic goals."
- "The Soviet Union and China, currently and in the future for a long historical period, will not have any conflicts of fundamental strategic goals."
- "China and Japan and China and the United States will certainly for a long period have potentially contradictory strategic goals."
- "Sino-Soviet cooperation and economic development will essentially crush Japan's fantasy of carrying out new colonialism in China."
- "Against the background of crises in natural resources and energy in the 21st century, Japan's strategic focus will turn to the East."
- "Japan and the Soviet Union very likely will cooperate to develop Siberian oil and gas natural resources, mineral resources and forest reserves."
- "At the same time, in the overall strategic arrangement, Japan will completely carve up and isolate China."
- "Casting off the United States, nibbling at China, fostering cordial relations with the Soviet Union, and striving for world hegemony very likely will be Japan's basic strategic global policy."

---

[70]He Xin, *Zhongguo fuxing yu shijie weilai* (China's rejuvenation and the world's future), (Chengdu: Sichuan renmin chubanshe, 1996), 1-3. After He Xin presented this article to the leadership, an abstract was published in *Zixue* (Independent Studies), no. 5 (1989).

Military Development

The discussion of future Japanese militarism sets the foundation for Chinese authors to analyze the country's military planning. Several authors point to Japan's growing defense budget as being indicative of efforts to become a military power: "It is . . . still increasing its military budget, which is already the second largest in the world."[71] Further, "Japan's defense expenditure has been increasing since 1991, though its economic growth is constantly declining."[72] Chinese analysts argue that the level and extent of Japan's military development reveal that it is moving beyond self-defense, to overseas operations and potential military expansionism. Liu Jiangyong of CICIR writes,

> The Japanese Government has repeatedly promised that "Japan will not become a military power threatening the security of other countries." Its actions, however, seem to indicate otherwise. In recent years, there are signs showing that Japan is no longer satisfied with a capability to defend its own security. More and more it shows an aspiration to involve itself in international military activities and to increase rapidly the power of its high-tech conventional forces. For this purpose, it plans to invest about U.S. $50 billion each year in the coming four years. Not long ago, the Japanese Institute for Defense Studies under the Ministry of Defense advocated that Japan should build its own nuclear-propelled submarines and have long-range troop projecting capability before the year of 2015. These will no doubt raise increasing concerns among its Asian neighbors.[73]

An immediate problem for China is the Japanese development of an antiballistic missile defense system in cooperation with the United States. Detailed Chinese commentary has also emphasized Japanese plans to acquire additional military airlift, aerial refueling, long-range antishipping fighter aircraft (the FSX), and other military acquisition plans as clear evidence of

---

[71]Yan Xiangjun, Yang Bojiang, Chu Shulong, and Dao Shulin, "A Survey of Current Asian-Pacific Security," 4.

[72]Chen Peiyao, "East Asian Security: Situation, Concept and Mechanism," *SIIS Journal* 3, no. 2 (July 1997): 4.

[73]Liu Jiangyong, "Japan in 1997," *Contemporary International Relations* 7, no. 1 (January 1997): 23.

Japan's gradual transition over the coming decade into a major military power, including the Japanese goal of acquiring nuclear weapons and two aircraft carriers within two decades.[74] Chinese analysts claim that Japan already has transport ships that "have the functions of an air-craft carrier" and are able to carry helicopters and vertical-flight jet fighters.[75]

Chinese authors also point out how being "militarily strong in technology" will put Japan in a beneficial position in developing the RMA.[76] For example, a Research Fellow at CIISS, which is sponsored by military intelligence, writes, "Japan is unwilling to lag behind the tide of the new military revolution. Using every opportunity, Japan has not only changed its practice of 'building the country through scientific and technological copying' to 'building the country through scientific and technological creativity,' but also put the emphasis of military reform on enhancing the five capabilities, i.e., the capabilities of intelligence, sea lane defense, island defense, theater missile defense, and long-distance transportation."[77] Even on the issue of nuclear weapons, some analysts predict that in the future, Japan will, like India, become a nuclear power:

> Evidence indicates that Japan is increasing its nuclear potential under the slogan of peaceful utilization of nuclear energy, and is possibly utilizing nuclear energy to serve its political and military goals. As one of the limited number of nuclear power countries in the world, Japan's nuclear power facilities make up over one tenth of the world's total. . . . The development of nuclear electricity is an indicator of the increase of nuclear potential. There is no doubt that Japan has the capacity to produce a nuclear bomb. . . . It should not be excluded that some day Japan can possibly start research on and produce nuclear weapons. . . . As the only country attacked

---

[74]Colonel Xu Weidi, "Post-Cold War Naval Security Environment," *World Military Trends* (Beijing: National Defense University, 1996).

[75]Li Jiensong, "Continued Naval Developments in Nations on China's Periphery" (in Chinese), *Bingqi zhishi* (Ordinance Knowledge)(May 12, 1997): 17-20.

[76]Zhang Changtai, "Some Views on the Current Situation in the Asia-Pacific Region," 27.

[77]Li Qinggong, "Dangdai de guoji junshi anquan xingshi" (The current international military security situation), *Guoji zhanlue yanjiu* (International Strategic Studies) 47, no. 1 (January 1998): 9.

by nuclear weapons in the world, Japan has a particular advantage in research on nuclear protection. From the viewpoint of technique, Japan has measures to avoid international supervision and undertake secret research on nuclear weapons. Inference can be drawn that Japan can increase the transparency of nuclear research by publicizing its plutonium storage, gaining trust from other countries, as well as imposing a deterrent. It is predicted that if North Korea possesses nuclear weapons, Japan will develop such weapons as well.[73]

INDIA

Chinese assessments of India's future development and international role frequently stress its dangerous military potential and the instability of Indian democracy. For many years, Chinese analysts have been attuned to the prospects of intense rivalry with India, another great ancient empire. In spite of a well-publicized agreement in September 1993 on confidence-building measures regarding disputed territory, Chinese authors recently have become concerned that there are countervailing manifestations of Sino-Indian geopolitical rivalry. They include Chinese M-11 missile component sales to Pakistan in response to concern about Indian nuclear and missile development; Chinese irritation about India's tacit support for Tibetan independence; Indian allegations about a disruptive Chinese role in the Kashmir dispute; and China's efforts to sell weapons to India's neighbors.[79] After May 1999, PLA authors such as Peng Guangqian of AMS warned that the United States will exploit India to contain China, adding another kind of "danger" from India. Writings from 25 Chinese authors are reviewed in the following section.

A Future Asian Great Power?

There is some debate among Chinese analysts about the position and role of India in the 21st century. As discussed in chapter one, orthodox and reform

---

[78]Ding Bangquan, "Adjustments and Trends in Japan's Military Strategy," *World Military Trends* (Beijing: Academy of Military Science, no date).

[79]J. Mohan Malik, "China-India Relations in the Post Soviet Era: the Continuing Rivalry," *The China Quarterly* (June 1995): 317-355.

views differ over whether or not Third World nations will rise in strength to occupy a significant position in the future multipolar world. Orthodox authors predict that today's developing nations will be crucial in transforming world politics, while reformists do not foresee that they will develop enough power to exert a major influence and compete with the five poles. India, as one of the major Third World nations, is at the center of this debate. At one end of the spectrum, Zhang Changtai, a Research Fellow at CIISS, writes, "Besides the five major powers, India is also a major power with great potential for development so far as population and territorial size and regional influence are concerned. It is expected that India will become a newly rising force not to be neglected in the upcoming structure of the Asia-Pacific."[80] Chen Qimao, former president of SIIS, believes that India's power "will greatly increase, but until the early 21st century (before 2010) there is no prospect for . . . [it] to become one of the world's poles."[81] On the other side of the debate is the view that India is too weak to contend in the future world structure. "After 50 years of development . . . India has not extricated itself from its status as a poor country, and its average output per capita is far down in world rankings. India has been demanding for a long time to become a permanent member of the U.N. Security Council, and to achieve an international status commensurate with having the second highest population in the world. In fact, however, India's international status has been continually declining in

---

[80]Zhang Changtai, "Some Views on the Current Situation in the Asia-Pacific Region," *International Strategic Studies* (English edition) 43, no. 1 (January 1997): 28.

[81]Chen Qimao, "Qianyan" (Introduction) in *Kua shiji de shijie geju de da zhuanhuan* (Major changes in the world structure at the turn of the century), ed. Chen Qimao (Shanghai: Shanghai jiaoyu chubanshe, 1996): 153-154. Hua Biyun of CICIR also discusses the subject: "India is a major Asian nation," not only strategically located on the Indian Ocean, a major thoroughfare, but in "area, population, and economic development level, common developing nations cannot compare with it. It possesses relatively strong Comprehensive National Power (including the factors natural resources, manpower, economics, science and technology, military power, and political and international influence). According to the research of specialists, in 1989 India's CNP was number 9 in the world, and it will rise to number 8 by the end of the century." Hua Biyun, "Indu lizheng chengwei xia shiji de jingji daguo" (India: striving to be an economic power in the next century) *Xiandai guoji guanxi* (Contemporary International Relations) 75, no. 1 (January 1996): 21.

recent years."[82] This debate about India will be echoed in chapter five, where orthodox and reform quantitative assessments of India's CNP predict very different placements for India in the hierarchy of the world's future major powers.

In general, when assessing India and its power, Chinese analysts emphasize that the country's development has both positive and negative factors. Ye Zhengjia of CIIS writes, "India is a very complex developing major nation, it has a dual nature in multiple areas. India has tremendous potential, and faces numerous grim challenges."[83] For example, in terms of India's economic development, Chinese assessments tend to discuss both that India has made great strides and that it still has a long way to go. Hua Biyun of CICIR, while noting that India's reforms "have attained spectacular results," and predicting continued accomplishments, also lists numerous "restricting factors" that will hinder rapid success:[84]

> 1. The people's standard of living is low. 2. Base facilities are poor and there is a serious shortage of energy resources. 3. After initial success in correcting financial imbalance, a relapse appeared. 4. Reform of state-owned enterprises is slow. 5. In a democratic system opposing parties often tie up government policy.[85]

---

[82]Hu Weimin, "India Uses the 'Nuclear Counter' to Bargain," *Renmin Ribao* (People's Daily) (Guangzhou South China News Supplement), July 28, 1998, 14, in FBIS-CHI-98-209, July 28, 1998.

[83]Ye Zhengjia, "Buru 21 shiji de Yindu" (India enters the 21st century), *International Studies* (English edition) 61, no. 3 (July 1996): 20.

[84]According to Hua, India's successes include, "the national economy has steadily grown . . . the state of international income and expenditures has improved . . . investment in private industry is brisk . . . the investment market has gradually been perfected." Hua Biyun, "Indu lizheng chengwei xia shiji de jingji daguo," 22-23.

[85]Ibid., 23-24. Ye Zhengjia makes a similar assessment: "Looking at the overall process of India's economic development in the 50 years since independence, its characteristics are that it has been both stable and slow. . . . In more than 40 years, India has already established a relatively complete national industry system, and industrial output value is at the world's forefront. The township and village middle class has reached about 200 million, and is one of the world's ten newly rising markets. However, on the other hand, India still is the country with the most people in abject poverty in the world." Ye treats India's science and technology in a similar manner, focusing on both the positive and the negative. "India's science and

When discussing the influence of India's economic development on China, Hua predicts that although "as a parallel rising market, India becomes China's main competitor in international funds, technology and commodity markets," theirs is "not a life or death relationship," because China's economy is stronger. "India's influence in Asia and the Indian Ocean will expand. From now until 2010, its economic development speed is predicted to be 6 to 8 percent, while China's will be above 8 percent. The two countries' development levels will grow further apart . . . therefore, India cannot become 'China's replacement market,' although its influence is rising."[86]

China's research on India's future also focuses on the range of divergent factors affecting stability in Indian politics and government. One Chinese concern has been the role played in Indian politics by religious extremist organizations, and the extent to which they will influence the orientation of Indian domestic and foreign policies.[87] One important article stresses that the Bharatiya Janata Party (BJP) may take over India and turn it toward intense, Hindu chauvinistic policies.[88] The rise of nationalism is another point of concern for Chinese analysts, because the BJP drew on Indian nationalism to gain support for the nuclear tests, and the government may draw on it again to boost its efforts to attain regional hegemony. One analyst asserts, "Great power ambitions form a strong contrast with the decline of real international status, and this is an important reason for the continual rise of nationalism in India in recent years. . . . The BJP, which rode this whirlwind of nationalism to take power, has seized the opportunity brought by the nuclear tests to play the 'people's will' card to the outside world and the 'interests of national

---

technology is in a leading position among developing nations," but there exist a number of "defects." Ye Zhengjia, "Buru 21 shiji de Yindu," 22.

[86]Hua Biyun, "Indu lizheng chengwei xia shiji de jingji daguo," 26.

[87]For example, see Jiang Yili, "Yindu jiaojiaopai zuzhi shijie Yindujiao dahui (VHP) pouxi" (An analysis of the VHP—A Hindu religious organization), *Nanya yanjiu* (South Asian Studies) 56, no. 3 (1994): 62-68. Jiang is in the Asia-Pacific Institute of CASS.

[88]Jiang Yili, "Dangdai Yindujiao" (Contemporary Hinduism), *Shijie zongjiao xue* (Studies in World Religions) 61, no. 3 (September 1995): 18. Ye Zhengjia also discusses the trend that Hinduism is gaining prominence in Indian politics. Ye Zhengjia, "Buru 21 shiji de Yindu," 21. See also Yang Xuexiang, *Indu wenhua shenmi zhi mi* (The riddle of India's cultural mystery)(Beijing: Jiefangjun wenyi chubanshe, 1994).

security card' for domestic consumption, and has used international pressure to further fan nationalist emotions."[89]

Political instability in general is predicted for India. "In the future a multi-party alliance government is very possible, representing different classes and interests, but India's historical experiences have proved that this type of government often is short lived. A turbulent situation could once again emerge in India. In addition, religious, ethnic, and gender contradictions are very complex, making it difficult for the country to maintain long term stability."[90]

One area where Chinese authors assess India as having significant power is in military affairs. For example, Hua Biyun asserts, "India's military strength is number four in the world."[91] Two CICIR analysts write, "During the past few decades, India has enhanced its military strength and rapidly developed its national defense industry." They explain that India's stress on the development of science and technology has been a key factor in developing its military power. "India currently has 3 million scientists and technicians, following only the United States and Russia, to be third in the world. These science and technology troops are India's precious 'intelligence resource,' and play a decisive role in national defense studies and war production." They predict that India's military power will continue to grow in the future:

> Through several years of continuous effort . . . India's national defense science and technology and war production has undergone a huge change, its reliance on other countries has been reduced, and its degree of self-sufficiency has increasingly risen. Now India has the capacity to build large vessels and submarines. It designs and produces aircraft carriers, nuclear submarines, missile destroyers, and equips Russian-made C-grade nuclear submarines with medium-range missiles. The new tanks produced by India

[89]Hu Weimin, "India Uses the 'Nuclear Counter' to Bargain."

[90]Hua Biyun, "Indu lizheng chengwei xia shiji de jingji daguo," 24. See also, Liang Jiejun, "Evolving Indian Political Scene," *Contemporary International Relations* 6, no. 6 (June 1996): 1-16.

[91]Hua Biyun, "Indu lizheng chengwei xia shiji de jingji daguo," 22. For other discussions about the prospects for India's future military development example see, Wu Hua and others, *Nanya zhi shi—Indu* (The lion of south Asia—India)(Beijing: Shishi chubanshe, 1997), and Gong Wei, "Yindu daodan neng dadao Beijing ma?" (Can Indian missiles hit Beijing?"), *Junshi wenchai* (Military Digest), no. 1 (1995): 43.

can resist high-speed armor piercing shells and anti-tank bombs, and are of world standard. India has started to manufacture modern light fighters, which will be put into operation in 2005. The light fighters have modern navigation and aiming systems, and can have the capacity of continuous flight and inflight fueling. Such fighters are equivalent to M-27s. . . . Before 2010 it will enter the ranks of the "top level world military powers."[92]

The strategic importance of the Indian Ocean has caused India to focus on naval development, and many analysts stress India's powerful Navy in their discussions of the country's military capabilities. "In order to attain its strategic objective of seeking regional hegemony and exercising control over the Indian Ocean, India has focused attention on strengthening its navy. India's Navy now ranks 7th in the world and it is one of a small number of countries in the world, and the only one in South Asia, to possess aircraft carriers." An article written following India's nuclear tests in 1998, stated, "The Indian Navy is the strongest one in the South Asian subcontinent, being charged with the missions of 'countering' the Pakistan Navy and controlling the Bay of Bengal and the Arabian Sea on the east and west wings of the Indian peninsula, and, when conditions permit, deterring the superpowers within Indian sea space." It details India's future development plan as forming:

> a sea-based, submarine-launched nuclear strike capability by the early 21st century. . . . By the late 20th century to the early 21st, the Indian Navy will add dozens of new warships of all types including 20-plus more advanced large and medium combat ships, with its naval might topping 100,000 troops. By that time, the Indian naval fleet will have extended its naval defense line 600 nautical miles beyond a blue-water fleet with a nuclear combat capability. . . . The Indian Navy's steadily stronger control of the Indian Ocean, particularly of the two strategic channels of the Persian Gulf and the Strait of Malacca, is likely not only to cause potential conflict with navies operating in the region and to affect the navigational order in the key

---

[92]Liu Xiaofei and Pan Xiaozhu, "Indu lizheng chengwei junshi gongye daguo" (India is striving to become a military industrial power), *Xiandai guoji guanxi* (Contemporary International Relations) 77, no. 3 (March 1996): 26-28.

international lanes of the Indian Ocean, but also to pose a threat to the maritime security of the Asia Pacific region.[93]

Instability in South Asia

As the Chinese see it, India's prospects seem to depend on the chances for resolution of its conflicts with Pakistan and its ultimate ambitions. Chinese authors urge caution, specifically recommending against China becoming a mediator between India and Pakistan. For example, Sheng Huipeng, a professor at Beijing University, argues that two of the "important purposes of India's nuclear policy are . . . to counter what it considered a possible nuclear threat from China; and . . . to use its status as a nuclear power to become a permanent member state of the U.N. Security Council."[94] Sheng is more generous toward Pakistan, which he says maintains its nuclear program because

> it is the most economical way of facing up to India. . . . It is said that Pakistan is able to produce 10-15 nuclear warheads and uranium raw materials. Pakistan's nuclear stance has become the pillar of its national defense strategy. . . . It is very difficult to break the nuclear deadlock between the two countries. From now on either party's imprudence on this issue will not only destroy any progress made in the security dialogue, but will probably push these countries to the brink of nuclear war.

He adds that the Kashmir issue

---

[93]Zhang Minhui, "The India and Pakistan Navies After the Nuclear Tests," *Jianchuan zhishi*, no. 7 (July 4, 1998), in FBIS-CHI-98-224, August 12, 1998.

[94]Ye Zhengjia of CIIS has put forward a similar argument, stating, "The goal of India's current defense and security strategy is to counter Pakistan . . . its long term goal is to counter China. . . . India's basic relations with other South Asian nations can be summed up as both interdependent and mutual contradictions and antagonism. This last aspect is a significant obstacle to India's efforts to establish a world power position. Of course, the fundamental factor determining whether India attains a world power position lies in India's own comprehensive power." (24) India has said, "now there is a 'multipolar world,' and thus has made itself one of the six world poles along with the United States, Russia, China, the EU, and Japan. On this basis it has put forward that India has the qualifications to become a permanent member of the U.N. Security Council." Ye Zhengjia, "Buru 21 shiji de Yindu," 25.

is more fundamental than the nuclear issue, and the solution to it is more difficult. The letter K in the name Pakistan stands for Kashmir. Thus, the Pakistanis believe without Kashmir, Pakistan holds the country as incomplete. . . . India claims that the legal position of Kashmir has already been determined, because soon after a partition, the ruler of Kashmir declared that Kashmir had joined India. Pakistan believes that Kashmir's Moslems belong with Pakistan; India believes it cannot recognize religious ethnic groups. . . . Hence in a sense fighting for Kashmir is equivalent to defending a faith. To both countries, to give up Kashmir means to give up not only territory, but also a principle and a belief.

Shang is not optimistic, noting that "there is a complete stalemate at the moment on Kashmir."[95] In the security dialogue between India and Pakistan, Shang advocates that "China should not try to serve as a mediator, but continue to provide advice on promoting the alleviation of tension."[96]

A new assessment of the India-Pakistan dispute in Kashmir comes from an article in the *Liberation Army Daily*, which "sees a U.S. conspiracy" in the conflict, and believes, "Fighting between India and Pakistan over Kashmir would benefit the United States regardless of the outcome." The editorial by Ding Zengyi depicted "the United States as 'sitting on a hill watching the tigers fight,' waiting to reap the benefits of their conflict." The current U.S. "South Asia strategy is to control India and Pakistan, maintain the balance of power in South Asia and use India to contain China." The article concluded that "In the present India-Pakistan armed clash over Kashmir, it would be hard to avoid a scenario where both parties are losers again. . . . This would result in a weakened Pakistan and a limited India for the United States. . . . As long as the exchange of fire between India and Pakistan does not turn into a nuclear war, it would benefit the United States' South Asia strategic scheme."[97]

---

[95]Shang Huipeng, "Indian-Pakistani Security Dialog and China's Policy Toward South Asia," in *Guoji xingshi genxi baogao, 1997-1998* (Study reports on the international situation 1997—1998)(Beijing: Zhanlue yu guanli chubanshe, 1998), 192. This was written before India and Pakistan tested their nuclear weapons in the summer of 1998.

[96]Ibid., 197.

[97]"PRC Sees U.S. Conspiracy in Indo-Pakistan Conflict," Hong Kong Agence France Presse, June 12, 1999, in FBIS-CHI-1999-0612, June 12, 1999.

China's analysts are clearly worried about either India or Japan becoming part of a future balance of power system in Asia that may emerge in response to a common perceived threat from China. They would have sufficient economic and military strength to join the United States to form a balance of power system. Forming such an anti-China coalition seems an unlikely possibility to Western analysts. At present, some idea of the pressure threshold required to drive together Asian nations can be observed in the failure of the ASEAN member nations to achieve any multinational security cooperation. In the decades ahead, an Asian multinational security coalition to deter China would have to include several larger powers, roughly equivalent to Chinese economic and military capacity. Using the CNP scores of Chinese analysts, for example, it could be calculated that Japan, Russia, and India would be needed to balance China. Rapid growth rates for Russia and India, however, may bring these two Asian nations into the same league as China and Japan. They would then be available as strong partners in a coalition in Asia, rather than weak states that would tend to ally themselves with the threatening power or seek isolation and neutrality. Because of their potential to affect the Asia balance of power, the quality of economic decisionmaking in New Delhi and Moscow in the near term will determine whether these powers will have the capability to form coalitions, let alone the intention to do so. Some Chinese authors have considered this possibility.

Historical Rivalries

Chinese authors debate whether the historical origins of India's rivalry with China can ever be resolved, or must inevitably remain a source of military conflict. On the optimistic side of this debate, some authors imply that this historical issue can be overcome and no longer be a barrier to improving future Sino-Indian relations. On the pessimistic side, however, far more authors emphasize the depth of Indian hostility. Even the optimists use the word "dangerous" to warn of the consequences if India does not revisit the past and see it the "right" way. For example, Ye Zhengjia, a Senior Research Fellow at CIIS, stated in an interview with the Indian magazine *Frontline*, "My personal view is that it is a precondition [for the development of Sino-Indian relations] to see the right situation in 1962," that the two sides "can not go forward smoothly without clarifying all the facts." He explains, "Because the

Indian side did not see the facts right in 1962, from a wrong notion, India and China came to conflict. The BJP government wants to force a boundary settlement on China on its terms. As a scholar, I would like to warn that if we do not take this boundary question on the right track, it could turn out to be dangerous." Another problem with historical roots discussed by Ye involves Tibet. He criticizes Prime Minister Nehru's reluctance "to recognize Chinese sovereignty over Tibet," and states that today,

> I do not think India is doing the right thing on the Dalai Lama. . . . In my personal view, the Tibetan problem is even more important than the boundary question. The British (imperialist Raj) perception, as it has influenced the mind of the Indian ruling classes, is very wrong and dangerous: 'when there is a problem in Tibet, raise it!' . . . but if you always think of interfering in Tibetan affairs, the future could be dangerous."[98]

At the height of the polemics in 1962, after China had attacked Indian frontier posts (claiming self-defense), the Chinese Government provided its opinion of why India had expansionist ambitions. The Chinese view of Indian motives was that Indian leaders had interbred with their British colonial occupiers, thereby absorbing "British imperialism" and leading to "a blood relationship" with the British.[99] China also implied that India's reliance on Western aid meant that India had been "bought" by the West. Finally, China quoted this sentence from Prime Minister Nehru's *Autobiography* to show his imperialist expansionist ambitions: "Though not directly a Pacific state, India will inevitably exercise an important influence there."

China claimed that this statement shows that the "goal pursued by this ambitious Nehru is the establishment of a great empire unprecedented in India's history." A small national state "can only be a vassal in Nehru's great empire." Nehru was not alone in his ambition, China stated, for the Indian middle classes "took over from British imperialism this concept of India as

[98]"Clarifying the Facts About 1962 is a Precondition," *Frontline* 15, no. 19 (September 12-15, 1998), http://www.the-hindu.com/fline/fl1519/15190170.htm.

[99]*The Sino-Indian Border Dispute*, 103.

the center of Asia" and "this has led to Nehru's idea of a great Indian empire. . . . India is the only country in Asia that has a protectorate."[100]

It might be imagined that China's rivalry with India may also be based on other historical factors, like the challenge of Buddhism to Chinese core beliefs, jealousy about the achievements of India's ancient empire, or India's large population and territory. There were also more immediate issues in 1962. Premier Zhou Enlai's public letter to Nehru said, "The Indian Government has stepped up its persecution of Chinese nationals in India . . . publicly spread seeds of hatred for the Chinese people."[101]

Another cause for China's hostility was the claim that India "instigated treason" in Tibet in 1950. While China's security was "seriously threatened by the U.S. aggression in Korea," India "brazenly did what the British imperialists had not dared to do. They forcibly occupied more than 90,000 square kilometers of China's territory." In 1959, "the fourth day after" Tibet started its rebellion in March, Nehru wrote to Zhou Enlai repeating the demand for 90,000 square kilometers and adding a claim for another 33,000 in the west, making the total area claimed three times as large as Holland.

China responded testily to Indian charges that China is an expansionist power, stating, "It is true that historically China had been powerful and had invaded other countries, but that occurred under the rule of the feudal landlord class."[102] Nehru's statements were "utterly outrageous" and "preposterous" and formed a slander campaign from 1959 to 1962, when Nehru made more than 300 speeches using "the most malicious language vilifying China," such as saying that China is "trying to flaunt her strength in a crude and violent way . . . to keep a foot on our chest." Nehru is "slandering China noisily" on the boundary question and "he has also tried in the most despicable sinister way to sow dissension between China and other countries."[103]

---

[100]Ibid., 97.

[101]Ibid., 33.

[102]Ibid., 106.

[103]Ibid.

Particularly galling for China was this statement by Nehru: "A strong China is normally an expansionist China. Throughout history this has been the case. . . . Even if we were 100 percent friendly with them, the fact remains that here is a mighty power sitting on our borders. That in itself changes the whole context, the whole picture. . . . The continuous failure of harvest has created an explosive situation." China replied that Chinese population pressure is less than in India, China's per square kilometer population being 67 and India's 148. China asked Nehru, "According to your logic, do you or do you not think that India's huge population is also a menace to other countries?"

A final motive for the activation of the rivalry was India's effort to protect Tibet from China's suppression of the Buddhist monks in the name of social progress. India's actions seemed closely related to the road to Tibet China had built secretly across the disputed territory prior to the 1959 Tibet uprising. India's effort in Tibet to protect Buddhism from a society that had rejected Buddhism was a source of hostile comments by China, especially because India seemed to be cooperating with the American CIA in this supposedly "religious" effort.[104]

China and India also had military skirmishes again in 1987. Despite the appearance of improved diplomatic relations, India and China cannot find common ground to settle their border dispute. Behind that dispute, an enduring rivalry exists that has been intensified by India's development of both nuclear weapons and a ballistic missile, which put much of China within range of Indian nuclear warheads.

The Enduring Relevance of History

Following its nuclear tests in May 1998, the Indian Government alleged a China threat—a clear manifestation of the continued influence of the historical rivalries in Sino-Indian relations. A *China Daily* article stated that Indian leaders "thought spreading the theory of a China threat was very useful. However, since they could not find any factual basis, they wracked

---

[104]Sun Keqin and Cui Hongjian, eds., *Ezhi Zhongguo—Shenhua yu xianshi* (Containing China—myth and reality)(Beijing: Zhongguo yanshi chubanshe, 1996). Chapter 2 discusses the CIA in Tibet. For U.S. articles on CIA operations in Tibet, see William M. Leary, "Secret Mission to Tibet," *Air and Space* (December 1997/January 1998): 62-71, and Jim Mann, "CIA Gave Aid to Tibetan Exiles in 60s, Files Show," *Los Angeles Times*, September 15, 1998.

their brains to come up with some age-old events in an attempt to confuse public opinion. In a letter to the U.S. President, the [Indian] Prime Minister slung mud at China, saying that China 'launched an armed invasion against India in 1962,' and that India's security environment has 'continued to worsen' for several years. That is to say, India was developing its nuclear weapons because of a China threat."[105]

Chinese authors reacted strongly to India's new China Threat Theory, blasting the government for creating the theory as an excuse for their nuclear tests, and to keep the BJP in power.[106] They were particularly disgusted because it "wrecked in a single day the results of improving relations between these two countries over the past 10 years and more."[107] A *Liberation Army Daily* article stated, "Unexpectedly, just as Sino-Indian relations are improving continually, the Indian authorities have insolently jumped out and raised a hue and cry about the China Threat Theory, openly regarding China as an obstacle to India seeking regional hegemony in an attempt to land China in a difficult position and boost its own morale. If this is not regional hegemonism, what is it then?"[108]

Yan Xuetong of CICIR expressed concern that India may try to turn the China Threat Theory into reality. "What merits attention is that India's vigorous spread of the China Threat Theory may betoken a new regional danger. For a long time India has repeatedly pushed forward its expansionist policy, threatening its neighboring countries in various ways. In 1962 it even started a large-scale border war against China; it also provided bases in Indian territory for the Dalai clique and encouraged them to engage in activities to

---

[105]"History Shall Not be Denied, Facts Speak Louder than Words," reprinted by Beijing Xinhua Domestic Service, May 18,1998, in FBIS-CHI-98-139, May 19, 1998.

[106]"One of the main purposes of creating a theory [China Threat Theory] is to keep a grip on political power. . . . It is now choosing to create an external threat to meet the needs of ultra-nationalist parties and thus keep them in the government." Yan Xuetong, "Why Has India Created a 'China Threat Theory'," *Guangming Ribao*, May 19, 1998, in FBIS-CHI-98-140, May 20, 1998.

[107]Li Wenyun, "India: Nuclear Tests Condemned, Lobbying Suffers Setbacks," *Renmin Ribao* (People's Daily), June 28, 1998, 3, in FBIS-CHI-98-187, July 6, 1998.

[108]Dong Guozheng, "Hegemonist Ambition is Completely Exposed," *Jiefangjun bao* (Liberation Army Daily), May 19, 1998, 5, in FBIS-CHI-98-140, May 20, 1998.

split China. People should wait and see whether the current Indian Government will create new trouble that may lead to a regional danger, to prove to the world a 'China Threat' really exists."[109]

At the same time India was using the China threat and the 1962 war as its excuse for conducting nuclear tests, Chinese analysts were employing arguments and phrases from the same era to respond to and criticize the tests. They frequently referred to Nehru's ambitions and India's British legacy as the sources of Indian aspirations of hegemony and its related goal of possessing nuclear weapons. For example, an article in the *Liberation Army Daily* stated, "The desire among some Indians to seek regional hegemony has swollen and they are bent on intimidating others and forcing neighboring countries to 'respect' India. . . . Prior to India's independence, Indian Congress Party leader Nehru pointed out in his book, *India's Discovery*: 'With its current position, India simply cannot play a secondary role in the world. India should either be vigorous or disappear from the scene.' "[110]

Far from disappearing from the scene, Chinese authors argue that "Through 50 years of efforts, India now boasts a mighty army," and its "military strategic targets" are "to seek hegemony in South Asia, contain China, control the Indian Ocean, and strive to become a military power in the contemporary world." One reason for India's "ambition of scrambling for military hegemony in the region" is that "it believes that since the Indian Ocean was formerly the 'lake of Britain,' it should now be included in the sphere of influence of India."[111]

Another article also mentions the British legacy in Indian aspirations, but argues that India lacks the real strength to achieve its goals. "In the contemporary era, India has always considered itself to be the 'natural successor to the great British empire.' It is dreaming of becoming a regional big nation and a world power as well. However, it is also a developing

---

[109] Yan Xuetong, "Why Has India Created a 'China Threat Theory.'"

[110] Ding Zengyi, "India's Attempt to Seek Hegemony has been Long-Standing—Interview with Liu Wenguo, A Member of the China South Asia Society."

[111] Liu Yang and Guo Feng, "What is the Intention of Wantonly Engaging in Military Ventures—India's Military Development Should Be Watched Out For," *Jiefangjun bao* (Liberation Army Daily), May 19, 1998, 5, in FBIS-CHI-98-141, May 21, 1998.

country. Of its over 900 million population (1993-1994), 169 million are impoverished, accounting for 19 percent of the total number." Therefore, the article argues, "It can only place its hope on wantonly engaging in military ventures and making a show of force. . . . Its fond dream of regional hegemony is a nightmare to the world!"[112] According to Chinese analysts, India believed the way to achieve its dreams of regional hegemony was to possess nuclear weapons. A *Liberation Army Daily* article states, "For a long time, succeeding Indian Governments have viewed nuclear weapons development as an important means to seek great-power status and to dominate South Asia and the Indian Ocean."[113] Wang Chiming of NDU agrees, although he argues that Pakistan's strong foreign ties, rather than India's domestic situation, are the factor hindering hegemony.

> India is self assured of being the South Asian region's number one major nation, its economic and military power has absolute superiority, and it has the objective conditions to serve as South Asia's 'hegemon.' Pakistan is the number two major nation on the South Asian subcontinent, and although its strength is far inferior to India's, it seeks a power balance on the South Asian subcontinent, and its determination to contend with India is great. To India, Pakistan still has the support of the United States and the Middle Eastern Muslim nations, so it is truly possible that it has the capability to present a challenge to India's senior position, thus destroying the strategic structure with India at the center, on the South Asian subcontinent. Therefore, India has tried to achieve its regional strategic goals through building a military force that has a powerful deterrent effect on the countries of South Asia, and nuclear weapons are . . . its tool.[114]

---

[112]Dong Guozheng, "Hegemonist Ambition is Completely Exposed."

[113]Zhang Changtai, "It Would be Hard for the Indian Government to Get Out of Its Dilemma by Conducting Nuclear Tests,"*Jiefangjun Bao* (Liberation Army Daily), May 20, 1998, 5, in FBIS-CHI-98-140, May 20, 1998.

[114]Wang Chiming, "Qian xi Indu kuayue 'he menkan' de beijing" (A brief analysis of the background of India's crossing the "nuclear threshold"), *Heping yu fazhan* (Peace and Development) 65, no. 3 (August 1998): 24.

FINDINGS

China's assessments of Japan and India are similar because both "fit" the analytic premises the Chinese use about nations that have territorial disputes with China, that are capitalist, and that are democratic. India is assessed as a sort of half-scale version of Japan. Chinese authors surveyed in this chapter suggest that Japan:

- Will achieve CNP equal to the United States by 2010
- Wants to restrain China's rising influence
- Seeks to foment conflict between the United States and China
- Will continue to have a militaristic, strategic culture
- Will struggle for resources in Central Asia and Siberia against the United States and Russia
- Will have ever-increasing conflicts with both Europe and the United States
- Will develop nuclear weapons eventually, earlier if Korea obtains them
- Will face a dangerous environment of potential conflict with Russia, Europe, and the United States
- Seeks (covertly) to become the military equivalent of the United States.

China's analysts write that India, as a smaller scale version of Japan, also has a militaristic, religion-based strategic culture, seeks to dominate its neighbors, has had covert nuclear ambitions for two decades prior to its nuclear tests in 1998, attempts to foment conflict between China and other nations, and has some areas of military superiority over China, such as its current navy. However, India's economic reforms are judged insufficient to catch up with China and enter the multipolar world as the sixth pole. India's CNP scores for 2010 place it no higher than number nine (AMS) or thirteen (CASS), only about half of China's CNP score in 2010.

4: A WEAK RUSSIA'S FUTURE

RELY ON CHINA

CHINA HAS MADE HIGHLY OPTIMISTIC FORECASTS about Russia's prospects for recovery and return to the ranks of the top five powers in the future security environment. Few analysts in the United States share this optimism about Russia's future, nor would Americans agree with the proposal of some nationalistic Chinese authors, like He Xin, that China must form a long-term strategic partnership with Russia in order to balance the rise of a militaristic Japan. One orthodox senior analyst explains that the geopolitical thinking is, "Russia needs to rely on China. Because both the United States and Japan regard Russia as a potential force to reduce their influence in the Asia-Pacific region, and Japan has territorial disputes with Russia, Chinese-Russian cooperation can, to a great extent, resist U.S. and Japanese forces, as well as maintain the power balance in Asia."[1]

Chinese military estimates of Russian national power by 2010 to 2020 place Russia as the second- or at least the third-ranking country in terms of overall military power. Applying the ancient statecraft of the Warring States, Chinese authors refer to the geopolitical nightmare of a powerful predatory Japan joining with a declining but still powerful America to isolate and contain China. A strong Chinese partnership with a recovering Russia is the preferred countermeasure. This chapter, which introduces the views of 55 Chinese authors on Russia, lists the factors they foresee Russia will face in its future dangerous security environment. In spite of these dangers, they believe Russia also has advantages, such as its potential partnership with China and advanced

---

[1]Gu Guanfu, "Russian Foreign Policy in Evolution," *Contemporary International Relations* 4, no. 11 (November 1994).

military concepts and technology, which cause China to assess the Russians as far more likely to exploit successfully the revolution in military affairs (RMA) than the United States. One military author argues that "Russia will use the RMA to maintain its military superiority . . . and is taking aim at America's commanding position in the RMA."[2] Another military author states that the Russian General Staff Academy is focusing on the RMA.[3] Ancient Chinese statecraft warns that a state needs powerful "partners" to survive in a multipolar environment. China's authors seem to see a rewarding Russian "partnership" in the decades ahead. This chapter also describes Chinese sympathy for the dangers that a weak Russia will face from Japan, Europe, and the United States as these three powers attempt to carve out part of the former Soviet sphere of influence in Central Asia and Eastern Europe.

DEBATES ON RUSSIA

According to interviews with civilian experts, after the collapse of the Soviet Union, it took 2 years for Chinese analysts to reach a consensus on the causes and future significance of the Soviet collapse (addressed at the end of this chapter). It is apparent from Chinese articles written since the consensus was reached that China has decided Russia's decline will end and that it will be able to play its assigned role as one of the five poles in the multipolar world foreseen by Deng Xiaoping and Huan Xian in 1986. Indeed, Russia may be aligned with China in the future multipolar world, now that Moscow is somewhat weakened from its Soviet days and has a smaller gross national product (GNP) than China. According to one author, Russia's GNP is fifth in Europe, or "the level of a medium country."[4] Additionally, because Russia has forsaken Marxism, Marxist ideology cannot be a source of conflict

---

[2]Zhu Xiaoli and Zhao Xiaozhuo, *Mei-E xin junshi geming* (America, Russia, and the revolution in military affairs)(Beijing: Junshi kexue chubanshe, 1996), 2.

[3]Gao Chunxiang, ed., *Xin junshi geming lun* (On the new revolution in military affairs)(Beijing: Junshi kexue chubanshe, 1996), 196.

[4]Yang Shuheng, "Lengzhan hou de Zhong-Mei-E guanxi" (Sino-U.S.-Russian relations after the Cold War," *Heping yu fazhan* (Peace and Development) 51, no. 1 (February 1995): 13-15, 42.

between the two countries, nor can Russia realistically ever again seek to dominate China.

The new consensus on Russia's promising future contrasts with past debates.[5] Since the early days of the Chinese Communist Party, even before Mao was Chairman, party leaders have debated the nature of the Soviet Union. The subject of Soviet communism and the Russian nation may be the most controversial among Chinese strategists. From alliance with the Soviets in the 1950s, to estrangement and then border clashes in the 1960s, Moscow has proved "hard to understand," in the words of one People's Liberation Army (PLA) officer interviewed for this study.

In spite of the collapse of the Soviet Union, Chinese analysts "officially" continue to portray the future role of Russia as one of the five equal "poles" (along with China, Japan, Europe, and the United States) that will shape the future world balance of power. Nevertheless, a few years ago, China's analysts saw Russia's immediate future as uncertain.[6] At least four scenarios were mentioned, although none of them would upset the "inevitable" trend toward a five-power multipolar structure laid down by Deng Xiaoping:

- *Further fragmentation* could bring warfare within and between many republics, including an independent Siberia.[7]
- *Chronic crisis* might bring neither a full collapse nor any real progress, but just gridlock and a continued limping along.
- *Successful transformation* built around the old Russian core, with stable relations among the republics and a territorial settlement with Japan,

---

[5]Gilbert Rozman, *The Chinese Debate About Soviet Socialism* (Princeton, NJ: Princeton University Press, 1987), 3.

[6]Yan Jin, Bai Xue, and Zhang Xingping, *Shuangtouying fei xiang hechu—guoji wutai shang de E'Luosi* (Where is the double-headed eagle flying—Russia on the international stage)(Beijing: Shishi chubanshe, 1995).

[7]The most dramatic scenario of an independent Siberia occurs in the first novel about future warfare that the PLA has published—Qiao Liang, *Mo ri zhi men—Danyuan zhe qizhong miaoshu de yiqie jie nan dou bu yao fasheng* (Door to doomsday—I hope the disasters described will not take place)(Beijing: Kunlun chubanshe, 1995). Siberian independence is declared to exploit the distraction of Chinese armed forces attempting to limit a war between India and Pakistan (in order to preserve a balance of power in South Asia, even though India has not invaded China). The author serves in the General Political Department of PLA.

would bring investment and trade opportunities, keeping Russia in play as a pole in the five-pole multipolar world structure and as a coalition partner to Japan or China.

● *Nationalistic regression* would resemble the results of the coup in 1991 against Gorbachev, had it succeeded. Hardliners impose martial law, followed by a halt to market reforms and democracy.

By 1995, Chinese writings about Russia became more optimistic.[8] Chinese military authors envisioned Russia increasing its military power in future decades by exploiting the RMA ahead of other nations. In any event, Chinese authors deny that the collapse of the Soviet Union caused future trends in world politics to "break" or be "transformed."[9] They asserted China had anticipated the end of the bipolar world as early as 1986, 5 years before the Soviet collapse.

Although there is a general consensus among Chinese authors about Russia's position as a pole in the future multipolar world, Chinese analysts suggest there are dangers to Russia in the decades ahead:

● The United States will continue to exploit a weakened Russia still coping with short-term domestic economic and political problems.

● Russian success in implementing the RMA ahead of others is not certain.

● As Russia rebuilds its Comprehensive National Power (CNP), it will be under pressure from the United States and Europe to the West and Japan to the East.

---

[8]An example of an optimistic assessment of Russia's future is Yu Sui, "Dui E'Luosi xingshi yu zhengce de ji dian kanfa" (Some observations on Russia's situation and policy), *Xiandai guoji guanxi* (Contemporary International Relations) 76, no. 2 (February 1996): 17-20.

[9]According to Zhu Chun, of the China Institute of International Strategic Studies, a think tank affiliated with Chinese military intelligence, "The maintenance of a balanced development of relations in the Asia-Pacific region by the four big powers, the United States, the Soviet Union, China and Japan is of great significance to peace and stability in this region." See "A Probe Into the Question of Security and New Order in the Asia-Pacific Region," *International Strategic Studies* (English edition) 19, no. 1 (March 1991): 14.

DEVELOPMENT AND RECOVERY

Chinese authors recognize that Russia will continue to have economic, political, and social turbulence in the short term but do not foresee these problems preventing Russia from assuming its position as a pole in the future multipolar world. Although its influence has weakened and it no longer is a superpower, Chinese analysts emphasize that Russia remains a major nation with extensive military strength. While today's crises have contributed to a decline in Russia's CNP, in the long run they forecast that its domestic difficulties will gradually be overcome.

At present, however, the Chinese view Russia as a factor of instability during the period of transition to a multipolar world. When assessing the overall situation in the Asia-Pacific, Zhang Changtai, a Research Fellow at the China Institute of International Strategic Studies (CIISS), writes:

> Russia remains an uncertain factor where there are still ups and downs in the political arena. . . . For the future, the struggle among all political factions around redistribution of powers will continue to develop and even intensify; the position of the military has declined with growing dissatisfaction, and it is a severe test for President Yeltsin and his government whether they can maintain stability in the armed forces.[10]

Chinese analysts also see economic problems precluding stability in Russia's current development and do not believe the economy will recover quickly.[11] A Shanghai Institute for International Studies (SIIS) analyst estimates, "In the short term it will be difficult for the Russian Federation's economic situation to take a turn for the better, economic recovery will necessitate a very long period of time . . . by the year 2005 it will be able to break even with the

---

[10]Zhang Changtai, "Some Views on the Current Situation in the Asia-Pacific Region," *International Strategic Studies* 43, no.1 (January 1997): 31.

[11]For an analysis of Russia's economic crisis see Sun Zhanlin, "News Analysis: Why Has the Russian Financial Crisis Occurred," Beijing Xinhua Domestic Service, September 16, 1998, in FBIS-CHI-98-264, September 25, 1998.

economy in 1990. The necessary time for Russia to build a comparatively complete and developed market economy will probably be even longer."[12]

A study of Russia's current and future development by the China Institute of Contemporary International Relations (CICIR) provides a representative orthodox view of Russia's overall near-term prospects. It both acknowledges serious problems and predicts a trend of inevitable gradual recovery and restoration. Stating that "for many years Russian society has accumulated a huge number of complex contradictions and problems," the study lists some of the most critical issues it is currently facing:

- "Economic depression has endangered political stability."
- "The state of social political order is becoming seriously worse," with the pervasive spread of crime and terrorist activities.
- "The trend of local independence and localities acting on their own is difficult to contain."
- The uncertainty of President Yeltsin's health.[13]

According to the study, the combination of the above problems "makes it very difficult for people to make an optimistic appraisal of Russia's political situation and the entire country's situation at the end of the century."[14] However, at least with regard to Russia's economic prospects, CICIR is more positive and puts forward a timetable predicting future development and reconstruction. It forecasts that 1997-98 will be "the true turning point for Russia's economy," 1999-2005 will bring "stable recovery," and after 2005, Russia will see "sustained growth."[15] This growth will permit gradual progress in attaining strategic goals to "restore its position as a great nation," to

---

[12]Dong Bainan, "Euluosi lianbang he qian Sulian diqu qita guojia de fazhan qianjing" (The development prospects for the Russian federation and the other countries of the former Soviet region), in *Kua shiji de shijie geju da zhuanhuan* (Major changes in the world structure at the turn of the century), ed. Chen Qimao (Shanghai: Shanghai jiaoyu chubanshe, 1996), 79.

[13]Wang Lijiu and Liu Guiling, eds., *Kua shiji de E'Luosi* (Russia today and in the next century) (Beijing: Shishi chubanshe, 1997), 78-80.

[14]Ibid.

[15]Ibid., 128-131.

"contain regional separatism," and to prevent "external forces" from penetrating Russia's sphere of influence.[16]

What Chinese analysts emphasize is that despite Russia's current and short-term difficulties, the "framework" of its former power and status still exists, and the country has definite potential for future development. The CICIR study concludes, "Currently, Russia's domestic political and economic relations still are not smooth and the restoration of its Comprehensive National Power will require time. However, the framework of Russia as a major nation and the factors of its actual strength have not disappeared; in particular, Russia possesses a huge nuclear weapons arsenal and armed forces that can not be belittled."[17] Similarly, Chen Qimao, former president of SIIS, writes, "In the short term it will be difficult for Russia to revive, but its potential cannot be underestimated. . . . From the long-term view, Russia will gradually recover and develop, and although it can not again become a superpower, it still will be a global power."[18] Yu Sui, of the Central Committee International Liaison Department, sums up Chinese analysts greater optimism about Russia's mid- to long-term prospects, saying, "We would rather assess that Russia will rejuvenate at an earlier date and at a quicker pace."[19]

DANGERS IN THE
FUTURE SECURITY ENVIRONMENT

Not only do Chinese analysts predict continued domestic problems during Russia's path to establishing its position as one of the five poles of the future multipolar world, but they also examine the numerous threats to its external security environment. One author writes,

> The correlation of forces is moving in an unfavorable direction for Russia. . . . Russia's geopolitical environment is becoming worse. . . . The western

[16]Ibid., 176.

[17]Ibid., 198.

[18]Chen Qimao, "Qianyan" (Introduction), in *Kua shiji de shijie geju da zhuanhuan*, 8.

[19]Yu Sui, "The Big Powers' Relationships in Northeast Asia," *International Strategic Studies*, 8, no. 3 (1994).

area of Russia has lost its strategic defense line by over a thousand kilometers. . . . Even more serious, the Pan-Turkic and Islamic Fundamentalists that tend to be against Russia are rapidly developing, which may possibly cause new conflicts and endanger the security of southern Russia.[20]

In general, most Chinese analysts focus on the United States and NATO as being the biggest challenges currently endangering Russia's security environment. In fact, some have blamed the West for contributing to Russia's continued domestic problems. For example, several authors assert that one of the reasons that Russia has not recovered more rapidly is "the stingy financial assistance provided by the Western powers."[21] The insufficient aid is explained by Chinese authors as the West's desire to keep Russia weak, so that it will not grow and once again be a challenge to America and NATO. "The United States and other Western countries . . . [have] continued their Cold War mentality, trying to take advantage of Russia's current political, economic and military weakness to pursue a policy of containment in order to weaken, westernize and split Russia and prevent it from restoring its position as a big power."[22]

However, Chinese analysts note that the West wants Russia to be "weak but not chaotic," and therefore must temper its efforts to inhibit the country's power.[23] Xue Gang, a Research Fellow at CIISS, explains, "The present U.S. attitude toward Russia is like this: on the one hand it continues to assist and support the present government in Moscow in order to stabilize the situation

---

[20]Li Haoyu, "Shixi E'Luosi de guojia anquan zhanlue" (A tentative analysis of Russia's national security strategy), *Heping yu Fazhan* (Peace and Development) 50, no. 4 (November 1994): 24.

[21]Song Yimin, "Dulianti de xianzhuang ji fazhan qianjing" (The Commonwealth of Independent States current situation and its future), *Heping yu fazhan* (Peace and Development) 50, no. 4 (November 1994): 21-23. Another article stressing how little aid the United States gave Russia is Zhang Yebai, "Meiguo dui E'Luosi de yuanju" (American assistance to Russia), *Heping yu fazhan* (Peace and Development) 49, no. 3 (August 1994): 44-48.

[22]Wang Rui and Zhang Wei, "A Preliminary Analysis of Russian Military Strategy," *International Strategic Studies* 45, no. 3 (July 1997): 39.

[23]Li Haoyu, "Shixi E'Luosi de guojia anquan zhanlue," 27.

in Russia, but on the other, it attempts to prevent Russia from becoming truly powerful so that Russia will not become a threat to it again in the future."[24]

The main thrust of the West's "policy of precaution, containment, and enfeeblement" toward Russia is through the NATO eastward expansion.[25] Feng Yujun of CICIR writes, "There are three objectives for the West to extend eastward: to fill up the security vacancy in Eastern and Central Europe so as to consolidate its victory won in the Cold War; to give an impetus to Westernization of the former Warsaw Pact nations so as to 'enlarge the community of democratic countries; and to complete strategic encirclement of Russia so as to prevent Russia from staging a comeback."[26] Consequently, Chinese analysts assert, "It is not a simple policy regression for the Russians to redefine NATO as its chief threat. It is an inevitable result of the fierce strategic collision between Russia and the Western powers to protect their respective strategic interests. . . . Containing NATO expansion naturally becomes a major goal of Russian military strategy."[27] However, the Chinese

---

[24]Xue Gang, "The Present Security Policy Framework of Russia," *International Strategic Studies*, no. 1 (1995). A CICIR analyst has noted that the United States cannot push Russia too far in its efforts to weaken and contain its development. "As for Washington, avoidance of a confrontation with Russia is also in its own strategic interests. Examination of Washington's Russia policy reveals its duality. On the one hand, it intends to guard against and contain Russia out of concern for Moscow's reviving potential and alleged 'imperial ambitions,' which may someday evolve into a regional dominating power threatening Washington's world leadership. As a matter of fact, the NATO eastern expansion is essentially a most important strategic move against such an eventuality. On the other hand, it attempts to appease and encourage Russia at the same time. Russia's position on the nuclear issue and the success or failure of Moscow's economic transition are closely related to U.S. strategic objectives. Under these circumstances, possible confrontation with Moscow on this issue would naturally harm vital U.S. interests." See Zhang Minqian, "Washington and NATO Expansion," *Contemporary International Relations* 7, no. 5 (May 1997): 4-5. Zhang is an Associate Research Professor at CICIR.

[25]Wang Naicheng, "Beiyue dongkuang dui Mei-E-Ou guanxi de yingxiang" (The impact of NATO's eastward expansion on relations between the United States, Russia and Europe), *Guoji zhanlue yanjiu* (International Strategic Studies) 46, no. 4 (October 1997): 20. Wang is a Senior Research Fellow at CIISS.

[26]Feng Yujun, "Moscow vs. NATO: Compromise Will Not Dispel Apprehensions," *Contemporary International Relations* 7, no. 5 (May 1997): 14. Feng is an Assistant Research Professor at CICIR.

[27]Wang Rui and Zhang Wei, "A Preliminary Analysis of Russian Military Strategy," 40.

forecast that the prospects for Russia's ability to prevent the eastward expansion are dim. A CICIR analyst, discussing how Russia was already forced to accept that Poland, Hungary, and the Czech Republic will join NATO, writes, "Confronted with such a powerful offensive, Moscow has evidently soft-pedaled its resistance. Acutely aware of the latent threats to its security, yet unable to reverse the trends, Moscow had no alternative other than swallowing the bitter pill."[28] Some analysts do not foresee that Russia will do much better at thwarting new Western aggression in the near term either: "Short of an evident increase in economic and military strength in the near future, Russia will still be in a passive position before the NATO eastward expansion."[29]

Chinese authors often seem genuinely worried and even sympathetic to the hostile security environment in which a weakened Russia will find itself for decades ahead until its comprehensive power is rebuilt. For example, Russia's current weakness in the face of NATO seems exaggerated in this statement:

> The disintegration of the Warsaw Pact Organization and the Soviet Union had already inflicted upon Russia a loss of a strategic depth of more than one thousand kilometers, and now NATO expansion would further push its military frontier eastward by more than 700 kilometers. It is known that the current strength of NATO conventional forces is three times that of Russia. If that of the first batch of members-to-be are also reckoned in, NATO would be militarily stronger than Russia by nearly 4 times, which would be a tremendous military pressure on Russia's western border. . . . Russia's position is restrained by its worsening national power. Politically, economically and militarily, NATO enjoys overwhelming advantage. The total GNP of its member states is 20 times that of Russia, and its military expenditure is 10 times Russia's. On the part of Russia, the erstwhile superpower is now not only crisis ridden economically and drastically weakened militarily, but also bogged down in domestic political strife. In consequence, its opposition to NATO expansion to Eastern and Central

---

[28]Zhang Minqian, "Washington and NATO Expansion," 5.

[29]Ji Zhiye, "Russia in 1997," *Contemporary International Relations* 7, no. 1 (January 1997): 31-32.

Europe is almost tantamount to a hope for the impossible, at least for the time being.[30]

Chinese analysts suggest that the real threat to Russia's security would occur if NATO decided to infiltrate the nations of the former Soviet Union, incorporating the Baltic states and Central Asian nations into its sphere of influence. They assert that such a move is part of the final NATO aim to completely encircle Russia and that the United States and Western European nations have already begun to lay the foundation for the ultimate stages of the eastward expansion. At present, they claim the West is penetrating the region through economic and military means. "The United States has decided to play a more active role in the ethnic and local conflicts in the region, and has refused to let Russia have special peacekeeping privileges in the region."[31]

A Senior Research Fellow at CIISS, Wang Naicheng, even argues that if NATO did eventually incorporate this area, such a development could mean the end of Russia's hope of becoming pole in the future multipolar world. "Further NATO expansion to the Baltic nations, Ukraine, and other Commonwealth of Independent States (CIS) countries will make Russia's space for strategic survival contract to the maximum. This would be no less than to strike at the root of Russia, for she might finally lose the important base upon which she could be an independent pole in the world." However, Wang asserts that Russia is doing its utmost to prevent this worst case scenario. "With the first line of defense in Central-Eastern Europe broken through, Russia is exerting every effort to build and entrench on the second line, tolerating no entry into the 'forbidden zone.' "[32]

Two articles written in 1998 foresee the three Baltic Nations—Lithuania, Latvia, and Estonia— becoming the next in line to fall into NATO clutches, citing the signing of the "U.S.-Baltic Charter of Partnership" in January and the first meeting of the Partnership Committee in July as preliminary steps. A *People's Daily* article asserts, "The formal launching of NATO eastward expansion shows that East Europe is being drawn into the west European

---

[30]Feng Yujun, "Moscow vs. NATO: Compromise Will Not Dispel Apprehensions," 10, 14.

[31]Li Haoyu, "Shixi E'Luosi de guojia anquan zhanlue," 27.

[32]Wang Naicheng, "Beiyue dongkuang dui Mei-E-Ou guanxi de yingxiang," 19.

sphere of influence and will not longer be under Russian control. Against this background, the United States has decided to push on in the flush of victory and regards the countries of the former Soviet Union as the next targets in expanding its influence." According to the article, the three Baltic states are the natural choices of NATO because they "were the first to break away from the Soviet Union and have never joined the CIS." Additionally, they have already tried to "fuse into Europe" in an effort to maintain their independence from Russian control.[33]

Other analysts see the Central Asian nations as the main countries targeted by the West. A CICIR study holds that "Western nations, with the United States at the head, have stood in the way of the CIS integration process, particularly toward Ukraine, and have actively carried out efforts to divide and disintegrate." U.S. invitations to Ukraine and Uzbekistan to join NATO are extremely dangerous to Russia's security interests, for Uzbekistan is considered to be an "important strategic partner" by the West, and in 1996, the Ukrainian Minister of National Defense expressed that at a necessary time, Ukraine "would not eliminate the possibility of entering NATO."[34] Additionally, Ukraine and a few Central Asian countries have signed "Peace Partnership Relationship" documents with NATO. One article asserts that it is through these Peace Partnerships that the United States will be able to increase its infiltration of the region, "on the pretext of 'mediating' regional conflicts, and, in the name of 'maintaining peace', dispatching U.S. and Western military forces to weaken and push out Russia's forces in this region." It concludes, "In essence it is a repeat of the 19th century 'fierce rivalry' among the great powers for Central Asia, and a way to turn Central Asian countries into the United States 'chess pieces.' "[35]

The future U.S. challenge to Russia is even more serious than efforts to contain Russia's power. In addition to luring former Soviet republics to join

---

[33]Xu Hongzhi, "The United States Upgrades Ties with the Three Baltic States," *Renmin Ribao* (People's Daily), July 21, 1998, 6, in FBIS-CHI-98-209, July 29, 1998. See also Tang Bingzhong, "Another Move by the United States on the Chessboard European Strategy," Beijing Xinhua Domestic Service, January 18, 1998, in FBIS-CHI-98-021, January 23, 1998.

[34]Wang Lijin and Liu Guiling, eds., *Kua shiji de E'Luosi*, 189-190.

[35]Wang Guang, "New U.S. Central Asia Strategy Evaluated" (in Chinese), *Xiandai guoji guanxi* (Contemporary International Relations), no. 11 (November 1997): 13-16.

NATO, the United States has targeted Central Asian oil and natural gas and is already "squeezing Russia out."[36] Yang Shuheng, of the Chinese Academy of Social Sciences (CASS), asserts, "The rivalry over the Caspian Sea region's oil and natural gas is . . . part of the U.S.-Russian rivalry over strategic interests and spheres of influence in the Eurasian hinterland. . . . The number of countries involved (in the struggle) will increase. . . . International forces covet the treasure chest that is Central Asia."[37]

RUSSIA'S RESPONSE

While some Chinese authors regard Russia as passive and weak in the face of these threats, others see Russia as taking a stand and adopting countermeasures against U.S. and NATO policies. For example, Li Qinggong, a Research Fellow at CIISS, states, "The plan of 'NATO eastward expansion' pursued by the United States and other Western countries has entered the stage of implementation, but Russia has not weakened its opposition; it has taken new countering actions in an attempt to build the Russia-France-Germany axis to oppose the control of the United States over European security affairs and offset the impact of 'NATO eastward expansion.' "[38] Liu Guilin, an Associate Research Professor in the Division for Russian and East Europe Studies at CICIR writes, "Clearly, Moscow intends to rely on the CIS as both the basis for its great power strategy and the bulwark against NATO eastern expansion." He believes that despite drawbacks and problems that exist in inter-CIS relations, such as worries about "Moscow's possible domineering intention," Russia will not lose out to the West in the struggle for influence over the nations of the former Soviet Union.[39] "Shared interests will sustain the CIS in the face of difficulties . . . (and) cooperation will remain the

---

[36]Yang Shuheng, "Lengzhan hou daguo he diqu liliang dui Zhongya de zhengduo" (The struggles over Central Asia by major nations and regional forces in the post-Cold War period), *Heping yu fazhan* (Peace and Development) 60, no. 2 (June 1997): 29.

[37]Ibid., 45.

[38]Li Qinggong, "Dangqian de guoji junshi anquan xingshi" (Current international military security situation," *Guoji zhanlue yanjiu* (International Strategic Studies) 47, no. 1 (January 1998):8.

[39]Liu Guiling, "Whither CIS?," *Contemporary International Relations* 8, no. 7 (July 1998): 29, 31.

mainstream due to economic and security interdependence. . . . Russia still retains strong deep-seated influence in the CIS in the forms of geographical proximity, traditional economic ties, and a Russian community of some 25 million scattered all over the region. All this cannot possibly be replaced by the West."[40] He writes that even the "strongly independence-minded Ukraine will still depend on Russia for a long time to come," citing the fact that 40 percent of its foreign trade is with Russia, and that Russia supplies much of its oil and gas.[41] Therefore, Liu predicts that CIS integration will proceed, although it will be gradual. Finally, he concludes,

> Looking beyond the current Russian financial crisis, it can safely be estimated that along with further improvement in overall conditions, the stronger Russia's urge to make bigger strides in winning back its original big power status in international life, the greater CIS cohesion and the higher the organization's profile in a multipolar world of the 21st century.[42]

Chinese analysts recognize that on international issues other than NATO eastward expansion, Russia also has strategic interests that conflict with those of the West. In the Iraqi weapons inspection crises, they assert that Russia came out ahead in its dispute with the United States over how to handle the problem:

> In resolving this conflict, there has been practically a struggle between Iraq and the United States, or a struggle between Russia and the United States, and Moscow has scored the most points. . . . All these efforts were made by Russia in an effort not only to head off a war in the Gulf region, but also to pave the way for strong economic ties with Iraq when the U.N. sanctions are eventually lifted. . . . Russia is, of course, aware that Washington does not like the strengthening of Russia's position in the Middle East and the increasing role of its diplomacy in the region."[43]

---

[40]Ibid., 33-35.

[41]Ibid., 34.

[42]Ibid., 36.

[43]Wang Dandi, "Russia's Role, Goal in Resolving Iraqi Crisis," Beijing Xinhua Domestic Service (February 24, 1998), in FBIS-CHI-98-055, March 3, 1998.

INFLUENCE OF THE KOSOVO CRISIS

The two different views regarding Russia's position and power in the world structure—that it is passive and relatively powerless against the current onslaught from the NATO eastward expansion, versus it is actively asserting itself and taking steps to counter the threat—are reflected in the divergent views put forward by Chinese analysts regarding Russia's response to NATO military strikes against Yugoslavia in spring 1999. Some authors focus on the dangers posed by NATO actions in the Kosovo crisis and Russia's weak response, while others emphasize Russia's eventual return to power and the ways this was manifested during the crisis.

Chinese analysts regarded NATO strikes against Yugoslavia as part of the plan of eastward expansion, an effort "to bring the strategic areas in the Balkans under control, in order to further contain and weaken Russia and prevent Russia from rising up again."[44] While one CICIR analyst merely stated that NATO "wanted to issue a warning to Russia, and further weaken its international standing," other authors were much more explicit.[45] An article in the *Liberation Army Daily*, claimed:

> The ultimate aim of the United States in launching air strikes against Yugoslavia is to remove the last obstacle on the 'crescent frontier' surrounding Russia and to further narrow Russia's strategic space. Sticking a knife in Russia's traditional sphere of influence not only contains Russia but gives Eastern Europe and the former Soviet countries a sense of crisis, making them realize that they are lacking military security assurance and forcing them to throw themselves more resolutely into the NATO fold. This move really kills two birds with one stone.[46]

---

[44]Wang Naicheng, "Failure of the New Strategic Concept," *Jiefangjun bao* (Liberation Army Daily), May 22, 1999, 4, in FBIS-CHI-1999-0601, May 22, 1999.

[45]Yuan Peng, "An Arrogant and Lonely Superpower—The Tradition and History of Hegemony," *Zhongguo Qingnian Bao*, May 26, 1999, 3, in FBIS-CHI-1999-0609, June 10, 1999. Yuan is at CICIR.

[46]Li Donghang, "Dangerous Attempt to Resist Multipolarization Process," *Jiefangjun bao* (Liberation Army Daily), May 26, 1999, 5, in FBIS-CHI-1999-0604, May 26, 1999.

Li Yonggang, a scholar at the Chinese Society for Strategy and Management, holds a similar view, "By dismembering the Federal Republic of Yugoslavia or forcing Milosevic to surrender, the external front of Russia will be brushed away, therefore, Russia will be further oppressed, which is the key step to finally annihilating Russia." He writes, "In addition to sharing the advantages of militarily and politically squeezing out Russia," one of the reasons "NATO European powers have been so enthusiastic" about their actions in Yugoslavia is that it is an "attempt to get through the Balkan corridor in the south and extend their sphere of economic influence to Central Asia and even further to a wider scope."[47]

Wang Naicheng, of CIISS, also considers power in Central Asia to be one of the goals of NATO: "If NATO succeeds in stationing its troops in Kosovo and taking up strategically important places to the east, it can make direct threats against Central Asia, thus weakening the control of Russia over the CIS and undermining its foundation." Wang even warned that NATO incursions could harm Russia's efforts to return to power. "If the strength and influence of NATO can drive straight into the scope of influence of the former Soviet Union through the Balkans, Russia is bound to be further weakened and will encounter more difficulties in realizing its overall state strategy of becoming a pole in the future multipolar world."[48]

Chinese analysts note how the United States exploited Russia's economic weakness during the Kosovo crisis, counting on Russia's dependency on loans to keep it from taking a stand against NATO actions. Zhang Zhaozhong, of NDU, writes, "The United States has already accurately gauged Russia's weak disposition. When it started bombing the FRY, it was feeling for Russia's cards and did not know what Russia would do." However, "they know that in dealing with Russia they only need to use economic methods and give them a bit of money, and everything will be fine. In addition, the European Union (EU) and the International Monetary Fund (IMF) also declared that they were willing to help Russia resolve its economic crisis and provide loans totaling

---

[47]Li Yonggang, "Looking at the U.S. World Strategy Against the Backdrop of the Kosovo Crisis," excerpt published in *Zhongguo Tongxun She* (Hong Kong), May 27, 1999, in FBIS-CHI-1999-0528, May 27, 1999.

[48]Wang Naicheng, "Failure of the New Strategic Concept."

over \$4 billion. They also knew that Russia would just murmur without really doing anything."[49] Colonel Liu Gang of the Academy of Military Science (AMS) similarly commented on Russia's weak response due to economic concerns, stating, "The fact that Russia has continually changed its role during the Kosovo crisis shows that when U.S.-led NATO encroached on Russian interests in Kosovo and affronted its dignity. . . . Russia showed that, for economic reasons, 'the spirit is willing but the flesh is weak,' and it had no alternative but to retreat." However, Colonel Liu points out that the United States was forced to make "certain concessions to Russia . . . because Russia is still a military power that cannot be lightly 'stirred up.' "[50]

Dr. Shen Jiru, a Research Fellow and Director of the International Strategic Research Section of the Institute of World Economics and Politics at CASS, argues that despite its weakened power, Russia will not be passive in the face of the NATO threat:

It is difficult for Russia to make any substantial moves. The fundamental reason for this is that its national strength is too weak. Its total domestic output is less than the military expenditure of the United States; its military expenditure is only about 1/45th that of the United States, or about \$6 billion. Consequently, few Russian army divisions are completely equipped nowadays. . . . Nevertheless, the Russian Government also understands that NATO's strategic aim is to further weaken Russia to make it become a third-class country with no chance to rise up again forever. . . . Russia's entrance into the 20th century was marked by its defeat in the Russian-Japanese War. This time, Russia is certainly unwilling to have its entrance into the 21st century marked by losing the Balkans without a fight.[51]

---

[49]Ma Ling, "The Attempt Behind the 'Bombing in Error'—Interview with Renowned Military Commentator Zhang Zhaozhong," *Ta Kung Pao* (Hong Kong), May 17, 1999, A4, in FBIS-CHI-1999-1518, May 17, 1999. Zhang is Director of the Science and Technology Teaching and Research Section of NDU.

[50]Liu Gang, "Why Has Russia Changed Its Role," *Renmin ribao*, June 23, 1999, 6, in FBIS-CHI-1999-0624, June 25, 1999.

[51]Hsu Tao-chen, "United States Still Makes Old Mistakes, Exclusive interview with Shen Jiru," *Hong Kong Ta Kung Pao*, May 21, 1999, A6, in FBIS-CHI-1999-0604, May 21, 1999. A similar view is presented in Xiao Feng, "World Trends Under U.S. Global Strategy, Part One of Two," *Renmin Ribao*, May 31, 1999, 6, in FBIS-CHI-1999-0601, May 31, 1999. "Since Russia

Other authors considered Russia's function as a mediator in the Kosovo crisis to be evidence of Russia's continued influence in international affairs. One explained, "In the political settlement of the Kosovo issue, Russia played a unique, important role. Regarding this, the United States expressed its 'thanks' to Russia superficially. In fact, it had a sour feeling. For a considerable period of time, the United States has adopted the policy of pressuring and intimidating Russia, weakening its role in international affairs. However, when the United States was in a dilemma over the Kosovo issue, it had to seek Russia's assistance. As a consequence, the latter played the role of mediator and increased its international status."[52] The fact that Russian troops entered Kosovo before NATO troops was viewed by the Chinese as even further evidence of Russian power and a sign of potential growth and influence in the future.

> Like magical soldiers descending from the sky, a spearhead detachment of the Russian peacekeeping force arrived in Pristina, capital of Kosovo in the Yugoslav Federation, at 0130 on 12 June. . . . It should be said that although Russia's national strength is weak at present, it is still very experienced in handling international affairs, and the action of its peacekeeping force in being the first into Kosovo has already scored highly in international politics. It shows to the whole world that Russia can still play a major role in international affairs, that Russia will continue to exert a major influence in postwar Kosovo issues, and that Russia can make things hot for NATO when necessary.[53]

---

is 'no longer what it was' and dares not break up with the West, it is forced to make concessions in a weak-kneed fashion. A nation which once defeated Napoleon and later defeated Hitler during World War Two cannot be ordered about for a long time. Russia's economic strength has been weakened and its political situation is unstable, but its military strength, especially its nuclear arsenal, is still there. Once it has recovered sufficiently to stand on its feet, its conflicts with the West, especially with U.S. hegemonism, are bound to sharpen. It will not accept the attempts of the United States to build a 'unipolar world.' "

[52]Ma Shikun and Zhang Yong, "United States: Winner or Loser?" *Renmin Ribao*, June 11, 1999, 6, in FBIS-CHI-1999-0611, June 11, 1999.

[53]Qi Changming, "Unusual Significance of the Russian Army's Stealing a March into Kosovo," *Jiefangjun bao* (Liberation Army Daily), June 13, 1999, 4, in FBIS-CHI-1999-0623, June 24, 1999.

SINO-RUSSIAN RELATIONS

Some Chinese analysts argue that one way for Russia to counterbalance the dangers to its security environment from the West would be to improve its relations with China. Chinese authors have noted a shift in Russia's foreign policy toward this direction, in the years since the collapse of the Soviet Union. Initially, in the early 1990s, they were critical of Russia for focusing too much on the West, for "leaning to one side."[54] In keeping with the Chinese foreign policy theory that only weak nations have alliances, Russia at that time was regarded negatively, "Because of dependency on the West, Russia's foreign affairs policy lacked independence, causing its international position to suffer a disastrous decline and incurring domestic criticism and opposition."[55] However, in the mid-1990s, the focus of Russia's foreign policy began to widen, with greater attention being given to other parts of the world.[56] Li Zhongcheng, a Research Professor in the China and World Studies Division at CICIR, writes, "Russia, bent on recovering its former status as a global power, will intensify its efforts in pursuing an omni-directional diplomacy so as to regain and expand its influence in the international community."[57]

Chinese analysts assert that it was the threats to Russia's security environment from the West that caused it turn to the East, making Asia in general and China in particular the new targets of its diplomacy. Li states, "While NATO was busy preparing its eastward expansion and the United States and Japan redefined the U.S.-Japan security treaty, which broadened the field of cooperative defense, China and Russia announced a plan to develop

---

[54]Gao Heng, "Lengzhan hou Mei-E-De sanbian guanxi" (The trilateral relations between the United States, Russia and Germany in the post-Cold War period"), *Heping yu fazhan* (Peace and Development), 60, no. 2 (June 1997): 10.

[55]Wang Lijiu and Liu Guiling, eds., *Kua shiji de E'Luosi*, 3.

[56]Several authors point to 1996 as the specific year in which Russia began to stand up to the West and shift the focus of its foreign policy to the East. For example, "The year 1996 marked a turning point in Russia's foreign policy." Ji Zhiye, "Russia in 1997," 31. See also Wang Lijiu and Liu Guiling, eds., *Kua shiji de E'Luosi*, 4.

[57]Li Zhongcheng, "World Politics in 1997," *Contemporary International Relations* 7, no. 1 (January 1997): 1-2.

a '21st-century-oriented strategic partnership of equality, mutual confidence, and mutual coordination.' "[58] Shi Ze, the Vice President of the China Institute of International Studies (CIIS), holds a similar view, emphasizing the benefits to Russia from improving its relations with China:

> For Russia, it is the most realistic and ideal choice to enhance its cooperation with China so as to enter the Asia-Pacific economic and political space as soon as possible. . . . After the disintegration of the Soviet Union, certain changes have taken place in the geopolitical situation which are unfavorable to Russia. From the west, the eastern expansion of NATO has taken on a strong momentum, while in the south it is facing infiltration by separatists. . . . Russia has made it a top priority to establish "good neighboring areas." Developing relations with China is significant not only for the improvement of Russia's surrounding environment, but also for the future prospect of its far east area.[59]

Chinese authors see the Sino-Russian partnership as benefiting both sides.[60] Not only does Russia gain by having a counterweight to NATO eastward expansion, but several studies also point to the economic advantages that can be derived through improved relations, because "the two sides are especially complementary in terms of resources, industrial structure, and

---

[58]Li Zhongcheng, "The Role of an Emerging China in World Politics," *Contemporary International Relations* 8, no. 2 (February 1998): 14.

[59]Shi Ze, "Lun xin shiqi de Zhong-E guanxi" (Perceptions on Sino-Russian relations in the new era)," *Gouji zhanlue yanjiu* (International Studies) 60, no. 2 (April 1996): 5-6.

[60]A CICIR study provides a positive assessment of Sino-Russian relations, pointing to four main reasons why Sino-Russian relations have made headway in the past several years and will continue to develop in the future. First, "No major disputes and problems exist between China and Russia." Neither country interferes in the internal affairs of the other, such as Taiwan, Tibet, and human rights. Second, both sides have learned from past historical experiences. Third, "On international issues, the two countries have numerous common understandings and common interests that are not mutually exclusive." Fourth, "Their advantageous geographical position and complementary economic structures create the conditions for the two countries' reforms and economic development." See Wang Liuji and Liu Guiling, *Kua shiji de E'Luosi*, 224-225.

development levels."[61] From China's point of view, it also intends to use Russia as a counterbalance to the West. Liu Jinghua of CASS writes,

> There are two possible prospects for Russia: One, Russia succeeds in its reforms and fits into the track that the West designs for it. Two, Russia fails in its reforms and chooses nationalism. In 10 years, Russia's future will be clear. Within the next 15 years, Russia will still be a strong force, but it will not be on its guard against China. . . . Hence maintaining a good Sino-Russian relationship will have a comprehensive effect for China to use Russia's market and restrain the West.[62]

Study Reports on the International Situation–1997-1998, a yearly compilation of the views of authors from a variety of institutes published by the Chinese Society for Strategy and Management, contained an article that argues why Russia and China are very natural strategic partners. The author, Zheng Yu, writes, "Even if the next Russian President takes office with pro-Western influence in the year 2000, Russia's unique diplomatic and cultural tradition, its consciousness as a great power, and the natural characteristics formed by the Orthodox Eastern Church will make it difficult" for Russia to be part of the West. The process of catching up for Russia has lasted "several hundred years, since Peter the Great, [and] has not made Russia entirely Westernized." He further points out, "Since 1992 pro-Western radicals in Russia have gradually lost power on the Russian political stage." This is a strategic cultural argument. According to Zheng, a good reason for Russia to help China is that "Russia has considerable influence in the continents of Europe and Asia and will undoubtedly promote the setting up of China's position of a political great power in the world."[63]

---

[61]Shi Ze, "Lun xin shiqi de Zhong-E guanxi," 12.

[62]Liu Jinghua, "Ershi yi shiji ershi sanshi niandai Zhongguo jueqi ji waijiao zhanlue xueze" (China's rise and diplomatic strategy in the twenties and thirties of the 21st century), *Zhanlue yu guanli* (Strategy and Management) 4, no. 3 (1994): 119.

[63]Zheng Yu, "New Changes in the Russian Security Environment and Chinese-Russian Strategic Partnership Relations (in Chinese)," in *Guoji xingshi genxi baogao—1997-1998* (Study reports on the international situation 1997-1998)(Beijing: Zhanlue yu guanli chubanshe, 1998), 137.

Additionally, Zheng advocates that in the 21st century China should increase its cooperation with Russia and Northeast Asia "with a view to disintegrating American manipulation to improve Japanese-Russian relations and draw Russia closer to the American-Japanese position on the question of security in the Northeast Asian region."[64] Concerning economic factors, creating closer ties to Russia would also benefit China.

> From the long-term view, the massive energy development projects in the next century already agreed upon will be an important source of supply for China's even greater energy demands in the early 21st century. In the inevitable economic recovery which Russia will have in the early 21st century, China will be a great market unmatched by the West, either because of its geographical advantage or its consistent demand for the same product mix of Russian goods. The absorption by China of Siberian chemical, metallurgical and energy products will play a big role as a market to support the development of Russia's Eastern Region.

Zheng also points out that "China's participation in the development of Russia Far East oil and gas fields will have an important strategic significance in the next century."[65] Military affairs is a final area where China could profit from improved relations. Zheng argues, "In Chinese-Russian military cooperation, China should absorb and use Russian achievements in long-term research on American weapons and combat methods in order to serve China in its struggle in Taiwan and to exercise Chinese sovereignty in the South China Sea."[66]

Chinese analysts do point out troubles that exist in Sino-Russian relations, which could become hindrances to continued improvement, and a few authors have warned Moscow not to interfere in Taiwan or take other steps to harm China's interests. The Vice President of CIIS put forward three main problem areas in the bilateral ties:

---

[64]Ibid., 138.

[65]Ibid., 137.

[66]Ibid., 138.

• "There often appear comments in the Russian society and media that are not conducive to the bilateral relations; some extreme Russian nationalists also have made trouble in the bilateral relations time and again. They disseminate the theory that 'Russia is getting weaker and China is getting stronger,' or 'China is carrying out population and economic expansion toward Russia.' Some even openly exaggerate that 'the development of China has constituted threats to Russia.' They are deliberately making rifts in the bilateral relations."

• "In the boundary areas, the two countries have resolved 99 percent of the boundary issues, but still a small number of borders are not determined. Some regional forces and politicians are obstructing the boundary delimitation work."

• "The issue of Taiwan still remains an important issue affecting Sino-Russian relations. While actively expanding economic and trade relations and people-to-people exchanges with Russia, the Taiwan authorities also are attempting to seek official relations with Russia, to which some political forces in Russia have given certain responses."[67]

Other authors cite similar issues, but argue that the current trend of improving relations will outweigh the problems. Feng Yujun, an Assistant Research Professor in the Division for Russian and East Europe Studies at CICIR writes,

> Side by side with deepening bilateral relations, there has arisen an anti-China undercurrent in Russia, which spreads such allegations against China as "population invasion," "economic penetration," "military challenges," and "geostrategic contradictions." It has affected somewhat the expansion of bilateral relations. Yet this frenzy remains after all only a tributary and is mixed up with many factors of Russian domestic politics. The mainstream in Russia's China policy still considers China as a reliable partner and gives top priority in Russian foreign policy to the expansion of relations with China.[58]

---

[67]Shi Ze, "Lun xin shiqi de Zhong-E guanxi," 15.

[68]Feng Yujun, "Reflections on the Sino-Russian Strategic Partnership," *Contemporary International Relations* 8, no. 8 (August 1998): 8-9.

In general, Chinese analysts put forward very positive assessments of the current and future development of the two countries' relationship. For example, the settlement and removal of problems that existed between China and the Soviet Union, such as ideology and border disputes, have contributed to the improvement of Sino-Russian relations, as Shi Ze asserts: "Compared with the relations between China and the Soviet Union, which experienced ups and downs and even military confrontations . . . the relations between China and Russia have been showing a positive momentum of stable development and full dynamic."[69]

Other authors write about how Sino-Russian relations will contribute to regional stability and the world's multipolar development: "The expansion of Sino-Russian strategic cooperation has given an impetus to adjustments in major power relations and a strong stimulus to the tendency toward a multipolar world."[70] Li Zhongcheng of CICIR even predicts that these improved relations will be better than those China has with the United States:

> In the near future, China's ties with Russia will be much closer than with the United States . . . There exist no "natural" or "artificial" barriers to friendly cooperation between China and Russia; China shares more common views on major world issues with Russia than China shares with the United States and the United States shares with Russia; China and Russia both stick to the Five Principles of Peaceful Coexistence.[71]

MILITARY DEVELOPMENT

Chinese analysts often point to Russian military power as one of the key factors contributing to its continued existence as a major nation in the world and believe that in international affairs it will rely on its military strength while it copes with its domestic economic and political problems. However, the Russian military, while strong, still can not compare to that of the Soviet Union. One author writes about Russia's current force: "Its military power has declined and its defense capability has seriously weakened. . . . Russia

---

[69]Shi Ze, "Lun xinshiqi de Zhong-E guanxi," 1.

[70]Feng Yujun, "Reflections on the Sino-Russian Strategic Partnership," 3.

[71]Li Zhongcheng, "The Role of an Emerging China in World Politics," 12.

inherited most of the former Soviet army's weapons and equipment, but less than 20 percent of those meet the requirements of modernization; its military power has seriously weakened."[72]

A CICIR study stated, "Following the collapse of the Soviet Union and the fall in Russia's Comprehensive National Power, Russia's armed forces sank into a severe decline." It went on to sum up several problems Russia will have to deal with in its efforts to modernize and develop its military:

- "The largest difficulty currently facing the Russian military is that funds are seriously insufficient."
- "The serious shortage of funds greatly influences the Russian military's work in troop training, logistics supplies, equipment renewal, professionalizing troops, and other projects."
- "Troop replenishment difficulties have brought the Russian military one disaster after another. Because of unrest in the Russian political situation and the low level of the troops' social position and living wages, young people's enthusiasm for participating in the military is universally low, and evading military service is extremely common."
- "Various objective factors are causing a sharp rise in the crime rate in the Russian armed forces."
- "In the war in Chechnya, the Russian military revealed that its command coordination was not at its best, its coordinated fighting was in chaos, its information reconnaissance was sluggish, its logistics safeguards were lacking, it had low officer-soldier morale, and there were many other weak points."[73]

However, according to the study, Russia's military reforms may speed up because of its problems in Chechnya, which "critically influenced Russia's military reform process," even though Russia still "lacks a clear military reform strategy." Failures during the war in Chechnya resulted in much

---

[72]Li Haoyu, "Shixi E'Luosi de guojia anquan zhanlue," 24.

[73]Wang Lijiu and Liu Guiling, eds., *Kua shiji de E'Luosi*, 285-289.

attention from Russia's highest decisionmaking levels, so that the entire plan for military reforms is also being "tensely deliberated and drafted."[74]

One area of Russia's military force that Chinese analysts assess as balancing these inadequacies is its arsenal of nuclear weapons. "On the one hand, Russia is still a major nuclear power and the second largest military power in the world; on the other hand, the shortage of military funds, the slow renewal of equipment and the irregular training have greatly lowered the Russian army's effectiveness."[75] Chinese authors point out that, "given the fact that Russian national power has dramatically declined and its conventional forces have been reduced on a large scale," Russia has no choice but to "stress the deterrent role played by the nuclear force in safeguarding its national security."[76] A *People's Daily* article stated,

> Russia, not reconciled to having been reduced to a "second-class country," tries hard to restore its status as a big country with its "nuclear shield." . . . After beginning to expand eastward, NATO has steadily closed in on Russia, and Russia has been reduced to an inferior position with regard to the balance between Russia and Western countries in conventional military forces. Thus, Russia should all the more attach importance to the nuclear weapons in its hands.

The article predicts that Russia will invest heavily in the development of nuclear technology so that it will retain its military power:

> To balance its nuclear weapons with those of the United States, Russia has still allocated a huge sum of money, despite its financial straits, in order to accelerate development of the "White Poplar M" intercontinental guided missiles. This year, Russia will deploy this new kind of guided missile to replace gradually the SS-25 powered intercontinental ballistic guided missiles. Russia is also developing a new series of fourth-generation nuclear submarines called "God of the North Wind," and the first modern nuclear

---

[74]Ibid., 289, 295.

[75]Wang Rui and Zhang Wei, "A Preliminary Analysis of Russian Military Strategy," 42.

[76]Ibid., 40-41.

submarine, named "Dorglooge," will be put into use between 2000 and 2003.[77]

A particularly negative assessment of Russia's military capabilities was put forward by Shen Jiru, Director of the International Strategic Research Section of the Institute of World Economics and Politics at CASS. He also believes that Russia's only option is to rely on its nuclear forces. He writes:

> Few Russian army divisions are completely equipped nowadays. As its navy cannot even afford fuel, its aircraft carriers have had to be sold as scrap metal. Under these circumstances, Russia can only barely manage to keep up its nuclear forces, but nothing else. Russian military personages have said that, in the future, Russia will have to be more and more reliant on nuclear forces. Therefore, in conducting any future military activities, Russia has lost the possibility of making choices. As far as Russia is concerned, it either fights or does not fight. But if the latter is chosen, it is very probable that it will have to use nuclear weapons, because any other weapons link for Russia is now incomplete. Russia would be unable to operate militarily in a normal way due to financial problems as well as a shortage of military staff. Frankly, it just lacks the material base to adopt any strategy and tactics which would escalate step by step.[78]

Despite Russia's weakened military force, Chinese analysts emphasize that it still is quite powerful when compared to that of other countries. According to Chinese assessments, Russia currently has the second most powerful military in the world after the United States, and in the short term no other country will be able to surpass it. For example, Yan Xuetong of CICIR writes, "Russia's superiority over China, Japan, and Germany in the areas of nuclear and conventional weaponry . . . can be preserved until early next century."[79]

---

[77]Tang Jinxiu, "Contest and Compromise Between Russia and the United States Over Nuclear Disarmament," *Renmin Ribao* (People's Daily), March 17, 1998, 6, in FBIS-CHI-98-083, March 25, 1998.

[78]Hsu Tao-chen, "United States Still Makes Old Mistakes, Exclusive interview with Shen Jiru."

[79]Yan Xuetong, *Zhongguo guojia liyi fenxi* (An analysis of China's national interests)(Tianjin: Tianjin renmin chubanshe, 1996), 55.

A comparison of the military power of six countries, done by Colonel Huang Shuofeng of AMS in 1996 as part of a study on CNP, found that Russia's military power was 67 percent of the U.S. score, a major decline from the assessment of the Soviet Union's military power by Huang in 1990, when it was 99.6 percent of the U.S. score.[80] However, Huang points out, "Although Russia currently has numerous economic difficulties, the progress of its armed forces reforms is uneven, its national defense expenditures have actually decreased by around 45 percent, and it has suffered a disastrous decline from its position as a military superpower to a very large extent; it can be said that Russia is a military power that is second only to the United States, and it is second only to the United States in terms of the highest military expenditures." China accordingly, still falls behind Russia in military power. Based on Huang's calculations, in 1996, China's military power score was 77.7 percent of the Russian score. In strategic weaponry, China's score was only 0.4 percent of Russia's; in national defense expenditures, China scored 8.7 percent; and in average national defense expenditures per person and annual per capita defense expenditures, China's scores were 4.7 percent and 1.0 percent, respectively.[81]

"SECRET" RMA EFFORTS

As Russia assumes its place as one of the five poles in the multipolar structure, Chinese military analysts believe Russia will also be exploiting the RMA, probably ahead of the declining United States. Two officers at AMS, authors of *America, Russia, and the Revolution in Military Affairs*, describe Russia's fall from its "superpower pinnacle" as the reason Moscow "temporarily will be unable to compete with the United States in this new RMA." They add: "In the new RMA tide that is currently rising in the world, the United States without a doubt is in the central position that is the focus of attention." However, they contend that several factors favor a surprise, and Russia may do better at the RMA than the United States: "Because military power has

---

[80]Huang Shuofeng, *Guojia shengshuai lun* (On the rise and fall of nations)(Changsha: Hunan Press, 1996): 405, and Huang Shuofeng, *Zonghe guoli lun* (On comprehensive national power) (Beijing: Zhongguo shehui kexue chubanshe, 1992): 218.

[81]Huang, *Guojiashengshuai lun*, 496.

today become practically the only pillar supporting Russia's position as a major nation, its strategists will place top priority on using the new RMA to maintain its military superiority in a position of top priority in its national strategy. Currently it is secretly taking aim at America's commanding position in the new RMA and actively planning, preparing, and carrying out the new RMA."[82] The orthodox view seems to be that Russia will achieve sustained growth after 2005, and recovery suggests to PLA authors that Moscow will be able to exploit the RMA rapidly, which would enhance Russian military power.

Russian military specialists invited to AMS find their works quoted favorably in Chinese journals.[83] Even though "up to now [Moscow] still has not completely implemented a new RMA plan . . . this does not indicate that the figures in Russia's military and political leadership and military doctrinal circles lack a full understanding and urgent desire regarding the RMA; also, it does not mean that Russia is willingly allowing its former opponent to get far ahead in the spring tide of this new RMA . . . they are trying to prepare for the future when Russia will enter the period when it completely carries out the new RMA."[84] Despite its current economic weakness, Chinese analysts such as Gao Chunxiang of AMS see that, "Russia's high-level military and political leadership continually make speeches on issues related to the RMA . . . [and] draw lessons from the new technology the United States needs to develop the RMA." The place in Russia where this is done is "the General Staff Military Academy and other military learning organizations." The Chinese are aware

---

[82]Zhu Xiaoli and Zhao Xiaozhuo, *Mei-E xin junshi geming*, 2.

[83]The views of General Vladimir Slipchenko, of the Russian Academy of Military Science, were suggested in *Komsomolskaya Pravda* October 15, 1996. He said that new weapons based on new physical principles "will form the basis of many states' armed forces in 10 to 15 years time. . . . Explosives are currently being developed which will be 30 to 50 times more destructive . . . . The main attack element will be five to eight times faster then sound air- and sea-launched cruise missiles . . . military lasers will be used to disable military space systems. . . . By directing energy emission at a target it is possible to turn an enemy division into a herd of frightened idiots . . . electromagnetic weapons . . . ionizing (plasma) weapons . . . our 'likely friends' in the West and the East are developing new weapons and means of employing them. Is Russia ready to take up the challenge of the times?" According to interviews conducted in Beijing for this study, Chinese military officers are now studying at advanced Russian military institutes, where they become aware of Russian views.

[84]Zhu Xiaoli and Zhao Xiaozhuo, *Mei-E xin junshi geming*, 139.

that Russian doctrine "points out that national defense research and development must first focus on developing new deep-strike weapons, information weapons, and electronic warfare equipment." Moreover, they know the Russian military is "putting forward concepts about 21st century Russian military structure and has already made public 'The Russian Military's Ten-Year Weaponry Development Long-Term Plan' and 'Twenty-First Century Soldier Equipment Plan.' "[85] Li Qinggong, a Research Fellow at CIISS, writes,

> With the introduction of the program of "three-phased military reform," Russia has begun to speed up the process of the new military revolution, with an even clearer objective, i.e., carrying out the professionalization of the armed forces, enhancing military scientific research, updating equipment on a large scale, and restoring its position as a major military power. To achieve this goal, Russia on the one hand is adjusting its military structure and reorganizing its military industries, and on the other hand is increasing its input in the development of military high technology, updating its nuclear force and promoting its conventional force. In order to deal with future information warfare, Russia specially held a roundtable meeting, which introduced the "doctrine of information security" and decided to step up its development of information weapons so as to achieve a "new balance of power."[56]

IMPLICATIONS OF THE SOVIET COLLAPSE

As noted in the Preface, Chinese "debates" about the security environment are quite different in style and content from the debates of Western scholars and public commentators. Debates about Russia have been particularly sensitive and secretive in the two decades since the death of Chairman Mao.

According to interviews in China, these past debates remain relevant and not all issues in them have been fully resolved. A secretive debate on the character of the USSR was carried out in the mid-1970s through allegorical references to Chinese ancient history by authors using pseudonyms for the individuals or groups involved. The authors pretended to hold "harmless"

---

[85]Gao Chunxiang, ed., *Xin junshi geming lun*,196.

[86]Li Qinggong, "Current International Military Security Situation," 10-11.

historical debates. Only after the deaths of Mao Zedong and Zhou Enlai and the subsequent arrest of the Gang of Four did China reveal that the allegorical debates had directly involved Politburo members. Apparently they instigated the scholars' attack on the policies of their political opponents using ancient historical figures in allegory.[87] From 1978 to 1982, a second debate on the USSR was also largely concealed. The result of the second debate was a sharp reduction in China's assessment of a Soviet military threat.[88]

The collapse of the Communist Party in the Soviet Union jolted China. China's leaders had difficulty maintaining their claim that socialism was a superior system that would eventually replace capitalism. Consequently, in the early nineties, a debate ensued over the causes of the collapse and the implications for China. In the first phase of the debate, from 1991-92, the United States was assessed to be completely responsible for the collapse of the Soviet Union through a process of containment and ideological subversion called "peaceful evolution." However, this view was overturned in the second stage of "scholarly" debate in 1992-93.[89]

AMERICAN SUBVERSION?

Close examination of Chinese commentary from 1990 to 1992 indicates a veiled debate took place among various institutes and individuals about the causes of the Soviet disintegration and its consequences for Chinese communism. The debates were initially restricted to internally circulated journals. Using an old Mao quotation, an initial explanation was attributed to an American strategy, dating back to John Foster Dulles, known by the characters for "peaceful evolution." An early assertion of this cause of the Soviet collapse appeared in Hong Kong in December 1991 in a newspaper affiliated with the People's Republic of China (PRC):

---

[87]See Michael Pillsbury, "Sino-American Security Ties: The View from Moscow, Tokyo and Beijing," *International Security* 1, no. 4 (Spring 1977): 124-142.

[88]Gilbert Rozman, *The Chinese Debate About Soviet Socialism*.

[89]For a review of several U.S. books on why the Soviet Union collapsed, see Lawrence G. Kelley, "Gorbachev and Beyond: An Empire Transforming?" *Parameters* 28, no. 3 (Autumn 1998): 141-149.

> The strategy of peaceful evolution created an opportunity for foreign forces, lead by United States, to meddle in, interfere with, and eventually dominate the political and economic affairs of the Soviet Union, and opened the door for them to impose their own political, economic and social values.[90]

Its author provides an explicit warning for China when he adds, "It is fair to say that without overt or covert support from the United States, the disintegration of the Soviet Union could not have been realized, nor could it have been achieved so successfully and so precipitously."

According to the "peaceful evolution" strategy, the levers the United States used against the former Soviet Union (and which would apply to China) were trade, economic cooperation, technology transfer, diplomacy, cultural and educational exchanges, religious freedom, and so on. Another scholar estimates that the West enjoyed a superiority in these "weapons." By the mid-1980s, the estimated advantage that the Western countries enjoyed over the socialist countries in material terms was calculated by the Chinese to be 3:1. However, in terms of mass media, the advantage was calculated to exceed 20:1. The analyst argued that Western countries have employed electronic media as a weapon to infiltrate socialist countries and disintegrate them.[91] One internal speech by a Chinese leader warns,

> In the wake of traumatic changes in Eastern Europe and the August 19 coup in the Soviet Union, the task of countering peaceful evolution has become ever tougher. The developed countries headed by the United States attempt to conquer the whole world in terms of ideology, imposing such Western values as democracy, freedom and human rights . . . they have already caused revolts in the Soviet Union and Eastern Europe. Now they naturally would target China.[92]

---

[90] *Ta Kung Pao* (Hong Kong), December 28, 1991.

[91] Wang Jiafu, "Strategic Analysis of the Internal Factors Affecting Traumatic Change in the Soviet Union," *Soviet Social Science Research*, no. 1 (1992): 2.

[92] Cited in Zhang Jialin, *China's Response to the Downfall of Communism in Eastern Europe and the Soviet Union*.

According to interviews conducted by the author, a book entitled *Western Politicians on Peaceful Evolution* contains articles warning about the American subversive strategy for dealing with China after the June 1989 Tiananmen breakdown.

MOSCOW'S OWN FAULT

The second thesis about the collapse of the Soviet Union was argued by Liu Keming, the former chief of the Liaison Department of China's Central Committee. Liu, a leading Soviet expert, criticized Mikhail Gorbachev's "new thinking" and his personality.[93] In Liu's view, when Gorbachev introduced a multiparty system and separation of powers, he completely negated 70 years of Soviet political structure and brought an end to the Communist Party in power. Gorbachev was a negative example for China; thus Liu asserts that China should avoid:

• The adoption of a multiparty system, which abandoned the leading role of the Communist Party
• A pluralist ideology, in which Marxist-Leninism no longer formed the only ideological foundation
• Talk of democratic socialism rather than communism as the final goal of the party
• Rejection of democratic central control of the Communist Party and its transformation into a loose political organization tolerating overt factions.

Liu's thesis holds that the neglect of politics and ideology by the Soviet leadership, together with Gorbachev's political errors and widespread corruption (including the bribery case of Leonid Brezhnev's son-in-law), all caused the downfall.

By mid-1992, however, a new analysis emerged. Scholars presenting this analysis challenged the idea of Western imperialists pushing peaceful evolution in the Soviet Union. If they had been at it since the 1940s, why did

---

[93]Liu Keming, "The New Thinking of Mikhail Gorbachev's Reform," *Soviet Social Science Research*, no. 1, (1992): 1.

it not succeed until the late 1980s? They asked how hostile international forces could peacefully subvert a 20-million-member Soviet Communist Party without encountering any resistance. Professor Luo Zhaohong, of the Institute of World Economics and Politics at CASS, directly criticizes the effort to blame Gorbachev alone for the Soviet disintegration. He also attacks the notion of peaceful evolution, arguing that foreign involvement could never play a significant role in the Soviet collapse. Professor Luo puts forward the view that it was an excess of Stalinism and poor budgetary management and errors in economic policy that caused the Soviet collapse.[94] According to Chinese analysts, the logic of the "peaceful evolution" thesis began to be attacked by many analysts in the second phase of the 1990-1992 debate.[95] For one thing, not a single American soldier had entered the Soviet Union. Chinese analysts instead suggest that problems such as agriculture were ignored; the ethnic issue was mishandled; and the Soviets were overcommitted, especially with the invasion of Afghanistan and generous aid to Cuba. In general, they said, economic factors were key to the collapse.

In an interesting twist, the new argument held that stagnation and isolation had caused the Soviet system to fall behind, along with its highly centralized planning and an excessive military budget. The implication of this diagnosis was that if China could avoid highly centralized planning, excess defense spending, and isolation, then China could also avoid the fate of the Soviet Union. Professor Luo Zhaohong also criticizes the economic theory of the Soviet Union because it left out of its theoretical foundation notions of value, profit, and competition and it overemphasized state-owned enterprises, which had no autonomy and had their production geared to an arbitrary state plan rather than market commands. This, he concludes, destroyed the vitality of enterprises and hampered the quantity and quality of production. There were no incentives to innovate. Technological progress and competition with the West were impossible.[96]

---

[94]Luo Zhaohong, "Disintegration of the Soviet Union and its Impact on the World Economic and Political Landscape" (in Chinese), *Shijie jingji yu zhengzhi* (World Economics and Politics), no. 10 (1992), 1. The author interviewed Professor Luo in January 1998.

[95]See Zhang Jialin, *China's Response*.

[96]Luo Zhaohong, "Disintegration of the Soviet Union," 5.

Professor Luo estimates the Soviet defense budget to have been at 20 to 25 percent of the GNP at the time of the USSR collapse, and almost all the research efforts of the Soviet industrial base served the military. He quotes former Soviet Prime Minister Nikolai Ryzhkov in saying that 75 percent of the government research and development budget had been appropriated for alternate use, and that the military share of electronics was as much as 50 percent. Thus Luo concludes that because the Soviet GNP was one-third that of the U.S. GNP, maintaining strategic parity with strategic weapons and surpassing the United States in conventional forces put an unbearable burden on the Soviet economy. The Chinese quote Gorbachev's admission in a speech in February 1981: "This is the most militarized economy in the world."[97]

Gorbachev's personality and policies may have accelerated the economic collapse, but in the Chinese view, decades of overly centralized planning and excessive military expenditures were the root causes of the collapse. The gap between American and Soviet living standards was 10 to 1, according to Chinese calculations, with the per capita GNP in the Soviet Union as low as about $2,000.

The conclusions for China of this new thesis were not that "peaceful evolution" should be cut off by seclusion and isolation from Western cultural influences; rather, the issues would be successful management of the economy to maintain ever higher living standards, further devolution of planning toward a market economy, and efforts to continue technological progress. After nearly 2 years of debate, in what seems to be a tradition in this policy process, a major conference was held in Beijing in May 1992. The record was published in the journal *World Economics and Politics*. An important element in this policy process was a statement made by Deng Xiaoping during his tour of Southern China in early 1992. In remarks conveyed through intermediaries, Deng supposedly said, "A planned economy does not equal socialism." Whether something is socialist or capitalist, Deng pointed out, depends on whether it will benefit the living standards of the people. He criticized anyone

---

[97]Liu Keming, "Formation, Development and Major Lessons of the Militarization of the Soviet Economy," *Soviet Studies*, no. 3 (1992): 6.

who opposed foreign capital investment in China or joint ventures with foreigners as "ignorant" and "lacking common sense."[98]

FINDINGS

Russia and the Soviet Union have always been a subject of debate in China. For example, in the 1970s and 1980s there were disagreements about the extent of the Soviet threat, while in the early 1990s a major debate ensued over the causes of the collapse of the USSR and its implications for China. Today, Chinese analysts see the Soviet decline as a cautionary tale but generally speaking they regard Russia with sympathy. In spite of its current extensive problems, Chinese analysts "officially" continue to portray the future role of Russia as one of the five equal poles that will shape the coming world balance of power. They forecast that its decline will eventually end, and that Russia will increase its military power by exploiting the RMA in advance of other nations. Although Russia's inevitable recovery and position as a pole are commonly accepted by Chinese analysts, what will happen to the country during the transition to a multipolar world is the subject of conflicting points of view. Authors recognize that Russia will continue to have economic, political, and social instability. What they disagree upon is how long the turmoil will prevail. Additionally, most analysts discuss the numerous threats to Russia's future security environment, but they differ in how they view its response to these dangers.

Chinese authors do not foresee Russia's severe crises and decline in CNP preventing it from assuming its position as a pole, because they emphasize that the framework of its former power and status still exists, and it has potential for future development. Some authors argue that promoting relations with China would be a way for Russia to improve its current circumstances. Not only would it be helped by strengthened economic ties to China, but a strategic partnership would also be a means for counterbalancing the dangers to its security environment, particularly by providing a counterweight to NATO eastward expansion.

It is Russia's past efforts and its future abilities to deal with serious threats from the U.S. and NATO that are the main subjects of debate about Russia.

---

[98] *Liaowang,* no. 7 (1993): 1.

Some analysts see Russia as passive and relatively powerless against NATO efforts to infringe upon the former Soviet sphere of influence. They point out that Russia has already lost Poland, Hungary, and Czechoslovakia to NATO and do not foresee that Russia will do much better at thwarting new Western aggression in the near term. The real threat to Russia's security would occur if NATO decided to infiltrate the Baltic states and particularly Central Asia, where the goal of the West is not only to contain Russia's power but also to obtain oil and gas. There have even been warnings that if Russia does not prevent these incursions, it could lose its foundation for becoming a pole. However, other analysts see Russia adopting countermeasures against U.S. and NATO policies that are commensurate with its current power and indicative of future influence.

Chinese discussions of Russian military strength tend to fall into two categories—those that focus on the negative aspects of its current status, and those that make positive predictions about the future. When assessing the Russian military today, many authors examine its numerous weaknesses, although its arsenal of nuclear weapons is often considered to balance some of its inadequacies. More optimistic assessments are made about Russian military affairs, when analysts examine the country's development potential. In particular, some authors assert that as Russia assumes its place as a pole, it will be developing the RMA, probably ahead of the declining United States. Analysts argue that its current military power is the key factor contributing to its continued existence as a major nation in the world, consequently the country will give priority to promoting the RMA. The belief is that once Russia inevitably overcomes its problems, gradual sustained growth will allow it to be able to rapidly exploit the RMA, enhancing both its military strength, as well as its overall CNP.

Senior Colonel Luo Yuan (left), son of Premier Zhou Enlai's intelligence director, and Senior Colonel Zhai Zhigang (right), who has analyzed U.S. weaknesses in the Persian Gulf War, are seen here standing at the entrance to the Academy of Military Science in Beijing.

Senior Colonel Huang Shuofeng of the Strategy Department, Academy of Military Science, is the author of the first book published on the key concept of Comprehensive National Power, which estimates that the rate of growth of Chinese national power will remain double that of the United States. In an interview with *Liberation Army Daily* on June 10, 1999, he stated that China has risen from number 20 in terms of Comprehensive National Power in 1950 to number 6 in 1999.

General Xiong Guangkai (center), Chairman of the China Institute of International Strategic Studies and PLA Deputy Chief of Staff for Intelligence. Writing in April 1998, he observed, "Any efforts for seeking hegemony and world domination can only result in accumulating contradictions and fermenting war." Dr. Chu Shulong (right), who served as Director of North American Studies at the China Institute of Contemporary International Relations, wrote in a June 1999 article, "In the U.S. Defense Department and the intelligence departments, there are a number of experts, strategists, and government officials who fabricate and publish all kinds of 'reports,' and stir up all kinds of 'cases' for which there is no factual evidence, in order to create strategic opinion for the 'China threat.'" The author, Michael Pillsbury, is seen at the left.

Liu Huaqiu (center) is Director of the State Council Foreign Affairs Bureau, Beijing's equivalent to the National Security Adviser to the President of the United States. Liu Shaoming (second from right) is deputy chief of the Chinese Embassy in Washington. Shen Qurong (left) is President of the China Institute of Contemporary International Relations. Shen noted in an article published in September 1996, "A military revolution (RMA) is underway. . . . the London-based International Institute for Strategic Studies says that along with the advance of this revolution, some small and medium-size nations will no longer be condemned to a perpetual inferior position relative to the Western world."

Senior Colonel Wang Baocun (right) of the Department of Foreign Military Studies, Academy of Military Science, has published a number of articles on information warfare. He is shown here with the former U.S. defense attaché to China, Admiral Eric McVadon, at Beijing's Fourth International Sun Zi Conference in October 1998.

Qin Lizheng, Secretary General of the China Futures Research Society, seen in his office at the Chinese Academy of Social Sciences.

193

Senior Colonel Zhu Chenghu is the Deputy Director of the Institute of National Security Studies at the PLA National Defense University. In June 1998, Zhu wrote that "Although the Asia-Pacific region has been relatively stable since the end of the Cold War, there are also many uncertainties there. If certain hot-spot problems are not handled properly they may cause conflicts, confrontations, and even war in this region, thus wrecking the peace, stability, and prosperity of the region."

Senior Colonel Chen Xiaogong is a well-known author whose articles have appeared in the journal of the China Institute of International Strategic Studies. He serves in a key role in PLA intelligence as director of the assessment and analysis division. In 1991, he said, "It is certain that the five major powers will be the focus of the world, but the relative strengths of the various poles will be unbalanced."

Yao Yunzhu, a senior colonel in the Foreign Military Studies Department at the Academy of Military Science, wrote in the Winter 1995 issue of the *Korean Journal of Defense Analysis* that there have been "heated debates" inside the PLA about the "international environment, the real and potential threats China will face, the kinds of wars that China is likely to be engaged in, and the ways and means to fight such wars." She concluded, "It would be too early to conclude that the PLA has abandoned its traditional doctrine altogether. . . . Most Chinese military analysts consider that the changes made so far are compatible with traditional doctrine, at least with the basic ideas it embodies. People's War and Active Defense are still directing the Chinese PLA in its long march toward modernization."

This office building in downtown Beijing houses most of the research institutes of the Chinese Academy of Social Sciences.

The "Book City" Building near Beijing University sells titles about the future distributed by major Chinese publishing companies.

Headquarters of the Commission on Science, Technology and Industry for National Defense in Beijing. Recently reorganized, the commission coordinates the defense industry complex and supports numerous institutes to assess the future.

Beijing headquarters of the PLA-sponsored China Institute of International Strategic Studies, chaired by General Xiong Guangkai.

195

Yang Dazhou, formerly of New China News Agency, now is an author at the Institute of American Studies, Chinese Academy of Social Sciences. Yang's June 1997 article in the journal *Peace and Development* challenged the views of the orthodox strategists in several ways. He criticized the view that a multipolar world structure is "already" restraining American hegemony. Instead, Yang stated the United States is the only global "pole," that China is not yet a "pole," and that three decades may be needed for a true multipolar power balance to develop.

Senior Colonel Wu Rusong, Academy of Military Science division chief for ancient military doctrines, is the author of many books and articles on Sun Zi's *Art of War.*

General Li Jijun has written that during the Persian Gulf War U.S. forces demonstrated many weaknesses. He argued that, "If the adversary of the United States was not Iraq, if the battle was not fought on the flat desert, if the Iraqi armed forces struck first during the phase when the U.S. Armed Forces were still assembling, or if Iraqi armed forces withdrew suddenly before U.S. Forces struck, then the outcome of the war might have been quite different."

The China Society for Strategy and Management, on the grounds of the former U.S. legation in Beijing, publishes a journal known for thoughtful articles on nationalistic themes, such as Zhang Wenmu's prediction that the United States will try to separate Tibet from China to gain access to oil supplies from Central Asia.

Beijing headquarters of the China Institute of International Studies, sponsored by the Foreign Ministry and headed by Ambassador Yang Chengxu. The historic building was formerly the embassy of Austria.

Senior Colonel Wu Chunqiu of the Strategy Department, Academy of Military Science, is the author of articles on grand strategy and the concept of Comprehensive National Power. He wrote, "China's wise ancient strategists never advocated relying only on military power to conquer the enemy, but emphasized combining military power with the nonmilitary power related to war in order to get the upper hand."

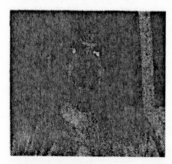

Wang Jisi is Director of the Chinese Academy of Social Sciences, Institute of American Studies, one of several institutions that analyze U.S. Affairs. The institute also publishes a journal, *Meiguo yanjiu* (American Studies). Educated at Oxford, he has published many articles on American foreign policy, U.S.-China relations, and U.S. strategy toward China.

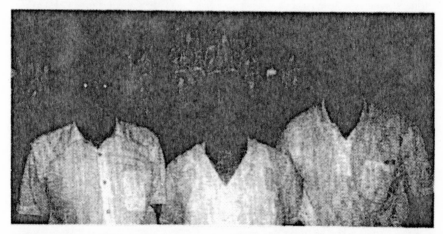

Chang Mengxiong (left) was senior engineer of the Beijing Institute of System Engineering of the Commission on Science, Technology and Industry for National Defense. Gao Heng (center) is the founder of the Institute of Grand Strategy and a well-known scholar at the Institute of World Economy and Politics, Chinese Academy of Social Sciences. Gao pioneered studies of multipolarity in 1986. In a more recent article in the journal *21st Century*, he wrote that if the United States and Japan intervene to protect an independent Taiwan, a major war will occur and will escalate, with "global and historic implications." On the right is Senior Colonel Wang Zhongchun of the Institute of National Security Studies, National Defense University, Beijing, who has authored several books on the United States.

General Yao Youzhi became Director of the Strategy Department of the Academy of Military Science in 1998. He is also the Secretary General of the Sun Zi Society and has written many articles on ancient military thought. In the summer 1999 issue of *China Military Science* he concluded, "The U.S. bombing of Yugoslavia and the Chinese Embassy in Belgrade challenges the global trend toward multipolarity."

Lieutenant General Liu Jingsong (center) was President of the Academy of Military Science and the former commander of Lanzhou and Shenyang Military Regions on the border with Russia. In a 1997 issue of *National Defense University Journal*, he advised, "Surprise and dominating the enemy by striking first are effective combat methods for seizing battlefield initiative, particularly when weaponry is inferior. Not only can you upset the enemy's war plan and operational preparations, you can strengthen the combat effectiveness of our own army's trump cards (shashoujian)." At right is Senior Colonel Peng Guangqian of the Academy of Military Science Strategy Department, who, in August 1999, stated in *Liberation Army Daily* that Taiwan President Li Denghui is "a test-tube baby manufactured by the West." The author is seen at the left.

Dr. Yan Xuetong is Director of the South and Southeast Asia Division, China Institute of Contemporary International Relations, and the author of a book on how to analyze national interests as well as co-editor of a book on the security environment facing a rising China. He has a doctorate from the University of California at Berkeley and is a frequent visitor to the United States. His chart on the probability of war between China and the United States in the next 10 years appears on page xli of this book.

Beijing headquarters of the China Institute of Contemporary International Relations, which has a staff of 500, a public journal, and its own press. It is sponsored by the State Council and Ministry of State Security. The Vice President of the institute, Song Baoxian (second from left), and Japan specialist Liu Jiangyong (left) welcome the author and Colonel Greg Man, USA (third from right), and his wife, Shirley Kan, from the U.S. Congressional Research Service.

Major General Pan Junfeng serves as director of the
Foreign Military Studies Department, Academy of Military
Science. Fluent in Japanese, he wrote in *China Military
Science*, "We can make the enemy's command centers not
work by changing their data system. We can cause the
enemy's headquarters to make incorrect judgments
by sending disinformation. We can dominate the enemy's
banking system and even its entire social order."

Senior Colonel Zhang Zhaozhong is director of the science
and technology teaching and research section at the PLA
National Defense University. Hong Kong's newspaper
Ta Kong Pao in May 1999 called him China's "leading
military commentator." In an interview he said, "The next
10 to 15 years will be the most difficult and most important
period in China's development. The United States has
already realized that this is the best period for containing
China. During this period, therefore, the United States
may devise all kinds of ways to cause trouble." Zhang
added, "The United States at present does not have the gall
to take the initiative in attacking China's territory. But we
must be vigilant."

The Shanghai Institute for International Studies occupies a modern building. The American
studies co-director, Yang Jiemian, is seen standing in the front row (second from left) next to
the author and U.S. specialist Ding Xinghao. The institute publishes journals, books, and an
annual review of world politics

Huan Xiang, national security adviser to Deng Xiaoping, wrote in 1986, "As the world moves toward a multipolar . . . five pole world, when the United States and the Soviet Union are considering problems, they must think about the China factor, and also the other poles." Japan, he continued, "not only wants to strive to be on equal footing with the United States economically and politically, but further, it is deliberately planning, when the time is ripe, to surpass the United States and replace America's world economic hegemony. Having economic hegemony, then political and military hegemony, would not be too difficult." In 1985 Huam listed four technologies for a technological revolution in military affairs: precision-guided tactical weapons, long-range strategic vehicles, a system formed by satellite communications and reconnaissance, and rapid and comprehensive data processing with computers.

He Xin, the author of several best-selling books, has written, "The world situation, after the severe changes in the Soviet Union and Eastern Europe, in form actually appears amazingly similar to the situation in the latter period of the Warring States, where there were six powerful countries facing each other and one country dominating. . . . In the early period [of the Warring States era], the six countries 'joined horizontally,' and for a number of decades effectively resisted the powerful Qin threat. However, in the later period, one after another they accepted Qin protection and were willing to become its satellite countries. The result was their collapse in 10 years. They were each destroyed by the Qin threat. . . . It is now necessary to form a modern strategy of 'joining horizontally'. . . . China must seek allies among all countries that could become America's potential opponents today or in the future."

Lieutenant General Richard A. Chilcoat, USA, President of the National Defense University (center), is shown here escorting his Chinese counterpart, Lieutenant General Xing Shizhong (left), during a visit to Nellis Air Force Base, Nevada, as part of a tour of U.S. military installations conducted under the Memorandum of Cooperation and Reciprocal Relations. At right is Major General Gong Xianfu, the PRC defense attaché to the United States.

5: GEOPOLITICAL POWER CALCULATIONS

A UNIQUE ASPECT OF CHINA'S STRATEGIC ASSESSMENTS of the future security environment is the "scientific" method used to predict power relations among the major nations. Chinese ancient statecraft from the Warring States era focused on how a wise leader made strategy according to the power of his state. Sun Zi warned that the outcome of war depends on the correct assessment of power through calculations and estimates of enemy strengths and weaknesses. Consequently, more so than most Western futurists, Chinese authors want to forecast the future international status hierarchy. The means by which they make such strategic assessments is through the measurement and comparison of Comprehensive National Power (CNP).

CNP (*zonghe guoli*) refers to the combined overall conditions and strengths of a country in numerous areas. During the Cold War and the U.S.-Soviet confrontation, a nation's power was largely determined by military force, but in the current transition period, as the world moves toward multipolarity, military might is no longer the main defining factor of strength. Instead, elements such as economics and science and technology have become increasingly important in the competition for power and influence in the world. An evaluation of current and future strength requires the inclusion of a variety of factors, such as territory, natural resources, military force, economic power, social conditions, domestic government, foreign policy, and international influence. CNP is the aggregate of all these factors, as Deng

Xiaoping stated: "In measuring a country's national power, one must look at it comprehensively and from all sides."[1]

Chinese assessments of CNP are done both qualitatively, in general discussions of country strengths and weaknesses, as well as quantitatively, through the use of formulas to calculate numerical values of CNP. China's forecasts of CNP reject using gross national product (GNP) indexes or the measurement methods of national power used in the United States. Instead, Chinese analysts have developed their own extensive index systems and equations for assessing CNP. It will be seen that their analytical methods are not traditional Marxist-Leninist dogma or Western social science but something unique to China.

Several assessments of the current and future CNP of a number of nations are provided in this chapter, including estimations of the rank order in the future security environment of 2010 and 2020. The conflicting findings reflect the differences seen in chapters 1 and 2 about both the rate at which the world is moving toward multipolarity and the rate of decline of U.S. national power. For example, of the 20 authors introduced in this section, some authors write, "It is certain that the five major powers will be the focus of the world, but the relative strengths of the various poles will be unbalanced,"[2] while others emphasize, "The strength and political gaps among the five powers are gradually getting closer."[3] This "debate" about CNP is also important to analysts of the RMA, because knowing a nation's CNP can determine which side will win a war and which side will better implement an RMA.[4] To sum up, the future CNP scores for major powers can help identify:

---

[1] Deng Xiaoping, quoted in *Renmin Ribao* (People's Daily), February 26, 1990, quoted in Huang Shuofeng, *Zonghe guoli lun* (On comprehensive national power)(Beijing: Zhongguo shehui kexue chubanshe, 1992), 7.

[2] Chen Xiaogong, "The World Strategic Pattern in the 1990s," *International Strategic Studies* 19, no. 1 (March 1991): 7.

[3] Yan Xuetong and Li Zhongcheng, "Zhanwang xia shiji chu guoji zhengzhi" (A perspective on international politics in the early next century), *Xiandai guoji guanxi* (Contemporary International Relations) 92, no. 6 (June 1997).

[4] According to Li Qingshan, "Through the analysis of belligerent countries' Comprehensive National Power, even before a war has begun, people frequently can know the results in

- The status hierarchy in world politics
- The power of potential rivals and potential partners
- Who will best exploit the RMA
- Which side will win a war.

Although numerous authors make predictions about future CNP, few provide detailed accounts about the measurement and evaluation process. This chapter focuses on two studies that contain elaborate descriptions of how their assessments were conducted, and which represent the orthodox and reform views. After the following overview of the two abovementioned studies, the chapter is divided into four main sections:

- The origins of the concept of CNP under Deng Xiaoping, and its historical antecedents in Chinese ancient statecraft
- Qualitative analysis of CNP as viewed from a variety of disciplines
- Methods for quantitatively assessing CNP
- The estimates made by several Chinese authors about the current and future rank order of the major powers.

ORTHODOX VERSUS REFORM

To illustrate how China assesses CNP, the findings of two books published by the Academy of Military Science (AMS) are contrasted with those of a book by the civilian Chinese Academy of Social Sciences (CASS). The publications of both institutes use premises established by Deng Xiaoping 15 years ago, and some of the authors were apparently directly involved with Deng's estimates. From AMS, this chapter draws on interviews with and the published work of Senior Colonel Huang Shuofeng. His orthodox findings differ from those presented in the reform assessment published by a team of CASS researchers. The reformers had as senior advisor noted author Gao Heng. According to interviews, Gao helped to invent the key Chinese concept

advance." Li Qingshan, *Xin junshi geming yu gao jishu zhanzheng* (The new revolution in military affairs and high-technology warfare)(Beijing: Junshi kexue chubanshe, 1995), 191-192.

of structural multipolarity, which he published in 1986, at the same time Deng Xiaoping's national security adviser announced the concept.[5]

The AMS books and the CASS book are similar in that they see America declining and an evolution toward a multipolar world, as the quantitative power gap between the United States and other major powers closes rapidly between 2000 and 2020. Additionally, they avoid describing the rise of China to superpower status. A decade ago, senior Chinese analysts pondered in public the implications of China's surpassing the United States; however, this is not mentioned by AMS or CASS authors. The publications of both institutes agree that China will, at most, become merely one pole among five equals, in spite of its much faster growth rate and much larger population and territory. Where the AMS and CASS books differ is mainly in how to assess the *rate* of China's rise and America's decline. They also differ in how they assess military power. By examining this "debate" about the future security environment, foreign observers can better understand how issues about the future are "argued" among both civilian and military analysts.

According to interviews in Beijing, the assessments of future power ratios by CASS and AMS are not projected beyond 2010 because to do so might aid the China Threat Theory. However, for this study, the AMS and CASS estimated growth rates and their baseline power scores for 2010 are used to project 2020 findings. It is apparent that CASS and AMS use very different rates—AMS growth estimates have China's CNP increasing seven times faster than the CASS pace; the CASS rate for Japan is also much slower. The CASS assessment has U.S. CNP decreasing 1 percent a year, to be overtaken by Japan, which is growing by 1 percent a year.

The estimates of the orthodox authors support the assertions of Deng Xiaoping and Li Peng that the multipolar world is approaching. By 2020, based on projected AMS scores, the United States and China will have roughly equal national power. However, the reform view published by the team from CASS predicts different results. Its CNP scores for the present suggest American unipolar superpower, not multipolarity. Projected CASS scores show that by 2020 Japan will be number one, followed closely by the United

[5] See Gao Heng, "Shijie zhanlue geju zhengxiang duojihua fazhan" (The strategic world structure is developing toward multipolarity), *Guofang daxue xuebao* (National Defense University Journal), no. 2 (1986): 32-33.

States, whereas China will still be only number eight in the world, not even one of the top major powers. China and Russia will be "half poles" because they will each have only about half the national power of Japan and America. These differences in CNP affect the debates discussed in other chapters of this study about which nations will be first to exploit the potential of an RMA.

ORIGINS

Ancient Chinese Strategists as Antecedents

Although the phrase "Comprehensive National Power" did not itself come into existence until the 1980s, the concept has ancient cultural roots and "evolved from the concepts of 'power,' 'actual strength', and 'national power.' "[6] Although a number of authors cite Marxist-Leninist theory as a foundation for CNP studies, even earlier discussions of the need to compare the overall power of different countries can be found in several Chinese ancient military classics. The studies of Herbert Goldhamer provide numerous examples of ancient Chinese strategists who emphasized the need to conduct calculations about the future.[7]

In his book *Grand Strategy*, Wu Chunqiu, a distinguished author at AMS, gives examples from Sun Zi's *The Art of War*, Wu Zi's *The Art of War*, and Guan Zhong's *Guan Zi*, to show how, "to a certain extent, the discussion of warfare in Chinese ancient literature embodies primitive, simple, and unsophisticated national power thought."[8] He explains, "In general, national power theories frequently (or above all) are closely related to issues of war." Therefore, measurements must include not only military strength but also other forces that have to do with carrying out a war. "China's wise ancient strategists," Wu writes, "never advocated relying only on military power to

[6]Wang Songfen, ed., *Shijie zhuyao guojia zonghe guoli bijiao yanjiu* (Comparative studies of the comprehensive national power of the world's major nations)(Changsha: Hunan chubanshe, 1996), 23.

[7]See Herbert Goldhamer, *The Adviser* (New York: Elsevier, 1978); and Herbert Goldhamer, *Reality and Belief in Military Affairs: A First Draft* (Santa Monica, CA: The RAND Corporation, 1979).

[8]Wu Chunqiu, *Guangyi da zhanlue* (Grand strategy)(Beijing: Shishi chubanshe, 1995), 98. The subsequent quotes in this paragraph are from the same page.

conquer the enemy, but emphasized combining military power with the nonmilitary power related to war in order to get the upper hand." Sun Zi advanced that there were "five things" and "seven stratagems" that governed the outcome of war. Weighing these components, which include politics, military affairs, economics, geography, and "subjective guidance," could forecast the results of a war in advance. Wu Zi wrote about six conditions under which, if the other side's strength was greater, war should be avoided. Wu Chunqiu writes, "These six points include the factors of national territory, population, domestic embodiment power, the legal system, servants, the quantity and quality of troops, as well as international aid. Even in an assessment based on modern views, these factors are relatively complete and are the epitome of Comprehensive National Power." Finally, the "eight views" discussed in *Guan Zi* are areas that, when assessed, show the size, strength, and development of a country's national power.

One of the largest and most famous geopolitical coalitions in ancient Chinese history was based on power calculations similar to assessments of CNP. The director of the military research division of the General Staff Department of the People's Liberation Army (PLA), Colonel Chai Yuqiu, recounts that in 334 B.C., during the Warring States era, the strategist Su Qin proposed that the six states of the vertical pillar of the strategic rectangle that made up the Warring States geopolitical game board unite against the hegemonic state of Qin. Su Qin explained that together, the land of the six nations was five times greater than the territory of Qin, and their combined military power was ten times greater than that of Qin. If the six nations united together to attack Qin, it would be destroyed. Su Qin successfully persuaded all six to "unite vertically" (*he zong*) to prevent their destruction, one by one, by Qin's hegemony. It was not until the next century that Qin's leading strategist was able to break up this coalition, which had been based on quantitative calculations of comparative power.[9]

Wu Chunqiu points out that the ancient Chinese stratagem of "victory without war" also has great relevance to the concept of CNP. The origin of the stratagem is a famous quotation from Sun Zi's *The Art of War*: "To subdue the enemy without fighting is the acme of skill." According to Wu, it means

[9]Chai Yuqiu, *Moulue Jia* (Strategists)(Beijing: Lan tian chubanshe, 1996), 511.

that, "Under certain military pressures, one can coordinate a political and diplomatic offensive, to psychologically disintegrate the enemy forces and subdue them."[10] Later, in *Xun Zi* and the works of other strategists, the concept is discussed further and condensed into "victory without war." Wu believes this strategy to achieve foreign policy goals without going to battle is even more applicable to the future security environment. He writes: "Victory without war does not mean that there is no war at all. The wars one must fight are political wars, economic wars, science and technology wars, diplomatic wars, etc. To sum up in a word, it is a war of Comprehensive National Power. Although military power is an important factor, in peacetime it usually acts as a backup force, and plays the role of invisible might."

Modern Beginnings

Compared to China, American studies of the future neglect geopolitical hierarchy and the rank order of the great powers. One reason may be the noble hope that war and geopolitics have become obsolete. Western studies have warned that errors in assessing power may explain why wars occur and that it is extremely difficult to assess geopolitical power accurately.[11] An almost poetic account is from the remark by the great English statesman, Lord Bolingbroke:

> A precise point at which the scales of power turn . . . is imperceptible to common observation . . . they who are in the rising scale do not immediately feel their strength, nor assume that confidence in it which successful experience gives them afterwards. They who are the most concerned to watch the variations of this balance, misjudge often in the same manner and from the same prejudices. They continue to dread a power no longer able to hurt them, or they continue to have no apprehensions of a power that grows daily more formidable.[12]

---

[10]Wu Chunqiu, *Guangyi da zhanlue*, 17. All other quotations in this paragraph are from pages 17-18.

[11]Geoffrey Blainey, *The Causes of War* (New York: The Free Press, 1973), 114.

[12]Quoted in Aaron Friedberg, *The Weary Titan* (Princeton: Princeton University Press, 1988), 14-15.

The Chinese focus on geopolitical calculations makes it crucial to them to have good estimates of the future. The idea of measuring and comparing CNP developed during the early 1980s, as Deng Xiaoping modified Chairman Mao's party line that "world war was unavoidable," by instead predicting that "world war probably can be avoided."[13] The Marxist-Leninist "foundation" of Deng's new assessment of the security environment was that "the growth of the world's forces of peace exceed the growth of the forces of war." Not only were the United States and the Soviet Union at a stalemate in their military struggle, but the strength of countries that were opposed to war was increasing. The international environment was changing, and the importance of economic issues and conflicts was growing. Military force was no longer the main index for judging a country's strength. Numerous other factors contributed to a country's power and were playing a greater role in warfare, such as economics, science and technology, and popular will. There needed to be a means for measuring the sum of the "forces restricting war," which included China. Deng wrote:

> If at the end of the new century China attains a "comparatively well off level," then there will be a major increase in the power restricting war. If China again goes through thirty to fifty years of construction, and comes close to the level of developed countries, then at that time it will be even harder for a war to be fought.[14]

In order to make more accurate assessments about the future balance of power, country strength had to be evaluated in a variety of areas.

Zhu Liangyin and Meng Renzhong of AMS write, "Deng Xiaoping used keen foresight and . . . established the theoretical basis for the emergence and formation of his Comprehensive National Power theory."[15] While Zhu and

---

[13]Zhu Liangyin and Meng Renzhong, "Deng Xiaoping zonghe guoli sixiang yanjiu" (A study on Deng Xiaoping's Comprehensive National Power thought), in *Xin shiqi junshi jingji lilun yanjiu* (Studies of new period military economic theory), eds. Li Lin and Zhao Qinxuan (Beijing: Junshi kexue chubanshe, 1995), 42. The subsequent quotes in this paragraph are from pages 43-44.

[14]Ibid., 44.

[15]Ibid., 43. All other quotes in this paragraph are from pages 44-46.

Meng never once quote Deng using the specific phrase "Comprehensive National Power," they set forth his "thought" on the subject, through analysis of his statements on the priorities of China's national construction and the significance of this development to the growth of China's strategic power. Deng's views that economic strength can be a force for peace and can counter military strength are used to show that "economic power is the most important and most essential factor in Comprehensive National Power." They go on to state that "Deng Xiaoping believes that military power is the basic means for ensuring that economic power will rise, protecting the nation's general interests, and carrying out global strategic goals. Therefore, while we on the one hand emphasize economic power as being the base of Comprehensive National Power, we must on the other hand devote ourselves to the development of military power, the element with the most direct role in Comprehensive National Power."

Zhu and Meng write that science and technology are considered to be "the guiding force in raising Comprehensive National Power."[16] This is established through Deng's emphasis on the need for scientific and technological research and advancement in the military and economic arenas. They claim Deng further developed the sacred classics of Marxist-Leninism by adding his unique idea of the "primary" productive role of science and technology. "Marx talked about science and technology being a productive force and this is very accurate, but perhaps today saying it that way is not sufficient, I think that they are the primary productive force."

Deng Xiaoping's new assessment of the security environment required a means to compare China to other countries. According to a book by Senior Colonel Huang Shuofeng of AMS, the specific phrase "Comprehensive National Power" was put forward by Colonel Huang himself as he worked with Deng. In *On Comprehensive National Power*, Huang describes how, in 1984, as part of a study on China's national defense strategy in the year 2000, Chinese scholars looked at the "national power equations" of Ray Cline and the West German professor William Fuchs as possible ways in which to analyze the international balance of power. After rejecting them based on their use of the concept of "power politics," the absence in their equations of a way

---

[16]Ibid., 49.

to evaluate the role of science and technology, and other issues, Chinese scholars began to create their own models and formulas for weighing and contrasting different countries' overall power. Colonel Huang writes that in 1984 he "put forward the concept of 'Comprehensive National Power,' and established a 'Comprehensive National Power dynamic equation' model aimed at comprehensively assessing the comprehensive power of different countries in the world, and conducted comparative analysis of the major countries Comprehensive National Power."[17]

In observing the discourse of the Chinese Communist Party, a clue about how important something is can come from the strained efforts to justify its creation with appeals to precedents from the sacred Marxist classics. It appears that Comprehensive National Power is sufficiently important to merit such claims. Colonel Huang Shuofeng cites Marx, Engels, and Mao as precedents for "guiding thoughts on studying Comprehensive National Power" and its relationship to warfare,[18] emphasizing Engels' discussion in *Anti-Duhring* on the important role of economics and other factors in military force. Huang also mentions Lenin's statement, "War is a test of every nation's complete economic and organizational power," and writes that Lenin's theory, "using the language of today," would be that war "is a test of every country's Comprehensive National Power."[19]

According to Colonel Huang, Chairman Mao Zedong also contributed to the development of the concept of CNP through his "strategy of grasping the situation as a whole," which applied Marxist-Leninist theory to China's military strategy. In his writings, Mao not only emphasized the role of concrete material components, such as military and economic power, in affecting the balance of power, but also the function of spiritual components, in particular the influence of leaders and popular will. In "Strategic Issues in China's Revolutionary War," Mao wrote, "Victory or defeat in war is mainly determined by both side's various military, political, economic and natural conditions; this is not an issue. However, it is not simply just that, it is also

---

[17]Huang Shuofeng, *Zonghe guoli lun*, 94.

[18]Ibid., 98.

[19]Ibid., 96-97.

determined by the subjective leadership capabilities of both sides in combat."[20] Both Huang and Wu Chunqiu laud Mao's *On Protracted Warfare* for its comprehensive comparison of China's and Japan's strengths during World War II and praised Mao's 1956 speech, "On the Ten Relationships," which was "a complete guide to strengthening Comprehensive National Power."[21]

QUALITATIVE FACTORS

The close connection between warfare and national power, which formed the basis of earlier Chinese strategic theory on the subject, of course remains a prominent issue today. However, because the foundation and means for exerting one's power and influence have diversified, because conflicts between countries are more focused on nonmilitary issues, and because they can be resolved through diplomatic and economic channels, Chinese scholars in a number of disciplines, both military and nonmilitary, today use the concept of CNP to make assessments in their particular areas. CNP scores can aid "warfare" today in general terms in an "all directional economic war,"[22] and more specifically in future warfare to predict "who is capable of winning a victory in a new RMA war."[23]

High-Technology Warfare

The basis of a discussion on employing the framework of CNP to analyze the outcome of future wars in *The New Revolution in Military Affairs and High-technology Warfare*, by Li Qingshan, a People's Liberation Army (PLA) colonel, is highly similar to the arguments put forward by China's ancient strategists. Sun Zi and Wu Zi both discussed how victory or defeat in war can be known in advance if a comparison is done of certain factors that contribute to a country's strengths. Li Qingshan agrees: "Through the analysis of belligerent countries' Comprehensive National Power, even before a war has begun,

---

[20]Ibid., 97.

[21]Wu Chunqiu, *Guangyi dazhanlue*, 99.

[22]Tong Fuquan and Liu Yichang, *Shijie quanfangwei jingji zhan* (The world's all directional economic war)(Beijing: Junshi kexue chubanshe, 1991).

[23]Li Qingshan, *Xin junshi geming yu gao jishu zhanzheng*, 191.

people can frequently know the results in advance."[24] However, Li adds that power changes during a war, because "Comprehensive National Power is a relatively dynamic concept." As a war develops, fluctuations and transformations will inevitably occur in the strengths and functions of the various component factors. Li states, "The outcome of war to a very large extent is determined by the contrast of the actual strength and potential of the two sides before the war begins, but what plays a direct role in the outcome of the war are the changes that take place in this comparison of forces during the process of military operations, as well as the results of diplomatic struggles, ideological struggles, and economic struggles."

Li's book asserts that the RMA will not override previously existing premises for making strategic assessments. Li claims that high-technology weaponry "can change the appearance of warfare, but it cannot change the laws of victory in warfare. Victory or defeat in war is, of course, related to the technological means used by the belligerents, but it is not the sole relationship. Historically, in numerous wars the victors have been both those who have technically inferior weaponry and those who have technically superior weaponry. Technology is not the only factor determining victory or defeat in war."[25] Li links the RMA to CNP. Lenin wrote, "War is a test of every nation's complete economic and organizational power," which Li asserts means that new RMA warfare "is still a comprehensive test of the level of countries' strength."

During development of the RMA, Li believes that CNP will continue to be composed of a country's strength in five major areas—politics, economics, military affairs, science and technology, and foreign affairs—each of which he discusses with regard to its influence and role in war. Beginning with political affairs, he states, "Warfare is the continuation of politics and reflects a country's strategic intentions, the desires of the people, organizational ability, and decision making ability."[26] According to Li, if a country's decisionmaking, organizational capability, or strategy is weak, unfocused, or defective, these factors will outweigh "actual" strength in determining the outcome of a war.

---

[24]Ibid., 192. All other quotes in this paragraph are from pages 191-193.

[25]Ibid., 191. All other quotes in this paragraph are from pages 191-193.

[26]Ibid., 192. The subsequent quotes in this paragraph are from 192-193.

Popular will expressed in opposition to a war can also reduce "actual" power. Pure military power "is warfare's most direct material force, it includes people, weaponry, strategy and tactics, organization and command, as well as various safeguards, etc. It is the most basic factor determining victory or defeat in war, and strength or weakness in any area will have a major role in war." Of course, in future RMA warfare, where "the entire process of war is permeated by the contest and match of technology," the extent of a country's scientific and technological development will be of major importance in attaining victory.[27]

Economic Rivalries

While Li Qingshan views the component factors of CNP from the perspective of their relevance to warfare, authors Tong Fuquan and Liu Yichang analyze them with more economic issues in mind. Tong and Liu's interest in evaluating and comparing countries' CNP stems from the role it plays in world conflicts and rivalries over "science and technology, industrialization, foreign trade, finance, and natural resources."[28] They divide CNP into four major parts—economics, politics, science and technology, and military affairs—placing economics in the most crucial position. "Actual economic strength," they write, "is, of course, the major component part of Comprehensive National Power, and to a certain extent, a country's actual economic strength represents its Comprehensive National Power." The other

---

[27] As discussed in chapter 2, Wang Zhengxi, a Senior Adviser at the China Institute of International Strategic Studies (CIISS), when writing about why other countries may exploit the RMA ahead of the United States, also links development of the RMA to CNP. "Counting on its technical superiority, the United States claims itself to be the forerunner in the military revolution and that it even has such a great lead of 30 to 50 years over other nations that no country can catch up and advance shoulder to shoulder with it before 2020. We say that military technology is an agent behind the military revolution, but not the only one. It depends on the combined action of social, political, economic, and scientific and technological factors for a military revolution to take place and proceed smoothly. . . . If the social, political, economic, scientific and technological, and military thought factors are taken into account, then it is not absolutely limited to the United States as the only country that can wage a military revolution." See Wang Zhenxi, "The New Wave of the World Revolution in Military Affairs," *International Strategic Studies* 44, no. 2 (April 1997): 8-9.

[28] Tong Fuquan and Liu Yichang, *Shijie quanfangwei jingji zhan*, 232. The subsequent quote in this paragraph is from page 232.

three areas are not discussed as independent factors but with regard to their relationship to economics.

Concerning politics, Tong and Liu write, "In general, political power and actual economic strength are linked together."[29] They believe a country with strong economic power will have powerful political influence, and a nation with unsubstantial economic strength will not have major political influence. However, they do grant an exception for Japan, whose great economic strength does not translate into a strong role in international political affairs. A similar relationship exists between the extent of a country's economic strength and the level of its scientific and technological development. While the authors recognize the importance of military power, they assess it based on its connection to the other factors:

> Actual military strength also is an area that can not be lacking in Comprehensive National Power; if a country's military power is not strong, it is out of the question that this country could have powerful Comprehensive National Power. In general, the size of military expenditures is both a reflection of whether a country's actual military strength is strong or weak, and an important sign of whether its economy is powerful, additionally, the development of military technology is related to actual scientific and technological strength. Therefore, in a certain sense, the enhancement of actual military strength is a strong symbol of a country's powerful Comprehensive National Power.[30]

Strategy and Structure

Sun Zi's emphasis on the importance of knowing and then attacking an opponent's strategy has also found its way into the study of CNP. "Prospects for the New World Structure," by Xi Runchang of AMS, is an effort to predict the future world structure based on each area that contributes to Comprehensive National Power—strategy, population and national territory, military affairs, economics, and international influence. However, in his discussion on evaluating and comparing CNP, Xi emphasizes one area that is of definite significance to the future security environment—the less concrete

---

[29]Ibid., 232.

[30]Ibid., 233.

component factors of CNP, especially strategy. Xi explains that his particular stress on the importance of strategy does not ignore the position of the other components, but is "done in order to give prominence to this important area that people often overlook."[31] According to Xi, national strategies need to be evaluated in three aspects. It must be determined:

- Whether or not a country's leaders have actually "established a national competition strategy, in order to participate in the international competition" and, if they have, how quickly it was implemented.[32]
- "Whether or not a nation's policymakers, when developing Comprehensive National Power's hard national power, put the main means for participating in the international competition in the most prominent development position."[33]
- How a country's leadership "effectively utilizes" its strategy. Xi writes, "In the current information age, for any major nation in the strategic competition, whether they take action early or take action late, is extremely important with regard to gaining the leading position."[34]

Today, according to Xi, the United States, Europe, and Japan, because of their "overwhelmingly ambitious" goals and because they have moved quickly to implement their strategies, are ahead of other countries. "By comparison, Russia and China, particularly Russia, are especially slow in the area of action. In a certain sense, this is an important reason why, in today's international competition, Russia and China are in defensive positions, or are said to have been late to enter the ranks of the major competing nations."[35]

---

[31]Xi Runchang, "Shijie xin geju zhanwang" (Prospects for the new world structure"), in *Shijie zhengzhi xin geju yu guoji anquan* (The new world political structure and international security), eds. Xi Runchang and Gao Heng (Beijing: Junshi kexue chubanshe, 1996), 46.

[32]Ibid., 44.

[33]Ibid., 45.

[34]Ibid., 45.

[35]Ibid., 46.

Grand Strategy

In *Grand Strategy*, Wu Chunqiu, of AMS, views the relationship between a country's strategy and CNP somewhat differently than Xi. He argues that CNP and grand strategy have an "unbreakable internal connection" of a "dual nature."[36] On the one hand, CNP is wielded to attain the goals of grand strategy, but on the other, because this requires strong CNP, its development becomes one of the aims of grand strategy. Wu therefore does not consider strategy to be a component of CNP. Rather, he breaks the main factors and their functions down in the following manner: "In the current age when peace and development have become the main trends in the world, numerous countries, to different degrees, recognize that economics are the foundation; science and technology, especially high technology, are the guide; education is the guide of the guide; national defense is the backup force; and national policies are the key factor playing a unifying and coordinating role."

Not only can studies of CNP aid a country in making strategic assessments of the international situation, but they also are an important tool for analyzing a country's own strengths and weaknesses. Furthermore, Wu explains that countries can learn from mistakes made by other countries by analyzing the development of both their national strategy and Comprehensive National Power. Like many Chinese authors, Wu cites the collapse of the Soviet Union as an example of a policy failure in the CNP competition.

QUANTITATIVE FACTORS

What exactly are the specific components of CNP? Some Chinese authors discuss CNP only in a qualitative sense, dividing it into a few broad areas. Others, however, engage in quantitative analysis with detailed definitions of the contents of CNP. Authors share certain factors, but there are also discrepancies. Wu Chunqiu writes, "Because different countries' national conditions are not the same, and researchers' personal goals are different, interpretations of the concept of national power vary. In the broadest sense, a country's power includes natural factors and social (manmade) factors; it includes material factors (hard national power) and spirit factors (soft national

---

[36]Wu Chunqiu, *Guangyi dazhanlue*, 94. The subsequent quotes in this paragraph are from pages 102 and 103.

power); it includes actual strength, as well as potential and the mechanism for turning potential into actual strength. It is all encompassing."[37] Two books propose quantitative approaches: *Comparative Studies of the Comprehensive National Power of the World's Major Nations*, by a team of analysts coordinated by Wang Songfen, of CASS, and *On Comprehensive National Power*, by Senior Colonel Huang Shuofeng, of AMS.

The CASS Index Framework

The current Foreign Minister of Russia once headed the Institute of World Economics and Politics (IMEMO), an influential Russian research institution. Since the 1950s, China has had its own IMEMO, the Institute of World Economics and Politics (IWEP), within CASS. *Comparative Studies of the Comprehensive National Power of the World's Major Nations* is the product of a group of researchers in the Office of Statistics and Analysis at IWEP. Published in December 1996, the book puts forward a detailed dissection of the characteristics and roles of the CNP component factors; describes measurement methods to evaluate them; and provides extensive data tables from the results of examining the CNP of 18 countries. The authors define their subject matter carefully:

> We believe that Comprehensive National Power is the organic sum of the different powers of a sovereign state during a certain period of time, it is the base which all countries rely on for existence and development, and it is the foundation on which world powers establish their international position and give full play to their influence and roles. Specifically, it is the condensed sum of the entire calculations of societies' various existence and development factors at a certain time, space, and under certain conditions.[38]

The book divides CNP into eight major areas: natural resources, domestic economics, foreign economics, science and technology, military affairs, government capabillity, foreign affairs capability, and social development.

---

[37]Ibid., 95.

[38]Wang Songfen, ed., *Shijie zhuyao guojia zonghe guoli bijiao yanjiu*, 25.

Three of the basic principles on which the authors relied to determine the above eight general factors include the following:

- Both material power (the concrete factors such as economics, military affairs, etc.) as well as spirit power (the intangible factors, such as international relations, politics, etc.) need to be included in an assessment of CNP.

- CNP is composed not only of actual power; latent or potential power also has a contributing role. Examples of the latter include the findings of scientific and technological research before being applied and utilized, or natural resources that exist but that have not yet been developed.

- The contents of CNP and the roles of these factors have changed throughout history and will continue to do so in the future; therefore, new aspects may be added or dropped when evaluating different time periods. Today, the rapidly increasing significance of information as a source of power is a case of a new factor of growing importance. The authors write, "In the current world, because of the development of new means of communication, different types of information about market trends can be promptly delivered to various places in the world, therefore, as a factor, in international relations, the role of information power is growing and can be compared with political and economic factors."[39]

In order to objectively assess the CNP of different countries, CASS needed measurable, unified standards. To this end, they sought (for each of the eight component factors) a set of specific indexes. The creation of an index system capable of evaluating countries at different development levels and with varying social, political, and economic systems meant that the indexes selected had to be general enough to be applicable to the diverse nations of the world; be representative of all the factors that constitute Comprehensive National Power; and have data sources that were systematic and feasible. The authors wanted to include "both indexes for total amount, and indexes for amount per person; both quantity indexes and quality indexes;

---

[39]Ibid., 36.

Table 3. *The Comprehensive National Power Index Framework*

Natural Resources

Man Power Resources: total population; life expectancy; the proportion of the economically active population in the total population; the number of university students per 10,000 people

Land Resources: the area of national territory; the area of cultivatable territory; the area in forest

Mineral Resources (reserves): iron; copper; bauxite

Energy Resources (reserves): coal; crude oil; natural gases; water energy

Economic Activities Capability

Actual Economic Strength (total): gross domestic product (GDP); industry production capability (electric energy production, steel output, cement output, logs output); food supply capability (total grain output, degree of self-sufficiency in grain); energy supply capability (volume of energy production, volume of energy consumption, crude oil processing capability); total cotton output

Actual Economic Strength (per person): GDP per person; industry production capability (electric energy production, steel output, cement output, logs output); food supply capability (total grain output, average calories per person); energy supply capability (volume of energy consumption)

Production Efficiency: social labor production rate; industry labor production rate, agriculture labor production rate

Material Consumption Level: volume of energy consumption based on GDP calculations

Structure: the proportion of the tertiary industry in the GDP

Foreign Economic Activities Capability

Total import and export trade; total import trade, total export trade

Total international reserves; international reserves (not including gold); gold reserves

Science and Technology Capability

Proportion of research and development in the GDP; number of scientists and engineers; the number of scientists and engineers per 1,000 people; proportion of machinery and transportation equipment exports in total exports; proportion of high-technology intensive exports in total exports

Social Development Level

Education Level: education expenditures per person; proportion of people studying in higher education; proportion of people studying in secondary school education

Cultural Level: adult literacy rate; number of people per one thousand who get a daily newspaper

Health Care Level: health care expenditures per person; number of people doctors are responsible for; number of people nurses are responsible for

Communications: number of people who have a telephone per 100 people

Urbanization: Proportion of the urban population in the total population

Military Capability

Number of military personnel; military expenditures; weapons exports; nuclear weapons (the number of nuclear launchers; the number of nuclear warheads)

Government Regulation and Control Capability

Proportion of final government consumption expenditures in the GDP; proportion of central government expenditures in the GDP; investigation through interviews asking nine questions

Foreign Affairs Capability

Uses ten factors in a "nerve network model" to carry out a broad assessment.

Source: Wang Songfen, ed., *Shijie zhuyao guojia zonghe guoli bijiao yanjiu* (Comparative studies of the comprehensive national power of the world's major nations)(Changsha: Hunan chubanshe, 1996), 69.

both efficiency indexes and consumption indexes."[40] Additionally, structural indexes were necessary in order to demonstrate the interrelations and inter-reliance of the different factors. Consequently, the authors divided the eight major areas into 64 indexes (table 3).

The AMS Index System

On Comprehensive National Power, by Colonel Huang Shuofeng, provides a detailed analysis of the major component factors of CNP and their numerous indexes. Huang writes, "Comprehensive National Power research is done in order to accurately analyze the international strategic situation and evaluate the comprehensive power of enemy states, allies, and one's own country for the purpose of scientifically planning one's own national strategic decision making."[41] Only relying on theoretical research is therefore inadequate for making this sort of assessment, and instead systems theory and mathematical methods must be utilized to develop qualitative and quantitative analysis. Consequently, Huang's objective in creating an index system is to "completely and systematically" describe the characteristics and development conditions of a country's CNP "in order to carry out scientific quantitative analysis."

Huang describes CNP as a large, complex system composed of many levels or subsystems, within which there are numerous interlinked component factors. He divides the CNP index system into four major index subsystems—the material power (hard) index subsystem, the spirit power (soft) index subsystem, the coordinated power index subsystem, and the environmental index subsystem:

> The material power and spirit power indexes mainly reflect a country's needed strength for existence and development; the coordinated power index mainly reflects the organization, command, management, and decisionmaking levels of the leadership mechanism; and the environmental

---

[40]Ibid., 64.

[41]Huang Shuofeng, *Zonghe guoli lun,* 159. All other quotes in this paragraph are from pages 155-157.

index mainly reflects the restricting conditions of Comprehensive National Power."[42]

Material power is made up of the "hard factors": natural resources, economics, science and technology, and national defense. These hard factors contain some aspects that are soft in nature, but for the purpose of analysis they are designated to a subsystem based on their dominant characteristic. For example, when viewed overall, national defense is a hard factor, but a few of its components, such as national defense ideology and military theory, are not. The "spiritual (including psychological) and intellect power soft factors" that "determine the effectiveness of the material form (hard) national power" include politics, foreign affairs, and culture and education.[43]

The coordinated power index subsystem is important because, in order for CNP to develop effectively, the factors that constitute material and spirit power "require macro adjustment and control, and coordinated development."[44] These functions are important both at the national level as well as at the lower levels of the specific areas. Although some of the soft power factors are contained both in their own system as well as in the coordinated power index, they operate differently in the capacity of the latter. As "spiritual" factors they influence the material form factors, but within the coordinated power index they regulate the relationship between the hard and soft factors. Finally, the environment index subsystem comprises three parts, the international environment (the world structure and the different balances of power), the natural environment (a country's natural resources, as well as its geographic and ecological conditions), and social environment (the political, economic and social systems and their stability). These three areas greatly influence, both negatively and positively, the development of all the other factors.

Each of the components of the four major subindexes is itself a sub-subindex, and together they all form what Huang refers to as a CNP appraisal index system. For each of these sub-subindexes, he provides detailed lists of

---

[42]Ibid., 162.

[43]Ibid., 164.

[44]Ibid., 165.

their contents, but only four of Huang's lists are seen here for comparison, two from the soft factor side, and two from the hard factor side:

"Political Power Subsystem: National strategy goals; political stability; policy level; the nation's leadership, organization, and decisionmaking capability; national embodiment power."

"Foreign Affairs Power Subsystem: Foreign political relations; foreign economic relations; foreign military relations; diplomatic activities capability; international contribution capability."

"Science and Technology Power Subsystem: Science and technology troops (scientists and engineers, technological personnel); investment in science and technology (total, proportion of the GNP); science and technology level (high science and technology, general science and technology); science and technology system; scientific and technological progress speed; scientific and technological progress contribution; scientific and technological results and applications."

"National Defense Power Subsystem: Standing army (nuclear, conventional) and reserve forces; national defense investment; national defense science and technology and national defense industry; national defense bases and installations; strategic material reserves and logistics safeguards; national defense education and training; national defense system establishment; the national defense ideology of the people and troop morale; military theory."[45]

After listing the above specific indexes, Huang writes, "The Comprehensive National Power index system is the concrete embodiment of the concept of Comprehensive National Power; it also is the qualitative basis for appraising Comprehensive National Power," and therefore is the foundation for his "Comprehensive National Power dynamic equation," which will be discussed later.[46] Before setting forth this equation, Huang first arranges his index system into a network structure so that it can be more easily quantified. However, in this diagram, "The Structural Network of the

---

[45]Ibid., 169, 170, 172.

[46]Ibid., 173. The subsequent quotes in this paragraph are from the same page.

Comprehensive National Power System," Huang outlines national defense power differently. He breaks it down into direct military power and indirect military power. Direct military power includes measures of nuclear forces and conventional forces. The components of the latter are: total armed manpower; soldier quality; weapons effectiveness; military installations and logistics support; organizational quality; strategic reserve capability; and the extent of weapons acquisitions.

Foreign Methods

Chinese authors often explicitly criticize foreign quantitative analysis methods. Three foreign formulas for assessing CNP frequently mentioned, both negatively and positively, are those created by Ray Cline, William Fuchs, and the Japan Economic Planning Department, Comprehensive Planning Office, in a study entitled *Japan's Comprehensive National Power.*

As noted earlier, according to Huang Shuofeng, Deng Xiaoping asked Chinese scholars in 1984 to analyze the future security environment, as part of a study on China's national defense strategy for the year 2000. They first examined existing Western formulas, but Huang rejected Cline's "national power equation" because it does not include a way to evaluate science and technology power; it is a static equation and therefore does not assess the variations in and development of a country's CNP over time; and Cline's means for judging the soft, intangible factors are not objective or unified. Huang finds fault with William Fuchs' formula because it measures only the hard material factors and completely ignores the soft ones. The Japanese study, done in 1987, is criticized by the authors of *The World's All Directional Economic War,* Tong Fuquan and Liu Yichang, because its index system and calculation methods are narrow and unscientific. They write that the research of the Japanese group was "done in order to serve the Japanese Government's established guiding principles and policy."[47]

As is common in China's assessment techniques, part of the foreigners' concepts may be borrowed. For example, in "Prospects for the New World Structure," in order to make "an objective and unassuming assessment" of

---

[47]Tong Fuquan and Liu Yichang, *Shijie quanfangwei jingji zhan,* 234.

Comprehensive National Power, Xi Runchang used Ray Cline's national power equation, $P = (C+E+M) \times (S+W)$. In the formula,

> P stands for national power
> C refers to population and territory
> E is economic power
> M stands for military power
> S refers to national strategy
> W is national will.[48]

In great contrast to General Huang's comments, Xi believes Cline's standards to be "relatively objective," including the standards for the soft factors, such as strategy, which is one of Xi's main areas of focus. CASS, for one of their measurement techniques (which will be explained in greater detail later), not only adapts aspects of Cline's method but combines it with features of the Japanese study.

One foreign study on the analysis and measurement of national power that is not criticized by Chinese analysts is the *International Competitive Power Report*, a yearly study conducted by the World Economic Forum and the Swiss Lausanne Management Institute. (A few Chinese institutes and university departments even contribute to it.) The Chinese periodical *Strategy and Management* praises the report, saying that it is "an important foundation which different countries' government circles and business circles refer to when making policy decisions, and has extensive authoritativeness."[49] Beginning in 1996, the magazine stated that each year it would publish the portion of the report showing the rank order of China's international competitive standing according to the various power indexes.[50]

---

[48]Xi Runchang, "Shijie zhengzhi xin geju," 44. The quote in the next sentence is from the same page.

[49]"Zhongguo guoji jinzhengli baogao" (China's international competitive power report), *Zhanlue yu guanli* (Strategy and Management), no. 2 (1996): 1.

[50]The report is often cited by Chinese authors, who refer to China's continued rise in the rankings. For example see Wu Zhaohong and Shui Jiayue, "Strive to Improve International Competitiveness," *Qiushi*, no. 6 (March 16, 1998): 32-34, in FBIS-CHI-98-126, May 6, 1998.

The CASS Weighted Index Plan

The researchers in the CASS Office of Statistics and Analysis at IWEP divide their measurement of CNP into two stages, the basic plan and the weighted plan.

The Basic Plan. The 64 indexes the researchers set forth as standards for evaluating CNP vary in size and character, so the basic plan is composed of several calculation methods, in order to cover and suit all of them. First, the data from the hard indexes are standardized through index calculation methods, which "combine R. S. Cline's comprehensive calculation method of assigning values and the comprehensive index calculation method used in *Japan's Comprehensive National Power.*"[51] Afterwards, it is separated into calculated unit values. The hard indexes are divided into two groups, direct indexes (those directly related to GDP growth per person) and indirect indexes (those inversely related to GDP growth per person). The former set take the biggest value as 100, the latter set takes the lowest value as 100 to "successively calculate the deserved value of the different countries for those indexes."

An investigation method of posing questions to specialists is utilized in the case of some of the intangible soft factors not easily measured. For example, in order to assess government regulation and control, the researchers asked some of the participants at the 1994 China World Economic Institute annual meeting questions about 9 aspects of government regulation and control in 18 countries. The answers from 59 specialists, scholars, and professors then underwent a computerized analysis. For foreign affairs, another soft factor, the group "designed a nerve network model with ten factors related to capability in foreign affairs activities—population, territory, natural resources, military affairs, economics, science and technology, politics, ideology, system of organization, and image—to make assessments and obtained vague data of the different countries' foreign affairs capabilities; afterwards the data were standardized." For all the standardized data, "a standardized, differentiated levels collection method was adopted to obtain the basic plan data model." Based on these different methods, the researchers

---

[51]Wang Songfen, ed., *Shijie zhuyao guojia zonghe guoli bijiao yanjiu*, 71. All other quotes in this paragraph are from pages 71-72.

calculated the numerical value of the 64 indexes, the eight major areas, and the CNP for 18 countries in the years 1970, 1980, and 1990. Looked at statically, the results can be used to compare the CNP of different countries; viewed dynamically, the results show the changes in a country's CNP over time.

The Weighted Plan. Certain problems and distortions arise, however, when calculations are made under the basic plan; this necessitates "appropriate revision [of the calculation techniques] through weighted methods."[52] First, those countries with extensive natural resources and comparatively small populations, such as Canada and Australia, receive high values of CNP that do not correspond to their actual economic strength and role in world affairs. Such results arise because in those countries per-person rates of a variety of economic and social factors are fairly high. Second, when assessing CNP, the authors assert it must be recognized that the importance and role of the various factors change over time. For example, during war, even during the Cold War, military strength and the various factors that contribute to it are the most crucial components of CNP. However, during peacetime, economic development, foreign trade, and social development rise in prominence. "Therefore, based on different time periods and different missions, revisions need to be made and weights need to be assigned to ensure the research conclusions are scientific and objective." Last, not only is the number of indexes in each of the eight major areas not equal—natural resources has fourteen, while foreign economic capability has only two—but each index, regardless of its value or importance, is allotted the same weight. Consequently, in the second stage of CNP measurement, the quantitative results of the basic plan are revised through qualitative analysis, by assigning weights to both the eight major component factors and their specific indexes.

In general, the researchers determined the weighted coefficients (table 4) for the different indexes based on the following principles:

- In times of peace, domestic and foreign economic activities are the most central and important part of CNP.
- The significance of science and technology in CNP and the international competition is growing.

---

[52]Ibid., 168.

- The level of social development is connected to people's quality of life, political stability, and social benefits.
- "Military capability is the basic content of studies of Comprehensive National Power, measuring international competitiveness and analyzing a comparison of forces; during peace times it also is an important factor in strengthening national defense and safeguarding peace."
- Natural resources are the "material base" of CNP.[53]

Table 4. *Weighted Coefficients of Major Component Factors*

National Power Factor	Weighted Coefficient
Total CNP	1.00
Natural resources	0.08
Economic activities capability	0.28
Foreign economic activities capability	0.13
Scientific and technological capability	0.15
Social development level	0.10
Military capability	0.10
Government regulation and control capability	0.08
Foreign affairs capability	0.08

Source: Wang Songfen, ed., *Shijie zhuyao guojia zonghe guoli bijiao yanjiu* (Comparative studies of the comprehensive national power of the world's major nations)(Changsha: Hunan chubanshe, 1996), 169.

Additionally, the different indexes within each of the major factors are also assigned weights. As examples, within the science and technology factor, the index for proportion of research and development in the GDP and the index for technology personnel both have weighted coefficients of 0.30; the index for the proportion of machinery and transportation equipment exports in total exports and the index for the proportion of high-technology intensive exports in total exports are both 0.20. All four indexes constituting the military factor—the number of military personnel, military expenditures, weapons exports, and nuclear weapons—are assigned equal weights of 0.25.

---

[53]Ibid., 169. The weighted coefficients for the factors and indexes are from pages 169-170.

Table 5. CASS 1990 CNP Scores

Country	National Power Factors			
	Natural Resources	*Economic Activities*	*Foreign Economic Activities*	*Science & Technology*
United States	4.3	24.3	12.8	8.8
Japan	1.2	14.3	7.3	11.9
Germany	1.3	11.1	9.3	8.0
France	1.3	10.6	5.7	6.4
Italy	1.1	9.8	5.9	4.9
England	1.4	8.5	4.6	7.2
Canada	2.6	9.3	2.7	5.1
Australia	2.6	8.0	1.3	2.4
S. Africa	0.9	3.6	0.3	1.3
USSR	5.7	9.4	1.9	10.3
Russia	4.2	6.7	1.3	9.4
China	4.0	7.5	2.2	4.5
India	2.1	4.8	0.5	2.3
Indonesia	1.6	3.1	0.7	1.0
Korea	1.2	4.3	1.6	7.0
Brazil	2.7	5.8	0.7	2.5
Mexico	1.6	4.1	0.8	2.6
Egypt	0.8	2.6	0.2	0.6

National Power Factors				
Social Development	*Military Affairs*	*Government Regulation and Control*	*Foreign Affairs*	*CNP*
7.8	7.1	6.1	8.0	79.1
7.3	0.4	5.7	4.8	52.9
8.0	0.8	6.8	5.1	50.3
7.2	1.1	6.9	4.6	43.8
6.7	0.4	6.5	4.2	39.5
7.4	0.9	6.4	6.4	42.7
8.1	0.2	5.9	4.0	38.0
7.0	0.1	5.6	3.6	30.6
3.3	0.1	5.4	3.0	17.9
5.8	9.9	5.3	6.0	54.3
6.1	6.6	3.5	5.3	43.1
2.0	2.5	4.8	5.0	32.3
1.7	0.9	4.6	4.2	21.0
2.0	0.2	4.3	3.0	15.9
5.3	0.5	5.3	3.5	28.7
3.4	0.2	4.5	3.8	23.8
3.8	0.1	4.2	3.4	20.8
2.6	0.3	5.0	3.3	15.6

Source: Wang , ed., *Shijie zhuyao guojia zonghe guoli bijiao yanjiu* (Comparative studies of the comprehensive national power of the world's major nations)(Changsha: Hunan chubanshe, 1996), 171-179.

Based on these weighted revisions and using the data generated for the 64 indexes under the basic plan, the numerical value of the eight major areas and then total CNP is recalculated for the 18 nations for the years 1970, 1980, and 1990. The results are shown in table 5. Under the basic plan, the authors write that the guiding principle was to "seek truth from facts," and the data reflected "the natural appearance of overall Comprehensive National Power and its objectives."[54] However, the combination of quantitative and qualitative analysis in the second stage of measurement causes "the results of the calculations to be closer to the specific national conditions of the different countries, making them more reliable and believable."[55]

Forecasted Weighted Plan. The researchers at CASS evaluated CNP for 1970, 1980, and 1990 and also made forecasts of what the CNP of the 18 nations will be in the years 2000 and 2010. Based on the principles of the weighted plan, they predicted the potential future role and influence of the different component factors and adjusted their weighted coefficients accordingly. Because of the growing significance of science and technology, education, and communications, the weighted coefficients for science and technology and social development level were raised from 0.15 to 0.17 and from 0.10 to 0.12, respectively. The natural resources category had the greatest reduction, from 0.08 to 0.06. Both government control and regulation capability, as well as foreign affairs capability, were reduced by 0.01 to weighted coefficients of 0.07, and the weights allotted to the two economic factors and military affairs capability remained the same. Once again, the data from the basic plan are taken as the base; using the new weighted coefficients, as well as data from projections of the 18 countries' GDP in 2000 and 2010, forecasts of future CNP are calculated. The projected CASS CNP scores and the CASS qualitative assessments of the future role and development of individual countries are discussed at the end of this chapter.

The AMS Dynamic Equation

Compared to the researchers at CASS, Huang Shuofeng of AMS provides a much more detailed analysis of his measurement and calculation methods for

---

[54]Ibid., 167.

[55]Ibid., 2.

CNP, including outlines of a number of his specific equations. As can be seen from the discussion in the previous section on Huang's CNP index system, he views CNP to be a large multilayered system composed of a number of interlinked subsystems and sub-subsystems. This complex system forms the framework for his calculation methods.

In establishing his equation, Huang emphasizes another characteristic of CNP—that it continually evolves. He writes, "Comprehensive national power not only changes with the passage of time and transformations in the world structure, but also through the interchange of energy flows, material flows and information flows of science and technology, economics, and foreign affairs, within the international environment."[56] Therefore, in order to best assess the developments and variations in CNP, a type of "motion equation" is needed. Based on the principles of systems theory, coordinated studies, and dynamics studies, Huang summed up: "The interconnections, inter-restrictions and interactions between the numerous subsystems must be analyzed to find the quantitative relations, and in order to arrange the entire system's evolution dynamic equation;" calculations are made using various methods; the results are used to compare the CNP of the different countries; and predictions are made about future trends in the "international Comprehensive National Power contest." Not surprisingly, Colonel Huang generates final calculations quite different from his civilian colleagues at CASS.

The CNP Function. Colonel Huang defines the growth and development process of CNP as "the process of taking a group of factors and turning them into output, under fixed domestic and foreign environments, and natural conditions." This process can be depicted numerically through a "Comprehensive National Power function":

$$Y_t = F(x_1, x_2, ..., x_n; t)$$

In the equation:

the CNP n component factors are $x_1, x_2, ..., x_n$

---

[56]Huang Shuofeng, *Zonghe guoli lun*, 175. The other quotes in this paragraph are from pages 185 and 188.

the amount of their inputs is combined, and the output volume—the CNP—is represented by Y,

t is the variable for time

$x_1, x_2, ..., x_n$ are functions of t.

According to Huang, because this equation shows the relationship between the input amount of the individual component factors and the total volume of output, it is "in keeping with the universal relations principle in the Marxist materialist dialectics theory system." In materialist dialectics theory, every material thing is an independent object, but through its connections and interaction with other objects it becomes a part of a "unified whole." Including too many component factors with their extensive data and numerous interconnections would make the national power function very complicated. Huang thus simplifies the function by using "macro variables . . . with the biggest roles in the allocation, control, and guidance of comprehensive national output Y_t." He selects three of the four major index subsystems from his CNP index system to be the variables: hard variables, represented by H_t; soft variables, indicated by S_t; and coordinated variables, depicted by K_t. The new national power function is then written:

$$Y_t = F (H_t, S_t, K_t)$$

So that calculations can be made using this new form of the national power function, it is rewritten using Newton's third law, where $\Sigma \times F = kma$:

$$Y_t = K_t \times (H_t)^\alpha \times (S_t)^\beta$$

In the above function:

H_t stands for the "mass" of CNP

S_t represents the "acceleration" of CNP

K_t is the coordinated coefficient

α is the "hard elasticity index"

β is the "soft elasticity index."

The two elasticity indexes establish country conditions in two basic areas: whether a country is a developed or developing nation (α), and whether a country is at war or has unrest, or whether it is at peace and is stable (β). Because α and β can really be only imprecisely calculated, "vague mathematics" are used to determine them. The above final form of the national power function shows how a country generates CNP by combining the input amounts of the component factors. Huang writes, "This establishes the basis for measuring and assessing Comprehensive National Power. However, the measurement of the Comprehensive National Power dynamic evolution process, requires studying the Comprehensive National Power dynamic equation."[57]

The Main CNP Dynamic Equation. Before setting forth his main equation, Huang explains that CNP is a complex system with many subsystems, with nonlinear interaction. "Therefore, when using dissipation structure theory to analyze the evolution and development process of the Comprehensive National Power system, you must use a nonlinear differential equation." Such an equation is:

$$\frac{dY_t}{dt} = \varrho Y_t \left(1 - \frac{Y_t}{M} \right)$$

Where:

Y_t stands for the national power function at time t
ϱ refers to the national power yearly growth rate
M is "the greatest value for a system variable that the environment (international, domestic and natural) will permit."

Just as the CNP system has numerous subsystems and sub-subsystems, so too, does the CNP dynamic equation have several layers of equations. Although Huang does not explain them all, he provides examples of subequations for population growth, gross national product, national income

---

[57]Ibid., 188-189. All quotes and equations in this section are from 189-191.

growth, scientific and technological power, and national defense power. Following is a discussion of the national defense power equation.[58]

National Defense Power Subequation. Huang believes that national defense power refers to both actual and potential defense power and includes not only military power but also various related factors from political, economic, and scientific and technological power. Consequently, national defense power has a number of different subequations. The formula he provides as an example is for military power, which he divides into strategic and conventional force. The former is "assessed on the basis of the composite index of the structure of attack forces, means of delivery and nuclear warheads' quantity and quality (precision, reliability, existence rate, *tufang* rate), and nuclear defense capability." The latter is "determined by troop combat ability, strategic maneuverability, and the extent of armament efforts." The equation is:

$$M_t = m_t \times \frac{1}{n} \sum_{i-1}^{n} a_i \times b_t + c_t$$
$$(i=1, 2, \ldots, n, n=4)$$

In the formula:

M_t indicates conventional military force in period t
m_t indicates the total number of troops in period t
a_1 indicates soldier quality
a_2 indicates weapons effectiveness
a_3 indicates logistics supplies and facilities quality
a_4 indicates organization and command quality
b_t indicates strategic reserve capabilities in period t
c_t indicates the extent of armament efforts in period t.

A country's military power also can be measured by using the two indexes of military expenditures and military capital.

Total military capital (including weapons and facilities) is calculated by adding the past military investment depreciation surplus total to that year's new investment total. Its equation is:

---

[58]Ibid.; all quotes and equations in this section are from 191.

$$K_t = (1\text{-}d) \, K_{t-1} + I_t$$

In the formula:

K$_t$ indicates total military capital during time t
d indicates the depreciation rate
I$_t$ indicates total military investment during time t.

Then total military investment I$_t$ can be calculated through its proportion in that year's gross national product. Its equation is:

$$I_t = S \times GNP_t$$

In the formula, S indicates, in year t, the new military investment total's proportion of that year's GNP$_t$."[59]

Four Assessment and Measurement Methods. After detailing his "Comprehensive National Power dynamic equation" and several of its subequations, Huang outlines four different assessment and measurement methods for evaluating CNP: the index number method, used to compute the hard factors of the dynamic equation; a specialist evaluation method, for the soft factors; weighted coefficients, assigned to the coordinated factors; and a vague judgment method, to assess some of the undetermined factors. Under the index number method, after the data have been generated through the different subequations of the CNP dynamic equation, index numbers are established for it. These index numbers are set based upon a unified ratio, in which the value of the U.S. data from each equation is given the index number of 100. The indexes of the other countries are then set accordingly. Afterward, using the new indexes, the CNP of the different countries is calculated using the national power function. The results of Huang's calculations are shown in table 6.

Huang also projects the future Comprehensive National Power of countries; however, the only explanation he provides of his methods is: "In order to forecast the future world strategic structure, we used the

---

[59]Ibid., 202. All quotes and equations in this section are from 202-203.

Comprehensive National Power developments equation model, using the 'leading trend analysis method' to make calculations."[60]

Calculating the Rise and Decline of Nations

In his second book, *On the Rise and Fall of Nations*, Colonel Huang Shuofeng further develops his qualitative and quantitative analysis of CNP in order to show its role in the prosperity and decline of nations. He writes, "The strengths and weaknesses of CNP are the measures for the rise and fall of nations," and uses the above discussed "Comprehensive National Power dynamic equation" as the starting point for conducting his new assessments.[61] Huang's explanation of his original equation is almost identical to that laid out in *On Comprehensive National Power*, except that he gives further details regarding the science and technology power subequation. Before elaborating on how the "Comprehensive National Power equation" can be expanded upon to measure the rise and fall of nations, Huang calculates the 1996 scores of overall CNP and its various factors for six countries. Unfortunately, he did not make any predictions about the future CNP for the different countries, as he did in his previous book. The results of his new quantitative analysis of the United States, Japan, Germany, Russia, China, and India differ from those he derived 7 years before. A clear trend is that (as a percentage of the U.S. score) the CNP of all countries analyzed is growing faster than was predicted in 1989. A comparison of Huang's statistics from his two books is shown in table 7.

The original "Comprehensive National Power dynamic equation" measures only a country's strength at a given time; it does not indicate how the level of this power and its component factors influence a country's development and well being. Its numerical results allow for the comparison of CNP for different countries, but they do not illustrate the outcome of the interaction and competition between these countries. In setting forth his new "rise and fall of national power equation," Huang explains that the CNP

---

[60]Ibid., 220.

[61]Huang Shuofeng, *Guojia shengshuai lun* (On the rise and fall of nations)(Changsha: Hunan chubanshe, 1996), 337.

Table 6. *Huang Shuofeng's CNP scores for 1989*

Country	National Power Factors								CNP
	National Resources Power	*Science & Technology Power*	*Economic Power*	*National Defense Power*	*Cultural & Education Power*	*Foreign Affairs Power*	*National Embodiment Power*	*Coordinated Power*	
United States	92	234	269	249	.54	.61	.43	1.59	593.33
USSR	98	156	192	248	.51	.60	.55	1.64	386.72
Japan	35	239	251	80	.55	.51	.52	1.54	368.04
Germany	64	238	246	96	.54	.45	.42	1.52	308.10
France	62	231	212	110	.51	.46	.48	1.54	276.35
China	98	102	101	194	.46	.48	.47	1.66	222.33
England	62	163	146	101	.48	.40	.41	1.41	214.08
Brazil	87	94	102	90	.45	.37	.38	1.40	156.05
India	81	95	102	96	.48	.39	.43	1.41	144.16
Canada	72	85	127	75	.40	.39	.35	1.46	136.64
Australia	51	65	117	62	.45	.39	.35	1.45	112.59

Source: Huang Shuofeng, *Guojia zhongshuai lun* (On the rise and fall of nations) (Changsha: Hunan chubanshe, 1996), 337.

Table 7. *A Comparison of Huang's CNP Statistics*

Country	Score			Rank			As % of U.S. Score		
	'89	2000	'96	'89	2000	'96	'89	2000	'96
United States	593	817	90	1	1	1	100%	100%	100%
Japan	368	537	67	4	4	2	62	66	74
Germany	378	558	62	3	3	3	64	68	69
France	276	385	–	5	6	–	47	47	–
England	214	281	–	7	7	–	36	34	–
Canada	137	177	–	10	10	–	23	22	–
Australia	113	148	–	11	11	–	19	18	–
USSR	387	648	–	2	2	–	65	79	–
Russia	–	–	58	–	–	4	–	–	64
China	222	437	48	6	5	5	37	53	53
India	144	274	35	9	8	6	24	34	39
Brazil	156	268	–	8	9	–	26	33	–

Source: The scores for 1989 and 2000 are from Huang, *Zonghe guoli lun*, 220-221. The scores for 1996 are from Huang, *Guojia shengshuai lun*, 405. Their scores as a percentage of the U.S. score were generated by the author for comparison purposes.

system is "just like the organic world, it is a competitive and developing evolutionary process, where both vigorous and declining phenomenon exist."[62] The goal of the new equation is to quantitatively analyze this "competitive and developing evolutionary process," in order to determine the laws of the rise and decline of nations. Huang divides his discussion of the "rise and fall of national power equation" into two parts, its use in evaluating an individual country by itself, and its use in assessing two nations that are in competition with each other.

In the first situation, which Huang refers to as "an environment where the initiative is in one's own hands," the equation can be used to analyze how a

---

[62]Ibid., 379.

country's power is influenced by domestic conditions and the international environment. Explaining that "the rise and fall of a country's CNP obeys the organic world's law of the survival of the fittest," Huang makes an analogy between the disappearance of the dinosaurs and the collapse of the Soviet Union.[63] "With regard to a species, when there are natural changes and an inhospitable environment," if some form of mutation does not occur in that species that would allow it to evolve, then "this old species must decline, and no matter how prosperous this species was in the past, it will be unable to escape its destructive fate, such as occurred with the dinosaurs."

In the case of nations, Huang writes, if a country has poor strategic decisionmaking, which "deviates from the development trends of the international and domestic strategic environment" (such as through pursuing hegemony and arms expansion and focusing too much of its economy in the military arena, which hurts civilian development and leads to social and political instability), then the country will fall.[64] Once again he states, "Regardless of how prosperous it was in the past, this country will be unable to escape its fate of complete collapse. The disintegration of the Soviet Union is a typical example." However, Huang explains, if the species can adapt to its changed environment, and if countries uphold policies that are in keeping with the needs of the domestic and international environments, then "a spark can start a prairie fire," and they both can gradually develop and strengthen.

The second part of Huang's discussion on the uses for the "rise and fall of national power equation" deals with how national strength is affected by the interaction between two forces in a "struggle for existence environment." Huang writes, "The modern international struggle for existence in the final analysis is the competition of Comprehensive National Power. The focus of the competition is the struggle for strategic resources, including scientific and technological resources, economic resources, natural resources, personnel resources, information resources, etc., the key elements of Comprehensive National Power."[65] One purpose for the equation, therefore, is to analyze the

---

[63]Huang, *Guojia shengshuai lun*, 382. All subsequent quotes in this paragraph are from the same page.

[64]Ibid., 382. All other quotes in this paragraph are from the same page.

[65]Ibid., 383-384.

influence of a struggle for the same resource, on the rise and decline of two countries. It can also be adapted to examine an internal struggle for power between a country's old state system and a new one with a new national strategy. Finally, the equation can be used to assess a situation where two countries are not vying for the same thing but are seeking different resources and one of the countries has developed a new type of resource. In this case, their competition is conducted in the global marketplace.

Huang writes that the application of the equation to the latter scenario allows him to illustrate, "the laws of a competition, in an international environment, between two arbitrary countries on the 'battlefield' of the Comprehensive National Power competition."[66] The potential results of such a competition he describes as falling into four general categories:

- Both countries could be "destroyed" through an event such as nuclear war.
- One country could force another into a "fatal position."
- There could be "unequal coexistence," where one country is dominated by another.
- Two countries could coexist and "promote the prosperity" of each other through "mutual cooperation and reliance."

The last possibility, which sounds similar to the "Five Principles of Peaceful Coexistence," is regarded by Huang to be "the model for the future 'new world order.' "[67] Unfortunately, Huang does not provide any numerical results from calculations using "the rise and fall of national power equation."

FORECASTS: WINNERS AND LOSERS IN 2020

CASS

Prior to presenting its projected CNP scores for the years 2000 and 2010, the CASS study sets forth some main findings about the future prospects of each

---

[66]Ibid., 385.

[67]Ibid., 386-387.

of the world's major powers and considers the roles they are likely to assume in the future international competition.

China. By 2010 China will draw closer to Britain's rank in CNP. Along with Korea, China is one of the two swiftest risers in the CASS study, but China's task is much harder than Korea's. Korea has been surpassing only developing nations, while China is closing in on the industrialized leaders of the world. China's CNP rank is not commensurate either with China's military strength or the gross size of its economy measured in terms of purchase power parity (PPP). At least a decade will be needed for PLA modernization to take effect. China's three strongest components of CNP are its natural resources, rapid growth rate, and military manpower and weapons. However, these are offset by two important weakness—its low level of science and technology and its low "social" development. China must focus on economic policy and raising both its science and technology and its national educational level. Using PPP and the forecasts from the models of "Global Economic Forecasts" and "Project Link," in 1990 China already had a GDP of over $2 trillion, which would be the second largest in the world. PPP, however, is misleading. Using official exchange or conversion rates, China would have only the 10th largest economy in the world, with about $369 billion, and an even lower average per capita rank order (17th). Additionally, China's per capita GDP is at best $1,950, ranking 16th in the world.

Germany. Germany will remain the third-ranking power in the world after Japan and the United States for several decades, but it will not play a political or military role equivalent to its economic status. Germany's gap in CNP with the United States will decrease. However, this will occur only because of the relative decline of the United States. Germany will likely fall further behind a faster growing Japan. Germany may perhaps be overtaken by faster growing France, now in fourth place in CNP. Only if Germany can overcome the misgivings of its neighbors and the United States, and only after 2010, can it develop its actual power and benefit from the superior science and technology in Europe, thereby closing the gap with Japan. There will then be a new competition to see who will be the world's second-ranked power. It is necessary to watch closely this competition for second place between Japan and Germany after 2010 because it will significantly affect the 21st century. Germany's prospects to increase its competitive standing depend in part on a sound economy (foreign reserves, exports, and foreign investments), but it faces two important restraints. First, it must continue to integrate eastern Germany into its economy and social welfare system. Second, Germany must try to overcome the misgivings and treaty limitations placed on its military power by neighbor states and the United States, which oppose Germany playing a military role.

Russia. Moscow has yielded its second-place ranking in the world to Germany and Japan. Russia will fall further behind both France and England. One source of Russian decline is that Russia is the target of efforts by NATO and the United States to further weaken its status. Only after 40 to 50 years will Russia be able to become once more the number-one European power, ahead of Germany, France, and Britain. However, before this can occur in the middle decades of the 21st century, Russia will continue to fall behind Japan and Germany in CNP even after 2010.

France. Since the 1970s, France has consistently placed sixth in the fierce global competition. France has the potential to improve its relative position in CNP in the decades ahead, if it reorients its trade from Africa to Asia and exploits its impressive base in science and technology. However, France must overcome a large national debt, weak industries, and high unemployment. If this is done, France can move ahead even to fourth place in the world by 2010.

Great Britain. Despite its ranking as eighth in the world in CNP, England scores very high in economic indexes. During the decade from 2000 to 2010, London will rank eighth. Even though Britain is challenged by its small territorial size, it makes superb use of its limited space and can improve its productivity. In military terms, even though Britain is a nuclear power, its role will decline, while the nonnuclear military forces of Japan and Germany will increasingly improve and close this military gap. Because of a variety of factors, Britain will probably be surpassed by Italy by 2010. Italy's CNP will give Rome a greater role as its surpasses Britain and rises to the world's seventh-ranking power.

India. Reforms in India began 13 years after those in China. The Indian reform process is still influenced by political instability. Politics will influence the extent of further reform. At the same time, India's defense spending will increase. Its state-owned enterprises are only slowly being privatized.

The Rank Order in 2000-2020. By 2010, China will have improved its rank order by only one level, rising from the world's ninth power in 1990 to number eight. Scoring higher in CNP than China in 2010 will be the United States, Japan, Germany, France, Italy, Russia, and England (table 8). Like China, Japan, Germany, France, and Italy will each move up one rank from 1990 to 2010. Korea, not China, will show the fastest rate of improvement, because since 1975 Korea has passed India, Brazil, Mexico, and South Africa in CNP. By 2010 Korea will also pass Australia and Canada, to the number nine position. The important "loser" is Russia, whose world rank in CNP will decline by 2010. India will remain in 13th place.

Although CASS predicts only what the CNP of the world's major nations will look like in 2010, by using their statistics from 1990, 2000, and 2010, it is possible to project forward the scores another 10 years to 2020. Based on the projections, in 2020 Japan will pass the United States to place number one in the world; China will move into seventh place, ahead of England; South Korea will pass China, jumping into the number six spot; and Russia will slip even further, to number nine. The rank of all other countries will remain the same.

The Future of Japan and the United States. Japan's CNP score by 2010 will be almost as high as that of the United States. Assuming Japan sustains its faster CNP growth rate, Japanese CNP in 2020 will surpass the United States by about 19 percent—an extraordinary finding of the CASS civilian team. It obviously fulfills the prediction by Deng Xiaoping's advisers in the mid-1980s that the United States will lose its hegemony as the multipolar structure arrives. Yet it seems to open the potential for a new hegemony by Japan.

The CNP scores of Japan and the United States are both twice as high as the scores for Russia and China—a situation that does not fulfill the predictions of five "poles" in a multipolar structure. Rather, it opens the possibility that a security alliance of the United States and Japan (combining their CNP scores) would score four times higher than China alone. Even if China and Russia could combine their CNP scores in an alliance, they would still have but half the score of the combination of the United States and Japan. A comparison of tables 8 and 9 shows that CASS findings contrast sharply with those of the AMS; this contrast becomes even greater when the scores are projected forward another 10 years. In order to compare the CNP estimates

Table 8. *Projections to 2020 of CASS CNP Statistics, Points and Rank by Year*

Country	1990	2000	2010	2020
United States	279 (1)	241 (1)	213 (1)	192 (2)
Japan	162 (3)	184 (2)	206 (2)	228 (1)
Germany	161 (4)	162 (3)	163 (3)	164 (3)
France	129 (5)	141 (4)	150 (4)	157 (4)
Italy	115 (7)	125 (6)	137 (5)	151 (5)
England	116 (6)	116 (7)	115 (7)	115 (8)
Canada	100 (8)	92 (9)	86 (10)	81 (10)
Australia	78 (10)	71 (11)	66 (12)	62 (12)
South Africa	36 (15)	34 (16)	32 (16)	30 (16)
USSR	184 (2)	–	–	–
Russia	(139) (4)*	131 (5)	121 (6)	108 (9)
China	94 (9)	102 (8)	110 (8)	118 (7)
India	51 (13)	53 (13)	55 (13)	57 13)
Indonesia	34 (16)	37 (15)	39 (15)	40 (15)
South Korea	70 (11)	87 (10) .	105 (9)	124 (6)
Brazil	62 (12)	69 (12)	75 (11)	80 (11)
Mexico	46 (14)	49 (14)	51 (14)	52 (14)
Egypt	30 (17)	26 (17)	23 (17)	21 (17)

*In original chart to denote what retro Russia projections might have been.
Source: The scores for 1990, 2000 and 2010 are from Wang Songfen, ed., *Shijie zhuyao guojia zonghe guoli bijiao yanjiu* (Comparative studies of the comprehensive national power of the world's major nations)(Changsha: Hunan chubanshe, 1996), 438. The scores for 2020 were generated by the author.

of CASS and AMS, it was necessary to calculate the CNP scores for each country as a percentage of the U.S. CNP score (table 10). Two of the biggest differences between the orthodox and reform calculation results that emerge from the comparison are:

- By 2020, CASS has Japan ahead of the United States by 19 percent, while AMS has Japan 27 percent behind the United States.
- By 2020, CASS shows the United States ahead of China by 39 percent; AMS shows the United States only 3 percent ahead of China.

AMS

Using an extensive system of equations, discussed earlier in the chapter, Colonel Huang of AMS also calculates the CNP of the major nations of the world, with results that are greatly different from those generated by CASS. Huang forecasts CNP scores only for the year 2000, but by using the future CNP growth rates he provides, it was possible to project forward his scores to 2010 and 2020. These estimates show China passing Japan in the year 2009, passing Germany in 2011, becoming equal with the U.S. in 2021, and then taking the number-one position in the CNP rank order in 2022 (table 9).

In his second book, Huang provides 1996 CNP scores that differ from those of *On Comprehensive National Power*, in that they show Japan's CNP as more powerful than Germany's. However, the revised 1996 scores do not alter the big differences in CNP forecasts between CASS and AMS concerning the rise of China and the decline of the United States.

CNP Versus GDP Forecasts

For comparison purposes it is useful to contrast predictions of future CNP with future Gross Domestic Product (GDP). Some analysts consider the GDP index to be an excellent indicator of a nation's power, but for others it simply is one factor contributing to overall CNP, and a country's GDP and CNP rankings are not always the same. While Huang Shuofeng did not provide any statistics on future GDP, part of the CASS process of forecasting CNP is to first estimate GDP (table 11). "As a comprehensive index that reflects a country's actual economic strength, GDP and Comprehensive National Power are closely interrelated, and GDP is an important component part of Comprehensive National Power . . . countries whose GDP growth is fast, also have comparatively clear strengthening of their CNP, and visa versa.

Accordingly, before forecasting CNP, it is essential to first observe and study future GDP trends."[68]

For the majority of the 18 nations analyzed by CASS, their predicted GDP and CNP rankings in 2010 are very similar (table 12), and they are forecasted to have the same rankings in both categories or off by one position. Four nations, though, have divergent estimated rankings. China, India, and Brazil are expected to place higher in GDP than in CNP, while Russia is forecasted to have the reverse outcome. According to the CASS estimates, China will rank number 4 in GDP in 2010, while it will be number 8 that year in CNP. The country with the biggest predicted difference in GDP and CNP rankings, however, is Russia. CASS calculations place Russia fifteenth in the 2010 GDP rankings, but sixth in those for CNP.

Table 9. *Score and Rank Projections to 2020 of AMS CNP Statistics*

Country	1989	2000	2010	2020	Yearly Growth Rate
United States	593.33 (1)	816.85 (1)	1066.21 (1)	1391.71 (1)	2.7%
USSR	386.72 (2)	648.34 (2)	--	--	--
Germany	378.10 (3)	558.23 (3)	772.36 (2)	1068.63 (3)	3.3%
Japan	368.04 (4)	537.39 (4)	736.35 (4)	1009 (4)	3.2%
China	222.33 (6)	437.35 (5)	768.57 (3)	1350.63 (2)	5.8%
France	276.35 (5)	384.93 (6)	507.36 (5)	668.73 (6)	2.8%
England	214.08 (7)	281.24 (7)	353.05 (8)	443.19 (8)	2.3%
Brazil	156.05 (8)	267.70 (9)	419.72 (7)	658.09 (7)	4.6%
India	144.16 (9)	274.08 (8)	468.15 (6)	799.67 (5)	5.5%
Canada	136.64 (10)	177.41 (10)	220.56 (9)	274.18 (9)	2.2%
Australia	112.59 (11)	147.91 (11)	185.67 (10)	233.07 (10)	2.3%

Source: The scores for 1989 and 2000, and the yearly growth rates are from Huang Shuofeng, *Zonghe guoli lun* (On comprehensive national power)(Beijing: Zhongguo shehui kexue chubanshe, 1992), 220-221. Scores for 2010 and 2020 were generated by the author.

[68]Wang Songfen, ed., *Shijie zhuyao guojia zonghe guoli bijiao yanjiu*, 432-433; the statistics are from 434.

Table 10. A Comparison of the CNP Scores of CASS and Huang
(as a Percent of U.S. CNP by Year) (U.S. = 100)

Country	1970	1980	1989/1990		2000		2010		2020	
	CASS	CASS	Huang	CASS	Huang	CASS	Huang	CASS	Huang	CASS
United States	100%	100%	100%	100%	100%	100%	100%	100%	100%	100%
Japan	34	50	62	58	66	76	69	97	73	119
Germany	42	52	64	58	68	67	72	77	77	85
France	33	46	47	46	47	59	48	70	48	82
Italy	26	34	–	41	–	52	–	64	–	79
England	34	42	36	42	34	48	33	54	32	60
Canada	33	35	23	36	22	38	21	40	20	42
Australia	26	29	19	28	18	29	17	31	17	32
USSR	64	77	65	66	79	–	–	–	–	–
Russia	–	–	–	(50)	–	54	–	57	–	56
China	25	33	37	34	53	42	72	52	97	61
India	15	19	24	18	34	22	44	26	57	30
S. Korea	10	19	–	25	–	36	–	49	–	65

Source: Huang Shuofeng, *Zonghe guoli lun* (On comprehensive national power) (Beijing: Zhongguo shehui kexue chubanshe, 1992)

249

While CASS argues that GDP is only one component factor in CNP and that forecasted GDP estimates do not necessarily correctly indicate a country's overall national strength, other authors rely on GDP as the foundation for their assertions of future power, particularly with regard to China. For example, after giving statistics from the Organization for Economic Cooperation and Development (OECD) regarding China's future GDP and other economic indicators, as well as quoting an OECD report that says China's economy could be the world's largest by 2020, Li Zhongcheng of CICIR states, "Whether the above cited estimates have errors or not, few people would disagree that China's overall national strength will still be far behind the United States, but may catch up with Japan and will be sure to exceed Russia."[69] Other Chinese authors also refer to the predictions and findings of Western organizations to backup their assertions of China's future power. Chen Zhongjing, former president of CICIR, agrees with a U.S. Department of Defense report that by 2010 China will be number 2 or 3 in GNP.[70]

Other Predictions

The team at CASS and Colonel Huang at AMS are not the only Chinese analysts to calculate and predict future CNP; in fact, virtually every article and book about international relations and the future security environment mentions the concept. The CASS and AMS studies are unique in that they provide extensive details and explanations about their assessment and calculation processes, as well as numerous data tables of their results. Most other Chinese authors only mention CNP in general terms or, if they make predictions, do not elaborate on how they derived their conclusions. However, despite their lack of details, it is important to set forth other calculations and forecasts as a contrast to those of CASS and AMS.

---

[69]Li Zhongcheng, "The Role of an Emerging China in World Politics," *Contemporary International Relations* 8, no. 2 (February 1998): 10.

[70]Chen Zhongjing, *Guoji zhanlue wenti* (Problems of international strategy)(Beijing: Shishi chubanshe, 1988).

Table 11. *CASS GDP Forecasts of the Major Nations*

	GDP (billion $U.S., 1990 price)			GDP Yearly Growth Rate (%)		
	1990	*2000*	*2010*	*1991-1994*	*1995-2000*	*2001-2010*
United States	5464.8	7101.5	9179.4	2.21	2.94	2.6
Japan	2932.1	3691.5	4865.3	1.61	2.81	2.8
Germany	1618.3	2092.6	2626.8	2.21	2.86	2.3
France	1194.8	1450.3	1785.1	0.73	2.78	2.1
Italy	1095.1	1325.7	1647.8	0.85	2.64	2.2
England	975.5	1182.7	1455.7	0.73	2.76	2.1
Canada	569.4	721.2	914.2	1.26	3.15	2.4
Australia	294.5	397.8	534.6	2.29	3.56	3.0
South Africa	102.1	119.2	149.8	-0.02	2.62	2.25
Russia	382.5	225.6	367.4	-16.2	2.97	5.0
China	369.9	928.2	2003.8	11.67	8.29	8.0
India	303.2	477.0	814.7	3.57	5.36	5.5
Indonesia	106.3	198.0	408.1	6.74	6.20	7.5
South Korea	244.0	487.2	976.4	7.00	7.26	7.2
Brazil	476.0	746.1	1215.2	2.52	6.0	5.0
Mexico	244.0	341.2	529.8	2.48	4.04	4.5
Egypt	48.0	65.9	92.95	3.06	3.34	3.5

Source: Wang Songfen, ed., *Shijie zhuyao guojia zonghe guoli bijiao yanjiu* (Comparative studies of the comprehensive national power of the world's major nations)(Changsha: Hunan chubanshe, 1996), 434.

Table 12. *CASS Predictions of Future GDP and CNP Rankings*

Country	GDP Rankings			CNP Rankings		
	1990	2000	2010	1990	2000	2010
United States	1	1	1	1	1	1
Japan	2	2	2	3	2	2
Germany	3	3	3	4	3	3
France	4	4	5	5	4	4
Italy	5	5	6	7	6	5
England	6	6	7	6	7	7
Canada	7	9	10	8	9	10
Australia	12	12	12	9	11	12
South Africa	16	16	16	15	16	16
Russia	9	14	15	–	5	6
China	10	7	4	9	8	8
India	11	10	11	13	13	13
Indonesia	15	15	14	16	15	15
South Korea	14	11	9	11	10	9
Brazil	8	8	8	12	12	11
Mexico	13	13	13	14	14	14
Egypt	17	17	17	17	17	17

Source: Wang Songfen, ed., *Shijie zhuyao guojia zonghe guoli bijiao yanjiu* (Comparative studies of the comprehensive national power of the world's major nations)(Changsha: Hunan chubanshe, 1996).

Hubei Science Commission Calculations. In the discussion of research on CNP by other Chinese analysts, the CASS study describes some earlier research conducted by Yu Hongyi and Wang Youdi of the Hubei Science Commission. Their formula for calculating CNP was given as "function (F), dimension (D), structure (S), level (L), and four-dimensional vector comprehensive national strength (CNS) measurement formula, in which CNS = F (FDSL)."[71] The calculation results of 12 countries based on the FDSL measurement formula are shown in table 13. In addition to Yu and Wang, the CASS study also briefly describes the work of Huang Shuofeng, but does not compare either his or Yu and Wang's analysis methods or results with its own.

CICIR Calculations. Yan Xuetong of CICIR also calculates CNP (table 14), which he breaks down into six factors: manpower, natural resources, economics, politics, military affairs, and history and culture. The only explanation he gives for his measurement process is that he uses "a simple index average value method . . . to conduct quantitative analysis."[72]

Although Yan does not calculate the past CNP scores of the five countries, or forecast their future CNP, he describes the "post-Cold War unbalanced power development trend" as a situation where "the CNP of China, Japan, and Germany is relatively tending toward strengthening, and the United States, Russia, England and France are moving toward decline." Yan's assessment of China's CNP is quite positive: "China's national power growth is particularly outstanding, accelerating the speed of the changes in the balance of strength." However, he does note that when viewed on a global scale, "China already is one of the world's great nations, but if a national power comparison is carried out among the five major post-Cold War powers, then China still is only a regional power," for "there is a very large gap between the indexes of China, Russia, Japan, and Germany, and that of the United States."[73] Yan is optimistic about the future development of China's CNP:

---

[71]Yu Hongyi and Wang Youdi, "Zonghe guoli cedu pingjie (Measuring the value of comprehensive national power)," *Keji jinbu yu duice* (Scientific and technological progress and ways of dealing with it) 1989, 5, in Wang Songfen, ed., *Shijie zhuyao guojia zonghe guoli bijiao yanjiu*, 50-51.

[72]Yan Xuetong, *Zhongguo guojia liyi fenxi* (Analysis of China's national interests)(Tianjin: Tianjin renmin chubanshe, 1996), 88.

[73]Ibid., 57, 94-95.

Looking back at the success of the reforms and opening since the December 1978 Third Plenary Session of the 11th Central Committee, we can find that the potential for China to raise its CNP is very great. It is possible that at the end of this century China will become a rising industrializing country, situated between developed and developing countries. By the twenties of the next century, China will probably become a great nation in the world, second only to the United States.[74]

Table 13. *Hubei Science Commission CNP Calculations (1985)*

Country	Function Dimension (F_D)	Structure Level L_S	CNP
United States	0.5049	0.9262	0.6838 (1)
Soviet Union	0.2048	0.8252	0.4111 (2)
Japan	0.1434	0.8815	0.3555 (3)
Germany	0.0854	0.8839	0.2748 (4)
England	0.0621	0.9178	0.2386 (5)
France	0.0609	0.8907	0.2329 (6)
China	0.0757	0.6409	0.2202 (7)
Canada	0.0489	0.9225	0.2123 (8)
Italy	0.0454	0.8757	0.1993 (9)
Australia	0.0207	0.9133	0.1374 (10)
India	0.0298	0.6256	0.1365 (11)
Egypt	0.0057	0.7509	0.0656 (12)

Source: Yu Hongyi and Wang Youdi, "Zonghe guoli cedu pingjie (Measuring the value of comprehensive national power)," *Keji jinbu yu duice* (Scientific and Technological Progress and Ways of Dealing with it) 1989: 5, in *Shijie zhuyao guojia zonghe guoli bijiao yanjiu*, Wang Songfen, ed., 50-51.

[74]Ibid., 89.

Table 14. *Yan Xuetong's Calculations of the Simple Average Value of the Major Nation's GNP*

	United States	Japan	China	Russia	Germany
Manpower	1	0.5	0.3*	0.5	0.3
Natural Resources	1	0.04	0.7	1	0.1
Politics	1	0.5	0.7	0.5	0.5
*Economics***	1	0.6	0.17	0.1	0.3
Miliary Affairs	1	0.14	0.3	0.6	0.11
Culture	1	0.9	1	0.9	0.9
Total	1	0.44	0.53	0.6	0.35

*In general it is believed that 200 million is most ideal for the population of a great nation. China's population is well over that, so it has a negative effect on national power growth, added to which, China's overall education level is lower than the four other countries, therefore its index is smaller than that of the United States, Japan, and Russia.

**The economic index is based on 1993 GNP; China's and Russia's indexes were attained by the average values of exchange and PPP calculations.

Source: Yan Xuetong, *Zhongguo guojia liyi fenxi* (Analysis of China's national interests)(Tianjin: Tianjin renmin chubanshe, 1996), 95.

1994 Confidential Calculations. According to the Hong Kong newspaper *Cheng Ming*, a confidential report, "War to be Won," about the period 2000 to 2010, was released in 1994 by the Policy Research Office of the Chinese State Council, the Policy Research Office of the Central Military Commission, and the Policy Research Office of the Communist Party Central Committee. Classified as confidential, it was a document to be studied by departments in Beijing and the provinces. The main points are that the two sides of the Taiwan Strait will be unified and the comprehensive national strength of China will be in the top three in the world. China's GNP, excluding Taiwan, is estimated to become six times the 1993 figure or, in 2010, approximately 18 trillion yuan, about U.S. $2.5 trillion.[75]

Swiss Calculations. Another useful source for comparison is to look at Western forecasts of national power. The *World Competitive Yearbook* , jointly published by the World Economic Forum and the International Institute for Management Development in Lausanne, Switzerland, is an annual evaluation report of international competitiveness. It assesses many more countries than any of the Chinese studies discussed in this chapter. The 1998 rankings for those countries they had in common, as well as a few additions, are the United States (1), Singapore (2), Hong Kong (3), Canada (10), Britain (12), Germany (14), Australia (15), Taiwan (16), Japan (18), France (21), China (24), Italy (30), Mexico (34), Korea (35), Brazil (37), Indonesia (40), India (41), South Africa (42), and Russia (46). For some of the above nations, major changes took place in comparison to their rankings from the previous year: Japan fell from 9 to 18, Korea from 30 to 35, and Brazil from 33 to 37. On the other hand, Taiwan rose from 23 to 16, and China from 27 to 24.[76]

FINDINGS

In the mid-1980s, Deng Xiaoping asserted that it was important to calculate future trends in CNP, a concept that helps guide China's reforms and includes economics, science, defense, and other factors. Although it was invented in 1984, Chinese authors justify the concept as stemming from ancient Chinese strategists as well as Chairman Mao. CNP scores are important for major powers because they can help identify:

- The status hierarchy in world politics
- The power of potential rivals and potential partners
- Who will best exploit the RMA

---

[75]According to Professor Allen S. Whiting, "Although *Cheng Ming* is a Hong Kong journal, it has a good track record of acquiring authentic PRC classified documents." Allen S. Whiting, "East Asian Military Securities Dynamics," Asia-Pacific Research Center, Stanford University, February 1995, 49, footnote 9. The article also stated that China will have two to four aircraft carriers and a PLA reduced to only 1.5 million from today's 3 million. By 2010, manned Chinese spacecraft will be launched and a space station will have been established.

[76]"World's Competitive Countries List," *The Associated Press*, April 21, 1998.

- Which side will win a war
- The trend toward world multipolarity and U.S. decline.

Two contending scientific teams in Beijing have calculated estimates of the CNP scores of the major powers in 2010. Both teams claim to use very sophisticated quantitative methods they say had to be developed because of the deficiencies in the methodological techniques used by the West and Japan to measure future growth rates in national power.

The military team's quantitative results are consistent with the orthodox Chinese view that a multipolar world structure is emerging and that U.S. hegemony is ending. In particular, according to the military estimate, the U.S. quantitative power score by 2010 shows a decreasing gap between the United States and the other major powers. By 2020, the U.S. score will equal that of China, assuming China's power growth rate continues to be 5.8 percent, double the U.S. rate of 2.7 percent. Germany and Japan will also have higher CNP growth rates than the United States, ranking third and fourth in world power after the United States and China in 2020. If these growth rates are extended another decade or so, China, Japan, and Germany will all three equal or surpass the United States in CNP, but the United States will remain ahead of Russia (which is not scored because of uncertainty) and India, the sixth in rank order of CNP.

The civilian team's results contradict the orthodox view about an emerging multipolar structure. The most striking contrast is the assessment of China's growth rate relative to the United States (table 15). The civilian team does not rank China equal to the United States by 2020 but merely ranks it number eight in the world, with a projected power score of only about half the U.S. CNP by 2010 and 2020. A second contrast is that the civilian team's quantitative results place Japan not number four in the world by 2010 but equal to the United States. Japan pulls ahead of the United States by 19 percent in 2020. China in 2020 will still rank only seventh in the world, trailing not only the United States and Japan, but Germany, France, Italy, and even South Korea in CNP.

These differences between the civilian "reform" and military "orthodox" estimates of the future geopolitical power hierarchy take on significance in light of the claims made by Deng Xiaoping and many Chinese authors about the importance of CNP. For example, Chinese writing on the RMA emphasizes how CNP will be a crucial ingredient in determining which nation will do the best in designing and implementing an RMA. The civilian team would seem to suggest that Japan and the United States will be the nations to watch with respect to developing RMA capabilities. China will be only a distant contender, not even one of the top five powers.

Table 15. *A Comparison of CASS and AMS Growth Rates*

	AMS	CASS		
Country	1989-2000	1990-2000	2000-2010	2010-2020
United States	2.7%	-1.36%	-1.16%	-.99%
Japan	3.2	1.36	1.2	1.07
China	5.8	.85	.78	.73

Source: Huang Shuofeng, *Zonghe guoli lun* (On comprehensive national power)(Beijing: Zhongguo shehui kexue chubanshe, 1992): and Wang Songfen, ed., *Shijie zhuyao guojia zonghe guoli bijiao yanjiu* (Comparative studies of the comprehensive national power of the world's major nations)(Changsha: Hunan chubanshe, 1996).

Chinese military authors assert that national power scores probably determine the outcome of wars. If so, the Chinese military team's quantitative results suggest China has little to fear from Japanese national power by 2010 and still less by 2020 when Japan will slip to fourth place. Better still, in terms of military threats to China, the military team's results suggest China will have three-fourths of the power score of the United States by 2010 and become co-equal to the United States by 2020.

6: FORECASTING FUTURE WARS

CHINA'S ASSESSMENT OF THE FUTURE SECURITY ENVIRONMENT is closely linked to its views of future warfare. This chapter introduces 55 military authors who may be divided into the three schools of thought in China today that analyze likely wars and recommend what types of preparation China should undertake.

WHERE WILL LOCAL WARS OCCUR?

Chinese articles and books describe the current "new era" as one of transition in which the new world strategic pattern is in the process of replacing an old one. They predict that regional wars will be a significant part of this process. "If large-scale armed conflicts and local wars happen . . . it can result in drastic changes in critical regional situations and immensely harm the global strategic situation."[1] Where will these wars break out? Several Chinese authors have suggested that the fault lines of future war in the multipolar security environment will not be the same as during the bipolar Soviet-American confrontation. Colonel Xu Weidi of the National Defense University (NDU) predicts that the two great zones of war will be the East Asian littoral (because of territorial disputes) and the Eurasian zone, including Central Asia and the Persian Gulf.[2] At present, half the world's 48 local wars are in Africa.

---

[1]Xia Liping, Wang Zhongchun, Wen Zhonghua, and Xu Weidi, "Shijie zhanlue xingshi de zhuyao tedian yu qushi" (The world strategic situation—characteristics and trends), *Heping yu fazhan* (Peace and Development) 47, no. 1 (February 1994): 18.

[2]Colonel Xu Weidi, "Post Cold War Naval Security Environment," *World Military Trends* (Beijing: Academy of Military Science, no date).

Shen Qurong, President of the China Institute of Contemporary International Relations (CICIR), writes, "The rise of power centers in Asia will not be synchronized, yet the time lag among them will not be so distant. . . . In the next decade, there will exist a variety of possibilities or options for the structure of power in Asia." Shen believes that "unipolar hegemony" will give way to "a traditional balance of multipolar forces" or "ad hoc strategic alignments revolving around key issues or geopolitical pivots."[3] Shen concludes, "While the balance of power will still play an important role, the pursuit of hegemonism will further destabilize the original fragile structure in Asia."[4] Hegemonism runs counter to the Asian reality of the rise of a number of power centers and comes into conflict with the ever-mounting Asian demand to be master of its own house. "It actually puts Washington in confrontation with these multiple forces." Shen criticizes Joseph Nye, former U.S. Assistant Secretary of Defense, by quoting him as being unwilling to change from American leadership to having an American role as a "balancer" of power in East Asia.

No matter where wars break out, Chinese authors suggest that one of the main causes of wars will be the struggle for economic resources. As Colonel Liu Mingde states, "The Marxists hold that the conflict of economic interests is the root of war." He explains that the Arab-Israeli dispute "has to do with Israel's heavy reliance on the Jordan River" and that Iran-Iraq war and the Gulf War were about petroleum. Similarly, the civil war in Yugoslavia is a war between "poor" Serbia and the "rich" Slovenia and Croatia. Liu concludes that "competition in Comprehensive National Power has aggravated the scrambling for resources among nations."[5]

A likely area for future wars will be Central Asia, where "abundant natural resources will become the target of a struggle" between the major powers. The United States wants the energy resources, but Russia is unwilling to "drop to the status of a second-rank country" and will resist the United States.

---

[3]Shen Qurong "May Earlier Maturity Come to Peace: Thoughts on Asia's Future," *Contemporary International Relations* 6, no. 9 (September 1996): 14.

[4]Ibid., 14.

[5]Liu Mingde, "The Implications of Changes in Warfare After the Disintegration of the Bipolar Structure," *Guoji zhanlue yanjiu* (International Strategic Studies) 24, no. 2 (June 1992): 7-8.

Germany and Japan will be "potential competitive opponents" of the United States. The U.S. goal is not only to pursue its economic interests, but also to squeeze Russia out:

> The rivalry over the Caspian Sea region's oil and natural gas is part of the U.S.-Russian rivalry over strategic interests and spheres of influence in the Eurasian hinterland. . . .The number of countries involved (in the struggle) will increase. The European Union also regards the Central Asian region as an energy resources base that can replace the Gulf in the future. . . . International forces covet the treasure chest that is Central Asia.[6]

WHAT KIND OF WARS COULD AFFECT CHINA?

Since 1994, several dozen articles have appeared in the Chinese press and in military journals that purport to discuss China's current and future defense strategy. These articles are not all in agreement. At least three and possibly more schools of thought may be distinguished.

People's War Scenarios

- The enemy—the United States, Russia, or Japan—will invade and seek to subjugate China.
- The war will last many years.
- China's leaders will move to alternative national capitals during the war.
- China's defense industrial base will arm millions of militia in protracted war until the enemy can be defeated by the main army.

---

[6]Yang Shuheng, "Lengzhan hou daguo he diqu liliang dui Zhongya de zhengduo" (The struggles over Central Asia by major nations and regional forces in the post-Cold War period), *Heping yu fazhan* (Peace and Development) 60, no. 2 (June 1997): 29, 45.

In the first school, authors refer to the enduring validity of Mao's concepts of People's War (*renmin zhanzheng*).[7] These authors imply that the 21st century may well see the outbreak of another world war, a major invasion of China, or the use of nuclear weapons. This Maoist school of thought is less frequently seen in Chinese military journals than the second school of thought, which may be called "Local War."

Local War Scenarios

- The opponent will not be a superpower.
- The war will be near China's border.
- The war will not be a deep invasion.
- China will seek a quick military decision.
- Rapid reaction forces will defeat the local forces of Japan, Vietnam, India, Central Asia, Taiwan, Philippines, Malaysia, or Indonesia.

Local war is identified by the authors' call for China to prepare not for a protracted People's War with national mobilization, but for a quick, smaller scale "local war under high-tech conditions," or simply Local War (*jubu zhanzheng*). These authors frequently cite a speech by Deng Xiaoping to the Central Military Commission in 1985 to explain the origins of the concept. Deng's speech flatly decreed that the world would not be seeing a global war or a major nuclear war for "a long time to come." In the decade since that speech, more than 30 conflict scenarios have been spelled out in articles by Chinese analysts from this school of thought, as well as in interviews by the

---

[7] A recent endorsement of People's War appeared January 9, 1998, in *Liberation Army Daily*. It quoted Defense Minister Chi Haotian, who at the National Defense University stated, "Under high-tech conditions, we still need to insist on People's War." Chi said that People's War "is the product of historical and dialectical materialism."

author with Chinese military officers.[8] Local War is not a good translation of what this second school of Chinese analysts has been discussing—unless the Korean War, Vietnam War, and Gulf War can be appropriately labeled local wars. Rather, Local War seems to include a broad range of scenarios, almost any war smaller in scale than a global or a major nuclear war.

RMA Scenarios

The opponent—perhaps the U.S., Russia or Japan—will have advanced weapons, satellites for communications and reconnaissance, stealth aircraft, nuclear weapons, and nanotechnology. Therefore China must:

- Close an " information gap."
- Network all forces.
- Attack the enemy C^3I to paralyze its operations.
- Pre-empt enemy attacks.
- Use directed energy weapons.
- Use computer viruses.
- Use submarine-launched munitions.
- Use antisatellite weapons.
- Use forces to prevent a logistics buildup.
- Use special operations raids.

The third school of thought probably dates only from 1994 and is represented by a few books and perhaps a few dozen articles, although interest in the RMA seemed to increase after the NATO bombing campaign against Serbia in 1999. However, its proponents include several generals who occupy (or are recently retired from) high positions in China's most influential military institutions. This third school of thought recommends that China prepare for future warfare along the lines of concepts first discussed by Russian and

---

[8]The author conducted over 60 interviews with Chinese military and civilian authors from March 1995 to October 1998.

American authors who forecast a potential revolution in military affairs (RMA), or *xin junshi geming*. According to one analyst, "The unfolding of the new military revolution worldwide is a prominent feature of the international security situation. . . . [It] involves such fields as military thinking, military strategy, operational doctrine, military organization, and arms development."[9]

Chinese writers in 1995 repeatedly referred to the "third military technical revolution" without actually footnoting the Soviet military journals that in the past decade have been discussing the same subject. The subject itself was not new; it had been discussed earlier in books such as General Mi Zhenyu's *Chinese National Defense Concepts*, published in 1988. What was new in 1995 in Beijing was the enthusiasm; even the official newspaper, *Liberation Army Daily*, began to publish almost weekly articles about the military-technical revolution and its implications for China. In October 1995, the official media announced a national conference had been held to discuss the implications of a potential revolution in military affairs.

Soviet military science and its Chinese counterpart explicitly require the use of "scientific" forecasts about the changing nature of future warfare. In other words, it is not optional but mandated by "military science" that strategists must concern themselves with the search for the emergence of "revolutionary" changes in warfare, brought about mainly by technological change, rather than falsely assuming that mere evolutionary trends will continue.[10]

---

[9]Li Qinggong, "Dangqian de guoji junshi anquan xingshi" (The current international military security situation), *Guoji zhanlue yanjiu* (International Strategic Studies) 47, no. 1 (January 1998): 9. Li is a Research Fellow at China Institute of International Strategic Studies (CIISS).

[10]One description of RMAs comes from a Senior Adviser at CIISS, who writes, "A relatively typical view in our country has it that human history has thus far witnessed five military revolutions: The earliest one emerged with bare-handed fights; the second one accompanied the extensive military use of 'cold steel' after the invention of metallurgy; the third radical change in the military field came to the fore when human society stepped into the era of hot arms, as gunpowder was invented and firearms were used militarily on a large scale; mankind found itself in the period of mechanized warfare following the manufacture of internal combustion engines and the fabrication and broad military utilization of mechanical weapons from the 19th century to the first half of the 20th century; and the fifth revolution in military affairs began to emerge during the second half of this century in company with the extensive military application of nuclear weapons, electronic and micro-electronic technology, computers, remote sensing and control technology, new material and energy technology,

According to the Soviet concept, as applied by the Chinese, "military science" covers not only military operational art but several other specific approaches included within the formal definition of "military art." According to Marshal Ogarkov and Marshal Sokolovskiy in 1968, such studies include "the conditions and factors that determine, at any given historical moment, the nature of a future war."[11]

There seems to be no American counterpart to Chinese "military science" and its related requirement to anticipate military revolutions and to "experiment scientifically" with organizations, exercises, and prototype equipment. Rather, American studies of how military innovation occurs tend to emphasize the somewhat accidental role of the relatively rare individual genius who invents a new concept, pushes a new doctrinal idea, or changes resource allocations together with his organizational allies.

Like the RMA school, the Local War school also borrows Soviet and American concepts. After the Gulf War in 1991, local war authors incorporated many aspects of American strategy into their concept of local war. More than 40 books, published by the Academy of Military Science (AMS) and NDU, drew on examples from the Gulf War in order to illustrate how China's concept of local war should be implemented in the 21st century. Most of this writing focused on how the Chinese military may have to defend itself from an American-style Gulf War offensive action. In a similar fashion, in the last 5 years the main Chinese military newspaper *Liberation Army Daily* has published several hundred articles attempting to describe local war doctrine and Chinese military exercises designed to cope with a "high-tech enemy." These articles and books leave little doubt that the weapons, equipment, and uniforms that will be possessed by this high-tech enemy will be the forces of the United States or its military allies.

These three schools of authors cannot be easily reconciled. With a limited budget it is hard to prepare for all three types of future warfare. The

---

oceaneering and bioengineering technology, and aerospace technology, as well as with the epochal character of the historical transition period and the evolution in the international situation." Wang Zhenxi, "The New Wave of Military Revolution in the World," *Guoji zhanlue yanjiu* (International Strategic Studies) 44, no. 2 (April 1997): 2.

[11]V. D. Sokolovskiy, *Soviet Military Strategy* (London: MacDonald and James, 1968), 18.

neo-Maoist, or People's War, school seems to recommend that China be prepared for a long war of many years at low-level intensity in which space can be traded for time, territory will be surrendered initially, and the population will be mobilized for guerrilla warfare against the invader and in support of the regular Chinese Armed Forces. Local War school authors advocate preparing for a short-warning attack in which the decision will come quickly, with no opportunity to activate the nation for a multiyear People's War. They explicitly describe future local warfare as concluding within a matter of days or weeks, in which there will be no time to mobilize the population; instead, there will be an intense tempo. Success will almost certainly require China to consider pre-emptive strikes against the enemy near or beyond China's borders in order to achieve an "early, decisive victory."

Since the early 1980s, foreign scholars have declared in a series of articles that local war has become the official strategic doctrine of China; these conclusions may have been premature. Not only have the neo-Maoist articles continued to appear, but in interviews conducted by the author, senior Chinese military officers have declared that local war doctrine has not been written for China's Armed Forces, nor has it been formally adopted by the Central Military Commission, at least as of 1995. Dennis Blasko, former Assistant Army Attaché in Beijing, has pointed out that there is no official People's Liberation Army (PLA) doctrine of Local War, in spite of all the articles since 1985:

> On two separate occasions in the fall of 1994 and early 1995, a major general and a senior colonel at the AMS (Academy of Military Science in Beijing) denied that what is known in the West as the "PLA's doctrine of Local War" even exists or is anything as formal as the U.S. Army doctrine defined by FM 100-5. . . . Indeed, no formal "Doctrine of Local War" has been formulated or even ordered to be developed by the General Staff Department. . . . While it is possible that these three different officers assigned to the AMS and numerous contributors to Chinese military publications are trying to deceive foreigners about the current state of Chinese military thinking, informal conversations with officers in the field

have provided no indication that grass roots level leaders are looking any differently at the future of war either.[12]

This divergence—between published articles and military exercises and a lack of an authoritative declaration that local war is the national strategy—constitutes a major puzzle. Further complicating the confusion, in the last 3 years observers have noted an increase in the attention the press has given to the further development of China's nuclear forces, which does not seem connected to Local War theory. Additionally, a series of books and articles has appeared advocating a Chinese blue water navy, which also seems to have no link to the Local War doctrine. PLA naval authors assert that local war at sea covers two large zones of "active defense." Within the first zone, from the PRC coast out to the "First Island Chain," there are three levels, each with its own naval forces providing a "multilevel in-depth defense at sea:"

- Out to 50 miles, which is defended by radar, missiles, and large coastal patrol boats such as missile speedboats and fast gunships, and where laying mines and clearing enemy mines are very important tasks
- From 50 to 300 miles from the coast, which is defended by missile destroyers and corvettes, including ship-based helicopters
- From the Korean peninsula to the Ryukyu and Spratly Islands, which is defended by submarines with advanced missiles and naval attack planes.[13]

The second island chain the Chinese Navy aspires to patrol extends along a line from the Aleutians through Guam and the Philippines. However, these "island chains" are not discussed by PLA Navy authors who write about the RMA.

---

[12]Dennis Blasko, "Better Late Than Never: Non-equipment Aspects of PLA Ground Force Modernization," in *Chinese Military Modernization*, eds. C. Dennison Lane, Mark Weisenbloom, and Dimon Liu (Washington: AEI Press, 1996), 131.

[13]Captain Chen Yungkang and Lieutenant Commander Chai Wenchung, "A Study of the Evolving PRC Naval Strategy," *China Mainland* (Taipei, September 1, 1997): 7-10, 13-20.

As if this were not enough confusion, since 1994 the third RMA school of thought has presented itself vigorously in advocacy pieces that do not directly attack Local War theory but do state that China must exploit a potential future RMA in order to avoid a growing gap in its military capabilities, as compared to America, Russia, and Japan. At least 30 articles have appeared advocating development by China of the capacity to conduct information operations, massive long-range precision strikes, attacks on enemy satellites in space, and efforts to paralyze an enemy's command and control system by nonnuclear attacks on its homeland. These articles and at least three major conferences that focused on a future potential revolution in military affairs cannot be neatly fitted into the framework of either the neo-Maoist authors or the advocates of "local war under high tech conditions."

INSTITUTIONAL AFFILIATIONS
OF THE THREE SCHOOLS

These three schools may be seen as independent viewpoints that any individual could hold. They may also reflect institutional "homes" where the schools' authors work. RMA advocates (who tend to be senior colonels and a few major generals) seem to be employed by the AMS or the large components of the Commission on Science, Technology and Industry for National Defense (COSTIND) complex, such as the China Aerospace Corporation and its research institutes like the Beijing Institute of System Engineering. Local war authors occupy most of the highest positions of the PLA and also are employed at the NDU, which trains almost all future generals. People's War school authors seem to be senior party officials, members of the General Political Department, and senior militia and People's Armed Police (PAP) leaders.

FORCE STRUCTURE AND THE THREE SCHOOLS

The three schools may also to some extent reflect the current state of China's existing force structure, its efforts in doctrinal development, the equipment in its inventory, and the types of conflict scenarios used as points of reference.

The relationship of the three schools to one another and to the Chinese force structure can be visualized as a triangle, or a pyramid, with three tiers.[14]

Figure 1. *Three Schools of Future Warfare*

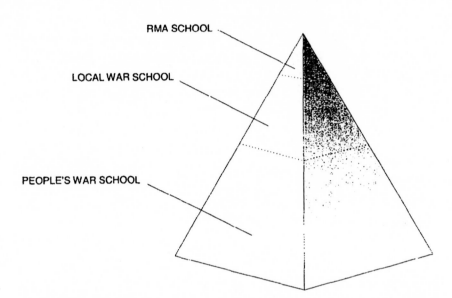

People's War School

According to Dennis Blasko, the base of the pyramid represents the People's War school, which encompasses the vast majority of the People's Liberation Army today. The military thought of Mao Zedong provides the theoretical foundation for this school.[15]

---

[14]In the following discussion of the force structure of the three schools, the author is deeply indebted to Dennis Blasko's observations. See Dennis J. Blasko, "A New PLA Force Structure," in *The People's Liberation Army in the Information Age*, eds. James C. Mulvenon and Richard H. Yang (Santa Monica, CA: The RAND Corporation, 1999), 258-288.

[15]For examples of Chinese writing on People's Warfare, see Liu Sheng'e and Miao Lin, *Xiandai jubu zhanzheng tiaojian xia de renmin zhanzheng* (People's War under the conditions of high-technology warfare)(Beijing: Guofang daxue chubanshe, 1996); Song Shilun, *A Preliminary Probe into Mao Zedong's Military Thought* (in Chinese)(Beijing: Junshi kexue chubanshe, 1983); Wang Pufeng, ed., *Mao Zedong junshi zhanlue lun* (On Mao Zedong's military strategy)(Beijing: Junshi

This doctrine has little utility beyond the borders of China, but a considerable portion of all Chinese military writing still must pay homage to the heritage of People's War. Probably about 80 percent of the PLA is best suited to fight a People's War and is equipped with weapons designed in the 1950s and 1960s that would be museum pieces in many countries. This school relies upon the use of "existing weapons to defeat an enemy equipped with high-technology weaponry." Professor Shen Kuiguan, of the Air Force Command Institute, explains that even a "superior" enemy can be defeated through the application of Mao's concepts, "In a high-tech war, one should still depend on the principles of people's war to defeat the superior enemy, for people's war can maximumly promote our combat superiority and degrade the enemy's superiority. In a high-tech war, as long as we persist in allying various armed forces, combining various combat forms and integrating armed operations with non-armed operations, we can employ the great role of people's war and isolate the enemy."[16]

These forces are trained to defend the mainland, its adjacent seas, and air space from invasion. They would fight along side the militia and swallow up an invader using concepts devised by Mao 60 years ago that have been only

---

kexue chubanshe, 1993); and Xia Zhengnan, *Mao Zedong junshi zhanlue lun* (Mao Zedong's military methodology)(Beijing: Junshi kexue chubanshe, 1995). See also the following six articles, all in Michael Pillsbury, *Chinese Views of Future Warfare* (Washington: National Defense University Press, 1997): Chen Zhou, "Zhongguo xiandai jubu zhanzheng lilun yu Meiguo youxian zhanzheng lilun zhi butong" (Chinese modern local war and U.S. limited war), *Zhongguo junshi kexue* (China Military Science) 33, no. 4 (Winter 1995): 43-47; Fang Ning, "Shilun woguo xin shiqi de guofang zhengce" (Defense policy in the new era), *Zhongguo junshi kexue* (China Military Science) 29, no. 4 (Winter 1994): 43-49; Shen Kuiguan, "Gao jishu zhanzheng zhong yilieshengyou de bianzhengfa (Dialectics of defeating the superior with the inferior), *Zhongguo junshi kexue* (China Military Science) 29, no. 4 (Winter 1994): 105-109; Wang Naiming, "Jianchi jiji fangyu, shixing xiandai tiaojian xia renmin zhanzheng" (Adhere to active defense and modern people's war)," in *Deng Xiaoping zhanlue sixiang lun* (On Deng Xiaoping's Strategic Thought), eds. Peng Guangqian and Yao Youzhi (Beijing: Junshi kexue chubanshe, 1994), 280-298; Wei Jincheng, "Information War: A New Form of People's War" (in Chinese), *Jiefangjun bao* (Liberation Army Daily), June 25, 1996; and Zhao Nanqi, "Xu" (Deng Xiaoping's theory of defense modernization), in *Deng Xiaoping zhanlue sixiang lun* (On Deng Xiaoping's strategic thought), eds. Peng Guangqian and Yao Youzhi (Beijing: Junshi kexue chubanshe, 1994), 1-12, foreword.

[16]Shen Kuiguan, "Gao jishu zhanzheng zhong yilieshengyou de bianzhengfa (Dialectics of defeating the superior with the inferior)," *Zhongguo junshi kexue* (China Military Science) 29, no. 4 (Winter 1994): 105-109, in Pillsbury, *Chinese Views of Future Warfare*, 218-219.

slightly modified to account for current requirements—"People's Warfare under modern conditions."[17] Fang Ning of the Department of Military Systems at AMS has described the new contemporary form:

> People's warfare is mobilized and carried out by the broad masses of people in order to seek liberation of the broad masses of people and to resist foreign aggression. People's warfare is the weapon that we have used to fight against domestic and foreign enemies, and to win the war. Because of the rapid development of science and technology and its wide application militarily, there have been many new changes and new characteristics in modern wars. But these changes and characteristics have in no way reduced the role and function of people's warfare in future anti-aggression wars. At the same time, the future people's warfare must also adapt to the characteristics of modern wars.[18]

The enduring legacy and utilization of Mao Zedong's military thought can be seen both in the continued publication of articles and books discussing his theories, as well as in its continued application in China's military strategy today. For example, in 1994, the six-volume *Military Writings of Mao Zedong* was published; it contains 1,612 military cables, orders, comments and remarks, reports, letters, and theoretical works on military affairs that Mao wrote between August 1927 and December 1972. The introduction published by the *People's Daily* on June 13 stated that most of the writings had never before been published and that the work is "the most systematic and comprehensive" of Mao's military writing.

A case where Mao's philosophy and strategies have been reaffirmed was reported by *China National Defense News* in 1994. An article entitled, "Discussions on 'Concentrating Forces to Fight a War of Annihilation' " disclosed:

---

[17]Wang Naiming, "Jianchi jiji fangyu, shixing xiandai tiaojian xia renmin zhanzheng" (Adhere to active defense and modern people's war). In *Deng Xiaoping zhanlue sixiang lun* (On Deng Xiaoping's strategic thought), eds. Peng Guangqian and Yao Youzhi (Beijing: Military Science Press, 1994), 280-298, in Pillsbury, *Chinese Views of Future Warfare*, 43.

[18]Fang Ning, "Shilun woguo xin shiqi de guofang zhengce" (Defense policy in the new era), *Zhongguo junshi kexue* (China Military Science) 29, no. 4 (Winter 1994): 43-49, in Pillsbury, *Chinese Views of Future Warfare*, 54-55.

Recently, leaders of a division . . . in Nanjing Military Region held discussions on the operational doctrine of Mao Zedong. Their answers were affirmative to the following questions: (1) whether such a doctrine still is valid in light of the tremendous changes in weaponry and in the patterns and means of operations that have taken place because of extensive applications of high and new technology; and (2) whether a war of annihilation can be fought under high-tech conditions. However, they contended that the forms of "concentrating forces" should be changed from "group" concentrations to "scattered" concentrations and from advance concentrations to mobile concentrations.[19]

Stratagem and deception are particularly important in People's War. The tactics these units practice are similar to those used in the War Against Japan (1937-45), the War of Liberation (1945-49), the Korean War (1950-53), and the 1979 conflict with Vietnam. The campaign against Vietnam was the last major PLA engagement against a foreign foe, and its shortcomings provided the stimulus for the military modernization efforts of the 1980s.

It is this segment of the PLA that will be reduced by 500,000 personnel, as announced by President Jiang Zemin at the 15th Party Congress in September 1997. A large portion of the 500,000-man reduction will be, or already has been, transferred to PAP. As defined by the March 1997 National Defense Law, PAP is part of the Chinese Armed Forces but is organizationally separate from the PLA. The National Defense Law defines the primary mission of the PLA as a defensive fighting mission, or external defense, while the primary mission of PAP is safeguarding security and maintaining public

---

[19]*China National Defense News*, June 3, 1994. More recently Xinhua reported, "The General Political Department entrusted the Nanjing Political Academy with the running of a session to study how to teach the course 'An Introduction to Mao Zedong Thought' in military academies and schools a few days ago. More than 130 teachers for political theory from academies and schools of the armed forces and the Armed Police Force carried out thorough study and discussion on how to improve the teaching of this course. The study and discussion session was aimed at seeking unity in the guiding ideology, purposes, and requirements of the teaching of the course 'An Introduction to Mao Zedong Thought,' energetically exploring the key points, difficult points, teaching methods, and teaching characteristics of the course, and raising the overall teaching level of the course 'An Introduction to Mao Zedong Thought' in all academies and schools of the armed forces." "Academy Runs PLA Session on Teaching Mao Zedong Thought," Beijing Xinhua Domestic Service, June 12, 1999, in FBIS-CHI-1999-0612, June 12, 1999.

order, or internal security. Beginning in late 1996, at least 14 divisions of the PLA were transferred to PAP, and more are expected to follow. This transfer should allow each force to focus more on its primary mission. Potentially, it could mean that a stronger, better trained PAP will be able to maintain domestic security without resorting to the use of excessive force. At the same time, it could minimize the need for the PLA to be used in an internal security role—decreasing the likelihood of a repeat of the tragedy at Tiananmen Square in 1989.

Local War School

The second tier of the PLA pyramid is the Local War school, which comprises maybe 15 percent of all army, navy, and air force units. The writings of Deng Xiaoping contain the theory that justifies this school.[20] In the 1980s, as the PLA began its modernization program, it developed rapid reaction units, experimental forces, and what has been labeled the "Doctrine of Local War." Local war is understood to be a limited war on the periphery of China that would be short but intense, utilizing advanced technology weapons, with units fighting in a joint and combined arms effort. It envisions an element of force projection (the ability to transport combat forces beyond China's borders), but by definition is regional, not global. Some rapid reaction and experimental units have been the recipients of the numerically limited imports of Russian hardware reported so vigorously by the media. Many units in this category are

---

[20]Six representative articles on local war by senior officers are: Liu Huaqing, "Yi shi wei jian jiaqiang guofang xiandaihua jianshe" (Defense modernization in historical perspective), *Zhongguo junshi kexue* (China Military Science) 29, no. 4 (Winter 1994): 7-8; Fu Quanyou, "Wojun houqin xiandaihua jianshe de zhinan" (Future logistics modernization), *Zhongguo junshi kexue* (China Military Science) 26, no. 1 (Spring 1994): 2-10; Yang Huan, "Woguo zhanlue he wuqi zhuangbei de fazhan" (China's strategic nuclear weaponry), in *Huitou yu zhanwang* (Retrospect and prospect: Chinese defense science, technology and industry)(Beijing: Guofang gongye chubanshe), 157-159; Wu Jianguo, "Gaojishu zhanzheng zhong de he yinying bu rong hushi" (Nuclear shadows on high-tech warfare), *Zhongguo junshi kexue* (China Military Science) 33, no. 4 (Winter 1995): 107-109; Chen Benchan, "Woguo zhuangjiabing wuqizhuangbei fazhan de huigu yu zhanwang" (Research and development of armor), in *Huitou yu zhanwang* (Retrospect and prospect: Chinese defense science, technology and industry)(Beijing: Guofang gongye chubanshe), 169-171; Ding Henggao, "Guofang keji gongye fazhan yu gaige ruogan wenti de sikao" (Reforming defense science, technology and industry), *Zhongguo junshi kexue* (China Military Science) 27, no. 2 (Summer 1994): 67-73; all in Pillsbury, *Chinese Views of Future Warfare.*

still equipped with outdated indigenous equipment and, like the People's War school, must devise ways to use their existing weapons to defeat a high-technology opponent. However, this segment of the PLA probably receives more training opportunities than do units dedicated to fighting a People's War.

China usually regards local war as its "next war," and the Persian Gulf War is often a point of reference for this school. According to Blasko, China has no combat experience in this type of conflict.[21] At this time, the development and dissemination of doctrine on how the PLA will fight such a war are extremely limited. The number of units actually prepared to live up to these modern standards is problematic, but this portion of the PLA is expected to grow in the future. There has been concern regarding China's need for development in this area; for example, in 1994, the Vice Director of the State Information Center, Wu Jiapei, admitted that China was 30 to 40 years behind the United States and the West in the technical levels of its information networks. He urged China to "speed up the technological renovation of its 'information highways' and improve its management over them."[22] Additionally, after the U.S. accidental bombing of the Chinese embassy in Belgrade, there may have been an increased concern among members of the Local War school to "improve the quality and speed of armament development."[23] An organizational change was announced as "Beijing's latest response to the Kosovo crisis and the Cox Report, both of which prompted calls from diplomats and military sources to upgrade the People's Liberation Army's combat capacity to check the United States-led Western Alliance's military status."[24]

---

[21]Dennis J. Blasko, "A New PLA Force Structure," 258-288.

[22]*S and T Daily*, April 16, 1994.

[23]For example, the Liberation Army Daily, June 9, 1999 quotes General Cao Gangchuan, director of the General Armament Department of the PLA speaking on the future navy.

[24]Cary Huang, "Beijing Sets Up Panel on High Tech Weapons," *Hong Kong Standard*, June 11, 1999, 6, in FBIS-CHI-1999-0611, June 14, 1999. The article further stated, " Beijing is . . . setting up a powerful task force . . . under the all-powerful Central Military Commission, it is a revival of the mainland's endeavor from the late 1950s to 1970s, when Marshal Ni Rongzhen was assigned by chairman Mao Zedong to head an army of leading scientists, engineers, technicians and intelligence officers to develop China's first nuclear bomb. The task force,

The RMA Advocates

The RMA school is at the top of the pyramid and is represented by only a very small portion of the PLA—strategists in its premier academic institutions, officers in COSTIND, some of its strategic missile units in what is known as the Second Artillery, and a few other units equipped with modern cruise missiles. Examples of this school are provided later in this chapter.

THREE MUTUALLY EXCLUSIVE SCENARIOS

Different types of conflict scenarios emerge from the debate among alternative Chinese schools of thought. In interviews with Chinese military officers, there are distinctive premises and assumptions made by each of the three schools of thought about Asian conflict scenarios. From the viewpoint of the eternal Mao framework, the most significant and likely scenario is the take-over of a major power by a madman bent on the invasion of China to "turn China into a colony." Whether Russian, Japanese, or American, this madman could successfully carry out the first phase of his invasion and penetrate several hundred miles into China along several axes of advance.

This school is obviously vulnerable to allegations of "fighting the last war." The example of a 7-year war (1937-45) against the Japanese invaders with a loss of over 20 million Chinese lives occurred during the lifetime of all Chinese military officers over the age of 55. This school of thought is particularly committed to the need to maintain a defense mobilization base and defense industry for production of weapons in the deep interior of China, where an alternative command center and national capital would be established for the years required to repulse the madman's invading forces.

The Local War school of thought focuses on entirely different scenarios. Its concern is to repel enemy forces infringing on Chinese territory or maritime resources. The associated authors refer to 30 islands already occupied by China's enemies, as well as China's disputed borders with nearly all its neighbors, including North Korea. They are also concerned about

---

headed by General Xiong Guangkai, deputy chief of the general staff in charge of the PLA intelligence and military research units, will comprise officials from several central military and civilian agencies."

275

separatists in Tibet and western China, who may receive terrorist or military support from China's enemies.

Figure 2. *People's War Scenarios*

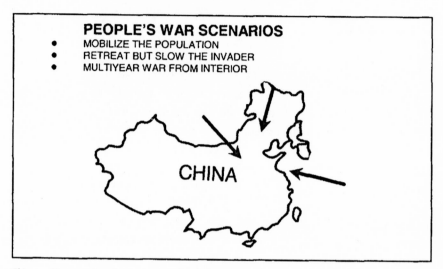

Chinese military authors have never repudiated the writings of Chairman Mao. The highest leaders still proclaim that People's War is the essence of China's military thinking.

Local wars may not be small. Examples cited by Local War authors include China's conflict with Vietnam in 1979 and with the United States in Northern Korea in 1950-51. In March 1979, China mobilized at least 200,000 ground forces, to achieve a 2:1 superiority over the 100,000 Vietnamese troops (mainly militia) and over 1,200 tanks and 1,500 heavy artillery pieces in support of the attack. No air or sea forces were involved. China suffered as many as 50,000 casualties, with 5,000 deaths. The Chinese offer for Vietnam to withdraw from Cambodia in return for a Chinese withdrawal from Vietnam was rejected by Vietnam.[25]

---

[25] A proximate cause for this Chinese invasion was Vietnam's seizing a number of strategic hilltops inside China and shelling Chinese nearby villages in December 1978. Other factors were harrassment of Chinese fishermen by the Vietnamese Navy, Vietnamese expulsion of at least 200,000 ethnic Chinese, Vietnam's invasion of Cambodia and liquidation of a pro-Chinese government there, and Vietnam's growing military alliance with the Soviet Union.

In Korea, China secretly sent 260,000 troops to surround and ambush a smaller 140,000 American and South Korean force, nearly achieving a 2:1 superiority. As this local war continued, a massive Chinese offensive in April 1951 cost China 70,000 casualties. By mid-1951, 700,000 troops on the China-North Korean side faced 420,000 U.N. troops. By the conflict's end in 1953, China had lost an estimated 400,000 troops.[26] The proximate cause of Chinese intervention in Korea as stated by China's spokesman was, "The American imperialists . . . directly threatened our northeastern borders. . . .The aim was not Korea itself but to invade China . . . to save our neighbor is to save ourselves . . . only resistance can make the imperialists learn the lesson."[27]

Figure 3. *Local War Scenarios*

Most Chinese authors in the past decade discuss Local War doctrine.

---

[26]Harvey Nelson, *Power and Insecurity: Beijing and Moscow and Washington, 1949-1988* (Boulder, CO: Westview Press), 12.

[27]The source is "Declaration of all Democratic Parties," November 4, 1950, in *The Great "Opposing America, Assisting Korea" Movement* (Beijing: New China Bookstore, 1954), 366-367. Later, General Wu Xiuquan at the United Nations Security Council described an American master plan to invade China that included bases and arrangements in Japan, South Korea, Taiwan, and the Philippines.

The third school of thought, which concerns itself with a potential RMA, seems to envision invasion conflict scenarios very different from the first two schools. For example, in "The Challenge of Information Warfare," General Wang Pufeng, after quoting Andrew W. Marshall,[28] urges that China develop three new missions: a strategic reconnaissance and warning system, a battlefield information network that brings all military branches into a single network for combat coordination, and long-range, precision-strike systems, including tactical guided missiles. In an implicit rebuke to Local War advocates and neo-Maoists, General Wang emphasizes, "In comparison with the strength of its potential enemies, the information technology and information weapons of the Chinese Armed Forces will all be inferior for quite some time." He also warns about the need to be the first to exploit a RMA:

> Those who perceive it first will swiftly rise to the top and have the advantage of the first opportunities. Those who perceive it late will unavoidably also be caught up in the vortex of this revolution. Every military will receive this baptism. This revolution is first a revolution in concepts.[29]

Other articles by the RMA school stress, "The submarine will rise in its status to become a major naval warfare force" with the "appearance of underwater arsenal ships and underwater mine laying robots." Space warfare will be conducted by navy ships which can destroy satellite reconnaissance and other space systems. Tactical laser weapons will be needed for antiship defense.

---

[28]Chinese authors frequently refer to Andrew Marshall, Head of the Office of Net Assessment, at the U.S. Department of Defense. For example, Peng Guangqian of AMS, after visiting the United States and meeting Marshall wrote, "He [Marshall] emphasized that China is a major power with tremendous potential, that is worth special attention, currently, although China still is behind the U.S. in military technology, if China makes a breakthrough in military theory innovation, then it is very possible that it will be in the leading rank of countries in the RMA. Peng Guangqian, "Meiguo junshi geming de jiji changdaozhe, Maxie'er" (The active initiator of the U.S. RMA, Marshall), *Junshi wenchai* (Military Digest) 4-5 (1996): 92-93.

[29]Wang Pufeng, "Yingjie xinxi zhanzheng de tiaozhan" (The challenge of information warfare), *Zhongguo junshi kexue* (China Military Science) 30, no. 1 (Spring 1995): 8-18, in Pillsbury, *Chinese Views of Future Warfare*, 317-326.

Long-range precision strikes at sea will cause "both sides to strive to make lightning attacks and raise their first strike damage rate."[30]

Figure 4. *RMA Scenarios*

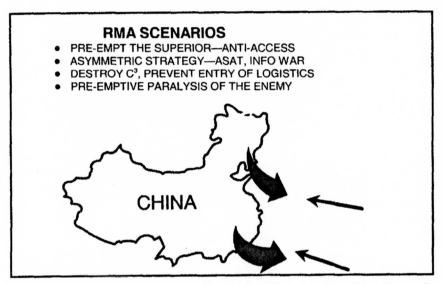

RMA SCENARIOS
- PRE-EMPT THE SUPERIOR—ANTI-ACCESS
- ASYMMETRIC STRATEGY—ASAT, INFO WAR
- DESTROY C³, PREVENT ENTRY OF LOGISTICS
- PRE-EMPTIVE PARALYSIS OF THE ENEMY

CHINA

In the 1990s, Chinese military authors began to address how the revolution in military affairs will change the nature of warfare. Their scenarios envisioned attacks on China by a superpower.

One theme of the RMA school is the need to change the measures of effectiveness used to design and develop military equipment and weapons, with one analyst proposing that future weapons systems and military organizations be judged largely on the basis of the "intensity with which they use information technology." It is apparent from this proposal that local war weapons and equipment now being procured in China would score at a very low level, if measured by the "Information Intensity Measure of Effectiveness." Thus, this article is a harsh criticism of the recommendations

---

[30]Shen Zhongchang, Zhou Xinsheng and Zhang Haiying, "21 shiji haizhan chutan" (21st-century naval warfare), *Zhongguo junshi kexue* (China Military Science) 30, no. 1 (Spring 1995): 28-32, in Pillsbury, *Chinese Views of Future Warfare*, 261-274.

of both the Local War and neo-Maoist schools.[31] Another critique comes from a *Liberation Army Daily* article:

> Meeting the challenge of the world military revolution demands that we give better play to our own advantages. The rich strategy of the east (*dongfang moulue*) is one of them. Over the past several years, our study and research of high-tech local wars and high-tech information war tend to show two tendencies: on the one hand, owing to their overestimation of the importance of technology and underestimation of the role of strategy, some people consider themselves to have nothing worthy of praise; on the other hand, however, with the belief that strategic principles can replace the development of technology, some are sure that the magic weapon passed down by their forefathers can bless them to win every battle. These two opposite tendencies are both lopsided views. This article puts forward the idea that the military revolution will push the military strategy of the east to a new level. Though some ideas in the article are open to discussion, the problems it raises warrant careful reflection.[32]

How should foreign observers assess and understand these contradictory Chinese strategic writings? The Asian conflict scenarios implicit in the RMA school of thought involve equipment and capabilities for China's future enemies that are not possessed by Vietnam, Outer Mongolia, North Korea, India, the Central Asian states, South Korea, or Japan at this time. The missions of long-range, precision strike, information warfare operations, and attacks against space satellite reconnaissance systems imply that either Russia or the United States is part of the scenario.

These three Asian conflict scenarios seem mutually exclusive. Is there a "strategic debate" underway that has not been resolved? Some authors refer to past debates on military strategy. According to Yan Xuetong of CICIR:

---

[31]Chang Mengxiong, "21 shiji wuqi he jundui zhanwang" (Weapons of the 21st century), *Zhongguo junshi kexue* (China Military Science) 30, no. 1 (Spring 1995): 19-24, 49, in Pillsbury, *Chinese Views of Future Warfare*, 249-260.

[32]Su Enze, "Strategy of the East is Advancing Toward a New Phase—Discussion on Welcoming the Challenge of a Military Revolution" (in Chinese), *Jiefangjun bao* (Liberation Army Daily), March 5,1996, 6.

In the 1980s there was a debate among Chinese military circles on the following questions: How to comprehend the exact meaning of "luring the enemy in deep?" Is it meant for battles or for the whole war? Should China fight a protracted or a quick war? Should China fight a full-scale war or a limited local war?

These questions imply the views of the local war school, which, in the 1980s, probably was the "reform" view opposed to the orthodox People's War view. The President of AMS apparently sided with the local war view. According to interviews in Beijing, the AMS actually "staffed" out the formation of the local war concepts. Yan continues the story to the late 1980s:

After the Cold War, a consensus has basically been reached on these questions among Chinese military circles, i.e., in order to ensure the safety of the country's economic achievements against war damages, the Chinese army must commit itself to the task of engaging the enemy outside of China's territory. Additionally, because wars China might be involved in during the post Cold War period will most probably be high-tech local wars, the Chinese army must acquire the ability of winning a high-tech local war so as to keep the enemy outside the country's territory.

Yan here introduces an evolution of the original local war view that focused on border disputes—by the early 1990s, the view emerged that China must fight local war beyond its borders. Yan writes:

Consequently, a strategy of active defense that lays stress on enhancing the army's rapid response capability and readiness for any high-tech local war has become China's current military strategy for national defense. The objective of this strategy is to prevent war from breaking out, or if failing that, to keep them outside of China's territory.[33]

Yan Xuetong's description of the debates in China's military establishment is supported by Yao Yunzhu, a senior colonel in the AMS Foreign Military Studies Department, who writes that there were "heated debates" before the

---

[33] Yan Xuetong, "China's Post-Cold War Security Strategy." *Contemporary International Relations,* 5, no. 5 (1995).

1985 switch to Local War doctrine, which were about the "international environment, the real and potential threats China will face, the kinds of wars that China is likely to be engaged in, and the ways and means to fight such wars."[34] She concludes, "However, it would be too early to conclude that the PLA has abandoned its traditional doctrine altogether. . . . Most Chinese military analysts consider that the changes made so far are compatible with the traditional doctrine, at least with the basic ideas it embodies. People's War and Active Defense are still directing the Chinese PLA in its long march toward modernization."[35]

Even with this insight about the 1980s, analysis in the 1990s remains difficult because the three groups under review decline to acknowledge each other. They do not "debate" in a Western sense of the word, and positions are not always clear cut. For example, People's War may be invoked to support the importance of information warfare, as is done by Wang Pufeng: "We must use a practical combination of information warfare and Marxist and Maoist military thought to guide information warfare and issues in military construction."[36] Another example where People's War and Information War are linked is given by Wei Jincheng, who writes:

> The concept of People's War of the olden days is bound to continue to be enriched, improved and updated in the information age to take on a brand-new form. . . . only by bringing relevant systems into play and combining human intelligence with artificial intelligence under effective organization

---

[34] Yao Yunzhu, "The Evolution of Military Doctrine of the Chinese PLA from 1985 to 1995," *Korean Journal of Defense Analysis* 7, no. 2 (Winter 1995): 57.

[35] Ibid., 80.

[36] Wang Pufeng, "Yingjie xinxi zhanzheng de tiaozhan," in Pillsbury, *Chinese Views of Future Warfare*, 325. Wang further clarifies his argument in a book on information warfare and the RMA stating, "Based on fighting an information war with existing weaponry, China's military is technically weak, but in the combat arena China's strength is People's War. Information warfare is warfare's technical form, it determines the large quantity of information technology used in war. People's Warfare is warfare's political form, it determines the righteous nature of warfare. Their content is different in nature, but on China's battlefield, China uses People's Warfare to fight information warfare, or in information warfare it fights a People's War, we must take these two different natured things and fuse them into a warfare furnace." Wang Pufeng, *Xinxi zhanzheng yu junshi geming* (Information Warfare and the revolution in military affairs)(Beijing: Junshi kexue chubanshe, 1995: 203-204.)

and coordination can we drown our enemies in the ocean of an information offensive. A people's war in the context of information warfare is carried out by hundreds of millions of people using open-type modern information systems."[37]

Chinese authors decline to admit the existence of a debate, preferring instead to claim there is merely a difference in "emphasis" among authors.[38]

However, in fact, there are clearly sharp, mutually exclusive differences among the three schools:

- Those who still champion Chairman Mao's People's War and "active defense" against likely opponents in the 21st century bent on invading China after a pre-emptive nuclear strike
- Those who (in the name of "Deng Xiaoping's new strategic thinking") want China to follow aspects of Soviet military models for conventional warfare with a balance among ground, naval, and air forces ready to repel limited aggression on Chinese territory
- A third (new and small) school that has been inspired by the writings of Ogarkov and the Soviet General Staff Academy about a potential "revolution in military affairs," which anticipates a world in the mid-21st century in which China will have the world's largest economy and be at least roughly equivalent in nuclear forces to Russia and America, a triangular nuclear equivalence never seen before, in which new measures of effectiveness will be needed to calculate the balance of military power.[39]

---

[37]Wei Jincheng, "Information War: A New form of People's War," *Jiefangjun bao* (Liberation Army Daily), June 25, 1996, in Pillsbury, *Chinese Views of Future Warfare.*

[38]An anthropologist has observed that Chinese involved in factional disputes carry on the conflict by denying to outsiders that the other factions even exist. Few Chinese analysts footnote other analysts or comment about other's work in any article or book. See Barbara L. K. Pillsbury, "Factionalism Observed: Behind the 'Face' of Harmony in a Chinese Community," *The China Quarterly,* no. 74 (June 1978): 241-272.

[39]This new third school has no senior leader like Mao or Deng to serve as a patron as yet. It tends to cite American specialists about the RMA (including Andrew W. Marshall), without reference to Mao or Deng. It will be important if the speeches of President Jiang Zemin ever incorporate this school rather than continuing (for the past 5 years) to endorse a vague mixture

These three schools of thought among military authors have counterparts among the civilian defense and foreign affairs community.[40] As has been discussed in detail, the civilians pursue unique techniques of strategic analysis to determine where future conflicts may involve China's national interests. They use a set of analytical categories different from their Western counterparts and do not anticipate that the United Nations or other well-intentioned security organizations will be that effective.

In contrast to the lack of debate on general warfare doctrine, "space warfare" appears to be an area for constructive debate among Chinese analysts. As would be expected, RMA advocates see "space warfare" as central to the outcome of future wars. However, the advocates of Local War and People's War seem to view "space warfare" as not particularly important to China. They suggest it was mainly important as part of the overall military balance that shifted back and forth during the Cold War competition between the United States and the Soviet Union. Some have taken note of the history of American and Russian antisatellite developments.

How do these analysts judge the future space balance?[41] Some have been extremely concerned about China's relative weakness in this area and have openly advocated a Chinese "space warfare headquarters" to command a future antisatellite capability and ballistic missile defense to break the "superpower monopoly" of space, in spite of China's current diplomatic position that antisatellite weapons (ASATs) should be banned and no weapons

---

of both the Mao and Deng approaches.

[40]Each of the three schools of thought identified above—People's War, combined arms and information warfare, and RMA—has certain themes that identify it. For People's War advocates, one clue is appeals for "defense conversion," or the production of commercial products (to assist with the politically correct goal of economic growth), but still carefully maintaining the capability to shift rapidly back to wartime intensity of production of light weapons to arm the millions who will be mobilized to defeat the invader.

[41]For a strategic framework, see Liu Mingtao and Yang Chengjun, *Gao jishu zhanzheng zhong de daodan zhan* (Missile wars during high tech warfare)(Beijing: Guofang daxue chubanshe, 1993).

permitted in space.[42] China Aerospace has published drawings of a space station and space shuttle for the future.

Other more cautious Chinese officers at least agree that ASATs and "space warfare" are important aspects of any strategic assessment. First, they look backward at the shifting balance in U.S. and Soviet efforts. Then they remark on the importance of China's enhancing its limited ability to manufacture satellites and to continue developing a robust launch capability at several sites with several reliable launchers; both a manned space program and a Chinese space station are budgeted. Articles have also discussed the importance of reducing satellite vulnerability by using very small satellites, the need for anti-ASAT capabilities to defend Chinese satellites, and the need to develop a capability to strike first at enemy space capabilities.

THE RMA IN CHINA

RMA Forecasts

In the view of those authors this study labels "RMA advocates," American decline will be further accelerated by an inevitable RMA that will drastically reduce the relative military power of any nation that does not pursue the RMA with great vigor.[43] The articles give no hint of any debate about this matter, but in the United States there has been a great deal of debate in professional military journals not only about how to exploit the next potential revolution in military affairs, but also about what it may mean.

Views on the RMA in the United States range from the assertion that the U.S. Air Force has already demonstrated the next RMA in the Gulf War, to the opposite view that no one has yet begun to appreciate what an RMA may look like in 20 years or more because the potential for change is so big as to

---

[42]Bao Zhongxing, "Jianshe tianjun gouxiang" (The notion of building a space army), in *Jundui xiandaihua jianshe*, NDU Research Department, Military Construction Research Institute, 431-442. Cited in Alastair Iain Johnston, "China's New 'Old Thinking': The Concept of Limited Deterrence," *International Security* 20, no. 3 (Winter 1995): 24.

[43]Wang Pufeng, *Xinxi zhanzheng yu junshi geming* (Information warfare and the revolution in military affairs)(Beijing: Junshi kexue chubanshe, 1995); Li Qingshan, *Xin junshi geming yu gao jishu zhanzheng* (The new revolution in military affairs and high-technology warfare)(Beijing: Junshi kexue chubanshe, 1995); Gao Chunxiang, ed., *Xin junshi geming lun* (On the new revolution in military affairs)(Beijing: Junshi kexue chubanshe, 1996).

be inconceivable at present. In between these views that "we have it now" and "we can't imagine it yet," there are many proposals in U.S. journals about what a potential RMA should be. Not so in China. Chinese analysts have even made predictions about the stages the RMA will go through in the future. For example, Wang Zhenxi, a senior advisor at CIISS, writes:

> The world military revolution will develop by and large into the senior stage around 2030 from the existing junior one. Then, there will be an overall qualitative leap in the military field of all countries—the possession by the military forces of high-quality personnel, integrated C⁴I systems, high-level training and education, intelligent arms, scientific system of organization and creative military doctrines. . . . It will enter a new phase when all the intelligent and new concept weapons such as robots, nonlethal weapons, psychological skill and precision-system defense technology are employed in actual combat and widely equipped in troops. There can be a good deal of the brand-new mode of warfare adopted in operations, e.g. the smart war, paralyzing war, space war, robot war, electronic war and knowledge war, etc.[44]

Some Chinese authors seem to leave open the possibility that China, not the United States, will be the first to exploit the RMA in two or three decades. Other authors emphasize instead the massive obstacles China must overcome. Civilians, too, forecast that any nation that exploits the RMA may be able to defy a superpower. Shen Qurong, president of CICIR, writes:

> A military revolution (RMA) is underway. . . . the London-based Institute for International Strategic Studies says that along with the advance of this revolution, some small and medium-size nations will no longer be condemned to a perpetual inferior position relative to the Western world. On the contrary, they will increasingly have the opportunity to obtain capabilities of offering direct opposition to Western military superiority in the 21st century.[45]

---

[44]Wang Zhenxi, "The New Wave of Military Revolution in the World," *Guoji zhanlue yanjiu* (International Strategic Studies) 44, no. 2 (April 1997): 2. Wang is a Senior Adviser at CIISS.

[45]Shen Qurong "May Earlier Maturity Come to Peace: Thoughts on Asia's Future", *Contemporary International Relations* 6, no. 9 (September 1966): 11.

As is evident from the essays in *Chinese Views of Future Warfare*, the Chinese are investigating the entire scope of new technologies and theories applicable to the RMA. Chinese defense industries are undertaking serious research efforts to identify areas upon which they should focus. However, no senior Chinese leader has lent his imprimatur to the RMA school.

The RMA and the United States

Open-source Chinese military writing on future warfare suggests that China may not be as friendly to the Pentagon as the Pentagon is to China. Indeed, numerous Chinese books and articles suggest an active research program has been underway for several years to examine how China should develop future military capabilities to defeat the United States by exploiting the RMA more effectively and more rapidly than the United States, particularly by tailoring new technology to "defeat the superior with the inferior" with a strategy of asymmetric warfare.

These two subjects, the RMA and asymmetric warfare, are closely related in some PLA writing. A book published in May 1996 by Major General Li Zhiyun, Foreign Military Studies Director at the National Defense University, contains articles by 64 PLA authors describing in detail an extended list of the weaknesses of the U.S. Army, Navy, and Air Force. This book represents a common theme in PLA views of future warfare—America is proclaimed to be a declining power with but two or three decades of primacy left. U.S. military forces, while dangerous at present, are vulnerable, even deeply flawed, and can be defeated with the right strategy, namely "defeating the superior with the inferior." Part of the recommended asymmetric approach in some of the PLA writing is the requirement for "the inferior" to pre-emptively strike the "superior" in order to paralyze his nerve centers and block his logistics.

Asymmetric War

The second aspect of PLA views of future warfare is the requirement to exploit the RMA so that China can even more rapidly and effectively "defeat the superior with the inferior." One statement never found in PLA open-source writing is any declaration that China will one day be the world's leading military power. Rather, the eventual end state of the current post-Cold War transitional period is always proclaimed to be "multipolarity" among five "equal" powers, each of which will have its own sphere of influence. One bold author explains that, by mid-21st century, even the declining United States will still be left its own sphere of influence, namely Latin America and Canada. Several PLA articles and a book published by the Academy of Military Science provide equations with which to calculate the future trends in CNP that will lead to this world of five equal powers.[46]

Advocates

To understand the RMA and to develop innovative defense programs, China announced in May 1996 that it had formed a strategic research center that would combine research on traditional Chinese statecraft with studies and experiments designed to generate innovative military operational concepts.[47] Several national conferences have been convened to assess the implications of the RMA for China, including whether traditional or ancient statecraft can be applied to exploit the RMA and asymmetrical strategy. The announcement of the new center in 1996 specifically praised several books by PLA authors that were previously published in the 1980s about the application of ancient strategy to future warfare.[48] Earlier, China announced the formation of an Institute of Grand Strategy, which would have responsibility for assessing the approaches of other major powers to security issues in the 21st century.

Both these new institutions (and several existing ones) take a task-force type of approach by assembling experts from a variety of Chinese military institutions to examine strategic alternatives more than one or two decades

---

[46]See chapter five.

[47]The importance of innovation in developing the RMA has been stressed by several authors. For example, Colonel Zhang Zhaozhong of NDU has stated, "If we have to face a war, how can we win the next war? Answer: Innovation is the soul of a nation's progress and development, and although China's economic strength does not match that of the developed countries, and our military expenditure cannot reach the level of the western countries, the more that this is so, the more we need the spirit of innovation." Ma Ling, "The Attempt Behind the 'Bombing in Error'—Interview with Renowned Military Commentator Zhang Zhaozhong," *Ta Kung Pao* (Hong Kong), May 17, 1999, A4, in FBIS-CHI-1999-1518, May 17, 1999. Zhang is Director of the Science and Technology Teaching and Research Section at NDU.

[48]Three were entitled, *A New Version of the 36 Stratagems, Strategy in the Three Kingdoms Era*, and *Eastern Zhou Strategies*.

ahead. Credit for some of these initiatives is sometimes given to Qian Xuesen, who made a speech in 1985 that brought prior Russian work on the RMA to the attention of China's senior military leadership. Qian, considered to be the father of China's missile programs, has a Ph.D. from Cal Tech and actually participated in the first major U.S. Air Force study of future warfare in the late 1940s, for which he authored several sections on future missile warfare. The contrast is striking between the orthodox authors, who since 1985 have advocated "active defense" and Local War programs, and the new articles since 1994 by Chinese military authors who urge that China must be the first, or among the first in the world, to exploit information and stealth technology, to acquire an entirely new type of armed forces that bears no resemblance to the 1985 program laid down by Deng Xiaoping.

Proposals and Programs

Books and journals put out by several military publishing houses in China suggest that at least 50 military officers now write about future warfare and the RMA. Some propose specific programs for China, such as developing means to counter U.S. stealth aircraft. Others suggest more general approaches that propose new doctrine and new weapons programs, or offer broad warnings about what will happen to China if it ignores the RMA.

Some articles by these "RMA advocates" seem to be reports of task forces formed within single service research institutes. The Air Force Command Institute authors focus on the crucial future role of "space forces" and praise the Israeli pre-emptive dawn attack that destroyed most of the Egyptian Air Force on the ground as an example of the "inferior" defeating the "superior" through a surprise attack. Similarly, Navy Research Institute authors state that the submarine will become the most important ship in the 21st century because of its stealthiness and its ability to destroy the large surface ships of a "superior" enemy navy.

PLA authors seem to have begun to assess the RMA almost 10 years ago,[49] even before the concept was well known in United States. Since the

---

[49]This highly tentative speculation could help to explain the many Chinese open-source references, recently uncovered by Mark Stokes, to previously unknown Chinese programs to develop laser weapons, antisatellite weapons, high-powered microwave weapons, electric rail guns, and other advanced technologies. Stokes examines them in his forthcoming study for the

mid-1980s, some senior AMS officers have repeatedly referred to the "third military technical revolution" without actually footnoting the Soviet military journals that discussed the same subject. In fact, Huan Xiang, Deng Xiaoping's national security advisor, discussed "the new technological revolution in military affairs" in a 1985 *Liberation Army Daily* article. Huan predicted, "In 10 years, it will be an era in which strategic nuclear weapons and strategic nonnuclear weapons both exist. Due to rising technology levels, non-nuclear weapons will become conventional strategic weapons . . . so that certain strategic targets can be reached." He suggests that there will be changes in military organization, and new military organizations, such as "strategic troops should be established." Huan listed four technologies for a technological RMA: precision-guided tactical weapons, long-range strategic vehicles, a system formed by satellite communications and reconnaissance, and rapid and comprehensive data processing with computers.[50] RMA articles by AMS authors began to appear at least as early as autumn 1988, with Wu Qunqiu's seminal article in *China Military Science* and AMS Vice President General Mi Zhenyu's book, *Chinese National Defense Development Concepts.*[51] It would be useful to review these representative articles and book chapters by the Chinese RMA advocates before discussing their implications.

China's National Defense Development Concepts, published by a team under the leadership of General Mi Zhenyu, a Vice President of the Academy of Military Science, is one of China's most important studies of future warfare. It suggests:

U.S. Air Force Academy Institute for National Security Studies.

[50]Huan Xiang, "Xin jishu geming dui junshi de yingxiang" (The influence of the new technological revolution on military affairs), in *Huan Xiang wenji* (The collected works of Huan Xiang)(Beijing: Shijie zhishi chubanshe, 1994), 1259. The article was originally published in *Jiefangjun bao* (Liberation Army Daily), June 7 and 14, 1985. See also Huan Xiang "Xin Jishu geming yu woguo duice" (The new technological revolution and china's decisionmaking), in *Huan Xiang wenji*, 1074-1088; and Huan Xiang, "Jiefangjun yaoyong yu yinjie xin jishu geming de tiaozhan" (The People's Liberation Army must bravely meet the challenge of the new technological revolution), in *Huan Xiang wenji*, 1089-1094.

[51]See Mi Zhenyu, *Zhongguo guofang fazhan gouxiang* (China's national defense development concepts)(Beijing: Jiefangjun chubanshe, 1988), in Pillsbury, *Chinese Views of Future Warfare,* 361-381.

- "China is in long-term competition with other major powers."
- "The gap between the weapons we now possess compared to those of advanced countries is 20 to 25 years."
- "If our objective is merely to shrink this discrepancy to 10 to 15 years, then from the point of view of effectiveness, it would seem to be higher than others. But from the point of view of competitive effectiveness, it would only be an impractical increase in quality, perhaps even a decrease."
- "When we compare the discrepancy of a half generation of weaponry in the year 2000 with the two- to three-generation discrepancies today, the difference in competitive effectiveness could be greater." "If we do not start today to plan to be better, *to be ahead of everyone,* how can we possibly make use of the opportunities, and become latecomers who surpass the old-timers?"[52]

National Conferences

In January 1996, the *Liberation Army Daily* recommended the next steps China should take with regard to the RMA. Here are some representative comments that illustrate typical optimism:

- "China is among those countries which had an early touch of the world's new military revolution. A nationwide campaign of emulating and studying the new technological revolution was started in China in 1983."
- "Shen Weiguang put forward the concept of information war as early as 1987."
- "In December 1994 and October 1995 COSTIND held seminars" for experts from inside and outside the Armed Forces on the RMA.
- Chinese seminar participants concluded the best approach to the RMA is to "set up a macro-control system," develop "scientific studies and demonstrations" and take steps to "build up combat laboratories (because the U.S. Army has built up six combat laboratories.)"
- China should develop "it's own unique lethal weapons" rather than "inlay the old framework with new technologies."

---

[52]Ibid.

- The armed forces of a wealthy country "will become extremely fragile and vulnerable when it completes the process of networking and then relies entirely on electronic computers."
- Through the RMA, underdeveloped countries can develop "a large number of secret weapons which can really throw financial systems and military command systems into chaos."[53]

ASYMMETRIC WARFARE

Strategy

In "Weapons of the 21st Century," Mr. Chang Mengxiong, the former Senior Engineer of the Beijing Institute of System Engineering of COSTIND, suggests "We are in the midst of a new revolution in military technology" and in the 21st century both weapons and military units will be "information-intensified."[54]

Chang has a keen eye for spotting American military weaknesses and suggesting asymmetric approaches in which "the inferior can defeat the superior." Chang writes that future C³I systems will be crucial, so that "attacking and protecting space satellites, airborne early-warning and electronic warfare aircraft and ground command sites will become important forms of combat." Like many Chinese authors, Chang sees new concept weapons such as lasers and high-powered microwave weapons to be the best way to conduct asymmetric attacks.[55]

In terms of asymmetric warfare, one of Chang's most vivid metaphors is of a Chinese boxer. "Information-intensified combat methods are like a Chinese boxer with a knowledge of vital body points who can bring an

---

[53]Zhang Feng and Libing Yan, "Historical Mission of Soldiers Straddling 21st Century—Roundup of Forum for Experts on How to Meet the Challenge of the World Military Revolution," *Jiefangjun bao* (Liberation Army Daily), January 2, 1996, 6, in FBIS-CHI-96-061, January 2, 1996.

[54]Chang Mengxiong, "21 shiji wuqi he jundui zhanwang," in Pillsbury, *Chinese Views of Future Warfare*, 249-260.

[55]Ibid.

opponent to his knees with a minimum of movement." Chang discusses some specific new concepts for weapons:

- High-power microwave weapons will be able to "destroy the opponents' electronic equipment."
- Information superiority is "more important than air and sea superiority."
- "We must gain air and sea superiority, but win information superiority first of all."
- Deterrence will be a new operational concept.[56]

Like nuclear deterrence, "information deterrence" will be vital, especially if "the power with a weaker information capability can deliver a crippling attack on the information system of the power with a stronger information system." In a very important point, Chang stresses, "Even if two adversaries are generally equal in weapons, unless the side having a weaker information capability is able effectively to weaken the information capability of the adversary, it has very little possibility of winning the war."[57]

Sea Power

In the first of two articles on 21st century naval warfare, Captain Shen Zhongchang and his coauthors from the Chinese Navy Research Institute suggest that "certain cutting-edge technologies are likely to be applied first to naval warfare."[58] They point out how China could adopt several asymmetric approaches to defeating a larger and more powerful navy. These approaches include disabling a more powerful navy by attacking its space-based communications and surveillance systems and even attacking naval units themselves from space. Shen writes, "The mastery of outer space will be a prerequisite for naval victory, with outer space becoming the new

---

[56]Ibid.

[57]Ibid.

[58]Shen Zhongchang, Zhang Haiying and Zhou Xinsheng, "21 shiji haizhan chu tan" (21st century naval warfare), *Zhongguo junshi kexue* (China Military Science) 33, no. 1 (Spring 1995): 28-32, in Pillsbury, *Chinese Views of Future Warfare*, 261-274.

commanding heights for naval combat." Ships at sea will carry out antireconnaissance strikes against space satellites and other space systems. "The side with electromagnetic combat superiority will make full use of that invisible killer mace to win naval victory." They believe that direct attacks on naval battlefields will become possible from outer space because "naval battle space is going to expand in unprecedented ways."[59]

A second asymmetric approach to defeating a more powerful navy is to use shore-based missiles and aircraft instead of developing a large (symmetrical) naval fleet: "As land-based weapons will be sharply improved in reaction capacity, strike precision, and range, it will be possible to strike formations at sea, even individual warships."[60]

A third asymmetric approach will be for China to pioneer in "magic weapons," such as tactical laser weapons, that "will be used first in antiship missile defense systems" and stealth technology for both naval ships and cruise missiles: "Lightning attacks and powerful first strikes will be more widely used."[61]

A fourth asymmetric approach will be for China to attack the naval logistics of the superior navy. Shen explains that the vulnerability of an American-style navy will grow in the future because future naval warfare will expend large amounts of human and material resources so that "logistics survival will face a greater challenge." He predicts that "future maritime supply lines and logistic security bases will find it hard to survive." He states that the Gulf War's daily ammunition expenditure was 4.6 times that of the Vietnam War and 20 times that of the Korean War, with an oil consumption rate of about 19 million gallons a day, suggesting American naval operations are vulnerable because of relatively unprotected supply lines.[62]

A fifth asymmetric approach will be for China to attack American naval command and information systems. In a second article, Captain Shen Zhongchang and his co-authors list new technologies that will contribute to

---

[59]Ibid.

[60]Ibid.

[61]Ibid.

[62]Ibid.

the defeat of the United States, explaining that protection of C³I is now so important that "the U.S. Defense Department has invested $1 billion in establishing a network to safeguard its information system."[63] However, Captain Shen writes that the American system may not be so safe from attack, because there are many ways to destroy information systems:

- Attacking radar and radio stations with smart weapons
- Jamming enemy communication facilities with electronic warfare
- Attacking communication centers, facilities, and command ships
- Destroying electronic systems with electromagnetic pulse weapons
- Destroying computer software with computer viruses
- Developing directed energy weapons and electromagnetic pulse weapons.

A sixth asymmetric approach to naval warfare is to use submarines with new types of torpedoes. Shen predicts that the most powerful naval weapon in future warfare will be submarines. He writes, "After the First World War, the dominant vessel was the battleship. In the Second World War, it was the aircraft carrier. If another global war breaks out, the most powerful weapon will be the submarine."[64] Torpedoes do not require a submarine and can also be launched from Chinese small patrol boats.

Air Power

In "The Military Revolution and Air Power," Major General Zheng Shenxia, President of Air Force Command College, and Colonel Zhang Changzhi make a case that the RMA will strengthen aerospace forces more than others.[65] They

---

[63]Shen Zhongchang, Zhang Haiying and Zhou Xinsheng, "Xin junshi geming yu haizhan ji haijun jianshe" (The military revolution in naval warfare), *Zhongguo junshi kexue* (China Military Science) 34, no. 1 (Spring 1996): 57-60, 82, in Pillsbury, *Chinese Views of Future Warfare*, 275-284.

[64]Ibid.

[65]Zheng Shenxia and Zhang Changzhi, "Xin junshi geming yu kongzhong lilian jianshe" (The miliary revolution in air power), *Zhongguo junshi kexue* (China Military Science) 34, no 1. (Spring 1996): 50-56, in Pillsbury, *Chinese Views of Future Warfare*, 297-309.

emphasize the growing importance of precision strike capability, stealth, night vision, longer range attacks, lethality of smart munitions, increased C³I capability, and electronic warfare. They were deeply impressed by the U.S. capability in the Gulf War to "capture all the high-frequency and ultrahigh-frequency radio signals of the Iraqi army and store information gathered by 34 reconnaissance satellites, 260 electronic reconnaissance planes, and 40 warning aircraft" and then "destroy the Iraqi communication system." They conclude that "this explains that information is the key to victory." According to General Zheng, China's future air force must integrate space, air, and air defense forces into one. Following the struggle for air control, he says, "Space control will become a decisive component of strategic initiative."

In "21st Century Air Warfare," Colonel Min Zengfu of the Air Force Command Institute argues, "The air battlefield will become decisively significant" in future warfare. He, too, stresses that China's air force must be "linked" to space forces. Min concludes that not only is it correct to say, "He who controls outer space controls the earth," but also "To maintain air superiority one must control outer space."[66]

Nanotechnology Weapons

An article by Major General Sun Bailin of the Academy of Military Science is particularly important because it illustrates how asymmetric attacks on U.S. military forces could be carried out with extremely advanced technology. General Sun points out that U.S. dependence on "information superhighways" will make it vulnerable to attack by microscale robot "electrical incapacitation systems."[67]

The targets would be American electrical power systems, civilian aviation systems, transportation networks, seaports and shipping, highways, television broadcast stations, telecommunications systems, computer centers, factories and enterprises, and so forth. Sun also suggests that U.S. military equipment

---

[66]Min Zengfu, "21 shiji kongzhong zhanchang guankui" (21st century air warfare), *Zhongguo junshi kexue* (China Military Science) 30, no. 1 (Spring 1995): 33-40, in Pillsbury, *Chinese Views of Future Warfare*, 285-296.

[67]Sun Bailin, "Nanotechnology Weapons on Future Battlefields," *National Defense* (June 15, 1996), in Pillsbury, *Chinese Views of Future Warfare*, 413-420.

will be vulnerable to asymmetrical attack by "ant robots." According to General Sun, these are a type of microscale electromechanical system that can be controlled with sound. The energy source of ant robots is a microscale microphone that can transform sound into energy. People can use them to creep into the enemy's vital equipment and lurk there for as long as several decades. In peacetime, they do not cause any problem. In the event of relations between two countries deteriorating, to the point that they develop into warfare, remote control equipment can be used to activate the hidden ant robots, so that they can destroy or "devour" the enemy's equipment.

"Magic Weapons"

In "Military Conflicts in the New Era," Major General Zheng Qinsheng points out that the well-known scientist Qian Xuesen "laid bare the essence of the military revolution" to be information technology.[68] Zheng, like Chang Mengxiong, advocates new measures of effectiveness.

In a rare remark that apparently criticizes Local War theorists, Zheng asks, "Where shall we place the nucleus of high-tech development? Where shall we put the main emphasis of local high-tech wars?" Zheng reveals that "a consensus on these issues has yet to be reached throughout the army. People still tend to place greater emphasis on hardware instead of software, and on the present instead of the future. Such a transitional 'optical parallax' is hindering us from gaining a correct grasp of major contradictions." Zheng concludes by recommending a conscientious study of the RMA, new ideas on military development, and "magic weapons" that can really serve our purpose.

COMBAT CONCEPTS

The COSTIND journal, *Contemporary Military Affairs*, published an article in March 1996 by Chen Huan, who calls for rapid technology development of

---

[68]Zheng Qinsheng, "Military Conflicts in the New Era," *Jiefangjun bao* (Liberation Army Daily) June 16, 1996, 6, in Pillsbury, *Chinese Views of Future Warfare*, 399-407.

information, stealth, and long-range precision strike capability.[69] Chen predicts new operational concepts will appear in future wars:

- Long-range combat: "There will be three main forms of long-range strikes in the future: the first is the one in which the air arm independently carries out long-range strikes; the second form is one in which the long-range strike combines with the long-range rapid movement of troops transported by land and sea with the vertical airdrops of airborne forces; and the third form is five-dimensional—air, land, sea, space, and electro-magnetic—long-range combat."
- Outer space combat: "The following new-concept weapons will come forth in a continuous stream—all these weapons will make outer space the fifth dimension—operational space—following land, sea, air, and electromagnetism:
  -Laser weapons
  -Ultrahigh frequency weapons
  -Ultrasonic wave weapons
  -Stealth weapons
  -Electromagnetic guns.

Because the efficacy of these new-concept weapons depends on the hard-shell support of a space platform, once the space platform is lost, their efficacy will be weakened and they will even become powerless. In this way, the two sides in a war will focus on offensive and defensive operations conducted from space platforms in outer space, and these operations will certainly become a new form in future wars. In the U.S. Armed Forces, a new service—the Space Force—is being discussed, showing that the idea of outer space combat is close to moving from theory to actual combat."[70]

---

[69]Chen Huan, "Di san ci junshi geming bijiang chansheng shenyuan yingxiang" (The third military revolution), *Xiandai junshi* (Contemporary Military Affairs) 30, no. 3 (1996): 8-10, in Pillsbury, *Chinese Views of Future Warfare*, 389-398.

[70]Ibid.

- Paralysis combat: By striking at the "vital point" of the enemy's information and support systems one can paralyze the enemy and collapse his morale with one blow.

- Computer combat: "Relevant data show that, before the outbreak of the Gulf War, American intelligence organizations put a virus into Iraq's air defense system, which led to the destruction of 86 percent of the Iraqi strategic targets in the first one or two days of the war. This also shows that making the computer an operational means of attacking the object of a strike has already become a reality . . . for example, concealing a virus source in the integrated circuits of enemy computers and, when necessary, activating the virus by electronic measures, then propagating and duplicating it. Again, for example, with the aid of electromagnetic waves, a virus can be injected from a long distance into the enemy's command and communication systems and into the computers on aircraft, tanks, and other weapons, causing nonlethal destruction."

- Radiation combat: "In the wars of the past, the power to inflict casualties mainly depended on the effects of kinetic energy and thermal energy, but the weapon systems produced by the third military revolution mainly use sound, electromagnetism, radiation, and other destructive mechanisms. The main radiation weapons are laser weapons, microwave weapons, particle beam weapons, and subsonic wave weapons; they possess enormous military potential."

- Robot combat: "The main types of military robots on active service or about to be put on active service in the armed forces of various countries of the world are vehicle emergency robots, minelaying robots, minesweeping robots, reconnaissance robots, transportation robots, electronic robots, and driver robots. Later, there will appear engineer robots, chemical defense robots, patrol robots, and even unmanned intelligent tanks, unmanned intelligent aircraft, and other robot soldiers."[1]

Ibid.

DEFENSE INVESTMENT DECISIONS

Resource Allocation

Western estimates of China's defense budget range from U.S. $8 billion to over $100 billion. Little is known with confidence about how it is allocated, but there is evidence that China's leadership cannot decide among several future paths that have been proposed by policy analysts and is therefore allocating resources among three distinct paths. Two of these paths represent reforms. Advocates of these two reform schools seem to be arrayed against a third group of conservative traditionalists who have been losing their share of the allocation of defense investments. There is muted debate among these schools and discussion about how to invest defense spending in the decade ahead. The outcome of this debate may shift the future balance in defense resource allocations.

Investments Recommended by RMA Advocates

Since at least 1994, RMA visionaries (represented in numerous articles and five books in 1997) have been calling for China to attempt to leapfrog the United States in the next two decades by investing mainly in the most exotic advanced military technology and in new doctrines and new organizations along the lines of American and Russian writings on a potential RMA. Judging by the tone of the authors in this RMA school, they have not yet been successful. One of their members complained in an unusual signed article in the main military newspaper in February 1998 that the recent rate of innovation in doctrine, technology and organization has not been sufficient. Books by these authors have warned that if China tries to match U.S. military technology in the short term (rather than by leapfrogging), after 20 years China will only be further behind. This warning has not been heeded by the second and more influential Local War school.

Investments Recommended by Power Projection Advocates

A second reformist school of thought, identified by its use of the concept of local war or power projection, seems to be somewhat more confident than RMA advocates that it has gained a significant share of new defense investment. Like the RMA advocates, this Local War school identifies itself as "reformers." They have tried to achieve their evolutionary reforms since the early 1980s. These reformers are caught between the traditional conservatives, who have the lion's share of the investment budget, and the RMA advocates, who, in the eyes of the Local War reformers, appear to be championing unrealistic goals. Local War advocates have written since the mid-1980s that China needs a power projection capability that will provide at least decisive force against challenges to China's borders.

This school counts among its members most of the current high command of the Chinese Armed Forces. However, Local War advocates, while satisfied at the *direction* of defense investment, seem discontent about the *level* of funding the central government is providing. Thus, the authors of this school express veiled criticism of the pace and scope of the development of China's power projection forces. They complain, for example, that all China's neighbors possess more advanced military technology. They complain of the slow pace of Chinese programs to develop aerial refueling, at-sea replenishment, airborne warning and control aircraft, a national command and control system, sufficient airborne and amphibious forces, an aircraft carrier program, and fighter aircraft. In the nuclear field, they express concern that U.S.-supplied theater missile defense will neutralize China's nuclear forces targeted on its Asian neighbors and the United States. This group of reformers is not comfortable with the level of investment of defense resources, even if they seem pleased at its goals. They may seek additional resources as China's economy prospers.

Investments Recommended by People's War Advocates

A third school of thought probably still commands the greater part of Chinese defense investment. They still endorse the concept of People's War, or active defense, and they benefit most by the status quo in China's Armed Forces. They probably resist the innovations of both the RMA advocates and the Local War reformers, because their main preference is to preserve the world's largest standing army and to maintain China's complete reliance on indigenous defense production; they oppose troop cuts and the purchase of foreign weapons systems. The PLA was 7 million strong in the early 1980s, and only after major controversy was it reduced to 3 million, with a recent promise (debated for the past 5 years) that another 500,000 may be cut by 2000. The

People's War school also prefers to maintain a national mobilization capability for wartime defense industry (to include production of light arms and ammunition). The People's War school may not be completely antagonistic to the reforms of the Local War advocates in the direction of limited power projection, as long as the expense does not compromise the large standing army and a suitable defense mobilization base and does not lead to dependence on foreign weapons or foreign technology.

FINDINGS

The debates and the competition for defense resources among the three schools can result in very different outcomes over a decade or two into the future. For example, the Local War or Power Projection school may eventually pose a challenge to U.S. naval and air forces in the Western Pacific. Over time, the Chinese have explicitly stated they intend to attain military influence out to the "first island chain" (roughly 500 to 1,000 miles from China) with their power projection forces. They cannot operate in this area today, yet Chinese authors emphasize that enormous natural resources await exploitation by China in this area. China's authors claim that China in the past century was humiliated by Japan and the Western imperialists because it lacked modern military technology. China particularly lacked advanced naval forces, and so it lost the province of Taiwan and other areas. Yet this school cannot obtain the necessary resources if the programs championed by the other two schools must also be funded.

In order to commit more resources to either power projection or developing RMA technology and doctrine, China must resolve or neglect a number of threats that will otherwise continue to claim the lion's share of defense investment. If these kinds of threats are reduced, then the RMA and Local War advocates can claim a larger share of defense resources. If China's economic growth rate continues to be three or four times faster than the U.S. economic growth rate (8 percent for China, 2.5 percent for the United States), then the estimates of the World Bank suggest that in the first quarter of the 20th century, China will have enormous resources with which to develop power projection and/or RMA capabilities. In some scenarios, the level of Chinese defense investment could exceed that of the United States within two decades.

Even with greater resources China's defense reformers of both the RMA and Local War schools need to free up those resources by resolving the threats and challenges that the programs of People's War school are designed to handle. Otherwise, conservatives will continue to dominate the defense investment process.

For example, a China with a GNP equal to the United States and focused on the RMA or advanced power projection forces would be a challenge to the United States. In contrast, a China focused on defense investments "turned inward" would be very different. China may decide to focus "inward" on:

- Layered strategic air defense
- Enhanced underground defense complexes
- Extensive ground forces around the national capital
- Border defense forces
- A large People's Armed Police for internal stability and counter subversion
- Inefficient defense industries located in interior provinces
- Fixed positional defenses for the largest energy project
- Deployments in the north to hedge against the revival of Russian nationalism
- Forces opposite Taiwan for amphibious invasion if Taiwan declares independence.

Much more needs to be known about China's secretive defense decisionmaking process before a thorough understanding is achieved about why China's leaders may select one path instead of another. This is probably worth attempting. Whether the People's War advocates continue to dominate China's military investment decisions may become an issue of some importance to the United States over the long term.

No Chinese author has yet publicly identified the relationship among the three different "schools of future warfare" and alternative future security environments. It is plausible that such debates are still too sensitive a subject for open publication. One could speculate, however, that a long-term security environment of "peace and development" would be a forecast that favors the RMA advocates and who propose that China should identify new technologies and new operational concepts and even set up new types of military organizations in order to leapfrog ahead a generation, as Mi Zhenyu and others advocate. Similarly, Local War advocates would welcome a second type of forecast about the future security environment over next two decades that emphasizes the high probability of local wars along China's frontiers. These local wars might include Taiwan's declaring independence, or maritime border disputes in the South China Sea or Central Asia. Such a forecast would mean that Beijing would have to invest heavily in the program of these advocates. Finally, one could imagine that People's War advocates would welcome Chinese authors who emphasize the threat of dismemberment, foreign subversion, or a land invasion by a future fascist Japan, or even the rise to power of a madman like Hitler in India, the United States, or Russia.

7 : CONCLUSIONS

MULTIPLE DEBATES

CHINESE ANALYSTS HAVE A CLEAR PICTURE of what the overall future security environment will look like—there will be a multipolar world structure, where the major nations have relatively equal Comprehensive National Power (CNP), international relations will be governed by the Five Principles of Peaceful Coexistence, and the world will no longer be dominated by power politics and hegemonic superpowers. However, the characteristics of the transition period to this multipolar world are not subject to the same clarity. As has been discussed, Chinese authors do not debate in the Western sense of the word. Not only do they rarely admit publicly to the existence of debates, their writings usually do not even refer to, let alone criticize, other author's views. However, through excerpts and quotes from the writings of over 200 civilian and military analysts, by allowing the authors to "speak for themselves," it becomes clear that Chinese analysts hold a variety of views on the features of the current and future security environment. These various and differing views, while they do not always constitute debates—they range from conflicting and opposing ideas, to merely a difference in emphasis—are important to our understanding the premises of Chinese national strategy. The basic "debates" are outlined below, followed by the book's major findings.

The Rate of Multipolarization
- First and foremost, the issue of the time frame of the transition era itself is uncertain. At what rate is the world moving toward multipolarity, how long will the transition last? Predictions range from vague forecasts about early next century, to more long-range outlooks of several decades.

- There is a question of whether or not the world is actually in a transition period, or if the current era, where there is "one superpower and four powers," can itself be actually described as a world structure.

The Pace of U.S. Decline

- Closely related to the issue of the rate of multipolarization, is the question of the pace of U.S. decline. The eventual U.S. fall from its current superpower status to become one of the equal poles in the future security environment is a given, a premise that is not debated. However, how long this process of decline will take is not a certainty. On one end of the spectrum authors argue that the United States is currently in a serious decline and that its power is weakening; at the other end, there is the view that the United States will be able to maintain its current supremacy for several decades. As was discussed in chapter one, after the NATO strikes in Yugoslavia and the bombing of the Chinese Embassy in spring 1999, a new feature was added to the debate when some authors began to predict that there would be further increases in U.S. power.

- The type of decline the United States is experiencing is described and depicted in different ways. As was seen in chapter two, there is a question of whether current U.S. decline is actual, or is merely relative when compared to the rise of other countries. A similar issue was manifested in the chapter on CNP, where the scores of Chinese Academy of Social Sciences (CASS) had U.S. CNP declining through 2020; versus Academy of Military Science (AMS) scores which had U.S. CNP increasing through 2020, but showed that the CNP of other countries was rising at much faster rates.

- Will the United States lose its allies? One of the key factors described as contributing to U.S. decline is that its relationships with Japan and Europe will deteriorate, and direct conflicts and struggles will eventually break up the partnerships. In chapter one, Yang Dazhou argues that the United States will maintain its alliances. However, although they differ in how long they expect it will take for friction to cause the alliances to crumble, in the views of most of the authors presented in chapter two, fierce rivalries are inevitable.

The Future Powers

● Who will be the poles in the future multipolar world? This question involves several issues. The first deals with the potential strength of the European nations—will Germany grow powerful enough to constitute a pole in its own right, or can that role be only held by the European Union? Another question is how many poles there will be in the multipolar structure? The most common premise put forward is that there will be five poles—the United States, China, Japan, Russia, and Europe. However, some analysts debate about what the role of the Third World will be. India in particular, as was discussed in chapter four, is the subject of opposing views over whether it will gain enough strength to become a potential pole.

● What will be the rank order of the major nations in the future multipolar world? In terms of comprehensive national power, will there actually be equality in the future multipolar world? Whose power will increase most rapidly during the transition period? Chapter five illustrated that the quantitative assessments of CNP conducted by CASS and AMS, as well as other individual analysts, result in very different pictures of the future security environment.

The Roles of Japan and Russia

● The main issue of debate concerning Japan is whether or not it will become a militarist power. Chinese analysts differ in whether they consider Japanese culture and society to be inherently militarist, or whether it is only conservatives in the government and some right-wing segments of society that want to lead the country back down the "road to militarism." Will the country's drive to be a world power and its growing military force affect its democracy and foreign policy? Will the general public be able to contain the portion of Japanese society and politics that advocates extreme nationalism?

● During the current transition period, Russia is generally described by Chinese as facing numerous dangers to its security environment, however, authors analyze very differently Russia's responses and ability to deal with these threats. Some analysts depict Russia as passive and weak in the face of NATO expansion (there are even some warnings about the danger of

Russia losing its foundation for being a pole); while others see Russia as taking a stand and adopting countermeasures against the United States and NATO.

Future Wars

- Regional wars and turbulence are expected to be constant features of the transition era, but will there be another world war? One of the common themes continuously repeated by Chinese authors is that "peace and development are the main trend" of the times, and that a major global war will not occur. However, after the Kosovo crisis and the bombing of the Chinese Embassy in Belgrade in spring 1999, the potential for a WWIII was mentioned by several authors.

- While it is generally accepted that regional wars will be prevalent during the transition period, their characteristics are subject to debate. Where will they occur? Where will be the major hot spots—Central and Eastern Europe, Africa, Central Asia, the Asia-Pacific? Who will be involved? Will there be wars among the major powers? Will China be involved in these wars, or even worse, will China be a source of war?

- Related to the questions of where the wars will occur, what they will be about, and what participants will be involved, is the issue of what kinds of war they will be. Will the doctrines of the People's War School, the Local War School, or the RMA School be needed to deal with these contingencies?

A CLEAR PICTURE

The public writings of Chinese authors from the major research institutes portray a clear picture of the future security environment. The *main trend* will be "peace and development" and a "multipolar world." But, there could also be wars and other future dangers for China from the same four nations that, back in the 1970s, Chairman Mao and Premier Zhou Enlai told Henry Kissinger threatened China—Russia, Japan, India, and America. Chinese analysts still study and respect Mao's essays and explicitly confirm that the line established by Deng Xiaoping in the 1980s about the coming "multipolar" world is still accurate. Chinese authors have added new details to Deng's assessment, however, and a few issues have become the subject of scholarly debates:

- The rate of relative decline of the sole superpower, the United States
- The types of local wars that may break out
- The precise hierarchy of major powers in 2010 or 2020, "scientifically" ranked according to the indices of Comprehensive National Power (CNP)
- Whether Japan or India will inevitably fall under control of militaristic leaders.

The Chinese assessment of the current and future security environment depicts the present world as being in an era of transition to a new world structure. During this period, great rivalries will emerge among the powers, and many local wars will be fought, as a "re-division of spheres of influence" and a struggle for world leadership takes place. Chinese analysts point to some examples of the current struggles to divide spheres of influence:

- The United States arranging the Bosnian settlement at Dayton to dominate further its European NATO allies.
- The United States forcing Japan to increase its financial support for U.S. bases and forces in Japan under the guise of the Defense Guidelines, so that it can challenge the Russian and Chinese spheres of influence from the east, while NATO challenges them from the west.
- Japan seeking to embroil the Unites States and China in a struggle that will weaken both Washington and Beijing.
- NATO air strikes against Yugoslavia in spring 1999 as a part of a U.S. plan to gain control over Eurasia.

After the transition to the multipolar world, a new "world system" will emerge to govern international affairs, one that will probably resemble the current Chinese proposal of the "Five Principles of Peaceful Coexistence." Chinese authorities assert that world politics since the 1800s always has had a "system" or a "strategic pattern." Under the rules of such a "system" or "strategic pattern" there is a competition among powers that includes a global division of spheres of influence. Chinese historical textbooks discuss the "Vienna System" of 1815-70; an intermediate system when Germany and Italy each unified and Japan launched the Meiji Reform; the "Versailles System" of 1920-45; the "Yalta System" of 1945-89; and the present "transition era."

Huan Xiang, Deng Xiaoping's national security adviser, first announced the features of the current view of the future security environment in early 1986, just after the U.S.-Soviet summit:

- "As the world moves toward a multipolar . . . five pole world, when the United States and the Soviet Union are considering problems, they must think about the China factor, and also the other poles."
- Japan "not only wants to strive to be on equal footing with the United States economically and politically, but further, it is deliberately planning, when the time is ripe, to surpass the United States, replacing America's world economic hegemony. Once it has economic hegemony, political and military hegemony would not be too difficult."

Chinese authors rarely refer to each other and almost never criticize other authors by name, but in 1997, two unusual articles broke this apparent taboo in two national journals. The episode began when Yang Dazhou, a well-known senior analyst at the Institute of American Studies of the Chinese Academy of Social Science (CASS), published a direct and detailed criticism of the orthodox assessment of the coming world of multipolarity. The article met with a vigorous response from a senior general in military intelligence, Huang Zhengji. In a departure from the tradition of merely stating a view without debating anyone else, the People's Liberation Army general actually quoted long passages from the reformer's article, then wrote that these views were ridiculous, without foundation, and unsupportable, and worst of all, they played into the hands of the United States. The two articles reflect a difference among the senior leadership of China about:

- The *pace* of the decline of the United States
- The *rate* of the rise of "multipolarity"
- Whether the U.S. will lose its allies
- What the future role of Third World nations will be.

In his article, Yang Dazhou heretically argues against each of the key features of the orthodox view of the future security environment, putting forward a reformist scenario:

- The United States will maintain its superpower status for at least three decades.
- The United States will maintain its alliances with Japan and Germany.
- There will not be a period of "uncertainty" in the next two or three decades.
- There will not be an extended transition period featuring a trend toward multipolarity.
- A "pluralistic" world structure of "one superpower and four powers" already exists.
- Only the United States is really a "pole" able to decide key issues in any region, as in the Dayton Accords. "The United States plays a leading role that no other nation can replace . . . the only country that is a 'pole.'"
- China "does not have sufficient qualifications to be a 'pole.'"
- For more than 20 years, no other nations, including those in the Third World, will emerge as major powers to challenge the five strongest, therefore the phrase used by many analysts "'one super many strong' is actually not appropriate."
- It is not likely large local wars will break out among nations.

General Huang quoted passages from Yang's article without directly citing it and reasserted the orthodox view on each of these points:

- U.S. decline is inevitable and continuing; U.S. global influence is already severely limited.
- Five-pole multipolarity is inevitable, especially as friction grows between the United States and Japan and Germany (as proved by the new summits between the European Union and Asia, which excluded the declining United States).
- The rise of the Third World has transformed world politics and will continue to restrain the United States.

- Local wars are certain, even though " 'peace and development' is the main trend" during the transitional period of uncertainty in the decades ahead.

The NATO strikes on Yugoslavia and the NATO bombing of the Chinese Embassy in Belgrade in spring 1999 have given prominence to the debate concerning the future world structure. One of the biggest outgrowths of the Kosovo crisis and the bombing is that they led to the reevaluation of previous assessments of the pace of U.S. decline and of the rate at which the world is moving toward multipolarization. It appears that the reformist view, represented by Yang Dazhou, has gained support as a result of U.S. and NATO actions in Yugoslavia. A clear post-Kosovo trend has been the number of Chinese authors admitting that the transition to multipolarity has been delayed. A key element in the new assessment is the issue of why the time frame for the transition to the new world structure has been greatly extended—the United States remains powerful. Not only are some authors no longer focusing on current U.S. decline, but rather they are predicting that its strength may even continue to increase. However, other Chinese analysts, while recognizing that the pace of the multipolarization process has slowed, also emphasize that the current trend does not mean that the United States will be able to establish a unipolar world. It is only a setback in the transition to a new world structure.

After the U.S. bombing of the Chinese embassy in Belgrade, some authors seemed to question whether the main trend of the times still is peace and development, and some authors even mentioned the possibility of a third world war.

Chinese analysts explain the outbreak of local wars in the 1990s as having two major causes: first, the ethnic, religious, historical, and territorial disputes previously covered up and restricted by the U.S.-Soviet confrontation were free to emerge following the end of the Cold War; and second, as the new world structure is forming, there is competition and contention for power, influence, and economic sources. Chinese analysts differ about where they see future local wars occurring. Some see the main local war "hot spot" as shifting to Africa or the Middle East, while others focus on Central Asia and the Asia-Pacific.

A number of analysts cite hegemonism and military interventionism as contributing to and exacerbating local wars. Following NATO military strikes against Yugoslavia in spring 1999, there was a tremendous increase in criticism and alarm about U.S. hegemonism being a source of war. In what is characterized as its pursuit of global hegemony and a unipolar world order, U.S. military intervention is expected to continue to occur throughout the transition period.

Chinese analysts suggest that a potential cause of war in the Asia-Pacific has to do with China's rise as a global power. Several authors have written about likely U.S. efforts in the next decade or two to contain China's development and prevent its rise in international affairs. They warn of potential conflicts between China and the United States, as China's power increases and the "desperate" United States struggles to maintain its leading position. These predictions conflict with Deng Xiaoping's assertion that China will never be a source of war—although apparently a war could be forced on China.

Debate about the future role of the United States concerns not only the decline of future U.S. capability, but also how other nations may affect U.S. policy. One author asserts China will face danger earlier because Japan (or some elements in Japan) is instigating long-term confrontation between the United States and China. He maintains Japan will do this in order to mask its own ambitions to replace the United States as the world's hegemon. Other Chinese authors claim to see through other conspiracies, pointing out that there are already many "hidden signs" of the struggles now shaping the future multipolar world. For example, U.S. officials use the China Threat Theory to scare Association of South East Asian Nations (ASEAN) into maintaining military relations with America. There are also "hidden signs" in Central Asia, Bosnia, and Eastern Europe that the United States is maneuvering to maintain its "hegemony" and "carve up" the former Soviet "sphere of influence." Chinese authors use words right out of Warring States texts to describe alleged U.S. strategies to maintain its position as "hegemon," the ancient name for the leading state in the Warring States era.

Deng Xiaoping himself used expressions from the Warring States and other ancient texts to advise future Chinese leaders on strategy. China, he said, must *"taoguang-yanghui"*—the literal translation means "Hide brightness, nourish obscurity" or, as the official Beijing interpretation translates the four-character idiom, "Bide our time and build up our capabilities." He suggested that China at present is poor and weak and must avoid being dragged into local wars, into any conflicts about spheres of influence, or into struggles over natural resources. Deng's advice is, "Yield on small issues with the long term in mind." Deng Xiaoping's additional word of advice was *bu chu tou*—never be the leader or, literally translated, "Don't stick your head out."

In the Warring States era, states that rose too fast suffered attack, dismemberment, and even complete extinction. In the final phase of the Warring States era, as every literate Chinese knows, Su Qin, a brilliant strategist, formed a coalition that stood for several years against the newly rising state of Qin. The United States and Japan, if provoked, could do this to a rising China. To counter this, nationalistic authors like He Xin want to take the initiative to form a coalition against the United States that "under the banner of opposing the hegemon," would align China with every anti-American nation in the world. Other proposals to protect a rising China from the ruthless hegemon are more defensive:

- China's forecasted energy needs will be enormous in 2020, which could make China vulnerable to the United States. Therefore, one author urges that China's energy must be sought through pipelines to Russia and Central Asia. He asserts that China's relative military superiority in ground forces can better protect these energy assets than if China purchases oil from the Persian Gulf and must rely on sealanes threatened by American or Japanese naval forces.
- President Jiang Zemin has issued traditional-style, poetic statements in sets of 16 Chinese characters that continue Deng's advice to avoid confrontation with the hegemon.
- Under Jiang Zemin, an additional set of writings (five books in 1996-97) has advocated that China's military programs be focused on the potential revolution in military affairs (RMA) rather than on improving current weapons. According to these books, the potential RMA will not "mature" until at least 2030, by which time Chinese military authors calculate that China (or possibly Japan) will score highest in the world in

CNP and be well positioned, as General Mi Zhenyu has written, to "get ahead of all the others."

WARRING STATES

The Warring States era in China gave rise to a series of classical texts on statecraft warfare that are currently being re-examined by Chinese analysts. According to China's authors:

- The current multipolar world is "amazingly" similar to the Warring States era.
- Ancient statecraft is useful and has been blessed by a commission of China's generals.
- As during the Warring States era, there is currently a great danger to national survival from deception and from falling victim to "strategic deception" by a major power. The United States and Japan are particularly active in strategic misdirection (*zhanlue wudao*). Chinese analysts maintain that the U.S. deception that caused Moscow to overspend on defense was a factor in the Soviet collapse, and Washington may even have tricked Saddam into invading Kuwait, according to the Vice President of the Academy of Military Science. Articles by two senior analysts at the China Institute of Contemporary International Relations and one at CASS assert that Japan may attempt strategic misdirection of the United States toward conflict with China, in order to mask its own ambitions of surpassing and replacing the United States as the world hegemon.
- In the Warring States era, successful leaders could divine the future and see through their rivals' conspiracies.

AMERICA'S DECLINE

Chinese national security specialists have been describing America's role in the future security environment in the same way for a decade: dangerous but declining. Chinese authors project a sharp decline in the global role of the United States, asserting:

- As the United States and Russia reduce nuclear forces, China will attain nuclear equivalence.

315

- U.S. "digitization" and other initial RMA efforts cannot be completed until 2050, by which time other nations will have surpassed the United States in the RMA competition.
- The United States will be involved in regional wars in the 21st century.
- China may have to use force if the U.S. attempts to "dismember" Taiwan, Tibet, or Xinjiang.

In the picturesque terms of ancient Chinese statecraft, America is a decaying hegemon whose leaders are as yet unaware that their fate is unavoidable. Authors claim the United States is pursuing strategies, such as:

- Attempting to limit Russia's recovery and access to resources
- Practicing limited containment of China's rising influence
- Fomenting conflict between China and Japan
- Investing (too slowly) in a potential RMA
- Using the Bosnia conflict to maintain domination of Europe
- Falsely spreading the China Threat Theory in ASEAN
- Seeking military bases and new NATO allies in Central Asia
- Aiding separatist movements in Tibet, Taiwan, and Xinjiang.

Other authors sound warnings. The Vice President of the Academy of Military Science urges vigilance because the declining United States will attempt "strategic deception" of other major powers, including China, as it did in the case of both the Soviet Union, with the phony "Star Wars" threat, and Iraq, with the invasion of Kuwait so the United States could dismantle Iraq's growing power. The Director of the Foreign Policy Center at China's largest security research institute warns that the United States may form a coalition to "strangle" China if the proponents of the neo-McCarthyist China Threat Theory become too strong in the United States.

Chinese assessments do not treat the United States as "weak" in any absolute sense at the present time, however. For example, a series of books on the U.S. Armed Forces asserts that the U.S. has military technological superiority in practically every field, despite U.S. reductions since 1991.

Nevertheless, the United States will fall behind in military innovation after 2010 for a variety of reasons.

FUTURE NATIONAL POWER

In the mid-1980s, Deng Xiaoping asserted that it was important to calculate future trends in Comprehensive National Power (CNP), the concept that helps guide China's reforms, and that CNP calculations should include economics, science, defense, and other factors. Although calculating CNP was developed in 1984, Chinese authors justify the concept as stemming both from ancient Chinese strategists and Chairman Mao. CNP scores are important for major powers because they can help identify:

- The status hierarchy in world politics
- The power of potential rivals and potential partners
- Who will best exploit the RMA
- Which side will win a war
- The trend toward world multipolarity and U.S. decline.

Two contending scientific teams in Beijing have calculated estimates of what the CNP scores of major powers will be in 2010. The military team's results parallel the "orthodox" authors' predictions about the future security environment:

- The U.S. quantitative power score by 2010 shows a decreasing gap between the United States and the other major powers.
- By 2020, the U.S. CNP score will equal China's, assuming China's power growth rate continues to be 5.8 percent, double the U.S. rate of 2.7 percent.
- Germany and Japan will also have higher CNP growth rates than the United States and will become the third- and fourth-ranking world powers after the United States and China in 2020.
- If these growth rates are extended another decade or so, China, Japan, and Germany will all three equal or surpass the United States in CNP.

However, the civilian team's "reformist" results contradict the orthodox view about an emerging multipolar structure:

- China's power score will be only about half the United States by 2010 and 2020.
- Japan by 2010 will equal the United States.
- Japan will score 20 percent higher than the United States in 2020.
- China in 2020 will be seventh, behind Japan, the United States, Germany, France, Italy, and even South Korea in CNP.

THREATS FROM JAPAN AND INDIA

China's assessments of Japan and India are similar because both "fit" the analytic premises the Chinese use about nations that have territorial disputes with China, and both are capitalist and democratic. India is assessed as a sort of half-scale version of Japan. Chinese authors suggest that Japan:

- Wants to restrain China's rising influence
- Seeks to foment conflict between the United States and China
- Will continue to have a militaristic strategic culture
- Will struggle for resources in Central Asia and Siberia against the United States and Russia
- Will have ever increasing conflicts with both Europe and the United States
- Will develop nuclear weapons eventually, and earlier if Korea obtains them
- Seeks (covertly) to become the military equivalent of the United States.

As a smaller scale version of Japan, China's analysts write that India, too, has a militaristic, religion-based strategic culture. They assert that it seeks to dominate its neighbors, had covert nuclear ambitions for two decades prior to its nuclear tests in 1998, attempts to foment conflict between China and other nations, and has some areas of military superiority over China, such as its current navy. However, India's economic reforms are judged insufficient to catch up with China and enter the multipolar world as the sixth pole. India's

CNP scores for 2010 place it no higher than ninth (AMS) or thirteenth (CASS), only about half of China's CNP score in 2010.

PARTNERSHIP WITH RUSSIA

Chinese analysts evidence sympathy for Russia in the wake of the Soviet Union's dissolution. That sympathy perhaps foreshadows interests in some form of future strategic partnership.

- China forecasts that Russia will return to the ranks of the top five powers in the future security environment.
- Some nationalistic Chinese authors like He Xin propose that China must form a long-term strategic partnership with Russia in order to balance the rise of a militaristic Japan.
- One orthodox senior analyst explains the geopolitical thinking involved: "Russia needs to rely on China. Because both the United States and Japan regard Russia as a potential force to reduce their influence in the Asia-Pacific region, and Japan has territorial disputes with Russia, Chinese-Russian cooperation can, to a great extent, resist U.S. and Japanese forces, as well as maintain the power balance in Asia."[1]
- Russia has advantages, such as its potential partnership with China and advanced military concepts and technology, that cause China to assess the Russians as far more likely to successfully exploit the RMA than the United States. One military author argues, "Russia will use the RMA to maintain its military superiority . . . and is secretly taking aim at America's commanding position in the RMA."[2] Another military author states that the Russian General Staff Academy is focusing on the RMA.[3]

---

[1]Gu Guanfu, "Russian Foreign Policy in Evolution," *Contemporary International Relations*, no. 11 (1994).

[2]Zhu Xiaoli and Zhao Xiaozhuo, *Mei-E xin junshi geming* (America, Russia and the revolution in military affairs)(Beijing: Junshi kexue chubanshe, 1996), 2.

[3]Gao Chunxiang, ed., *Xinjunshi geming lun* (On the new revolution in military affairs)(Beijing: Junshi kexue chubanshe, 1996), 196.

FORECASTING FUTURE WARS

China's authors appear to be debating several future paths for defense spending, two of which represent reforms. Advocates of these two reform schools seem to be arrayed against a third group of conservative traditionalists who have been losing their share of the allocation of defense investments. The outcome of this muted debate among these schools may affect defense resource allocations.

- *Investments Recommended by the RMA Advocates.* Since at least 1994, RMA visionaries (represented in numerous articles and five books in 1997) have been calling for China to attempt to leapfrog the United States in the next two decades by investing mainly in the most exotic advanced military technology and in new doctrines and new organizations along the lines of American and Russian writings on a potential RMA. Judging by the tone of the authors in this RMA School, they have not been very successful.

- *Investments Recommended by the Power Projection Advocates.* A second reformist school of thought, identified by its use of the concept of local war, or power projection, has advocated evolutionary reforms. These evolutionary reformers are caught between the traditional conservatives, who currently have the lion's share of the investment budget, and the RMA advocates, who appear to be championing unrealistic goals in the eyes of the Local War reformers. Local War advocates, while satisfied at the *current direction* of defense investment, seem discontented about the *level* of funding the central government is providing.

- *Investments Recommended by the People's War Advocates.* A third school of thought probably still commands the lion's share of Chinese defense investment. It still endorses the concept of People's War, or Active Defense, and opposes troop cuts and the purchase of foreign weapons systems. The People's War school may not be completely antagonistic to the reforms of the Local War advocates regarding limited power projection, as long as the expense does not compromise the large standing army and a suitable defense mobilization base and does not lead to dependence on foreign weapons or foreign technology.

China's defense reformers of both the RMA and Local War schools need to free up resources by resolving the threats and challenges that the programs of the People's War school are designed to handle. Otherwise, conservatives will continue to dominate the defense investment process.

SENSITIVE DEBATES

No Chinese author has yet publicly identified the relationship among the three different "schools of future warfare" and alternative future security environments. It is plausible that such debates are still too sensitive a subject for open publication. One could speculate, however, that a long-term security environment of "peace and development" would be a forecast that favors the RMA advocates and those who propose that China should identify new technologies and new operational concepts and even set up new types of military organizations in order to leapfrog ahead a generation. Similarly, Local War advocates would welcome a second type of forecast about the future security environment over the next two decades that emphasizes the high probability of local wars along China's frontiers. These local wars might include Taiwan's declaring independence, or maritime border disputes in the South China Sea or Central Asia. Such a forecast would mean that Beijing would have to invest heavily in the program of these advocates. Finally, one could imagine that People's War advocates would welcome Chinese authors who emphasize the threat of dismemberment, foreign subversion, or a land invasion by a future fascist Japan, or even the rise to power of a madman like Hitler in India, the United States, or Russia.

ACRONYMS

ACDA	U.S. Arms Control and Disarmament Agency
AMS	Academy of Military Science
ASATs	antisatellite weapons
BISE	Beijing Institute of Systems Engineering
CASS	Chinese Academy of Social Sciences
CICIR	China Institute of Contemporary International Relations
CIIS	China Institute of International Studies
CIISS	China Institute of International Strategic Studies
CIS	Commonwealth of Independent States
CMC	Central Military Commission
CNP	Comprehensive National Power
COSTIND	Commission on Science, Technology and Industry for National Defense
CSCE	Conference on Security and Cooperation in Europe
CSSM	Chinese Society for Strategy and Management
DOD	Department of Defense
FISS	Foundation for International Strategic Studies
GDP	gross domestic product
GNP	gross national product
GSD	General Staff Department
IMEMO	Institute of World Economics and Politics (Moscow)
IWEP	Institute of World Economics and Politics (Beijing)
MSS	Ministry of State Security
NCNA	New China News Agency
NDU	National Defense University
PAP	People's Armed Police
PLA	People's Liberation Army
PPP	purchase power parity
PRC	People's Republic of China
QDR	Quadrennial Defense Review
RMA	Revolution in Military Affairs
SIIS	Shanghai Institute for International Studies

CHINESE LANGUAGE BIBLIOGRAPHY

RMA, HIGH-TECHNOLOGY WARFARE, AND LOCAL WARFARE

Feng Changhong. *Waijun gao jishu yu xiandai junshi jiangzuo* (A course on foreign military high technology and modern military affairs). Beijing: Junshi kexue chubanshe, 1994.

Gao Chunxiang, ed. *Xin junshi geming lun* (On the new revolution in military affairs). Beijing: Junshi kexue chubanshe, 1996.

Gao jishu jubu zhanzheng yu zhanyi zhanfa (High-technology local warfare and campaign fighting methods). Guofang daxue keyan bu (National Defense University, Scientific Research Department). Beijing: Guofang daxue chubanshe, 1993.

Guan Jiefu, Zhang Feng, and Ling Yong. *Jun yuan da huo bao—Dangdai gao jishu jubu zhanzheng jing hui* (Explosive stories—contemporary high-technology local warfare collection). Beijing: Guofang daxue chubanshe, 1993.

Li Jie. *Gao jishu yu xiandai haijun* (High technology and the modern navy). Beijing: Junshi kexue chubanshe, 1994.

Li Qingshan. *Xin junshi geming yu gao jishu zhanzheng* (The new revolution in military affairs and high-technology warfare). Beijing: Junshi kexue chubanshe, 1995.

Li Zhishun and Sun Dafa. *Gao jishu zhanzheng moulue* (High-technology warfare strategy). Beijing: Guofang daxue chubanshe, 1993.

Liang Biqin and Zhao Lujie. *Gaojishu zhanzheng zheli* (High-technology warfare philosophy). Beijing: Jiefangjun chubanshe, 1995.

Liu Mingtao and Yang Chengjun. *Gao jishu zhanzheng zhong de daodan zhan* (Guided missile war in high-technology warfare). Beijing: Guofang daxue chubanshe, 1993.

Liu Sheng'e and Miao Lin. *Xiandai jubu zhanzheng tiaojian xia de renmin zhanzheng* (People's War under the conditions of modern local warfare). Beijing: Junshi kexue chubanshe, 1996.

Liu Yichang, ed. *Gao jishu zhanzheng lun* (High-technology warfare). Beijing: Junshi kexue chubanshe, 1993.

Luo Youli, Zhu Kuiyu, and Hou Luliang. *Gao jishu jubu zhanzheng zhanfa tansuo* (Exploring high-technology local warfare combat methods). Beijing: Junshi kexue chubanshe, 1994.

Su Yansong, ed. *Junjie redian juji—Gao jishu jubu zhanzheng gailun* (A collection of military hot points—an outline of high-technology local warfare). Beijing: Guofang daxue chubanshe, 1993.

Wang Pufeng. *Xinxi zhanzheng yu junshi geming* (Information warfare and the revolution in military affairs). Beijing: Junshi kexue chubanshe 1995.

Yang Lizhong and Yang Junxi. *Xiandai gao jishu zhan* (Modern high-technology warfare). Beijing: Junshi kexue chubanshe, 1993.

Yang Lizhong, Yang Junxi, Bie Yixun, and Le Junhuai. *Gao jishu zhanlue—kua shiji de tiaozhan yu jiyu* (High-technology strategy—trans-century challenges and opportunities). Beijing: Junshi kexue chubanshe, 1991.

Yang Yi. *Gaojishu tiaojian xia zuozhan fangshi, fangfa yanjiu yu sikao* (The research and thinking on combat forms and methods under high-technology conditions). Beijing: Junshi kexue chubanshe, 1997.

Yin Zhen and Su Qingyi, eds. *Gao jishu yu xiandai kongjun* (High technology and the modern airforce). N.p.: Junshi kexue chubanshe, 1993.

Yu Gaoda and Gao Wenyuan, eds. *Gao jishu zhanzheng houqin* (High-technology warfare logistics). Beijing: Guofang daxue chubanshe, 1995.

Yu Huating and Liu Guoyu, eds. *Gao jishu zhanzheng yu jundui zhiliang jianshe* (High-technology warfare and force quality development). Beijing: Guofang daxue chubanshe, 1993.

Yu Yongzhe, ed. *Gao jishu zhanzheng houqin baozhang* (High-technology warfare logistics protection). Beijing: Junshi kexue chubanshe, 1995.

Zhang Liuhua. *Shei zhuzai weilai zhanchang ?—Gao jishu zhanzheng zhong de jun bingzhong* (Who will dominate future battle fields?—the armed forces of high-technology warfare). Beijing: Guofang daxue chubanshe, 1993.

Zhang Yufa, Shou Xiaosong, Yu Qifen, Hu Guangzheng, Zhang Ji, Xiao Xianshe, Wang Yimin, and Ma Shanying. *Jubu zhanzheng gai lan—1945 nian 9 yue—1987 nian 12 yue* (General readings on local warfare—September 1945-December 1987). Beijing: Jiefangjun chubanshe, 1988.

Zhao Hongfa and Zhang Yuliang, eds. *Gao jishu jubu zhanzheng yezhan fangkong* (High-technology local warfare air defense operations). Beijing: Guofang daxue chubanshe, 1993.

Zhu Youwen, Feng Yi and Xu Dechi. *Gaojishu tiaojian xia de xinxizhan* (Information warfare under high-technology conditions). N.p.: Junshi kexue chubanshe, 1994.

MILITARY SCIENCE AND STRATEGIC STUDIES

Bretnor, Reginald. *Juedingxing zhanzheng—junshi lilun yanjiu* (Decisive warfare—a study in military theory). Translated by Junshi kexue yuan waiguo junshi yanjiu bu (Academy of Military Science, Foreign Military Affairs Research Department). Beijing: Junshi kexue chubanshe, 1989.

Chen Liheng, ed. *Junshi yuce xue* (Military forecasts). Beijing: Junshi kexue chubanshe, 1993.

Chen Weiren, ed. *Junshi moulue xue* (Military strategy studies). Beijing: Guofang daxue chubanshe, 1990.

Gao Tiqian. *Zhanzheng yu zhanlue* (War and strategy). Beijing: Junshi kexue chubanshe, 1994.

Jiang Shunxue, ed. *Lun wuchan jieji junshi kexue* (On proletariat military science). Beijing: Junshi kexue chubanshe 1997.

Li Jijun. *Junshi lilun yu zhanzheng shijian* (Military theory and warfare). Beijing: Junshi kexue chubanshe, 1994

Li Jijun. *Junshi zhanlue siwei* (Strategic thought). Beijing: Junshi kexue chubanshe, 1996.

Li Lin and Zhao Qinxuan, eds. *Xin shiqi junshi jingji lilun yanjiu* (New era military economic theory studies). Beijing: Junshi kexue chubanshe, 1995.

Liang Biqin, ed. *Junshi zhixue* (Military philosophy). Beijing: Junshi kexue chubanshe, 1995.

Liu Jixian. *Junshi lilun yu weilai zuozhan* (Military theory and future combat). Beijing: Guofang daxue chubanshe, 1992.

Liu Shanji and Qian Junde. *Dangdai waiguo junshi sixiang* (Contemporary foreign military thought). Beijing: Jiefangjun chubanshe, 1988.

Liu Yechu, ed. *Junshi jingji xueshuo shi* (The history of military economic theory). Beijing: Junshi kexue chubanshe, 1995.

Liu Yichang, Wu Xizhi, Tong Fuquan, and Sun Zhenhuan. *Guofang jingji yanjiu* (National defense economics studies). Beijing: Junshi kexue chubanshe, 1993.

Lu Jingzheng, Fu Shangkui, and Song Enmin, eds. *Dangdai zhanlue zhinan* (A guide to contemporary strategy). Beijing: Guofang daxue chubanshe, 1994.

Lun zhanzheng yu junshi kexue (On warfare and military science). Translated by Junshi kexue yuan jihua zuzhi bu (Academy of Military Science, Planning Organization Department). N.p.: Junshi kexue chubanshe, 1990.

Luobofu, B.H. *Zhanzheng zhong de moulue* (Strategy in war)(in Russian). Translated by Wu Guangquan, Wu Xia, Lin Yiqun, and Liu Gang. Beijing: Jiefangjun chubanshe, 1992.

Ma Jinsheng. *Junshi qipian* (Military deception). Jinan: Junshi kexue chubanshe,1992.

Nuofu, Pa, ed. *Zhanzheng yishu shi* (The history of the art of warfare)(in Russian). Translated by Li Jing and Yuan Yanan. Beijing: Junshi kexue chubanshe, 1990.

Pan Shiying, ed. *Dangdai Zhongguo junshi sixiang jing yao* (The essence of contemporary Chinese military thinking). Beijing: Jiefangjun chubanshe, 1992.

Peng Guangqian and Wang Guangxu. *Junshi zhanlue jian lun* (A general discussion on military strategy). N.p.: Jiefangjun chubanshe, 1989.

Shi Yichen, Yao Jie, and Sun Xianzhi. *Moulue zhisheng* (The strategy of getting the upper hand). Beijing: Junshi kexue chubanshe, 1991.

Su Zhisong. *Kua shiji de junshi xin guandian* (New military points of view at the turn of the century). Beijing: Junshi kexue chubanshe, 1997.

Sun Jizhang. *Zhanyi xue jichu* (The foundation of campaign studies). Beijing: Guofang daxue chubanshe, 1990.

Sun Lushi, ed. *Junshi weilai xue* (Military future studies). Beijing: Guofang daxue chubanshe, 1988.

Wang Pufeng. *Xiandai guofang lun* (Modern national defense theory). Chongqing: Chongqing chubanshe, 1993.

Wang Shouyi, Wang Hui, Wang Bingxian, Wang Jian, Lu Yangshan, Geng Bingzhong, Gao Kun, Guo Shengwei, and Geng Zhixian. *Zhanshu mofang—moubian zhisheng de yishu* (Tactical magic—the art of dominating strategm). Beijing: Junshi kexue chubanshe, 1996.

Wu Chunqiu. *Guangyi da zhanlue* (Grand strategy in a broad sense). Beijing: Shishi chubanshe, 1995.

Xue Lan. *Moulue siwei yishu* (The art of strategic thinking). Beijing: Junshi kexue chubanshe, 1993.

Yang Qiming, Yao Wen, Yang Ning, and Zheng Jie. *Guowai junshi moulue baili* (100 examples of foreign military strategy). Beijing: Junshi yiwen chubanshe, 1997.

Yu Changhai. *Junshi xitong juece yanjiu* (Military systems policymaking studies). Beijing: Junshi kexue chubanshe, 1994.

Zhang Jian, ed. *Guofang yu zhengzhi* (National defense and politics). Beijing: Guofang daxue chubanshe, 1997.

Zhang Jinbao and Liu Yongjie, eds. *Dangdai zhanshu zhinan* (A contemporary tactics guide). Beijing: Guofang daxue chubanshe, 1994.

Zhang Junbo, ed. *Zhong-xi junshi zhexue bijiao yanjiu* (Comparison studies of Chinese and Western military philosophy). Beijing: Junshi kexue chubanshe, 1993.

Zhang Rong, and Sha Jingsong. *Junshi moulue cidian* (A dictionary of military strategy). Beijing: Jiefangjun chubanshe, 1992.

Zhang Yufa. *Junshi kexue yanjiu gai shu* (A general report on military science studies). Junshi kexue chubanshe, 1991.

Zhang Yufa, Ren Liansheng, Yu Yanmin, Wang Yimin, and Xiao Xianshe. *Junshi kexue ge xueke yanjiu xianzhuang ji fazhan quxiang* (The current state and development trends in the study of military science disciplines). Beijing: Jiefangjun chubanshe, 1993.

Zhang Zuiliang, Li Changsheng, Zhao Wenzhi, and Ding Fuli. *Junshi yunchouxue* (Military operations research). Beijing: Junshi kexue chubanshe, 1997.

Zhanlue xue (Strategic Studies). Edited by Junshi Kexue Yuan (Academy of Military Science). Shanxi: Junshi kexue chubanshe, 1987.

Zheng Wenhan, ed. *Junshi kexue gailun* (An introduction to military science). Beijing: Junshi kexue chubanshe, 1994.

Zhu Meisheng, ed. *Junshi sixiang gailun* (An introduction to military thinking). Beijing: Guofang daxue chubanshe, 1997.

MILITARY FORCES

Bantianjunwen. *Junshi weixing—Wexing jiandie zhan he jianduan wuqi* (Military satellites—satellite spy wars and sophisticated weapons)(in Japanese). Translated by Qin Rongbin. Beijing: Junshi kexue chubanshe, 1990.

Cai Renzhao. *Zouxiang Weilai* (Heading towards the future). Shanghai: Shanghai renmin chubanshe, 1997.

Chen Yalai. *Waijun C³I xitong* (Foreign military C³I systems). Beijing: Jiefangjun chubanshe, 1989.

Clancy, Tom. *Zhuangjia qibing tuan zhi lu* (Armored cav: a guided tour of an armored cavalry regiment)(in English). Translated by Zhuang Shengxiong. N.p.: Hainan chubanshe, 1997.

Cui Jinjiu and Bu Weili. *20 shiji zhongda junshi weiji shuping* (A review of major 20th-century military crises). Beijing: Junshi kexue chubanshe, 1995.

Delurining, Fu Fu and De Si Kuntuoluofu. *Junshi xitong gongcheng wenti* (Military systems engineering problems)(originally in Russian). Junshi kexue yuan zuozhan yunchou fenxi yanjiu shi (Academy of Military Science, Combat Operations Analysis Research Office). Chinese People's Liberation Army plant #1201, 1984.

Gan Yanping. *Guoji haizhan fa gaiyao* (An outline of international sea warfare methods). Beijing: Haichao chubanshe, 1993.

Han Shengmin, ed. *Zouxiang 21 shiji de waiguo jundui jianshe* (Foreign military construction as the 21st century draws near). Beijing: Junshi kexue chubanshe, 1996.

Hu Shigong, Shen Liping, Lu Keqin and Huang Yanli. *Guowai lujun zhanshu C³I shouce* (Foreign armies' tactical C³I handbook). Beijing: Bingqi gongye chubanshe, 1990.

Huang Yanfeng and Liu Shengjun, eds. *Yatai de xuanwo: Yatai diqu junshi fazhan yuce xueshu yanlunhui lunwen ji* (The Asia-Pacific vortex: a collection of papers from the Asia-Pacific region military development forecast symposium). Compiled by Zhongguo junshi weilai yanjiu hui (Chinese Military Future Research Society). Beijing: Junshi kexue chubanshe, 1989.

Jiang Fu'an, ed. *Jiceng junguan suzhi xiuyang* (Basic level officer quality training). Beijing: Junshi kexue chubanshe, 1995.

Jiang Zhijun and Zhang Fan. *Haiyang douzheng yu haishang liliang de yunyong* (Ocean combat and the utilization of sea power). Beijing: Jiefangjun chubanshe, 1994.

Jilu yanming (Be highly disciplined). Edited by *Jiefangjun bao* junshi gongzuo xuanchuan bu (*Liberation Army Daily*, Military Work Propaganda Department). Beijing: Changzheng chubanshe 1996.

Jundui zhihui lilun jijin—quanjun shou jie jundui zhihui lilun yantao hui lunwenji. (Outstanding examples of armed forces command theory—a collection of the papers from the first whole army symposium on armed forces command theory). Edited by Guofang daxue jundui zhihui jiaoyanshi (National Defense University, Armed Forces Command Teaching and Research Section). Beijing: Guofang daxue chubanshe, 1992.

Li Defu. *Daoguo kun bing—Riben* (The poor island military—Japan). Beijing: Shishi chubanshe, 1997.

Li Hongzhi. *Guoji zhengzhi yu junshi wenti—ruogan shulianghua fenxi fangfa* (International political and military problems—a number of quantitative analysis methods). Beijing: Junshi kexue chubanshe, 1995.

Li Ligang, Jia Junming and Wang Jian. *Taikong zhan* (Space warfare). Harbin: Heilongjiang renmin chubanshe, 1995.

Li Peicai. *Taikong zhuizong—Zhongguo hangtian ce kong jishi* (Outer space tracking—China's space tracking telemetry and control activities). Beijing: Zhonggong zhongyang dangxiao chubanshe, 1995.

Li Qingshan and Wang Xuhe. *Jinglei wei zha—Yilake wuqi he cha weiji jishi* (The unexploded surprising thunder—a record of the Iraq nuclear weapons inspection crisis). Beijing: Junshi kexue chubanshe, 1998.

Li Yanming and others. *Chenlun juren—E'Luosi* (The sinking giant—Russia). Beijing: Shishi chubanshe, 1997.

Ling Xiang and Li Jie. *Dangdai hangkong mujian daguan* (The magnificent sight of modern aircraft carriers). Beijing: Shijie zhishi chubanshe, 1993.

Liu Guifang and Feng Yi. *Gao jishu tiaojian xia de C^3I—Jundui zhihui zidonghua* (The C^3I under high-technology conditions—armed forces command automation). Beijing: Guofang daxue chubanshe, 1994.

Liu Jian and Liu Yang. *Kexue jishu yu weilai jundui jianshe* (Science and technology and future armed forces construction). Beijing: Guofang daxue chubanshe, 1997.

Liu Jinjun and Chen Baijiang. *Lu-kong xietong zuozhan gailun* (An introduction to land and air coordinated battles). Beijing: Jiefangjun chubanshe, 1996.

Liu Jingsong, ed. *Jundui jiceng guanli jiaoyu gaiyao* (The essentials of armed forces basic level management education). Beijing: Junshi yiwen chubanshe, 1996.

Liu Puhua, ed. *Zhongguo changgui wuqi huicui* (A collection of Chinese conventional weapons). Beijing: Bingqi gongye chubanshe, 1991.

Liu Qing, ed. *Waiguo zhongyao junshi zhuzuo dao du* (Readings in important foreign military writings). Beijing: Junshi kexue chubanshe, 1992.

Liu Wannian and Xu Zhenbang. *Denglu zuozhan zong-heng tan* (A free discussion on landing operations). Beijing: Haijun haichao chubanshe, 1995.

Liu Xiaokun, Huang Mingkai, and Chen Huaide. *Dangdai shijie junshi redian toushi* (Perspectives on contemporary world military hot spots). Beijing: Junshi kexue chubanshe, 1996.

Liu Zhenwu, ed. *Xiandai jundui zhihui* (Modern armed forces commands). Beijing: Guofang daxue chubanshe, 1993.

Liu Zhiyong and Leng Ying. *Zhanshen zhizi: Shijie wangpai juntuan* (The war god's son: the world's elite army groups). Beijing: Shishi chubanshe, 1997.

Liu Zhongkai. *Feidie, cineng, yongdongji* (Flying saucers, magnetic energy and perpetual motion machines). Beijing: Bingqi gongye chubanshe, 1998.

Lu Hui. *He hua sheng wuqi de lishi yu weilai* (The history and future of nuclear, chemical, and biological weapons). Beijing: Junshi kexue chubanshe, 1991.

Lu Kemou, ed. *Zhongwai zhihui yishu bijiao* (A comparison of Chinese and foreign command skills). Beijing: Jiefangjun chubanshe, 1996.

Lu Yan, ed. *Hangkong huoli kongzhi jishu* (Aviation fire control technology). Beijing: Guofang gongye chubanshe, 1994.

Meng Zhaoying, Zhang Jian, Liu Wei, and Zhang Pengfei. *Kexue jishu yu weilai jundui zhihui* (Science and technology and future armed forces command). Beijing: Guofang daxue chubanshe, 1997.

Mi Zhenyu, *Zhongguo guofang fazhan gouxiang* (China's national defense development concepts). Beijing: Jiefangjun chubanshe, 1988.

Min Zengfu, Lin Jiaqian, Yao Wei, and Cao Kuofa. *Kongzhong liliang de fazhan he zuozhan fangfa de bian>ge* (The development of aerial strength and the transformation of combat methods). Beijing: Jiefangjun chubanshe, 1994.

Newhouse, John. *He shidai de zhanzheng yu heping* (War and Peace in the nuclear age) (in English). Translated by Junshi kexue yuan waiguo junshi yanjiu bu (Academy of Military Science, Foreign Military Research Department). Beijing: Junshi kexue chubanshe, 1989.

Pan Zhenqiang, ed. *Guoji caijun yu junbei kongzhi* (International disarmament and arms control). Beijing: Guofang daxue chubanshe, 1996.

Pan Zhenqiang and Xia Liping, eds. *Shijie junshi da qushi* (World military megatrends). Beijing: Guofang daxue chubanshe, 1994.

Pang Zhihao. *Taikong mo xing* (Magic stars in outerspace). Beijing: Hongqi chubanshe, 1995.

Pang Zhihao. *Tian yanshen xing—shijie junyong weixing jie mi* (Magic satellites and eyes in the sky—uncovering the secrets of the world's military satellites). Beijing: Yejin gongye chubanshe, 1996.

Peng Xunhou and Lin Ye. *Sulian junshi gaige yanlun ji* (A collection of speeches on Soviet mililtary reform). Beijing: Jiefangjun chuanshe, 1988.

Rijun yezhan canmou qinwu (Japanese army field operations staff officer duties)(in Japanese). Translated by Junshi kexue yuan waiguo junshi yanjiu bu (Academy of Military Science, Foreign Military Research Department). Beijing: Junshi kexue chubanshe, 1993.

Shang Jie. *Xiandai dimian zuozhan liliang de fazhan yu yunyong* (The development and utilization of modern ground combat strength). Beijing: Jiefangjun chubanshe, 1994.

Shen Weiguang. *Xin zhanzheng lun* (On new warfare). Beijing: Renmin chubanshe, 1997.

Sui Dongsheng. *Bingyi zhidu gailun* (An introduction to military service systems). Beijing: Junshi kexue chubanshe, 1996.

Sui Youjie, Nie Yun, Guo Xuexin, Sui Zhigang, Shen Weili and Liu Zhijun. *Lantian xiong ying: Shijie wangpai hangkongdui* (Powerful eagles in the blue sky: the world's elite air forces). Beijing: Shishi chubanshe, 1997.

Teng Jianqun, Wu Weiman, and Yu Peizhi. *Fengyan san jin kan haiwan—Shijie ge guo dui haiwan zhanzheng he lengzhan hou guoji anquan de kanfa* (Scattered beacons regard the Gulf—the views of various countries in the world on the Gulf War and international security after the Cold War). Beijing: Junshi kexue chubanshe, 1995.

Wang Huilin. *Xiandai zhanzheng de qimou he qishu—Quwei junshi* (Modern warfare's surprising stratagems and surprising tactics—interesting military affairs) Nanchang: Jiangxi jiaoyu chubanshe, 1996.

Wang Lianfa and Zhao Moyan. *Guangxue boli gongyi xue* (Optical glass technology). Beijing: Bingqi gongye chubanshe, 1995.

Wang Qianxiang. *Houqin fanglue* (A logistics general plan). Beijing: Junshi kexue chubanshe, 1995.

Wang Yamin, ed. *Tong xiang fuquo qiangbing zhi lu—jingji fada diqu minbing, yubeiyi* (Opening the road to a rich country and strong army—a collection of papers from the symposium on economically developed regions' peoples militias and reserve duty work theory). Beijing: Guofang daxue chubanshe, 1991.

Wang Yiju and Li Dajun, eds. *E'luosi junqing liaowang* (Observation of Russia's military situation). Beijing: Guofang daxue chubanshe, 1998.

Wang Ying and Ma Fuxue, ed. *Xin gainian wuqi yuanli* (Principles of new concept weaponry). Beijing: Bingqi gongye chubanshe, 1996.

Wang Ying, Zhi Yu, Zhi Tao, and Xiao Ping. *Xin gainian wuqi* (New concept weaponry). Beijing: Bingqi gongye chubanshe, 1998.

Wang Yongnian, Zhu Liangsheng, and Sun Longhe. *Toukui xianshi/ miaozhun xitong* (Helmet-mounted sight system). Beijing: Guofang gongye chubanshe, 1994.

Wang Zhiyi. *Wuzhuang liliang tizhi gailun* (An outline of armed forces systems). Beijing: Junshi kexue chubanshe, 1991.

Wei Guanghui, Yang Pei, and others. *Jiguang jishu zai bingqi gongye zhong de yingyong* (The use of laser technology in the arms industry). Beijing: Bingqi gongye chubanshe, 1995.

Weilai luzhan (Future Land Warfare). Translated by Zongcanmoubu wuqi zhuangbei zonghe lunzheng yanjiusuo (Headquarters of the General Staff, Weapons Testing Research Institute). Beijing: Bingqi gongye chubanshe, 1989.

Wu Hua, ed. *Bahai kuangbiao: Shijie wangpai jiandui* (The hurricane dominating the seas: the world's elite naval forces). Beijing: Shishi chubanshe, 1997.

Wu Hua, Shen Weili, and Zhen Hongtao. *Nanya zhi shi—Indu* (The lion of South Asia—India). Beijing: Shishi chubanshe, 1997.

Wusite, Halaerde, and Luyi Feidinande Xinbao. *Junshi zhihui xinxi xitong* (The military command information system)(originally in German). Translated by Junshi kexue yuan waiguo junshi yanjiu bu (Academy of Military Science, Foreign Military Research Department). Beijing: Junshi kexue chubanshe, 1989.

Xiao Tianliang. *Kexue jishu yu weilai junshi zhanlue* (Science and technology and future military strategy). Beijing: Guofang daxue chubanshe, 1997.

Yang Jingyu, Wu Yongge, Liu Leijian and Li Genshen. *Zhanchang shuju ronghe jishu* (Battlefield data fusion technology). Beijing: Bingqi gongye chubanshe, 1994.

Yu Chuanxin and Zhang Yupeng. *Kexue jishu yu weilai wuqi zhuangbei* (Science and technology and future weaponry). Beijing: Guofang daxue chubanshe, 1997.

Yu Guohua and Chen Shiguang. *Kexue jishu yu weilai jundui jiaoyu xunlian* (Science and technology and future armed forces education and training). Beijing: Guofang daxue chubanshe, 1997.

Yu Juliang, ed. *Riben junqing liaowang* (Observation of Japan's military situation). Beijing: Guofang daxue chubanshe, 1998.

Yuan Yuchun, Tian Xiaochuan and Fang Bing. *Hangkong mujian yu zhanzheng* (Aircraft carriers and warfare). Beijing: Guofang gongye chubanshe, 1997.

Zeng Guangjun, ed. *Guofang yuyan lu* (A record of national defense predictions). Beijing: Changzheng chubanshe, 1992.

Zhang Li. *Zhongguo wuguan* (Chinese military officers). Beijing: Jiefangjun chubanshe, 1992.

Zhang Shiping. *Jundui zhihui xitong gailun* (An outline of the armed forces command system). Beijing: Junshi kexue chubanshe, 1993.

Zhao Jie and Luo Xueshan. *Jundui zhihui zidonghua* (Armed forces command automation). Beijing: Junshi yiwen chubanshe, 1997.

Zhao Wenhua, Liu Youshui, and Meng Peipei. *Kexue jishu yu weilai zhanyi zhanshu* (Science and technology and future battle tactics). Beijing: Guofang daxue chubanshe, 1997.

Zhao Zhifa, Lu Daohai, and Ran Longke. *Xiandai zhanshu tongxin xitong gailun* (An introduction to modern tactical communication systems). Beijing: Guofang gongye chubanshe, 1998.

Zheng Hongtao and Li Xiujuan. *Xuezhan xianfeng: Shijie wangpai tezhong budui* (The vanguard of the bloody battle: the world's elite special troops). Beijing: Shishi chubanshe, 1997.

U.S. MILITARY

Chen Haihong. *Meiguo junshi liliang de jueqi* (The rise of American military strength). Huhehaote: Nei Menggu daxue chubanshe, 1995.

Chen Haihong. *Meiguo junshi shi gang* (An outline of U.S. military history). Beijing: Changzheng chubanshe, 1991.

Cui Shizeng and Wang Yongnan. *Meijun lianhe zuozhan* (U.S. military joint operations). Beijing: Guofang daxue chubanshe, 1995.

Hu Siyuan and Chen Hu. *Meijun hangtian zhan* (U.S. military space warfare). Beijing: Guofang daxue chubanshe, 1995.

Hu Siyuan and Dai Jinyu. *Xiandai Meiguo kongjun* (The modern U.S. Air Force). Beijing: Guofang daxue chubanshe, 1995.

Jiang Shaochong, ed. *Meijun zuozhan shouce* (The American military combat manual). 2 vols. Academy of Military Science, Foreign Military Affairs Research Department. Beijing: Junshi kexue chubanshe, 1993.

Li Zhiyun, ed. *Meijun lianhe zuozhan lilun yanjiu* (Studies on U.S. military joint operations theory). Beijing: Guofang daxue chubanshe, 1995.

Liu Bo, ed. *Huluobo jia dabang—Erzhan hou Meiguo chubing jishi* (Carrots and a big stick—a record the U.S. sending troops abroad in the post World War Two era). Beijing: Shishi chubanshe, 1997.

Meiguo guofangbu baogao—I luiwan zhanzheng (U.S. Department of Defense reports—the Gulf War)(originally in English). Translated by Junshi kexue yuan waiguo junshi yanjiu bu (Academy of Military Science, Foreign Military Research Department). Beijing: Junshi kexue chubanshe, 1991.

Pan Xiangting and Sun Zhanping, eds. *Gao jishu tiaojian xia Meijun jubu zhanzheng* (American military local warfare under high-technology conditions). Beijing: Jiefangjun chubanshe, 1994.

Wang Baofu. *Meiguo tezhong zuozhan budui yu tezhong zuozhan* (U.S. special combat units and special combat). Beijing: Guofang daxue chubanshe, 1995.

Wang Fang and others. *Shiji chao ba—Meilijian* (The century's ultra-tyrant—America). Beijing: Shishi chubanshe, 1997.

Wang Guoqiang. *Meiguo youxian zhanzheng lilun yu shijian* (U.S. limited warfare theory and practice). Beijing: Guofang daxue chubanshe, 1995.

Wang Xiaojian, ed. *Meiguo junqing liaowang* (Observation of the United States' military situation). Beijing: Guofang daxue chubanshe, 1998.

Wang Zhongchun and Xia Liping. *Meiguo he liliang yu he zhanlue* (American nuclear power and nuclear strategy). Beijing: Guofang daxue chubanshe, 1995.

Wang Zhongchun, Zhao Ziyu, and Zhou Bailin. *Xiandai Meiguo lujun* (The modern U.S. Army). Beijing: Guofang daxue chubanshe, 1995.

Wang Zhuo. *Xiandai Meijun houqin* (Modern U.S. logistics). Beijing: Guofang daxue chubanshe, 1995.

Yadeli, Hebaite O. *Zai mimi weimu beihou—Meiguo hei wu de tezhong xingdong* (Behind the secret heavy curtain—the special operations of America's black room)(originally in English). Translated by Cai Jianyong. Beijing: Jiefangjun chubanshe, 1989.

Yin Chengkui, Gao Guixiu, Li Ligang, and Su Yusheng. *Meijun gao jishu wuqi zhuangbei yingyong yu fazhan* (Use and development of U.S. high-technology weaponry). Beijing: Guofang daxue chubanshe, 1995.

Yin Gu, Li Jie, and Lei Xiangping. *Xiandai Meiguo haijun* (The modern U.S. Navy). Beijing: Guofang daxue chubanshe, 1995.

Zhen Xi. *Kelindun junshi zhanlue yu di er ci Chaoxian zhanzheng shexiang* (Clinton's military strategy and the tentative idea about a second Korean War). Beijing: Junshi kexue chubanshe, 1996.

Zhu Xiaoli and Zhao Xiaozhuo. *Mei-E xin junshi geming* (The new revolution in military affairs in the United States and Russia). Beijing: Junshi kexue chubanshe, 1996.

CHINESE ANCIENT MILITARY THOUGHT AND HISTORY

Central Television Station Military Department and the Navy Political Department Propaganda Department. *Sanshiliu ji gujin tan* (Ancient and modern discussions on the thirty-six stratagems). Jinan: Huanghe chubanshe, 1995.

Chai Yuqiu, ed. *Moulue jia* (Strategists). Beijing: Lan tian chubanshe, 1995.

Chai Yuqiu, ed. *Moulue ku* (A strategy storehouse). Vol. 2. Guangxi: Guangxi renmin chubanshe, 1995.

Chen Xuekai. *Zhisheng taolue—Sun Zi zhanzheng zhixing guanlun* (The military strategy of getting the upper hand—Sun Zi's views on knowledge and action in war). Jinan: Shandong renmin chubanshe, 1992.

Du Bo and Wen Jiacheng, eds. *Bu zhan er qu ren zhi bing—Zhongguo gudai xinlizhan sixiang ji qi yunyong* (Weapons that subdue people without fighting —ancient Chinese psychological warfare thought and usage). Beijing: Junshi kexue chubanshe, 1997.

Gao Liansheng. *Junshi shixue fangfa lun* (On military historiography methods). Beijing: Junshi kexue chubanshe, 1994.

Gao Rui. *Zhongguo shanggu junshi shi* (Chinese ancient military history). Beijing: Junshi kexue chubanshe, 1995.

Huang Zhixian, Geng Jianzhong, and Guo Shengwei. *Sun Zi jingcui xinbian* (A concise new edition of Sun Zi). Beijing: Junshi kexue chubanshe, 1993.

Huang Zhixian, Guo Shengwei, Geng Jianzhong, and Gao Kun. *Sun Zi bingfa yu shichang jingzheng* (Sun Zi's *The Art of War* and market competition). Beijing: Ba yi chubanshe, 1993.

Li Bingyan. *Sanshiliu ji xinbian* (The new edition of the thirty-six stratagems). Beijing: Jiefangjun chubanshe, 1995.

Li Zhishun. *Zhongguo lidai zhanzheng gailan* (An outline of warfare in past Chinese dynasties). Beijing: Junshi kexue chubanshe, 1994.

Liu Ruifang. *Zhongguo huangdi shi* (The history of Chinese emperors). Beijing: Guofang daxue chubanshe, 1993.

Liu Tinghua. *Xin sanshiliu ji* (The new thirty-six stratagems). Beijing: Zhongguo shehui chubanshe, 1997.

Liu Xiren, ed. *Quanmou shu—Shujia yu yingjia de jiaoliang* (Political trickery—a contest of losers and winners). Beijing: Lan tian chubanshe, 1995.

Lu Zhongjie. *Sun Zi bingfa yu sanshiliu ji* (Sun Zi's the art of war and the thirty-six stratagems). Jinan: Huang he chubanshe, 1996.

Ma Senliang. *Sanshiliu ji* (The thirty-six stratagems). Changsha: Hunan chubanshe, 1997.

Pu Yinghua and Huang Qibao. *Baihua sanshiliu ji* (Vernacular thirty-six stratagems). Beijing: Shishi chubanshe, 1994.

Ren Yuan. *Zhisheng bijian—Zhuge Liang de chengbai deshi* (Getting the upper hand must be examined—Zhuge Liang's successes and failures). Changan: Xibei daxue chubanshe, 1997.

Tao Hanzhang. *Sun Zi bingfa gailun* (An introduction to Sun Zi's *The Art of War*). Beijing: Jiefangjun chubanshe, 1985.

Wang Zihong. *Sanshiliu ji tan gu shi* (Using the 36 stratagems to explore the stock market). Beijing: Junshi kexue chubanshe, 1995.

Wu Rusong, ed. *Zhongguo gudai bingfa jingcui* (The essence of the ancient Chinese art of war). Beijing Junshi kexue chubanshe, 1988, 1996.

Wu Rusong, ed. *Zhongguo gudai bingfa jingcui lei bian* (The essence of the ancient Chinese art of war, concise edition). Beijing: Junshi kexue chubanshe, 1988.

Xie Guoliang and Yuan Dejin. *Zhongguo gudai junshi sixiang gailun* (An introduction to Chinese ancient military thought). Beijing: Jiefangjun chubanshe, 1994.

Yan Tingrui. *Weizhen Taihai: Kangxi tongyi Taiwan jishi* (Inspiring fame and fear in the Taiwan Strait: a record of Kangxi's integrating Taiwan). Beijing: Jiefangjun chubanshe, 1998.

Yang Shaojun, ed. *Sun Zi bingfa de diannao yanjiu* (Computer studies on Sun Zi's *The Art of War*). Beijing: Jiefangjun chubanshe, 1992.

Yun Xi and Yi Fei. *Gudai junshi geyan shang xi* (A selection of readings on ancient military mottos). Beijing: Junshi kexue chubanshe, 1995.

Zhang Dahe and Zhang Chen. *Ershiwu li junshi moulue gushi jingxuan* (A selection of 25 stories on historical military strategy). Beijing: Junshi kexue chubanshe, 1997.

Zhang Tieniu and Gao Xiaoxing. *Zhongguo gudai haijun shi* (Chinese ancient naval history). Beijing: Ba yi chubanshe, 1993.

Zhang Yu'an, Tang Mengsheng and Xue Keqiao, eds. *Shijie zhimou gushi jingcui* (The world's best stories of resourcefulness). Beijing: Lan tian chubanshe, 1995.

Zhao Feng. *Zhongguo junshi lunli sixiang shi* (The history of Chinese military ethics ideology). Beijing: Junshi kexue chubanshe, 1996.

Zou Yuanchu. *Zhongguo gudai jiangshuai yaolu* (The essential collection of China's commanders in chiefs). Beijing: Haichao chubanshe, 1996.

Zou Yuanchu. *Zhongguo jianchen yaolu* (The essential collection of China's treacherous court officials). Beijing: Haichao chubanshe, 1996.

Zou Yuanchu. *Zhongguo zaixiang yaolu* (The essential collection of prime ministers in feudal China). Beijing: Haichao chubanshe, 1995.

THE MILITARY THOUGHT OF MARX, MAO, AND DENG AND TWENTIETH-CENTURY CHINESE MILITARY HISTORY

Chen Hongyou, Wang Chengye, and Lu Yunbin, eds. *Makesi zhuyi junshi zhexue shi* (The history of Marxist military philosophy). Beijing: Junshi kexue chubanshe, 1993.

China Military Science Institute and Chinese People's Liberation Army Academy of Military Science. *Dang de sandai lingdao jiti yu jundui zhiliang jianshe—Zhongguo renmin jiefangjun jianjun 70 zhounian zhengwen* (The Party's third generation leadership collective and armed forces quality construction—articles on the 70th anniversary of the founding of the Chinese People's Liberation Army). Beijing: Junshi kexue chubanshe, 1997.

Fu Liqun, ed. *Zhidao Zhongguo geming zhanzheng de renshilun fangfa lun* (The epistemology and methodology guiding China's Revolutionary war). Beijing: Junshi kexue chubanshe, 1997.

Gu Hailiang. *Makesi zhuyi yuanli xinbian* (The new edition of the principles of Marxism). Beijing: Guofang daxue chubanshe, 1997.

Hong Xuezhi. *Kang-Mei yuan-Chao zhanzheng huiyi* (Recollections of the war to resist American aggression and aid Korea). Beijing: Jiefangjun wenyi chubanshe, 1991.

Jia Qiyu, ed. *Weida de junshijia Zhou Enlai* (Zhou Enlai, the great strategist). Beijing: Junshi kexue chubanshe, 1997.

Lei Yuangao, ed. *Zhongguo jindai fan qinlue zhangzheng shi* (The history of modern Chinese opposition to war of aggression). Beijing: Jiefangjun chubanshe, 1988.

Liu Xianting. *Mao Zedong junshi bianzhengfa lun gang* (An outline of Mao Zedong's military dialectics). Beijing: Jiefangjun chubanshe, 1993.

Peng Guangqian and Yao Youzhi. *Deng Xiaoping zhanlue sixiang lun* (On Deng Xiaoping's strategic thought). Beijing: Junshi kexue chubanshe, 1994.

Qi Dexue. *Kang-Mei yuan-Chao jishi* (The record of resisting America and aiding Korea). Beijing: Huaxia chubanshe, 1996.

Shen Zonghong and Meng Zhaohui, eds. *Zhongguo renmin zhiyuanjun Kang-Mei yuan-Chao zhan shi* (The history of the Chinese People's volunteers during the war to resist American aggression and aid Korea). Beijing: Junshi kexue chubanshe, 1990.

Wang Pufeng, ed. *Mao Zedong junshi zhanlue lun* (On Mao Zedong's military strategy). Beijing: Junshi kexue chubanshe, 1993.

Wu Jiezhang, Su Xiaodong, and Cheng Zhifa, eds. *Zhongguo jindai haijun shi* (Modern Chinese naval history). Beijing: Jiefangjun chubanshe, 1989.

Xia Zhengnan. *Mao Zedong junshi fangfalun* (Mao Zedong's military methodology). Beijing: Junshi kexue chubanshe, 1995.

Xu Gengming. *Zhongguo yuanzhengjun zhan shi* (The war history of China's expeditionary army). Beijing: Junshi kexue chubanshe, 1995.

Yao Yanjin and Liu Jixian, eds. *Deng Xiaoping xin shiqi junshi lilun yanjiu* (Deng Xiaoping's new period military theory studies). Beijing: Junshi kexue chubanshe, 1994.

Zhang Yongmei. *Meijun bai yu wo shou* (The U.S. military was defeated by my hand). Beijing: Jiefangjun chubanshe, 1995.

Zhang Zeshi. *Meijun jizhongying qinli ji* (A record of personal experiences in a U.S. military concentration camp). Beijing: Zhongguo wenshi chubanshe, 1995.

Zhang Zishen and Xue Chunde. *Zouxiang shen she de aige: Ri jun biming lu* (The elegy sung on the walk to the Yasukuni: the record of those killed by the Japanese Army). Beijing: Jiefangjun chubanshe, 1994.

CHINESE SECURITY POLICY AND DIPLOMACY

Chai Chengwen. *San da tupo: Xin Zhongguo zouxiang shijie de baogao* (Three big breakthroughs: reports from new China as it moves toward the world). Beijing: Jiefangjun chubanshe, 1994.

Ding Xinghao and Thomas Robinson, eds. *Zhong-Mei guanxi de xin sixiang he xin gainian* (New thinking and ideas about Sino-U.S. relations). Shanghai: Shanghai jiaoyu chubanshe, 1995.

Dong Mei, ed. *Zhong-Mei guanxi ziliao xuanbian (1971.7-1981.7)* (Selected materials on Sino-U.S. relations, July 1971-July 1981). Beijing: Shishi chubanshe, 1982.

Gu Qingguo. *Zhongguo bu jinjin shuo bu—wei shixian de hejie: Lengzhan chuqi de Zhong-Mei guanxi neimu* (China did not merely say no—unrealized reconciliation: the inside story of China-U.S. relations during the early days of the Cold War). Beijing: Zhonghua gongshang lianhe chubanshe, 1996.

He Xin. *Wei Zhongguo shengbian* (Arguing for China). Jingnan: Shandong youyi chubanshe, 1996.

He Xin. *Zhonghua fuxing yu shijie weilai* (China's rejuvination and the world's future). 2 vols. Chengdu: Sichuan renmin chubanshe, 1996.

Liu Liandi, ed. *Zhong-Mei guanxi zhongyao wenxian ziliao xuanbian* (A selection of important documents and materials on Sino-U.S. relations). Beijing: Shishi chubanshe, 1996.

Pan Shiying. *Nansha qundao. Shiyou zhengzhi. Guoji fa. "Wan an bei—21" Shiyou hetong qu weiyu Zhongguo guanxia haiyu wuyong zhiyi* (The petropolitics of the Nansha Islands—China's indisputable legal case). Hong Kong: Xianggang jingji dao baoshe chubanshe, 1996.

Pei Jianzhang, ed. *Mao Zedong waijiao sixiang yanjiu* (The study of Mao Zedong's foreign affairs thought). Beijing: Shijie zhishi chubanshe, 1994.

Peng Qian, Yang Mingjie and Xu Deren. *Zhongguo weishenme shuo bu?—Lengzhan hou Meiguo dui Hua zhengce de wuqu* (Why does China say no?—the mistakes in American foreign policy toward China after the Cold War). Beijing: Xin shijie chubanshe, 1996.

Song Qiang, Zhang Zangzang, and Qiao Bian. *Zhongguo keyi shuo bu—Lengzhan hou shidai de zhengzhi yu qinggan jueze* (China can say no—political and emotional choices in the post-Cold War era). Beijing: Zhonghua gongshang lianhe chubanshe, 1996.

Sun Keqin and Cui Hongjian, eds. *Ezhi Zhongguo—Shenhua yu xianshi* (Containing China—myth and reality). Beijing: Zhongguo yanshi chubanshe, 1996.

Tao Wenzhao, Yang Kuisong, and Wang Jianlang. *Kang-Ri zhanzheng shiqi Zhongguo duiwai guanxi* (Chinese foreign relations during the anti-Japanese war). Beijing: Zhonggong dang shi chubanshe, 1995.

Wang Junyan. *Zhong-Mei-Su sanguo yanyi* (China, the United States, and the Soviet Union, the romance of the three kingdoms). Beijing: Shishi chubanshe, 1996.

Wang Tingyue. *Jueqi de qianzou—Zhonggong kangzhan shiqi duiwai jiaowang jishi* (The prelude to the rise of China—A record of Chinese Communist Party foreign contacts during the war of resistance against Japan). Beijing: Shijie zhishi chubanshe, 1995.

Xie Qimei, specially invited ed. and Wang Xingfang, ed. *Zhongguo yu Lianheguo—Jinian Lianheguo chengli wushi zhou nian* (China and the United Nations—commemorating fifty years of the United Nations). Beijing: Shijie zhishi chubanshe, 1995.

Xue Juntu and Lu Zhongwei, eds. *Mianxiang ershiyi shiji de Zhongguo zhoubian xingshi* (Prospects for China and her neighbors in the 21st century). Beijing: Shishi chubanshe, 1995.

Yang Yong. *E'zhi yu fan e'zhi: Zhong-Mei-Su(E) da juezhu* (Containment and anti-containment: the big Sino-U.S.-Soviet (Russian) rivalry). Beijing: Shishi chubanshe, 1997.

Yang Zhengguang, ed. *Dangdai Zhong-Ri guanxi sishi nian (1949-1989)* (Forty years of contemporary Sino-Japanese relations, 1949-1989). Beijing: Shishi chubanshe, 1993.

Zhao Feng, ed. *Qiang tan ershiyi shiji: Zhongguo diyi* (Scrambling for the shoals of the 21st century: China is number one). Beijing: Shishi chubanshe, 1997.

FUTURE SECURITY ENVIRONMENT AND COUNTRY PROFILES

2000 nian de guoji jingji yu riben (The international economy and Japan in the year 2000). Edited by Riben jingi yanjiu zhongxin (Japanese Economics Research Center). Beijing: Shishi chubanshe, 1992.

Cao Xilong. *Weilai shijie geju—Xifang de yuce* (The future world structure—Western forecasts). Beijing: Shijie zhishi chubanshe, 1992.

Chen Bin, Wang Ke, Yu Kejie, and Lu Lei. *Meilijian chaoji zhi mi* (The riddle of super America). Beijing: Jiefangjun wenyi chubanshe, 1994.

Chen Binjin, Feng Xiaoqi and Er Dong. *Jingji konglong—Zouxiang 21 shiji de kuaguo gongsi* (Economic dinosaurs—transnational companies as they head toward the 21st century). Beijing: Shishi chubanshe, 1985.

Chen Chaogao. *Xifang kuaguo gongci jingying zhanlue* (The management strategies of Western transnational companies). Beijing: Shishi chubanshe, 1996.

Chen Peiyao, ed. *1995 Guoji xingshi nianjian* (1995 survey of international affairs). Shanghai: Shanghai jiaoyu chubanshe, 1995.

Chen Qimao, ed. *Kua shiji de shijie geju da zhuanhuan* (Major changes in the world structure at the turn of the century). Shanghai: Shanghai jiaoyu chubanshe, 1996.

Chen Zhongjing. *Guoji zhanlue wenti* (Problems of international strategy). Beijing: Shishi chubanshe, 1988.

Chu Shulong, ed. *Kua shiji de Meiguo* (The United States in this century and the next). Beijing: Shishi chubanshe, 1997.

Curridge, Nicholas. *Zhi laohu* (Paper tiger). Translated by Wang Zhong. Guangzhou: Guangdong jiaoyu chubanshe, 1997.

Du Gong, ed. *Zhuanhuan zhong de shijie geju* (The world structure in transformation). Beijing: Shijie zhishi chubanshe, 1992.

Guoji zhengzhi xin zhixu wenti (Problems in the new international political regime). Edited by Zhongguo xiandai guoji guanxi yanjiusuo (China Institute of Contemporary International Relations). Beijing: Shishi chubanshe, 1992.

Hou Ruoshi. *Zhanlue xuanze yu ziyuan peizhi* (Strategy choices and the allocation of natural resources). Beijing: Shishi chubanshe, 1990.

Huang Shuofeng. *Guojia shengshuai lun* (On the rise and fall of nations). Changsha: Hunan chubanshe, 1996.

Huang Shuofeng. *Zonghe guoli lun* (On comprehensive national power). Beijing: Zhongguo shehui kexue chubanshe, 1992.

Li Cong. *Di san shijie lun* (The third world). Beijing: Shijie zhishi chubanshe, 1993.

Li Yanming, Yuan Zhanguo, Xu Zisong, Cheng Kuaile and Liu Fang. *Diehai shenfeng: Shijie wangpai diebao jigou* (The world's elite espionage organizations). Beijing: Shishi chubanshe, 1997.

Li Zhengtang. *Weishenme Riben bu renzhang—Riben guo zhanzheng peichang beiluwang* (Why doesn't Japan admit what it has done?—Japan's national war compensation memorandum). Beijing: Shishi chubanshe, 1997.

Li Zhongcheng, ed. *Kua shiji de shijie zhengzhi* (Trans century world politics). Beijing: Shishi chubanshe, 1997.

Liang Shoude and Hong Yinxian. *Guoji zhengzhixue gailun* (General theory of international politics). Beijing: Zhongyang bianshi chubanshe, 1994.

Lin Huisheng. *Gei shanmu dashu suan yi gua* (Telling uncle sam's fortune). Beijing: Shishi chubanshe, 1995.

Liu Jiangyong, ed. *Kua shiji de riben—Zhengzhi, jingji, waijiao xin qushi* (Japan across the century—new political, economic, and foreign relations trends). Beijing: Shishi chubanshe, 1995.

Liu Ling and Hong Yuyi, eds. *Guoji guanxi shi jianbian—Ban ge shiji shijie fengyun* (The concise history of international relations—half a century of unstable world conditions). Beijing: Shijie zhishi chubanshe, 1986.

Liu Tihe, ed. *Dong Ou shichang jingji zouxiang* (Eastern Europe market economy trends). Beijing: Shishi chubanshe, 1993.

Lu Lei, Wu Youchang, and Hu Ruoqing. *Riben fu guo zhi mi* (The riddle of Japan, the wealthy country). Beijing: Jiefangjun wenyi chubanshe, 1994.

Lu Zhongwei. *Xin-jiu jiaoti de dongya geju* (The new structure replaces the old in East Asia). Beijing: Shishi chubanshe, 1993.

Lunwen zhaiyao xuanbian, ying yi ben (Selected excerpts from research papers, English version). Beijing: Guoji jishu jingji yanjiusuo, 1993.

Luo Rongsheng. *Quanqiu da zhendang: zhanwang 21 shiji jinji xuanyan* (Major global vibrations: forecasts of 21st century economic declarations). Beijing: Shishi chubanshe, 1997.

Mei-Ou-Ri yu disan shijie (The United States, Europe, Japan and the Third World). Edited by Xiandai guoji guanxi yanjiusuo (China Institute for Contemporary International Relations). Beijing: Shishi chubanshe, 1991.

Mei Ren, ed. *Meiguo liren zongtong* (The U.S. presidents). Beijing: Shishi chubanshe, 1997.

Mo Huilin, Yi Jinwu, Xu Xianqi, and Xu Zuolin. *Dangdai zibenzhuyi —pouxi yu jiejian* (Contemporary capitalism—analysis and lessons). N.p.: Junshi kexue chubanshe, 1993.

Pan Shiying. *Xiandai zhanlue sikao—lengzhan hou de zhanlue lilun* (Thoughts on modern strategy—post-Cold War strategic theory). Beijing: Shijie zhishi chubanshe, 1993.

Peng Qian, ed. *Mengxing ba, Riben! —Riben zhengzhi zouxiang jingshilu* (Wake up to the truth Japan!—Japan's political trends alarm). Beijing: Xin shijie chubanshe, 1996.

Shen Zhixun and Ding Kuisong. *Yi ge quanli shidai de jieshu—Qiaozhi Bushi zhuan* (The end of an era of power—a biography of George Bush). Beijing: Shishi chubanshe, 1994.

Song Zhangjun. *Riben guo xianfa yanjiu* (Studies on Japan's constitution). Beijing: Shishi chubanshe, 1997.

Su Jingxiang. *Meiguo jingji zhong de waiguo touzi* (Foreign investment in America's economy). Beijing: Shishi chubanshe, 1995.

Tang Hui and Liang Ming. *Dahe "chaoba" meng* (The great dream of "supremacy"). Beijing: Shishi chubanshe, 1995.

Tong Fuquan and Liu Yichang. *Shijie quan fangwei jingji zhan* (The world's all directional economic war). Beijing: Junshi kexue chubanshe, 1991.

Wan Guang. *Meiguo de shehui bing* (U.S. social diseases). Chengdu: Sichuan renmin chubanshe, 1997.

Wang Jisi, ed. *Wenming yu guoji zhengzhi—Zhongguo xuezhe pi xiang tingdun de wenming chongtu lun* (Civilization and international politics—Chinese scholars critique Samuel Huntington's civilization conflict theory). Shanghai: Shanghai renmin chubanshe, 1995.

Wang Jinbiao, ed. *Kua shiji de Ouzhou* (Europe in this century and the next). Beijing: Shishi chubanshe, 1997.

Wang Songfen, ed. *Shijie zhuyao guojia zonghe guoli bijiao yanjiu* (Comparative studies of the comprehensive national power of the world's major nations). Changsha: Hunan chubanshe, 1996.

Wang Yizhou. *Dangdai guoji zhengzhi xi lun* (Contemporary international politics analysis). Shanghai: Shanghai renmin chubanshe, 1995.

Wang Zaibang. *Baquan wending lun pipan—Buleidun senlin tixi de lishi kaocha* (A critique of the hegemonic stability theory—a study of the history of the Breton Woods system). Beijing: Shishi chubanshe, 1994.

Wu Guifu, ed. *Meiguo quanqiu zhanlue tiaozheng* (U.S. global strategy adustments). Beijing: Guofang daxue chubanshe, 1996.

Xi Runchang and Gao Heng, eds. *Shijie zhengzhi xin geju yu guoji anquan* (The new world political regime and international security). Beijing: Junshi kexue chubanshe, 1996.

Xiaochuanhejiu, Shiyuanzhenshentailang, and Dubushengyi. *Riben hai yao shuo "bu"—Ri-Mei jian de genben wenti* (Japan still should say "no"—the basic problem between Japan and the United States)(in Japanese). Translated by Junshi kexue yuan waiguo junshi yanjiu bu (Academy of Military Science, Foreign Military Research Department). Beijing: Junshi kexue chubanshe, 1992.

Yan Jin, Bai Xue and Zhang Xingping. *Shuangtouying fei xiang hechu—guoji wutai shang de E'Luosi* (Where is the double headed eagle flying—Russia on the international stage). Beijing: Shishi chubanshe, 1995.

Yang Baihua and Ming Xuan. *Zibenzhuyi guojia zhengzhi zhidu* (The political systems of capitalist countries). Beijing: Shijie zhishi chubanshe, 1984.

Yang Xuexiang. *Indu wenhua shenmi zhi mi* (The riddle of India's cultural mystery). Beijing: Jiefangjun wenyi chubanshe, 1994.

Yang Zheng. *2000: Shijie xiang hechu qu ?* (2000: Where is the world going?). Beijing: Zhongguo guangbo dianshi chubanshe, 1996.

Yang Zugong, and Gu Junli. *Xifang zhengzhi zhidu bijiao* (A comparison of Western political systems). Beijing: Shijie zhishi chubanshe, 1992.

Zhang Jiliang, ed. *Guoji guanxi xue gailun* (An introduction to international relations). Beijing: Shijie zhishi chubanshe, 1989.

Zhang Tuosheng, ed. *Huanqiu tong ci liang re—Yi dai lingxiumen de guoji zhanlue sixiang* (Simultaneous global temperature shifts—one generation of leaders' international strategic thought). Beijing: Zhongyang wenxian chubanshe, 1993.

Zhong-Ao Yatai diqu anquan guoji yantao hui xueshu lunwen ji. (A collection of the papers from the Sino-Australian workshop on Asia-Pacific security). Beijing: Zhongguo guoji youhao lianluo hui heping yu fazhan yanjiu zhongxin/Aodaliya gelifeisi daxue ao-ya guanxi yanjiu zhongxin, 1996.

Zhou Rongkun, ed. *Kua shiji de shijie jingji* (Trans-century world economics). Beijing: Shishi chubanshe, 1998.

Zi Shui and Xiao Shi. *Jingti Riben junguozhuyi* (Be on guard against Japanese militarism). Beijing: Jincheng chubanshe, 1996.

Zi Zhongjun, ed. *Zhanhou meiguo waijiao shi—Cong Tulumen dao Ligen* (The history of postwar American foreign relations—from Truman to Reagan). Beijing: Shijie zhishi chubanshe, 1994.

CHINA'S CURRENT SITUATION AND FUTURE

Feng Lin, ed. *21 Shiji Zhongguo da yuce* (Major forecasts for 21st century China). Beijing: Gaige chubanshe, 1996.

He Xin. *Weiji yu Fansi* (Crisis and introspective thinking). Beijing: Guoji wenhua chubanshe, 1997.

Hu Angang, Wang Shaoguang and Kang Xiaoguang. *Zhongguo diqu chaju baogao* (Regional disparities in China). Shenyang: Liaoning renmin chubanshe, 1995.

Huan Xiang. *Huan Xiang wenji* (The collected works of Huan Xiang). Beijing: Shijie zhishi chubanshe, 1994.

Li Kefei and Peng Dongmei. *Mimi zhuanji shang de lingxiumen* (The leadership on the secret private plane). Beijing: Zhonggong zhongyang dang xiao chubanshe, 1997.

Ling Xingzheng. *Shensheng de shanhu jiao—Nansha jishi* (The sacred coral reef—report from Nansha). Beijing: Haichao chubanshe, 1994.

Liu Guoguang, ed. *Hainan jingji fazhan zhanlue* (Hainan's economic development strategy). Beijing: Jingji guanli chubanshe, 1988.

Ma Hong and Sun Shangqing, eds. *Jingji baipishu: Zhongguo jingji xingshi yu zhanwang: 1995-1996* (Economic white paper: China's economic situation and prospects: 1995-1996). Beijing: Zhongguo fazhan chubanshe, 1996.

Shi Bike. *Zhongguo da qushi* (China megatrends). Beijing: Hualing chubanshe, 1996.

Wang Jiacheng. *Zhongguo nengyuan: chengji, wenti, zhengce he zhanwang* (China's energy resources: achievements, problems, policy and prospects). Beijing: Jingji guanli chubanshe, 1994.

Wang Jinglun. *Mao Zedong de lixiangzhuyi he Deng Xiaoping de xianshizhui—Meiguo xuezhe lun Zhongguo* (Mao Zedong's idealism and Deng Xiaoping's realism—the views of U.S. scholars on China). Beijing: Shishi chubanshe, 1996.

Weng Jieming, Zhang Ximing, Zhang Tao and Qu Kemin, eds. *1996-1997 Nian Zhongguo shehui fazhan zhuangkuang yu qushi* (China's social development situation and trends, 1996-1997). Beijing: Zhongguo shehui chubanshe, 1996.

Weng Jieming, Zhang Ximing, Zhang Tao and Qu Kemin, eds. *Zhongguo 1997-97 qianhou de zhengzhi jingji fenxi yu yuce* (China 1997-97 political and economic analysis and forecasts). Beijing: Shehui kexue wenxian chubanshe, 1997.

Wu Jie. *Deng Xiaoping sixiang lun (yingwen)* (On Deng Xiaoping thought). Beijing: Waiwen chubanshe, 1996.

Xin Xiangyang. *Hongqiang juece—Zhongguo zhengfu jigou gaige shenceng qiyin* (Red wall policy decisions—the deep origins of the reform of the Chinese government organizational structure). Beijing: Zhongguo jingji chubanshe, 1998.

Xu Shijie, ed. *Hainan sheng—ziran, lishi, xianzhuang yu weilai* (Hainan province—nature, history, current conditions, and future). Beijing: Shangwu yinshuguan, 1988.

Yan Changdong, ed. *Zhongguo nengyuan fazhan baoguo (1997 nianban)* (China's energy development report, 1997). Beijing: Jingji guanli chubanshe, 1997.

Yan Xuetong. *Zhongguo guojia liyi fenxi* (An analysis of China's national interests). Tianjin: Tianjin renmin chubanshe, 1996.

Zhao Yi and Zhao Keyi, eds. *Zhongguo shangye yinhang yewu yu caozuo* (The business and operation of the China Commercial Bank). Beijing: Zhongguo shijie yu chubanshe, 1994.

TAIWAN

Mei Zi, ed. *Mei-Tai guanxi zhongyao ziliao xuanbian* (A selection of important materials on U.S.-Taiwan relations). Beijing: Shishi chubanshe, 1996.

Tai Baolin. *Taiwan shehui qiwen daguan* (The unheard of magnificent spectacle of Taiwan society). Beijing: Hongqi chubanshe, 1992.

Taiwan yanjiu wenji (Collected works on Taiwan research). Edited by Zhongguo shehui kexueyuan Taiwan yanjiusuo (Chinese Academy of Social Sciences, Taiwan Institute). Beijing: Shishi chubanshe, 1988.

Wei Xiutang. *Huashuo Taiwanren* (Talking about the Taiwanese). Beijing: Shishi chubanshe, 1997.

THE FUTURE

Cohen, I. Bernard. *Kexue geming shi* (Revolution in science). Translated by Yang Aihua, Li Chengzhi, Li Changsheng, and Chen Dan. Beijing: Junshi kexue chubanshe, 1992.

Li Qinggong. *Gei diqiu jishang anquandai* (Fasten the earth's seatbelt). Beijing: Shishi chubanshe, 1995.

Qiao Liang. *Mo ri zhi men—Danyuan zhe qizhong miaoshu de yiqie jie nan dou bu yao fasheng* (Door to doomsday—I hope the disasters described will not take place). Beijing: Kunlun chubanshe, 1995.

Zhong Shukong. *21 Shiji de tiaozhan yu jiou—Quanqiu huanjing yu fazhan* (Challenges and opportunities in the 21st century—the global environment and development). Beijing: Shijie zhishi chubanshe, 1992.

APPENDIX 1:
The Definition of Strategic Assessment

STRATEGIC ASSESSMENT IN
COMPARATIVE PERSPECTIVE

There is intense secrecy about Chinese national security matters, but comparisons with other nations' processes of strategic assessment can increase our understanding of how China may assess its future security environment.[1] How have major nations conducted strategic assessments of the security environment? Studies of this question by more than 30 authors have been sponsored by the Director of Net Assessment, U.S. Department of Defense, to uncover lessons that may be of value to the production of American strategic assessments. One lesson is that there are different national styles of making strategic assessments. By viewing China in comparative perspective, it may be possible to understand better how China deals with its assessment problems.

DEFINITION OF STRATEGIC ASSESSMENT

What is strategic assessment?[2] It is sometimes confused with intelligence analysis of foreign forces and international trends. The major difference is that strategic assessment is an analysis of the *interaction* of two or more national security establishments both in peacetime and in war, usually ourselves and a potential enemy. It is the interaction of the two belligerents that is the central concept, not an assessment of one side alone. In historical analysis, it is possible prior to the outbreak of past wars to observe what the highest level of leadership on each side did to "assess" the outcome and nature of the war

---

[1] Readers may be surprised about how secretive China remains in the national security area in spite of openness in all other areas. After all, China is one of the most open nations in the world in many respects. In 1966 it had over $100 billion of foreign direct investment, the largest in the world after the United States, and was the second most popular destination for foreign tourism, after France.

[2] Two colonels at the Academy of Military Science define "strategic assessment" as used by Sun Zi in the *Art of War*. Their new translation into English faults the well-known translation in 1963 by Brigadier General Samuel Griffiths for "serious errors," including using the word "estimates" instead of "strategic assessment." See Pan Jiabin and Liu Ruixiang, *Art of War: A Chinese-English Bilingual Reader* (Beijing: Junshi kexue chubanshe,1993), 123-124.

that was coming. In fact, a widely praised explanation for the causes of war is precisely that strategic assessments were in conflict prior to the initiation of combat—one side seldom starts a war knowing in advance it will lose. Thus, we may presume there are almost always miscalculations in strategic assessments of varying types according to the nature of the national leadership that made the assessment.

In retrospect, it is often easy to discern the sources of errors in strategic assessment. For example, it is a mistake to examine static, side-by-side, force-on-force comparisons of numbers of weapons and military units without analyzing the way these weapons and units would actually interact in future combat. It is another mistake to fail to define correctly who will be a friend and who a foe in wartime, so the question of international alignments or alliances cannot be ignored. Another error is to deduce incorrectly from an opponent's peacetime training exercises, published military doctrines, and peacetime military deployments what may be the way forces actually conduct themselves in combat, especially in a war of many months or years that goes beyond the original plan of war that was drafted at the outset: the longer a war, the more time for factors involving the entire national society and economy to be brought into play and the less important the initial deployments, doctrines, and plans become. Another mistake is to use analytic routines or rigid measures of effectiveness designed for day-to-day management of efficiency in meeting budgetary or other standards to judge future military effectiveness during a war, which may bear little relationship to peacetime management problems.

Professor Stephen Peter Rosen of Harvard University has presented a set of examples of these errors. For example, between August 1939 and June 1940, the U.S. Navy senior leadership strategic assessments of the adequacy of the military capabilities of the United States paid little attention to how a future war might unfold. It mainly satisfied U.S. Navy peacetime criteria using "simple comparisons of the number of U.S. Navy and Imperial Japanese Navy ships . . . no sense of the possible wartime interaction between the two fleets let alone between the two nations."[3] The static use of counting numbers and

---

[3]Stephen Peter Rosen, "Net Assessment as an Analytical Concept," in *On Not Confusing Ourselves*, eds. Andrew W. Marshall, J. J. Martin, and Henry S. Rowen (Boulder, CO: Westview Press, 1991), 288.

units was at fault in the French military assessment of a potential German attack in 1939. The military balance measured in quantitative terms between the German forces opposite France and the French forces involved in that theater was almost equal, even slightly favoring France. The armored fire power of France and its allies exceeded that of the Germans by one-third, although German air power was nearly double that of France. Quantitative modeling could not have suggested that the Germans could achieve a four-to-one advantage in the sector in which they achieved a breakthrough; that the Germans could make rapid, deep penetrations to destroy rear areas in France; that the French concept of operations after World War I had been for slow infantry movements behind preplanned, centrally directed artillery barrages dependent on fixed headquarters with fixed telephone lines; and that the German Air Force would completely neutralize French air power and achieve absolute air superiority. Only a strategic assessment focusing on these qualities of the interaction of the two belligerents would give any indication of the outcome of the war.[4]

In the broadest definition, "strategic assessment" implies a forecast of peacetime and wartime competition between two nations or two alliances that includes the identification of enemy vulnerabilities and weaknesses in comparison to the strengths and advantages of one's own side. According to Professor Rosen, "The military theoretician Carl von Clausewitz probably deserves credit for being the first to try to delineate the general character of net assessment at the level of national military interaction."[5] One section of Clausewitz' book *On War* asks a simple question: How can the national leadership know how much force will be necessary to bring to bear against a potential enemy? Clausewitz replies,

> We must gauge the character of . . . (the enemy) government and people and do the same in regard to our own. Finally, we must evaluate the

---

[4]Rosen, 296-297; *Assessing the Correlation of Forces: France 1940* (Washington: BDM Report for the Office of Net Assessment, June 18, 1979).

[5]Rosen, 286.

political sympathies of other states and the effect the war may have on them.[6]

Clausewitz warns that studying enemy weaknesses without considering one's own capacity to take advantage of those weaknesses is a mistake. Clausewitz emphasizes the importance of identifying the enemy's "center of gravity," a feature that if successfully attacked, can stop the enemy's war effort. Assessment requires considering the potential interaction of the two sides. According to Clausewitz, "One must keep the dominant characteristics *of both belligerents* in mind."[7]

DEPARTMENT OF DEFENSE NET ASSESSMENTS

The practice of strategic assessment by the U.S. Department of Defense in the past 25 years has been divided into six categories of studies and analysis. The first involves efforts to measure and forecast trends in various military balances, such as the maritime balance, the Northeast Asian balance, the power-projection balance, the strategic nuclear balance, the Sino-Soviet military balance, and the European military balance between NATO and the former Warsaw Pact. Some of these studies look 20 or 30 years into the future to examine trends and discontinuities in technology, economic indicators, and other factors.

A second type of assessment focuses on weapons and force comparisons, with efforts to produce judgments about military effectiveness that sometimes "revealed U.S. and Soviet differences in measuring combat effectiveness and often showed the contrast between what each side considered important in combat."[8]

The third set of studies examines lessons of the past using historical evaluations as well as gathering data on past performance of weapons used in the context of specific conflicts. A fourth set analyzes the role of perceptions

---

[6]Carl von Clausewitz, *On War*, eds. and trans. Michael Howard and Peter Paret (Princeton: Princeton University Press, 1976), 586.

[7]Ibid., 595.

[8]George F. Pickett, James G. Roche, and Barry D. Watts, "Net Assessment: A Historical Review," in *On Not Confusing Ourselves*, 169-171.

of foreign decision makers and even the process by which foreign institutions make strategic assessments. As Andrew Marshall, Director, Net Assessment, wrote in 1982 about assessing the former Soviet Union,

> A major component of any assessment of the adequacy of the strategic balance should be our best approximation of a Soviet-style assessment of the strategic balance. But this must not be the standard U.S. calculations done with slightly different assumptions . . . . rather it should be, to the extent possible, an assessment structured as the Soviet would structure it, using those scenarios they see as most likely and their criteria and ways of measuring outcomes . . . the Soviet calculations are likely to make different assumptions about scenarios and objectives, focus attention upon different variables, include both long-range and theater forces (conventional as well as nuclear), and may at the technical assessment level, perform different calculations, use different measures of effectiveness, and perhaps use different assessment processes and methods. The result is that Soviet assessments may substantially differ from American assessments.[9]

Studies analyzing perceptions are difficult because the data used often must be inferred from public writings and speeches. Implicit biases of Americans based on our own education and culture must also be avoided.

A fifth effort of American net assessment sponsors studies that search for new analytical tools, such as developing higher "firepower scores" than may be used for the Air Force and Navy as well as the initial inventor, the ground forces. In the early 1980s, a multiyear effort was funded at The RAND Corporation to develop a Strategy Assessment System (RSAS) as a flexible analytic device for examining combat outcomes of alternative scenarios.

A sixth category of studies is professional analyses of particular issues of concern to the Secretary of Defense that may involve identifying competitive advantages and distinctive competencies of each size military force posture; highlighting important trends that may change a long-term balance; identifying future opportunities and risks in the military competition; and appraising the strengths and weaknesses of U.S. forces in light of long-term shifts in the security environment. Past practitioners from the Office of the Secretary of

---

[9]Andrew W. Marshall, "A Program to Improve Analytic Methods Related to Strategic Forces," *Policy Sciences* (November 1982): 48.

Defense have underscored the need for American strategic assessment to focus on long-term historical patterns rather than on short-term trends and to appraise strengths and vulnerabilities of both the United States and its potential opponents as they would interact in future conflicts as well as during peacetime competition.

ASSESSMENTS BEFORE WORLD WAR II

An insightful set of seven historical examples of strategic assessment from 1938 to1940, produced for the Office of Net Assessment, allows for the comparison of the styles of strategic assessment practiced in Britain, Nazi Germany, Italy, France, the Soviet Union, the United States, and Japan. A number of "lessons learned" are relevant to any effort to understand how the Chinese leadership conducts strategic assessment of its future security environment. Marshall specified four categories of strategic assessment:

- Foreseeing potential conflicts
- Comparing strengths and predicting outcomes in given contingencies
- Monitoring current developments and being alerted to developing problems
- Warning of imminent military danger.[10]

Sun Tzu proclaimed full confidence in the "calculations" he made in "the temple" before hostilities. "Modern net assessment follows Sun Tzu's principles, if not his confidence in outcomes. The important allusion is to 'the temple' and the role of faith."[11]

The main problem was how to frame assessments, particularly with regard to political-military factors such as who were the potential threats and potential allies, and what international alignments would be vital to the outcomes of future wars. Purely military issues were how to weight different types of combat power, especially new concepts of operations like tactical air power in the Blitzkrieg or the role of submarines. Errors and successes came

---

[10]Ernest R. May, ed., *Knowing One's Enemies* (Princeton: Princeton University Press, 1986), 5.

[11]Williamson Murray and Allan R. Millett, *Calculations: Net Assessment and the Coming of World War II* (New York: Free Press, 1992), 2.

from answers to large framework questions of what to include, what to ignore, and how to "think about" the military balances that form the security environment.

Both assessing wartime international alignments and finding new measures of effectiveness to assess new types of military power were fraught with errors in pre-World War II strategic assessments. Professor Paul Kennedy of Harvard points out that Britain failed to assess the role the Soviet Union could play as a second front for Hitler. The French made both types of error: they neglected the scenario that Germany might first conquer France's East European allies and underestimated the role of air power in the Blitzkrieg, despite detailed reports from French intelligence. The Soviets correctly assessed the potential for Japan to remain neutral and correctly saw that Hitler would invade along a southern approach toward the Baku oil fields, by Stalin's use of alternative scenarios in annual war games.

U.S. errors were "big picture" problems. Although the United States eventually in 1940 developed five alternative scenarios (RAINBOW 1 to 5), from 1920 to about 1935, it initially mistakenly believed it had only one potential enemy (Japan) and therefore planned for only one major military scenario—Plan ORANGE—for war in the Pacific to liberate the Philippines from a Japanese attack. The Naval War College played this scenario in annual and other war games an estimated 120 times. Then, with the rise of Hitler, 15 years of American assessments had to be discarded when the strategic focus shifted to winning first in Europe, while staying on the defensive in the Pacific.

The most relevant comparison for China may be the Soviet Union, but this is also the most secret. As Professor Earl Ziemke put it, after three decades of research on Soviet military affairs, even when he tried to use historical data to look back from 1990 to 1940:

> The Soviet net assessment process cannot be directly observed. Like a dark object in outer space, its probable nature can be discerned only from interactions with visible surroundings. Fortunately, its rigidly secret environment has been somewhat subject to countervailing conditions. . . . Tukhachevsky and his associates conducted relatively open discussion in print.

Comparing the Soviet structure with Chinese materials in the 1990s, it is apparent from the way in which Soviet strategic assessment was performed in the 1930s that a number of similarities, at least in institutional roles and the vocabulary of Marxism-Leninism, can also be seen in contemporary China. The leader of the Communist Party publicly presented a global strategic assessment to periodic Communist Party Congresses. The authors of the military portions of the assessment came from two institutions that have counterparts in Beijing today and were prominent in Moscow in the 1930s: the General Staff Academy and the National War College. Another similarity was that the Communist Party leader chaired a defense council or main military committee and in these capacities attended peacetime military exercises and was involved deciding the details of military strategy, weapons acquisition, and war planning.

APPENDIX 2:
Assessment Institutions

For more than 20 years, American scholars from major universities and privately endowed research organizations like the Brookings Institution, Heritage Foundation, American Enterprise Institute, and Council on Foreign Relations have all been received by their apparent "counterparts" in Beijing for discussions on foreign policy and defense issues. However, the Chinese institutions are quite different. Although their staff produce journals and books, and participate in international conferences, much as their U.S. "counterparts," do, they have additional roles.

Cited Authors at the Seven Main Institutes

CIIS	CIISS	NDU	SIIS
Jiang Yuechun	Chen Feng	Bao Zhongxing	Chen Peiyao
Shi Ze	Chen Xiaogong	Li Zhiyun	Chen Qimao
Ye Zhengjia	Huang Zhengji	Liu Chunzi	Ding Xinghao
Song Yimin	Hu Ping	Pan Zhengqiang	Wang Houkang
	Li Qinggong	Wang Zhongchun	Xia Liping
	Liu Mingde	Wen Zhonghua	Zhang Jialin
	Lu Dehong	Xu Weidi	
	Sa Benwang	Yang Xuhua	
	Shen Guoliang	Yu Guohua	
	Wang Naicheng	Zhang Zhaozhong	
	Wang Zhenxi	Zhu Chenghu	
	Xie Wenqing		
	Xiong Guangkai		
	Zhang Changtai		
	Zhang Taishan		
	Zhu Chun		

Cited Authors at the Seven Main Institutes (continued)

AMS	CASS	CICIR
Chen Zhou	Chen Shao	Bing Jinfu
Fang Ning	Feng Zhaokui	Cao Xia
Gao Chunxiang	Gao Heng	Chen Zhongjing
Gao Rui	He Fang	Chu Shulong
Han Shengmin	Jiang Yili	Dao Shulin
Huang Shuofeng	Liao Yonghe	Feng Yujun
Huang Yingxu	Liu Jinghua	Gan Ailan
Li Jijun	Luo Zhaohong	Gu Guanfu
Li Qingshan	Shen Jiru	Guo Chuanlin
Liu Gang	Wang Jisi	Hong Jianjun
Liu Jingsong	Wang Jincun	Jin Dexiang
Liu Tinghua	Wang Songfeng	Li Yiyan
Luo Yuan	Wu Guoqing	Li Zhongcheng
Meng Renzhong	Xi Runchang	Liu Guiling
Mi Zhenyu	Xiao Lian	Liu Jiangyong
Pan Jiabin	Yang Dazhou	Lu Zhongwei
Pan Junfeng	Yang Shuheng	Ouyang Liping
Peng Guangqian	Zhao Jieqi	Qi Dequang
Sun Bailin		Shen Qurong
Wang Naiming		Song Baoxian
Wang Pufeng		Wang Liuji
Wang Xuhe		Wang Zaibang
Wu Chunqiu		Xu Zhixian
Wu Rusong		Yan Xiangjun
Yao Youzhi		Yan Xuetong
Yao Yunzhu		Yang Bojiang
Zhai Zhigang		Yang Mingjie
Zhao Nanqi		Yu Xiaoqiu
Zhao Xiaozhuo		Yuan Peng
Zhen Xi		Zhang Liangneng
Zhu Liangyin		Zhang Minqian
Zhu Xiaoli		Zhang Wenmu

The primary difference between these Chinese institutes and American research institutes is their "ownership." Research institutes are "owned" by the major institutional players in the national security decision making process in China. Their staffs in many cases have access to what in the US would be considered government classified information such as cables from embassies abroad. Unfortunately, it is difficult to be precise about these differences. Members of these institutes often decline to discuss in any detail the exact nature of their internal reports. They are not puppets, however, and many research institutions are important in their own right for the creative ideas they produce. Their leaders carry great prestige and have high rank in the Communist Party.

CHINA INSTITUTE OF CONTEMPORARY INTERNATIONAL RELATIONS

China Institute of Contemporary International Relations (CICIR) analysts do not hide their affiliations with the Ministry of State Security, the Chinese leadership, and their access to classified materials, but they like to stress their open source research and publications. They are proud of their openness to foreign visitors, their extensive travel abroad, their foreign language capabilities, and their record of publishing short-term predictions about foreign political events, things that more cautious analysts do not have. CICIR also hosts many U.S. visitors to China.

CICIR employs about 500 professional analysts, slightly larger than the Academy of Military Science (AMS) and much larger than the Shanghai Institute of International Studies (SIIS), the China Institute of International Strategic Studies (CIISS), and the China Institute of International Studies (CIIS), but dwarfed by the 5,000 at the Chinese Academy of Social Science (CASS). CICIR has a campus-like compound in northwest Beijing to which dozens of open-source materials are air mailed daily. In the United States, an equivalent institute might cost $50 million or more annually to operate. CICIR maintains its own publishing house (Shishi chubanshe) and book store and publishes a monthly journal in Chinese, *Xiandai guoji guanxi* (Contemporary International Relations). One or two articles are selected from the 10 or more in each issue to be translated and distributed free for exchange to foreign counterparts.

CICIR seems to focus on analysis and forecasts based largely on open source publications and interviews with foreign leaders. It has its own training college. Numerous foreign visitors have been impressed with the quality of CICIR briefings and articles. CICIR analysts can disagree with each other and conduct limited debates, even in the presence of foreign visitors. CICIR is well known for its boldness in making forecasts about political, economic, and military trends. A recent collection of articles by the director of the East Asia Division examined Japan in the 21st century. The author-editor complained that he could find no counterpart studies of Japan's future in the United States or Europe.

CHINA INSTITUTE OF INTERNATIONAL STUDIES
and
SHANGHAI INSTITUTE
OF INTERNATIONAL STUDIES

These two research institutes are under the budgetary control of the Foreign Ministry. Graduates of China's Foreign Affairs College may be assigned to the CIIS and SIIS. Each institute is much smaller than CICIR, neither exceeding 100 professional staff. They publish journals and use the Foreign Ministry's press for publishing books and research reports. The CIIS journal *Guoji wenti yanjiu* (International Studies) features articles by its staff, who often are diplomats on rotation. The SIIS has numerous publications, including the annual *Guoji xingshi nianjian* (The Yearbook Survey of International Affairs), the biweekly *Guoji zhanwang* (World Outlook), and *Guoji wenti* (International Review), as well as two journals of English language translations of selected articles from the main journal, *SIIS Paper* and *SIIS Journal.*

SIIS focuses on future issues more boldly than CIIS, where the diplomats/analysts seem more comfortable with research on the recent past and near-term trends. Both institutes avoid dealing with military or future warfare issues. Each has an impressive building and happily receives foreign visitors, CIIS in Beijing and SIIS in Shanghai. There are five main SIIS research departments: American Studies, Japanese Studies, European Studies, Asian-Pacific Studies, and Comprehensive Studies, which focuses on global issues.

CHINESE ACADEMY OF SOCIAL SCIENCES

Once part of the Chinese Academy of Science, the Chinese Academy of Social Sciences (CASS) was established in 1977. It occupies a 12-story building in downtown Beijing and maintains a professional staff of 5,000 scholars and has its own publishing house for books. It houses five institutes: the Institute of World Economics and Politics, the Institute of American Studies, the Institute of Russian Studies, the Institute of Japan Studies, and the Taiwan

Institute. Each institute publishes its own journal. The academy's library on the ground floor has specialized collections for each institute. CASS scholars and institute directors can advocate policies in the national press. CASS is viewed as being highly influential. Li Tieying, who was appointed by the State Council as the president of CASS in March 1998, is also a member of the Political Bureau of the Central Committee of the Communist Party and serves as a State Councillor. An article in the *Hong Kong Ta Kung Pao*, a state-owned newspaper, reported recently, "According to the conference held in Beijing today to discuss information-related affairs of the Chinese Academy of Social Sciences, last year central leaders and other high-ranking officials read and commented on hundreds of CASS research reports, some of which were republished in documents of the Central Committee of the State Council, and research results were studied and applied by relevant departments."[1]

CASS research is oriented toward the future, both in terms of China's domestic development and the world structure. In 1998, CASS was reported to be focused on establishing a new set of research projects that deal with "major historical challenges and opportunities facing China after five or ten years or after even several decades in the next century. . . . At present, a 'research plan on major issues in 2010' is being discussed and shaped, including the following aspects: the experiences and lessons of the rise and fall of the Soviet Union, development trends of modern capitalism, the formation of property rights system and public ownership in a market economy, financial globalization and national economic security, the mechanism for achieving socialist democracy, problems of central and west China, and problems of corruption."[2]

Many of China's most famous human rights activists after the Tiananmen incident in 1989 came from CASS, such as the former director of the Institute for Marxist Leninist Studies and the former director of the Institute of Political Science, Su Shaozhi and Yan Jiaqi, who are well known leaders of the

[1]"Central Leadership Attaches Importance to 'Think Tanks'; Heeds the Views of Experts of the Chinese Academy of Social Sciences Before Making Major Decisions," *Ta Kung Pao*, March 3, 1998, in FBIS-CHI-98-062, March 7, 1998.

[2]Zhu Huaxin, "Provide Theoretical Support for China in the 21st Century—New Explorations in Reforms at the Chinese Academy of Social Science," *Renmin ribao* (People's Daily), September 18, 1998, 5, in FBIS-CHI-98-265, September 24, 1998.

democracy movement in exile. In the early 1980s, CASS leaders lead the economic reform effort. In the mid-1990s, Liu Ji, as deputy CASS director, has encouraged reform and published books about Jiang Zemin's reform concepts. It was reported in the Western press in July 1998, that CASS was one of the institutes tasked by Jiang Zemin to study the political systems of other nations. The Wall Street Journal quoted a CASS researcher as saying that "the U.S. [system] obviously made an impression" on Jiang. Upon his return from his summit in the U.S. in October 1997, "Jiang asked the academy to draft a manual on democracy for mandatory reading by high-ranking officials. The manual to be passed out with booklets on human rights and the rule of law, will feature sections on the historic development of democracy, Western models of democracy and China's own democratic path."[3] However, a recent shakeup in the top leadership of CASS, in October 1998, may be moving the institution in a more conservative direction. The *Hong Kong Standard* reported that the retirement of four vice-presidents, including Liu Ji, was, "a move seen by many as consolidating academy president Li Tieying's power."[4]

ACADEMY OF MILITARY SCIENCE

Founded in 1958, the Academy of Military Science (AMS) produces journals, books and classified reports for the Chinese military strategic planning process. Of all the research institutes, AMS is the most secretive and least visited by foreigners. It occupies a large compound northwest of Beijing and employs more than 500 professional military staff (a 10-minute walk from the National Defense University). AMS has no students (other than a new small graduate student program). It performs analysis for the Central Military Commission and the General Staff Department. It participates in task forces organized by other important organizations such as the Commission on Science, Technology and Industry for National Defense.

The president of the Academy of Military Science is usually a full general, equivalent to a Deputy Chief of Staff. This would translate roughly in

---

[3]Kathy Chen, "China to Test Waters of Political Reform," *Wall Street Journal*, July 27, 1998.

[4]Fong Tak-ho, "Politburo Reshuffles Chinese Academy of Social Sciences," *Hong Kong Standard*, October 26, 1998, 6; translated FBIS-CHI-98-299. See also, "CPCCC Changes CASS Party Committee into Party Group," *Zhongguo xinwen she*, October 26, 1998, in FBIS-CHI-98-300.

American protocol terms to an Under Secretary of Defense combined with a four- star flag officer. The current commandant of AMS, appointed in 1998, is General Liu Jingsong, former commander of the PLA Lanzhou military region. The AMS has its own publishing house (Junshi kexue chubanshe) and publishes an estimated 50 books a year. Its open source journal is *Zhongguo junshi kexue* (China military science), published by the AMS editorial board; its restricted journals are *World Military Trends* and *Military Thought*. AMS leaders acknowledge a counterpart relationship with the General Staff Academy in Moscow.

The AMS has 10 departments, each of which has 50 or more officers, and a few of which publish their own journals: Planning and Organization Department; Strategic Studies Department; Operations and Tactics Department; Military Systems Department; Military History Department, which publishes the bi-monthly *Military History*; Foreign Military Studies Department, which publishes the monthly *World Military Review*; Military Encyclopedia Department; Center for Mao Zedong Military Thought; Center for Political Education of the People's Liberation Army (PLA); and Center for Operations Research, which publishes the quarterly *Military System Engineering*. According to the introductory brochure describing the institute, AMS is the "national center for military studies; AMS plans and coordinates for the army all the research programs concerning military science. . . . AMS has made good progress in war gaming, command automation, machine translation, and military data bases. It has formed its own operational and tactical simulation systems, military experts systems, and specific research models."

AMS seems to be more closed to foreigners than the National Defense University (NDU)—its staff rarely travel abroad, and no foreign delegations receive permission to visit the AMS Compound without an extensive review by the unit called the General Staff Foreign Affairs Bureau, one mission of which is to control contact between foreigners and sensitive Chinese military organizations. An article in May 1998 commemorating the 40th anniversary of the founding of the AMS mentioned, however, that since it has been under the leadership of Chairman Jiang Zemin, the institute has "gradually improved contacts with foreign institutions and organizations for military scientific research, and enabled a setup of research open to the outside world to take place." The article, however, praised the institute for "having completed more than 1,000 research projects" in its 40 years of existence, especially those written of late:

> In recent years, aiming at the forward positions of military reforms in the world, the Academy of Military Science presented more than 200 research reports on such major realistic issues as strategies for border security, guidance for strategies and battles under high-technology conditions, and the regularization of our army under the new situation.[5]

The strategy department of AMS publishes books on military doctrine and strategy with a focus on the military thinking of Chairman Mao. In the past decade, it added books on the strategic thinking of Deng Xiaoping. A recent book by the former president of the Chinese Academy of Military Science, *The Categories of Military Science* by General Zheng Wenhan, offers numerous footnotes to Soviet works on the same subjects and employs the categories established in Soviet military science publications. Chinese authors never explicitly acknowledge their debt to Soviet military science and to Soviet military terminology. Readers are not made aware of the Soviet tutorial role in China in the early 1950s because there were political penalties paid by senior Chinese general officers in the 1950s for assuming policies civilian Communist leaders deemed to be pro-Soviet. Perhaps this is one reason Chinese military authors still do not refer to their deep Soviet roots in some matters of doctrine and terminology.

The Chinese Academy of Military Science has a mission to understand future warfare and the future security environment. Like its former Soviet counterpart, it still must use Marxist-Leninist "military science," which includes the notion of "dialectics" in analyzing technological influence on military doctrine. According to both Soviet and Chinese authors, the operation over time of "military dialectics" will more or less automatically change the nature of warfare quite drastically as a completely new synthesis is formed from the clash of thesis and antithesis. To examine the future of warfare, a

---

[5]Xiao Pu and Jiang Wenming, "Be A Good Forerunner of Great Military Reform—Military Scientific Research Undertakings Advance in a Pioneering Spirit Thanks to the Concern of Three Generations of the Party's Core Leadership," Beijing Xinhua Domestic Service, May 19, 1998, in FBIS-CHI-98-139, May 21, 1998. The article provides a history of AMS research under Mao Zedong, Deng Xiaoping, and Jiang Zemin.

vital task of military science is to anticipate and to identify the "dialectical" arrival of "military-technical revolutions." These military-technical revolutions are neither produced nor accidentally discovered by a single genius. They must occur with historical inevitability as science and technology progress forward. Military strategists must therefore be diligent to detect an approaching military technical revolution, because it will require the re-design of obsolete military doctrine.

Although the AMS does not have regular classes, in 1988 six of China's most important military strategists created a doctoral program in military science at the AMS, authorized by the State Council. It is significant that one of the two major fields for doctoral degrees is "Future Warfare." The program director is General Li Jijun, who has had a long association with the Academy. Significantly, General Li supervised the 38th Group Army near Beijing from 1983 to 1988, when it was the test bed for the new Chinese concept of the mechanized group army (corps). Prior to that experimental work, General Li had been with Academy of Military Science for many years, particularly in the field of foreign army studies. He compared strategic concepts in the Soviet Army with U.S. joint force doctrine. There are five senior officers of the AMS in charge of the new doctoral program: General Mi Zhenyu, former Deputy Commandant; General Wang Zhenxi; General Wang Pufeng, a former Director of the Strategic Research Department; Senior Colonel Qian Junde of the Strategy Department; and Zhang Zuiliang. General Mi was Deputy Commandant of the AMS beginning in 1985 and is the author of an important book on Chinese national development concepts published in 1988 and described in chapter 6. General Wang Zhenxi is a specialist in foreign military studies, who served as military attaché in both Yugoslavia and Romania, from 1977 to 1983. He became head of the Foreign Military Studies Department in 1986. General Wang Pufeng was the Deputy Director of the Strategy Research Department at the AMS in 1991. In an interview in *China Daily*, October 10, 1992, General Wang called for more attention by the PLA to the challenge of information warfare. He has been a prominent author on the revolution in military affairs (RMA).

Since 1992, there has been a limited restoration of contact between China's Academy of Military Science and its Soviet model, the General Staff Academy. A former Vice President of the Soviet Academy was even invited to come to Beijing for a year for research on the significance of the revolution in military affairs that has been a major subject at the Russian academy for 20 years.

NATIONAL DEFENSE UNIVERSITY

China's National Defense University (NDU) was formed in 1985 by combining three colleges, one for logistics instruction, one for political/commissar instruction, and a more general military academy. Unlike AMS, the NDU trains hundreds of students annually. It also has its own publishing house (Guofang daxue chubanshe) that produces 50 or more books annually, including textbooks. Much more open than the AMS, NDU has in the past decade hosted hundreds of foreign military delegations. NDU staff travel widely abroad. An exchange of letters between the U.S. NDU in Washington and the Chinese NDU in Beijing established an exchange program between the two institutions on the premise that they are roughly counterparts.

Operating under the Central Military Commission, NDU has two main functions: to train military commanders, officers, and government officials and, as described by the brochure handed out to visiting foreigners, to "conduct research into the modernization of national defense in order to advise the Central Military Commission and other military headquarters in making decisions." Its 13 teaching divisions "specialize in: strategic studies; operational art of war; command and management; arms and services; foreign military studies; Marxist theories; political work; international economics and politics; logistics studies; science and technology; foreign languages; foreign training; and audiovisual teaching."

In the past decade, a Scientific Research Department at NDU and its subordinate Institute of National Security Studies (INSS) have been increasingly involved in efforts to redefine Chinese military strategy and doctrine. A comparison of the two major journals produced by NDU and the Academy of Military Science shows they have different perspectives and methodologies. The *Guofan daxue xuebao* (NDU Journal) seems more interested in local war issues and has published very little on the potential RMA compared to the AMS journal. Perhaps to correct the NDU near-term focus, it announced in 1996 the formation of a center for military research on future warfare issues, including the RMA as well as traditional statecraft. General Pan Zhenqiang and Colonel Zhu Chenghu, director and deputy of the NDU INSS, publish articles on the security environment in national newspapers and frequently attend foreign conferences.

CHINESE SOCIETY FOR STRATEGY AND MANAGEMENT

Founded in 1989, the Chinese Society for Strategy and Management (CSSM) occupies a building in the former U. S. Embassy compound, made famous during the 55-day Boxer Siege in Beijing. It publishes a lengthy quarterly journal, *Zhanlue yu guanli* (Strategy and Management), containing articles forecasting the future security environment. According to the brochure describing the institute, "Many famous veteran national leaders, diplomats, and writers who have made great contributions to China's modernization serve as its senior advisers." The chairman of the CSSM is former Vice Premier of the State Council Gu Mu, and one of the Vice Chairmen is former Defense Minister Zhang Aiping, who is perhaps best known in China for his successful management of the Chinese nuclear weapons program. Indeed, CSSM articles have been described by some as more nationalistic than the journals of CASS and CICIR.[6] CSSM journal articles have discussed the rise of Chinese nationalism.[7] In 1996, the journal announced it would annually publish China's ranking in the various international indices of competitiveness and Comprehensive National Power. In 1997 and 1998, CSSM issued an annual strategic assessment, written by authors from CICIR, CASS, and the AMS.

---

[6]The East West Center in Honolulu published a study in 1996 on the rise of Chinese nationalism, the sole references of which were to "nationalistic" articles from this journal.

[7]For example, see Wang Hui and Zhang Tianwei, "Wenhua pipan lilun yu dangdai Zhongguo minzu zhuyi wenti" (Cultural criticism theory and the issue of contemporary Chinese nationalism), *Zhanlue yu guanli* (Strategy and Management) 5, no. 4 (1994): 17-20; Xiao Gongqin, "Minzu zhuyi yu Zhongguo zhuanxing shiqi de yishixingtai" (Nationalism and the ideology of China's period of change), *Zhanlue yu guanli* (Strategy and Management) 5, no. 4 (1994): 21-25; and Dong Zhenghua, "Minzu zhuyi yu guojia liyi" (Nationalism and national interests), *Zhanlue yu guanli* (Strategy and Management) 5, no. 4 (1994): 26-27.

FOUNDATION FOR
INTERNATIONAL STRATEGIC STUDIES

The Foundation for International Strategic Studies (FISS) was founded in the last few years by Chinese military officers on leave or retired from active duty and is authorized to engage in business as well as strategic studies. It publishes a few books a year and a journal and actively seeks "counterparts" overseas with whom to co-host conferences on political/military issues, including the future of the security environment. As a result of its close connection with both the Foreign Ministry and Chinese Military Intelligence, FISS can sometimes take more controversial positions than other better known research institutions. For example, in 1995 FISS published *Can Taiwan Become Independent?*, a book other research institutions and publishing houses had declined to print because it was too controversial in concluding that a major danger existed in Taiwan's movement toward independence.

COMMISSION ON SCIENCE, TECHNOLOGY,
AND INDUSTRY FOR NATIONAL DEFENSE

The Commission on Science, Technology, and Industry for National Defense (COSTIND) coordinates at least six ministry-level defense industrial complexes, which seem to be responsible for both production and research and development for future defense weapons and equipment. They publish magazines and books with assessments of the future. COSTIND has its own publishing house, newspaper, and series of journals, most of which are not released publicly. Some Chinese interviewed complained that COSTIND shrouds itself in secrecy not so much to prevent foreign observation but to maintain its autonomy from the Chinese military services and the General Staff.

There is apparently resentment that hundreds or thousands of COSTIND employees wear military uniforms and are assigned military ranks even though they have never participated in military units or received formal training. One General Staff officer said COSTIND officials can be spotted on the street by their nonuniform socks, coats, sweaters and general nonmilitary appearance even while wearing PLA uniforms. The COSTIND headquarters building in

Beijing is a long distance from the rest of the military compound and General Staff buildings. Another example of the COSTIND little concealed autonomous style can be seen in the two books it has released about its history since the 1950s that clearly distinguish between COSTIND and the Chinese military, for whom it produces weapons and equipment.[8]

COSTIND oversees a vast conglomerate of research institutions, factories, and government organizations that may employ more than 3 million people. COSTIND has published a series of books on the history of China's defense science and technology since the 1950s. One theme is the need to have "three moves on the chess board," a Chinese metaphor for the need to have weapons acquisition plans thought through in terms of an action-reaction sequence of possible opponents.

China Aerospace Science and Technology Corporation (CASC)

In addition to the central research institutes of COSTIND, assessments of the future security environment are also prepared by a number of other large research institutes in the complex, such as the CASC.

China Aerospace is not a corporation in the Western sense. It controls the ministries and firms that manufacture weapons and civil-use equipment in aviation and missiles.[9] It is particularly important in providing published assessments of the future of space warfare.[10] The Chinese Aerospace Corporation complex, together with the Ministry of Electronics, may be the two organizations most interested in the RMA. Chinese analysts interpret the RMA as a reduction in emphasis on armor, artillery, large naval vessels, and manned fighter aircraft that are all "products" of other parts of COSTIND, not China Aerospace. According to the version of 21st-century warfare

---

[8]COSTIND is being restructured. See Harlan Jencks, "COSTIND is Dead, Long Live COSTIND! Restructuring China's Defense Scientific, Technical, and Industrial Sector," in *The People's Liberation Army in the Information Age*, eds. James C. Mulvenon and Richard H. Yang (Santa Monica, CA: The RAND Corporation, 1999), 59-77.

[9]See *China Today Defense Science and Technology* (Beijing: National Defense Industry Press, 1993), vol. 1; and Mark Stokes, "China's Strategic Modernization," U.S. Army War College, Strategic Studies Institute, forthcoming.

[10]A restricted journal, *Space Electronic Warfare*, has been published for several years and is described in Mark Stokes.

described in some COSTIND and AMS publications, it will be the capability to link "sensors" with "shooters" while preserving the "invisibility" of both that will be decisive.

CHINA INSTITUTE OF INTERNATIONAL STRATEGIC STUDIES

The China Institute of International Strategic Studies (CIISS) is an important public research institution subordinate to the General Staff's Second Department. CIISS publishes a quarterly in Chinese and English, *Guoji zhanlue yanjiu* (International strategic studies). However, CIISS is located far from the secretive General Staff Department of the PLA. Its chairman is Deputy Chief of the General Staff for Intelligence General Xiong Guankai (whose speech at Harvard in December 1997 on the future security environment is described in chapter 1). Because of China's traditional secrecy about military matters, a few retired military attachés and a few civilians at the CIISS provide the sole "window" on general staff and military intelligence assessments.

It is unfortunate that foreign visitors are not permitted to visit the General Staff Department. The GSD, several blocks from the Zhongnanhai Compound facing the lake at Beihai Park, may have over 2,000 officers. In the 1950s the GSD had Soviet advisors resident for several years. Its internal structure probably resembles the former Soviet General Staff. The First Department manages operations and probably is the national command center for all PLA forces. The Second Department is the military intelligence service and has its own headquarters building. Its chief is usually a deputy chief of staff of the PLA and is a prominent representative sent abroad on public diplomacy missions. Unlike the well-known Second Department of the GSD, its Third Department is the "no such agency" of China and apparently is responsible for signals intelligence, which foreign experts such as Desmond Ball believe may be the world's third- or even second-largest communications intelligence organization after the United States and possibly Russia.[11] The

---

[11] The sole source on this matter seems to be Desmond Ball, "Signals Intelligence in China," *Jane's Intelligence Review* 7, no. 8 (August 1995): 365-370.

Fourth Department is the most recently established part of GSD; since 1990 it has been responsible for electronic warfare and early warning analysis.[12]

Of these General Staff departments, the Operations Department is probably the largest and most important in terms of its direct responsibilities for military operational planning and the program of annual exercises. However, the Second Department (the Chinese equivalent of the Soviet intelligence agency, GRU) is apparently also quite large, with some estimates as high as 2000 analysts and professional staff, according to one interview. The Second Department and possibly the Third have their own headquarters compounds in northern Beijing. According to interviews, the Second Department's director, as a Deputy Chief of the General Staff, apparently serves as the PLA representative in foreign policy discussions below the Politburo level. It would be a mistake to see the GSD Second Department as a counterpart to the American Defense Intelligence Agency because of this policy role the DIA lacks. Rather, the GSD Second Department seems to perform not only the functions of DIA foreign intelligence collection and analysis but also the policy deliberation role played by the 300 professional staff under the U.S. Assistant Secretary of Defense for International Security Affairs. Thus, the CIISS quarterly journal merits attention.

---

[12]Nicholas Eftimiades, *Chinese Intelligence Operations* (Annapolis, MD: Naval Institute Press, 1994).

INDEX OF CHINESE AUTHORS

ABOUT THE AUTHOR

Michael Pillsbury is a Visiting Senior Fellow at the Institute for National Strategic Studies, National Defense University, and an Honorary Councilor of the Atlantic Council of the United States, where he is sponsored by the Office of Net Assessment, Department of Defense. During the Reagan administration, Dr. Pillsbury was the Assistant Under Secretary of Defense for Policy Planning; under President Bush he was Special Assistant for Asian Affairs in the Office of the Secretary of Defense, reporting to Andrew W. Marshall, Director of Net Assessment. Previously he served on the staff of several U.S. Senate Committees.

In 1975-76, while an analyst at The RAND Corporation, he published articles in *Foreign Policy* and *International Security* recommending that the United States establish intelligence and military ties with China. The proposal, publicly commended by Ronald Reagan, Henry Kissinger, and James Schlesinger, later became U.S. policy.

Dr. Pillsbury studied Mandarin Chinese for two years at the Stanford Center in Taipei, Taiwan, under a doctoral dissertation fellowship of the National Science Foundation. He earned a B.A. from Stanford University and a Ph.D. from Columbia University. He has taught graduate courses in Chinese foreign policy at Georgetown University, the University of California at Los Angeles, the University of Southern California, and the Naval Postgraduate School. Dr. Pillsbury is a member of the Council on Foreign Relations and the International Institute for Strategic Studies.

The author gratefully acknowledges the research assistance provided by Samantha Blum on this book and on *Chinese Views of Future Warfare*, also published by NDU Press. Ms. Blum earned her B.A. in East Asian Studies from the College of William and Mary and her M.A. in East Asian Studies from the University of Illinois and was a research assistant to Professor Patricia B. Ebrey for the book *The Cambridge Illustrated History of China* (Cambridge University Press, 1996). She studied Chinese at the Beijing Language Institute and at the Johns Hopkins University-Nanjing University Center for Chinese and American Studies.

Printed in the United States
31952LVS00006B/8